Supply Chain for Liquids

*Out of the Box Approaches
to Liquid Logistics*

The St. Lucie Press Series on Resource Management

Titles in the Series

Supply Chain for Liquids

Out of the Box Approaches to Liquid Logistics

Wally Klatch

Auerbach Publications
Taylor & Francis Group

Boca Raton   London   New York   Singapore

Supply Chain for Liquids®, RFID for Liquids®, Liquid Lens^{SM}, SCFL^{SM}, CPVR^{SM}, Coordinated Procedures for Visibility Response^{SM}, Complementary Supply Chains^{SM}, Complementary Supply Chains for Liquids^{SM}, Thinking Liquids^{SM}, Supply Pipe^{SM}, Participatory CRM^{SM}. Service Marks Olami Inc.

Internet sites: www.SupplyChainForLiquids.com and www.RFIDforLiquids.com

Published in 2005 by
Auerbach Publications
Taylor & Francis Group
6000 Broken Sound Parkway NW, Suite 300
Boca Raton, FL 33487-2742

© 2005 by Olami Inc.
Auerbach is an imprint of Taylor & Francis Group

No claim to original U.S. Government works
Printed in the United States of America on acid-free paper
10 9 8 7 6 5 4 3 2 1

International Standard Book Number-10: 0-8493-2853-5 (Hardcover)
International Standard Book Number-13: 978-0-8493-2853-4 (Hardcover)
Library of Congress Card Number 2004066074

Library of Congress Cataloging-in-Publication Data

Klatch, Wally.
    Supply chain for liquids : out of the box approaches to liquid logistics / by Wally Klatch.
        p. cm. -- (St. Lucie Press series on resource management)
    Includes bibliographical references and index.
    ISBN 0-8493-2853-5 (alk. paper)
    1. Business logistics. 2. Physical distribution of goods. 3. Liquids. I. Series.

HD38.5.K525 2005
660'.042'0685--dc22   2004066074

Taylor & Francis Group
is the Academic Division of T&F Informa plc.

Visit the Taylor & Francis Web site at
http://www.taylorandfrancis.com

and the Auerbach Publications Web site at
http://www.auerbach-publications.com

To Dorit

and Sam, Ben, Asaf, Uriel, and Talya

Acknowledgments

Many tributaries, large and small, fed into the *Supply Chain for Liquids* stream. Some provided churning energy, others flowed with quiet wisdom. I thank each:

- *Rich O'Hanley*, publisher at Taylor & Francis, for his solid and deeply appreciated support for this project, and *Bill Walker*, series editor, whose clear and incisive input was instrumental from the development of the proposal through the completion of the work
- *Ed Frank* for his always-welcome guidance on topics large and small
- *Frank Parker* and *Fred Walsh*; *Roger Fountain* and *Bob Hiscock* of Watford, U.K.; and *Roseann Bellettieri* and *Kathy Osborn*, companions and partners on this journey
- *John Watson,* whose insightful analytical thinking is always as stimulating as it is enlightening
- *Jim Klatch, John Cramer,* and *David Kaplan* for their ongoing insights and support
- *John Lacus* for sharing both his knowledge and his passion
- *Colonel Joseph Walden, Dick Morley, Wilbert Platzer, Andrew Bielby,* and *Ed Walczak*, who very generously took of their time to contribute from their own very deep knowledge and experience

Their contributions were all most constructive, productive, and positive; any lapse in this book is solely my responsibility.

About the Author

Wally Klatch has been "thinking liquid" for nearly 25 years in executive and consulting roles at manufacturing and distribution companies in the United States and Europe. He received his bachelor's degree from Indiana University and his MBA from Purdue University, and he is CPIM-certified by the American Production and Inventory Control Society. Wally has authored articles and given presentations on operations and business topics for numerous professional and trade organizations. His next book, *RFID for Liquids*, focuses on that aspect of the supply stream for liquid products. Wally's e-mail address is Operations@SupplyChainForLiquids.com.

Contents

Preface

Some years ago, a sheet-metal fabrication operation was sold with all of its associated capital equipment, including 40-ton punch presses, brakes, and shears. Each piece of heavy machinery had to be removed from the premises by a particular date so that the new tenants could move in. Everything had been removed except the very last nut bolting the very last machine, a large shear, securely to the concrete floor. The owner had tried everything, but the nut just would not budge. Finally, in desperation, the owner hired a specialist, a rigger, to finish the job. The rigger arrived in an all-chrome tractor-trailer with a 20-ton forklift chained on the trailer. An industrial-strength toolbox mounted to the back of the cab held every imaginable size of wrench. The rigger himself was a big man at about 6 foot and maybe 220 pounds. He walked to the shear, got down on his hands and knees in just the right position, and unscrewed that last nut with his bare hand! Removing the shear was not about applying brute force to the nut; removing the shear was all about applying leverage to the nut.

Supply Chains for Liquids is a book about leverage. It teaches the reader how to think differently to leverage the inherent properties of liquids. It pulls the reader into a new perspective, showing the critical leverage points that have escaped discrete supply chain experts who see liquids merely as an exercise in packaging. Using discrete supply chain methods to build networks of packaged liquids is just brute force. This book advances the state of the art in supply chain management. It starts from a recognition that liquids are pervasive throughout the supply chain. [Was it mentioned that the shear had to be drained of its lubricating oil before being moved?] Wally Klatch reveals new methods that readers can use to take advantage of a liquid's properties to build networks of liquid products that flow to the customer.

Supply Chains for Liquids is fun to read. Wally draws from his extensive liquid-products experience, as both practitioner and consultant, to entertain the reader with amazing stories while instructing the reader on the practicalities that maximize the financial return in a liquid products business. Every supply chain network uses some form of liquids, and many supply chain networks are true hybrids, planning and controlling equal proportions of discrete and liquid products. Wally's point of view is so fresh that it is fair to say that this book offers something worth learning for every supply chain professional.

William T. Walker, CFPIM, CIRM
St. Lucie Press Series on Resource Management
Series Editor and Supply Chain Architect

Foreword

Supply Chain for Liquids: The Invisible Science

If your company produces or uses liquid products — and there are many millions of you in this category, including many who do not realize how involved you are with liquids — it is a fair certainty that you are missing out on one of the greatest logistical tools available to you — Supply Chain for Liquids®. Like screwdriver drill bits and anti-flea pet collars, Supply Chain for Liquids is such a patently obvious idea that it is completely invisible until somebody points it out. How invisible is Supply Chain for Liquids? Let us take the standard measure of reference in today's Internet-centric world — the number of "hits" the phrase returns from Google. In all of the search engine's four billion plus Web pages, the phrase "supply chain for liquids" *does not appear even one single time*! If life means appearing in Google and death means being a broken link, what does non-appearance mean? Even the phrase "supply chain for dummies" appears twice. Don't liquids rate at least what dummies get?

Even if we decide to loosen up a bit and go after something a little broader — the phrase "liquid logistics," for example — the pickings stay mighty slim. Out of the relative handful of responses that come back from a search for this phrase, many relate to bulk shippers and oceangoing freight or specific products involved with transporting liquids of various types. A few software companies include the phrase "liquid logistics" in their descriptions, but on the whole this search only reinforces the feeling that results from the search for "supply chain for liquids": this is not an area that is being paid much attention, much less one that has been explored and developed in all its richness.

Having failed to find Supply Chain for Liquids in the broad world, we turn reluctantly to the specific area in which we would expect the topic to be raised and focused on — the world of process industries. We say "reluctantly" because even though Supply Chain for Liquids is part and parcel of daily operations in process industries, our contention (and the contention of this book) is that Supply Chain for Liquids applies across many industries that do not consider themselves process industries. Liquids are also part of the products, processes, and practices of the largest and most common discrete and service industries, as we shall see further on. Even so, we find that the concept of liquid logistics even within process industries is more the realm of software vendors and equipment or service providers than it is of practitioners and companies who are looking at what they are doing and seeking to gain the best advantage for their liquid products. Process industries focus on the production process; Supply Chain for Liquids focuses on the entire logistics flow.

So not only is "Supply Chain for Liquids" virtually non-existent, but the whole concept of liquids as an industry entity does not exist. If we take a standard list of industries and start at the beginning, the list will look something like this:

- Aerospace and defense
- Agribusiness
- Airlines
- Alcoholic beverages
- Automotive

These entries are just the "A's," and the list goes on from here. But in all the lists of industries we examined, the word "liquid" never appeared. Even in the list of 71 American industries recognized by the U.S. Department of Commerce, the word "liquid" is absent. Clearly, the world does not want to think of liquids as an entity or as an industry unto itself. Liquids are "hidden" within whatever other industry represents the final product, be it construction equipment or baby products. To paraphrase the axiom "What gets measured gets improved," we could say that what is recognized gets paid attention to. This phenomenon occurs in many spheres, the medical world being an obvious example. Many people may suffer from a similar condition, but only when it is recognized and labeled does it start getting addressed. People who were "losing it" when they got older, or children who were "disruptive," were viewed as social problems until Alzheimer's disease and attention deficit disorder were identified. It was only then that people who suffered from these diseases began to get the help they needed. One suspects that if Asperger syndrome were better known, more children and adults would be related to differently.

The status of Supply Chain for Liquids could be viewed in the spirit of the song *Alice's Restaurant* — if one person does something out of the ordinary, they think he's really sick; when two people do it, they

Exhibit F.1 Many Types of Liquids Are Used in Many Types of Businesses

won't take either of them seriously; but when three people start talking about it, it's already a significant finding and will be recognized and related to as such.

In fact, you would be hard-pressed to find an industry in which liquids do not play a key role. Most products have liquid components or ingredients, whether a direct component, a chemical used to treat a direct component, or the die or paint used to provide coloration for the product. Liquids are used to lubricate the machines of production as well as to clean the production and office facilities of industrial companies. Liquids are consumed universally, both directly in the form of beverages and also in the liquid ingredients contained in most food products. Finally, any type of product transport is dependent on fuels and lubricants to keep them moving. Exhibit F.1 presents some common liquids and some of the many types of businesses that use liquids extensively. Despite this, the presence of liquids as an entity remains hidden for the most part and, as described above, liquids are virtually ignored in our literature and our thinking.

In declaring our independence from this way of thinking, we hold this truth to be self-evident: that liquids are all around us, and any company in pursuit of profit would do well to recognize the potential benefits of strong liquid logistics. As we shall see in this book, the "thinking" part is as important a part of Supply Chain for Liquids as the "doing" part. In many cases, introducing a Supply Chain for Liquids approach will be considered revolutionary or, at least, outside-the-box thinking. The motivation for any effort involving change is the opportunity to achieve a truly large benefit, and this benefit is in fact available from Supply Chain for Liquids. Let us take a moment to look at this hidden world of liquids to discover how important it is.

First, let us see if we can start to recognize the world of liquids, like suddenly starting to find the hidden pictures inside of a drawing. Revisiting the industries listed above, we can quickly see that liquids are deeply involved in the core processes related to each of these industries, even though at first blush we would have thought that most of them are discrete or even service industries. Let us take a look at how this lifeblood of liquids is flowing through the veins of our national industries:

- *Aerospace and defense*: Within this industry there is large-scale distribution, storage, and usage of liquids of every type including fuels, vehicle lubricants, beverages, cleaning fluids, chemicals, and many more types of liquids either supplied by private industry or managed by companies serving as contractors to the military. The Pentagon is the largest single consumer of petroleum in the world; over five billion gallons per year get moved around the military system to support its 150,000+ land vehicles, 22,000 aircraft, and over 300 ocean-going vessels. To provide perspective on how much it uses, two days of oil consumption by the military equals the entire amount used during a full year by the nation's urban bus systems. On the beverage side, water consumption is supplemented by soda, beer, and other beverages. As an example, the 5,000-member crew of the aircraft carrier USS *Abraham Lincoln* consumes 600 gallons of milk and 13,000 sodas each day — a veritable floating supply chain. Extrapolating from this data across the 1,400,000 active-duty personnel worldwide makes clear the magnitude of the liquid flow for beverages in the military.

- *Agribusiness*: Liquid consumption in agribusiness includes fertilizers, pesticides, and other chemicals. Over two billion gallons of nitrogen liquids are sold each year for field fertilization, and pesticides account for a volume of over 330 million pounds of usage nationwide each year. Farm operations are based on mechanical equipment, including machinery used to prepare, plant, spray, and harvest the fields; the equipment used to support raising livestock; and other machinery involved directly in the agricultural process. The flow of fuels, lubricants, and other maintenance fluids needed to support this equipment — nearly five million farm tractors with the corresponding quantity of related farming equipment —

constitutes a large and intense, if widespread, liquid Supply Chain. On top of this is an entire transportation network for dairy, grain, livestock, and other farm-origin products. For example, one of the major agribusiness companies alone operates a transportation system on four continents that includes 19,500 rail cars, 800 tractor trailers, 2100 barges, and 75 tow boats.

▪ *Airlines*: Fuels, lubricants, and other fluids keep airplanes in the skies. The nation's airlines consume over 35 million gallons of fuel each day for domestic flights alone, in addition to a large array of other liquids. The supply chains for these liquids flow from the producers, mainly of petroleum products, to users at the nation's airports as well as nearly 2500 aviation maintenance facilities nationwide that regularly utilize maintenance fluids in the course of their work. The airline industry represents as well as any the liquid element hidden within discrete activity. Nothing is more "discrete" than an airplane, each a highly identified and serialized unit with many parts that are also individually, serially tracked. But running through this discrete jungle of 8000 commercial aircraft in the United States is a veritable Amazon River of liquids. The aircraft make nine million departures each year, carrying over 600 million passengers an average of 1000 miles each between 5000 airports. Each commercial aircraft uses a variety of liquids, as shown in Exhibit F.2, and the 200,000+ general aviation aircraft at 14,000 private airports across the country use a subset of these liquids. The Supply Chain for Liquids in the airline industry is a large and important process that coexists with, although in many ways is hidden by, the traditional Supply Chain for discrete products in the industry.

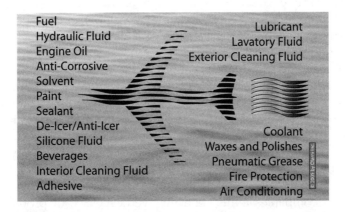

Fuel
Hydraulic Fluid
Engine Oil
Anti-Corrosive
Solvent
Paint
Sealant
De-Icer/Anti-Icer
Silicone Fluid
Beverages
Interior Cleaning Fluid
Adhesive

Lubricant
Lavatory Fluid
Exterior Cleaning Fluid

Coolant
Waxes and Polishes
Pneumatic Grease
Fire Protection
Air Conditioning

Exhibit F.2   Many Liquids Are Used Even in the Most Discrete of Products

- *Alcoholic beverages and tobacco*: Americans down over 19 million gallons of alcoholic beverages each day, for a total of over six billion gallons per year. In this case, the liquid element of the supply chain is clear.
- *Automotive*: "Automotive" covers many industries such as manufacturing, automobile dealerships, quick-lube centers, automobile repair, and many more. Common to many of these are the liquids that are used in these types of operations — lubricants, fuels, paints, maintenance fluids, and cleaning fluids, to name a few. The quantities of liquids used in these industries show the magnitude of "automotive" as a liquid industry: over 600 million gallons of motor oil and nearly 200 million gallons of hydraulic fluid flow each year into vehicles in the United States.

Extending the quantities of liquids shown in the industry segments mentioned across the whole industries listed above, and further across all industries in general, gives an idea of the importance of liquids and the size of the overall Supply Chain for Liquids. With so many billions of dollars worth of liquid products flowing through the economy — and with the potential for efficiencies, revenue enhancements, and cost savings as described in this book — the opportunities for economic benefit both on the macro scale and on the micro/per-company or per-supply chain scale are truly enormous. Except for "alcoholic beverages and tobacco," none of the industries listed above would be considered liquid in nature. Defense, agriculture, airlines, and automobiles are not normally thought of in liquid terms, and for the most part, the products produced by these industries are not liquids. This, however, is exactly the point. The many billions of gallons of liquids that are produced, moved, and consumed just in the examples described above show us that there is a liquid element in even the most discrete industries, and companies will benefit from recognizing that element and relating to it differently than it does to its main discrete products.

Let us make an important point about the universal nature of Supply Chain for Liquids: different kinds of liquids have a lot in common despite the diverse "nominal" industries in which they may be identified. Many of the core principles involved in the operational flow of pesticides to a farm are applicable to the logistics behind delivering brake fluid to an automobile repair shop. Thus we need to look at a completely different slice of operations when talking about Supply Chain for Liquids. Specifically, we need to focus on the "horizontal" slice of liquid logistics across all types of companies rather than the "vertical" slice of production and other logistics processes within any particular industry. Like the thin slice of onion on the hamburger that we do not notice until we bite into it,

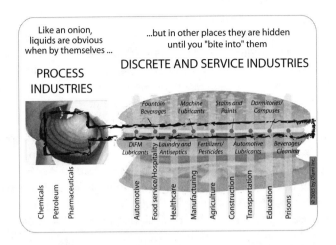

Like an onion, liquids are obvious when by themselves ...

...but in other places they are hidden until you "bite into" them

DISCRETE AND SERVICE INDUSTRIES

PROCESS INDUSTRIES

Fountain Beverages Machine Lubricants Stains and Paints Dormitories/ Campuses

DIFM Lubricants Laundry and Antiseptics Fertilizers/ Pesticides Automotive Lubricants Beverages Cleaning

Chemicals Petroleum Pharmaceuticals Automotive Food service/Hospitality Healthcare Manufacturing Agriculture Construction Transportation Education Prisons

© 2005 by Olami Inc.

Exhibit F.3 Liquids Are Found in Many Industries That Are Not Thought of as Liquids Oriented

the thin slice of liquid logistics does not appear until we become sensitive to it. Exhibit F.3 gives a taste of this concept. On the other hand, once we recognize liquids as a target of logistical analysis, we can (and in this book, we do) lay out some generalized principles related to Supply Chain for Liquids that can be readily adapted to liquid logistics in a broad variety of industries, companies, and liquid applications.

Another reason liquids are often hidden from sight is that they are frequently considered "tag-along" products related to discrete goods. A purchasing person ordering a dozen drive belts and five one-gallon jugs of floor wax does not even consider the fact that one product is discrete and the other is in essence a liquid. This hints at a concept discussed in detail further in this book — that liquids are invisible because it is the packaging, and not the product itself, that serves as the basis for viewing the liquid. A one-gallon jug of floor wax is logistically a solid, that is, the one-gallon jug itself is what is handled rather than the liquid inside the jug. Logistics has "neutered" the fact that the floor wax was manufactured as a liquid and will ultimately be used as a liquid, but in the middle, we forget that it is a liquid!

An additional barrier to working with liquids is that it requires a skill set that is outside the routine of the people who normally work with discrete products. It has been said that if you want to know a people, you should study their language. Like Eskimos who have 49 words for snow and the British who have 40 words for rain, people who have a particular experience create a vocabulary and a methodology for relating to that experience. The Eskimo words for snow, for example, describe several aspects of snow — the snow flakes themselves, the fallen snow, various snow formations, and snow events. Similarly, a person working with discrete products is familiar with bills of material, pallet sizes, inventory counts, production lines, components, and the rest of a complete vocabulary and way of relating to products. At the most basic level, simply using the corresponding liquids-based terms for the exact same concepts — recipes, tank capacities, liquid-level measurement, blending tanks, and ingredients — already throws an "unnatural" feeling into the process. Working with liquids per se goes much further out of the ordinary. As described in this book, it involves at the very least tweaking and adjusting systems that have been created for discrete items, and in its purest sense it involves building systems that are much different from those used for discrete products. Indeed, discrete products would not even be able to pass through these liquids-based systems. The language, the methodology, in short the entire logistics experience acts as a barrier to thinking about and gaining the benefits that are available from strong liquid logistics.

Finally, the treatment of liquids has remained "as is" because the forces of inertia like to keep things that way. When progress moves operational functionality forward to higher levels of efficiency and effectiveness, somewhere along the line someone pays a price. This is the nature of business and of life itself. "Survival of the fittest" applies to companies and supply chains as well as to turtles and dandelions. The theory says that it is not the smartest or the fastest that will survive and thrive, but the one who is best able to adapt to a changing environment. In an environment in which most players operate in more or less the same way, it is the adaptive company that will succeed in the fierce competitiveness of the business wilds.

At the beginning of this section, why did we refer to Supply Chain for Liquids as a "science"? Assuming that science, religion, and art are all variations on a single theme — a way of relating to things and an approach to doing things — we could have referred to Supply Chain for Liquids as an art or a religion as well. Each in its own way tries to strip away the extraneous, focus on the essence, and provide a frame of reference, just as Supply Chain for Liquids does. But as we shall see, Supply Chain for Liquids is a science in the sense that it establishes a methodology and an approach, the Liquid Lens^{SM}, that describes a process that leads to a result that is not known in advance. For this reason, we think of Supply Chain for Liquids as a science, and up until now, as an invisible science.

Having said this, we take an approach in this book that is common to science, religion, and art; we illustrate our thinking by telling the stories that make up the history and diversity of this topic. Although this book is very much anchored in the realities of day-to-day logistics, its parallel goal is to create outside-the-box thinking that comes from lifting your head up out of the day-to-day and looking at a broader horizon. This does not mean that this book will necessarily provide a "Eureka!" experience (which, by the way, is very liquids-connected — see Chapter 3), but it does mean that by looking at how people have faced and resolved liquids-related problems in the past we can open our minds to seeing things differently than we do now. We will tell stories of liquids-related people, products, and methods throughout the book, including the history, science, myth, and meaning of liquids in different times and places. By intermixing the discussion of today's liquid-logistics practices with these "get your head above the water" (it just comes naturally!) segments, we hope to achieve the goal of presenting as well as stimulating outside-the-box approaches to liquid logistics. The power of this approach cannot be overestimated. Dale Carnegie writes that, in preparing one of his books, he read many thousands of documents on the words and actions of famous people, including over 100 biographies of Theodore Roosevelt alone. He was not satisfied with one view or one theory or even one set of facts; he knew that the broad perspective is a great foundation for focusing on the very specific. Having choices means having power, and letting ideas from the past help us generate ideas for today and tomorrow is a great way to give ourselves choices. To rework an old phrase that puts it in the negative, we could say that those who do not pay attention to the past are condemned to live in it. This book brings the stories, rather than the results, because the meaning and the results will be different for each reader based on his or her own perspective and situation. Our objective is to provide a forum for readers to create their own outside-the-box solutions, in addition to those we suggest ourselves.

We believe that the use of history in a discussion of liquid logistics is more than justified; it is essential. The connection between the transportation of liquids and the nature of the liquids goes back far and deep. Lost in history is the creation of cheese, but it is easy to imagine what might have happened. Some ancient made a bladder out of the guts of an animal and decided to take some milk to a nearby village. Bracing the bladder full of milk on the back of a donkey, the rider set out and bounced along the rough path, stopping occasionally but continuing on until reaching the village. Expecting to pour out tasty milk, the rider would have been surprised and perhaps dismayed to see that it had turned into a curdy lump. Our proto-cheese creator was curious enough to taste the stuff, as were others, who quite enjoyed it. So the act of moving milk led to the creation of a whole new product.

The history of the nectar of the gods is similarly transportation-related. Despite some disagreement over who invented barrels for the transportation of liquids, at some point wine was put in wooden casks for transportation from place to place. Over time, people came to realize the effect that the wood was having on the wine, and the barrels changed

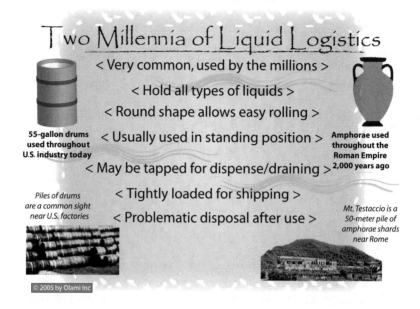

**Exhibit F.4   Liquid Logistics Has Been Around — and Facing the Same Issues —
for a Long Time**

from a transportation method to a storage/processing method. Moreover, to the benefit of all of us bourbon lovers, the effect of wood storage on other liquids also became apparent. So what started out as a method of moving liquid ended up creating a whole set of new liquid products.

The effects of transportation can also be seen in the use of "liquid gold," as Homer referred to olive oil. Olive oil was highly valued in ancient Rome and was accepted as a form of payment of taxes and tribute from the provinces. The freshest, highest quality oil was used as food and medicine. For oil that was lower quality or that had been affected by the long journey to Rome from the many locales from which it was sent, there were many other uses. Olive oil was used for cleaning and personal hygiene, to light lamps, to grease wheels and machines, and to prepare the dead for their final journey. The scale on which olive oil was transported to Rome is demonstrated by the 150-foot height of Mt. Testaccio near Rome, as shown in Exhibit F.4. Mt. Testaccio, the Hill of Broken Jars, is made up entirely of broken pieces of amphorae that were off-loaded from ships at that point on their way to Rome. The amphorae served as intermediate bulk containers (IBCs) for the long journey from overseas, and at Mt. Testaccio the olive oil was transferred to smaller jars for local distribution. The amphorae were an ancient version of bulk transport — the shape of the jars was such that their necks and looping carrying handles would fit between the jars on the next higher level during extended transportation. The olive oil trade in ancient times was truly of bulk proportion — the potsherds at Mt. Testaccio alone represent the movement of over a billion gallons of olive oil.

Given all of the forces described earlier that are at work against recognition of the operational aspects of liquids as liquids, it is little wonder that the value of Supply Chain for Liquids has not been recognized, much less exploited, in the business community. This is a reversible condition, as soon as we show the incredible power, flexibility, and — not incidentally — savings that are available from the proper use of Supply Chain for Liquids concepts. If you are one who does not find a way to adapt and apply at least some of these principles to your business, you may be the kind of person to whom the business thought applies, "I would like this person as my main competitor." This book does demand quite a lot from you — that you put some of your standard assumptions into a little box on the side while you look to see if other understandings may be valid; that you fight against what Malcolm Frank, president and CEO of CXO Systems, calls the "conspiracy of consultants, academics, and pundits that have produced … mechanisms more for their own goals than those of their clients"; that you look at a bigger picture than what you may be used to looking at or even have all the tools right now to look at. It even demands of you the greatest price it can ask you to pay — your time: time to think and to discuss and to envision, time without which new ideas and new methodologies are not even conceived, much less born. But as you will see, the rewards for your effort are significant or even dramatic, both for creating new revenue opportunities and for reducing product and operating costs. If you do see ways of moving your business forward based on some of these ideas, then welcome aboard. It is a heck of a voyage.

Introduction

Liquids are fantastic products to work with. As we shall see in this book, they can move without being moved, be inventoried without being counted, and be prepared without being processed. Anyone who works with liquids should be thrilled to have the good fortune to work with liquid products rather than (or at least, in addition to) discrete products. Liquids have marvelous characteristics that offer massive logistics advantages to anyone who knows how to use them.

Unfortunately, for a variety of reasons, it is common practice to completely ignore these advantages. Our training in "things" — widgets and gizmos and any other discrete items — has led us to think of liquids in terms of a "bottle of cleaning fluid," a "jug of cider," or a "drum of lubricant." In fact, for liquid-logistics purposes, these are not liquids at all. Our "things"-based world has desensitized us to the behavior, the opportunities, and the advantages that liquids offer in the world of logistics. We are so out of practice at looking and actually seeing that we need a special lens, a la Sherlock Holmes, with which to view liquid logistics. The lens, which we refer to as the Liquid Lens^{SM}, is actually a whole methodology for relating to liquid logistics that emphasizes such topics as the elementary nature of liquid-logistics processes and the unity of a liquid-logistics system. The Liquid Lens is described in detail in Chapter 3. Anyone who works with liquids — anyone who manufactures, buys, sells, moves, or uses them — who does not look at logistics through a Liquid Lens is working partially blind.

Another barrier to recognizing and implementing logistics methods that exploit the liquid nature of products is our approach to fixing problems — problem arises, problem fixed, end of problem. Like holistic medicine for the human body, though, an all-inclusive approach to business processes can discover relationships between different parts that are not readily obvious. Traditional problem fixing uses a process of isolation and

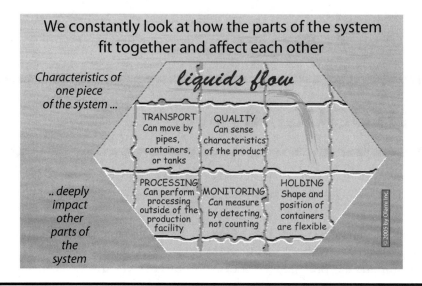

Exhibit I.1   A Full System Takes into Account the Characteristics of Each of Its Pieces

segregation, of identifying a "broken part" and fixing that part. When the washing machine does not drain properly, you clean out the pump without thinking to look for the gap in the drum that lets the lint through to the pump, and when the technician comes for the fourth time to fix the Internet connection, you know she is looking only at the smallest part of the problem.

On the other hand, the process of designing a full system such as Supply Chain for Liquids® involves continually connecting each piece to the whole and the whole to each piece. This method of thinking is built on the idea that a small change in one place is going to impact a process elsewhere in the system, or as this book shows, this minor piece here opens up all those opportunities over there. These changes are not necessarily related to problems — things may be running "fine" — but through education or technology, the user may realize that there is another way to perform a specific task within the system. Exhibit I.1 illustrates a common example of the relationship between pieces of a system and the whole system. The evaluation of alternative approaches to a specific activity should include identifying the implications and results on the rest of the activities in the overall process. Spot-fixing is not enough; we need to think in terms of adjusting systems. Incidentally, these two points (large impact of small changes and systemwide behavior) are two characteristics of the fascinating science that is called chaos theory. Chaos theory lurks constantly around liquid logistics, from these conceptual points to the turbulence in a liquid going through a bend in a pipe, although a detailed integration of liquid logistics and chaos theory is beyond the scope of this book.

It is not by accident, however, that we have come into the habit of spot-fixing problems or viewing global systems in a very local manner, and it would be overly simplistic to suggest that we stop doing it. One cannot be expected to rise above the limitations of his or her own knowledge and "comfort zone"; as the old Japanese proverb says: to a man with a hammer, everything looks like a nail. It is unreasonable to expect that the warehouseperson whose expertise is loading the trucks would be aware of the information-systems implications of changing carton sizes. On the other hand, part of liquid thinking is that all members of the team — the warehouseperson, the information-systems person, and all the rest — relate to their own areas in terms of the liquid nature of the product they are dealing with. This will provide the common foundation so that when the players come together to address situations and opportunities that have arisen, they will have this common liquids-based view of the entire system of which they are all a part.

In addition to connecting all the members of the internal team together, the approach described here assumes that another voice is heard — the voice of the customer. As we will see in our discussion of the Liquid Lens, the voice of the customer is not just heard, but rather in our methodology it is a driving force in designing the system we want to create. The "voice of the customer" in our context does not refer only to routine operational activities — the customer wants to accept deliveries in the morning and not in the afternoon, the customer wants preattached labels, etc. It refers to the customer's vision for the customer's own business, where it is going, what opportunities the customer would like to explore but does not yet have the capability. Supply Chain for Liquids offers logistics possibilities that do not exist without it, but these possibilities only come to full fruition when they are translated into business activities that provide advantages in the marketplace. The Supply Chain for Liquids approach provides a forum for relating strategically to customers, in a way that is beneficial to everyone involved in the supply stream.

This book does not attempt to present the "one right answer" to liquid logistics, because there is no such thing. A system that works wonders in one company might be a disaster in another company. There are many factors that come into play in determining what the Supply Chain for Liquids should look like for any particular company, and one of the joys of Supply Chain for Liquids is that it does not dictate a single rigid set of rules but rather consists of a methodology that is adaptable across a wide variety of companies, industries, and cultures. For example, one company might opt for one type of liquid monitoring technique described in Chapter 8, and another company might decide that a different technique is more appropriate. This type of variability does not affect the fact that both companies are fully utilizing the Supply Chain for Liquids method. Further, within a company, the definition of Supply Chain for Liquids can treat different liquid products differently. One set of liquids might be included in a comprehensive and sophisticated Supply Chain for Liquids system, a second set in a simpler system, and a third set might be handled in a "discrete" manner and not included in Supply Chain for Liquids at all. Again, there are many factors that are taken into account in coming to this decision, as is described in the planning process using the Liquid Lens (Chapter 3). This diversity of approach does not even prevent a company from achieving "optimal Supply Chain for Liquids" status, in that this status is achieved through a combination of a highly effective planning process and a highly effective execution process.

This book does not claim that one method or combination of methods is the "one right answer." But what this book does try to present is the concept that "the right answer is one," that is, the best way to approach Supply Chain for Liquids is a single unified approach to the entire system that best exploits the liquid nature of the product. For many companies in many industries, this is little-explored territory that offers great riches from a properly run effort.

This book is also not intended to present "all the answers." It does not touch on many standard Supply Chain issues that are the same for liquid or discrete products, as there is already a sizable volume of literature that covers the breadth of "Supply Chain" under its many definitions. This book is not a basic handbook of Supply Chain management or execution, and in fact assumes that the reader is already familiar with fundamental Supply Chain concepts as well as the general nature of logistics for liquid products. This book does serve as a survey of the issues associated with liquid products in a Supply Chain, and in particular those issues that differentiate liquid logistics from those of discrete products. It is the incremental element of liquid processes over or apart from discrete processes that serves as the focus of this book. Because of its breadth, some parts of the book will be too detailed for some readers, repetitive for others, and lacking in granularity for still others. Those who feel this way are missing perhaps the most important function of this book — to put Supply Chain for Liquids issues on the table in the context of companies who buy, sell, use, transport, or otherwise deal in liquid products. Each reader can define his or her own "take away" from the book, if not in the specific details then in raising liquids-related issues for the reader to apply to his or her own situation.

This book limits itself also in terms of the industries it touches on. Although there are specific applications of Supply Chain for Liquids in at least 24 different industries, as shown in Exhibit I.2, we use only a small

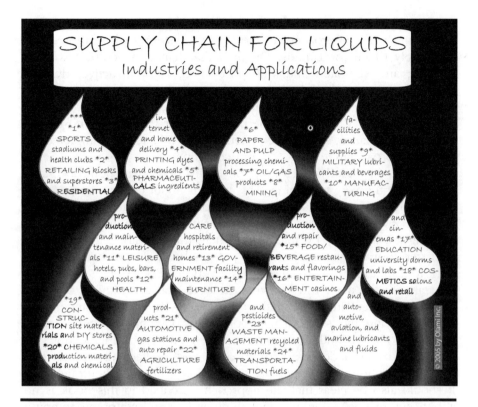

Exhibit I.2 Two Dozen Industries and Applications of Supply Chain for Liquids

number of industries throughout this book to demonstrate the planning, implementation, and operation of the Supply Chain for Liquids methodology. As described in this book, each industry brings a different "flavor" to Supply Chain for Liquids. Many industries have a strong "driver," be it the producer, the distributor, or the retailer, and the initiation and design as well as in some ways the operation of the system will depend on who the power player is in the relationship. The 80-20 rule is stronger in some industries than others, so some industries will benefit by including a small population of liquids in Supply Chain for Liquids, and others will see the value of a broader installation. Some industries are primarily B2B (business to business), and others are more clearly B2C (business to consumer), and the nature of the logistics flow is quite different between them. Of course, the nature of the liquids themselves will have an impact on the detailed design of the system and the exact functionality that will be included in it. Some mature industries will be caught in a typical paradox presented by systems such as Supply Chain for Liquids. On the one hand, the mature status of the industry means that competitive advantage does not come from product differentiation or new applications, but rather from paradigm-shifting approaches to the logistics system, such as represented by Supply Chain for Liquids. On the other hand, the current ways of working are well-oiled and well-entrenched, and the active, dynamic search for new methodologies that characterizes newer industries may well be lacking. Supply Chain for Liquids takes this into account by presenting many variations on the basic configuration, each with its own cost-benefit balance, so that the system can be adapted and implemented to meet a broad range of needs and conditions.

There is an underlying assumption in this book that should be stated explicitly at the very beginning. This book is about change, and in some cases significant change to the way a company operates. If things are going very well for your company and for now you are more focused on keeping the company on track rather than thinking about or taking the next step forward, you may want to put this book on the shelf and come back to it in a few months. It is often a very hard decision as to whether to deal with the devil you know or the devil you don't know, or to put it differently, deciding which risk you prefer — the risk of change or the risk of staying the same. This book offers incremental steps toward significant change and does not demand grandiose reengineering, but having said that, it does require an open and intellectually honest look at your operations and the ability to envision "things as they might be." It should also be clear that the approach described in this book is not about "automating" — taking something as it is and wrapping computer programs or high technology around it. It is about looking at a very different way of running the logistics of the liquids-related side of your business. As described in Chapter 3, you might think of it as the exact opposite of automating your business. Instead of adding an additional layer of complexity, such as often occurs during the process of automation, one of our objectives is to simplify the logistics process and reduce or eliminate complexity — with its associated costs and problems — from the system.

The first step in the process of change is recognition; you must have a reasonably clear picture of where you are and where you want to go in order to get an idea of the process of change. A key aspect of recognition is realizing the liquid nature of the industry you are in. As described in Chapter 4, even businesses that are usually thought of only in discrete terms contain a very large liquid aspect. Identifying the liquids that are used in your business — be it as part of the product, part of the production process, part of the overhead activities such as building maintenance, part of the transport system, etc. — gives you the first stage of recognition and the platform from which to build strong liquid logistics. Assuming we are better prepared than Alice in Wonderland, who did not really know where she wanted to go (which led the Cheshire Cat to point out that it did not really matter which road she took to get there), we should be able to develop a clear picture of the liquids that are used in our business and the scope of their usage. Using the concepts in this book, you can undertake the process of defining where you want to go as well as drawing the map of how you plan to get there. The key point for starters, though, is identifying the liquids you use and where and why they are used. These will be your focus as you pursue Supply Chain for Liquids.

Finally, it is important to keep our "eyes on the prize" as we go through this book. To provide as full a description as possible, this book touches on many topics, from a detailed description of the functionality of liquid-level sensors, to the strategic corporate benefits that can be gained from new marketing channels that Supply Chain for Liquids opens. Each reader will connect with different elements that are presented and feel most comfortable with his or her area of knowledge and experience. The many aspects of Supply Chain for Liquids are presented not to bore the reader in the areas of nonfamiliarity, but in the spirit of the major underlying theme of Supply Chain for Liquids — that it is a unified system that puts together its diverse pieces in what is in total the most effective manner. This ultimate purpose is best served by having all of the departments and disciplines in a company understand the others that are presented in this book. The breadth of topics is intended to help break down the sectorial approach that limits the effectiveness of and the benefits that result from so many business advancement efforts.

About This Book

Our journey through the ideas of liquid logistics is, of course, only the first step toward realizing the tremendous benefits that a truly liquids-based system has to offer. We will start this journey by looking at techniques that are currently used for liquid logistics in a variety of settings — upstream, B2B, and B2C, as well as common logistics practices within a company. Using existing practices as a starting point, we introduce the concept of the four levels of liquid logistics:

- Supply Chain
- Adapted Supply Chain
- Supply Chain for Liquids®
- Optimal Supply Chain for Liquids

Before going through each level in detail, we will set the stage for Thinking Liquid^{SM} by describing the Liquid Lens^{SM}. The Liquid Lens is not just an approach to designing a liquid-logistics system; it is a way of thinking in core liquids-based terms rather than translating discrete systems into usage for liquids. We also take a look at the world to understand the truly gigantic scope of liquid usage across many industries, far beyond the "process industries" that are normally considered the sole domain of liquids, and into the massive product and process presence of liquids in many industries.

Having laid the groundwork we will then get into the four types of liquid logistics systems in detail. A Supply Chain can evolve into an Adapted Supply Chain for liquid products, but from there it is a complete switch in thinking and approach to move to Supply Chain for Liquids. Once there, it is an additional evolutionary approach to reach the pinnacle of liquid logistics, that of Optimal Supply Chain for Liquids.

Having laid out the different types of systems, we will look at them from the perspective of each activity in the supply stream — production, distribution, and customer/user. After exploring in detail each of these perspectives, we look at some of the exceptions and special considerations that frequently must be taken into account related to liquid logistics.

To understand the organizational and management processes associated with liquid logistics, we take a look at issues related to managing Supply Chain for Liquids systems. These include designing/implementing/maintaining the system, implementation of RFID for Liquids® and a dynamic method for intercompany collaboration called Coordinated Procedures for Visibility Response^{SM} (CPVR^{SM}). We also look at other aspects of managing the Supply Chain for Liquids such as integration with other information systems and outsourcing specific aspects of system operation.

We round out the study of liquid logistics by looking at additional major business benefits of Supply Chain for Liquids, including the strategic, financial, and environmental areas. To keep our sights looking forward, we will discuss the achievement of Optimal Supply Chain for Liquids — what this status means, how Supply Chain for Liquids activity is measured, and how we can benefit from the Supply Chain for Liquids Society. And as the final step in this circuit, we will come back full circle to discuss the application of Supply Chain for Liquids principles to discrete products, returning to our "source" with a completely different understanding of the logistics possibilities that are available to us. Like the precipitation/evaporation cycle, this loop ends up near to where it started, but having offered plenty of benefit and plenty of opportunity for growth along the way.

Although this book is constructed according to the logical flow described here, the reader may find it useful to reference chapters not in the sequence in which they are presented. This might be because some chapters are of particular interest to the reader while others are less so, or it might be because some topics are treated in a generalized way at one point and in more detail later on. Chapter 11, for example, examines in detail the marketing, financial, and environmental issues that are referred to in a general way earlier in the book, so the reader who wants to gain a deeper understanding of this material may want to read some of those chapters when they are referenced.

In addition to this book, information regarding Supply Chain for Liquids and many of the methods related to it are found at the Internet site for Supply Chain for Liquids: www.SupplyChainForLiquids.com. A parallel site, www.RFIDforLiquids.com, focuses on the RFID for Liquids element of Supply Chain for Liquids.

Chapter 1

Current Liquid-Logistics Techniques

We start our voyage into the world of liquid logistics with a survey of liquid logistical techniques currently in use. This is just the beginning of the journey. Once we have gone over current practice, we can look further afield and push to new horizons. However, we have several objectives in looking at where things stand now:

- There is value in seeing the techniques that other people and other industries use for handling liquids. Improvement or innovation often occur after people observe how something is done that is completely unrelated to their own interests, and then adapt some of the underlying principles to their own needs. The area "outside the box" already exists; we just need to be willing to look there to take advantage of it. Consider Hermann Hollerith, who adapted the method for controlling weaving looms to develop a machine to process the 1890 U.S. census, or Lord Timothy Dexter, who used New England bed warmers as molasses strainers in the West Indies earlier in that century. Knowledge from outside our own area of focus can be very valuable. Our review here does not really even go so far outside the box. The intention is to provide insights into the various ways that liquids are currently handled from a logistics perspective, and then to provide ideas about how they may be handled in other fields.

- We can identify advantages and disadvantages of different methods, which provide direction regarding characteristics to avoid or characteristics to pursue regarding our own logistics flow. For example, if the external-pressure option of the liner method, as described below, provides advantages that we need for our operations, we may want to consider utilizing a portion of that methodology in our current systems. Seeing the benefits or drawbacks of other ways of doing things can put a different light on our way of doing things, and lead to the creative thinking that will help us do what we do better.

- We can also use a discussion of the benefits and drawbacks of different liquid-logistics methods to provide direction in developing a truly liquids-based logistics system that capitalizes on the characteristics that distinguish liquids from discrete products. That is, the list we compile of best practices, of methods that provide operational or other advantages, and of problems to avoid will guide us in designing the most appropriate liquid logistical system for our company, within the overall framework of Supply Chain for Liquids®.

What does the world of liquid logistics look like? There are many ways to view it, so let us jump in and see what we find.

Upstream/Source Liquid Practices

Starting at the beginning, the first segment we observe is the liquids at their source, or the upstream stage of the logistics flow. At this point, the liquids are being produced and moved in very large quantities. From the oil fields to the refineries, from the mining/mineral processing plant to the chemical manufacturer, from the agricultural ingredients supplier to the processing facility, these liquids move by pipeline, ship, or rail by the hundreds of thousands or millions of gallons. The order of magnitude of liquids moving through these channels — 50 million gallons per day through the Alaska pipeline, and much more than that through the capacity of today's supertankers, for example — means that only very-large-capacity methodologies are appropriate at this stage of the logistics flow.

At first blush, this last statement seems patently obvious, but if we stop to think about it for a moment, there is something interesting lurking there. "For liquids moving in large quantities, only large-capacity methods are appropriate." In a positive sense, this statement seems quite true, to the point that thinking in any other way seems absurd. Because we have gotten used to the idea of the supertanker, it would not make much sense to fill 50 million balloons with a gallon each of oil and then ship them on a container ship. If we can pour the liquid directly into the supertanker, why bother with packaging? It does not add any value to the product, or promote the logistics process, or serve a safety or some other purpose. Quite the opposite — any space that the packaging would take up would be "wasted" from a logistics perspective, so the introduction of packaging where it is not necessary would actually be counterproductive. In thinking about the loading and unloading of a supertanker versus a container ship, it is clear that the movement of five million gallons per hour through the filling or emptying process of a supertanker is much more efficient than those giant dockside cranes placing 20-foot trailers, with 6000 gallons of liquid capacity each, onto a container ship one at a time. A supertanker does not lose flexibility within its massive capacity, as the compartments within the ship are separated and can hold different liquids.

For all of these reasons and plenty more, these large-capacity methods such as supertankers, pipelines, or rail cars are the only way that it makes sense to move large quantities of liquids. The question that comes up, though, is the flip side of this statement: given the advantages of these methods for large quantities of liquids, does it not make sense to use these techniques where possible for smaller quantities of liquids? If the advantages described here — efficient use of space, efficient movement of product — were applicable only to large-scale product movement, the question would not come up. But given that these efficiencies are important for any liquid in any logistics situation, are there things we can learn from large-scale liquid-logistics methods that would be beneficial in smaller-scale environments? Or to look at our statement in the negative, is it only for liquids moving in large quantities that large-capacity methods are appropriate? The mind can immediately jump to an absurd image, a 1000-foot-long supertanker sailing down Elm Street to deliver a few cold beers to the local bar. Of course, we are not referring to the specific vehicle, but what we are referring to is the possibility of utilizing the logistics techniques of high-volume upstream liquids to make the downstream liquid flow more efficient.

Another ultrahigh-volume liquid-logistics technique is pipes or tunnels. Two well-known systems are among the largest for their respective liquids. The 800-mile-long Alaska pipeline mentioned above was built aboveground to protect the permafrost layer. In contrast, New York City's water-supply system consists of underground tunnels that bring water from 120 miles away through a series of underground tunnels to the tune of over 800 million gallons per day. In a sense, each of these systems attempts to mimic the natural flow of liquids, the river. A river, of course, makes its own "container," with the laws of nature dictating where the river channel will be, unless it is altered through man-made construction. From

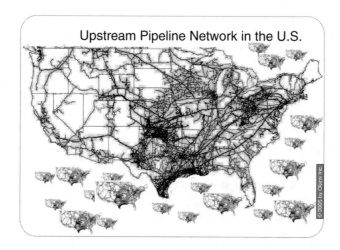

Upstream Pipeline Network in the U.S.

Exhibit 1.1 Large-Scale Principles Are Applicable to Smaller-Scale Liquid-Logistics Operations

a logistics perspective, pipelines (like supertankers) minimize or eliminate the handling of individual units of the liquid, and in fact relate to the liquids as a flow rather than as identifiable, discrete units. The New York City water tunnels further utilize the liquid characteristics of the "product" by using gravity flow to move the water from its source to virtually all of its users. These additional techniques of large-scale systems, viewing liquids as a flow rather than as discrete units and utilizing the characteristics of liquids that can be useful for logistics purposes, also enter our thinking as we consider liquid-logistics situations on a smaller scale. Just because these pipes and tunnels are rarely seen, we should not make the mistake of ignoring their presence or what we can learn from them. For example, Exhibit 1.1 gives an idea of the massive scale and extent of the gas pipeline network currently operating in the United States.

The two large-scale methods, supertankers and pipes/tunnels, have an important distinction that is useful to consider as we think in terms of liquid logistics. The supertanker and its compartments represent the largest form of "packaging" we can create for the liquid, and having created the largest packaging that we are able to, we avoid creating smaller packaging or grouping segments. Even with this, the supertanker and its compartments move with the liquid, that is, the liquid flows in and out of the tanker but not through the tanker. This is in contrast with a pipe or tunnel, which remains in a fixed position while the liquid flows through it. This is the ultimate efficiency in terms of the liquid flow. To the degree to which we are moving liquids alone, and not investing our resources to move nonproduct elements such as packaging, these large-scale liquid flows work most effectively. The example of the overall flow of oil demonstrates the connection between these two forms. Oil flows from the fields through the Alaska pipeline overland to Valdez, at which point it is loaded onto tankers for its seagoing journey. Each technique has its own place, but in combination, it would be difficult for us to think of a more effective way to move the liquids. Again, this sounds like a concept to keep in mind as we look at logistics systems for liquid products.

Not incidentally, we can also use these mass-movement liquid techniques to demonstrate the changes in our thought processes that are required for liquid-logistics development. The earliest settlers in what is now New York got their water from the streams and springs that dotted the area or from individually dug wells, and this was sufficient in the early years. As the population increased and these water sources could not keep up with demand, the settlers were forced to ask the question: what do we do for water now? The paradigm shift at that point led to the construction of deeper public wells to serve the population, and that solution lasted about 100 years. The next "leap" in thinking was the construction of reservoirs around what is now lower Manhattan, which again was satisfactory until population pressures both dried up the resources and polluted what was left. Because "doing without" was not an option when dealing with water, city planners came up with the "next-generation" solution, and in the mid-1800s they built an aqueduct from what is now Westchester County to reservoirs at 42nd and 86th streets. This Croton system was later extended to the Catskills system to bring the water supply to its current condition. What is important from our perspective is that we can sit here, at a distance of time and space from these events, and see the enormous leaps in logistics techniques that occurred as the need arose — moving from natural springs and fountains to private wells, then from private to public wells, then moving from wells to local reservoirs, then moving from local reservoirs to aqueducts — in each case stretching far beyond the thought and logistical boundaries of the previous technique. Another difference in perspective is that, in the case of New York City, they *had* to find a solution; being without water is not a problem you can sweep under the rug. Both of these traits — making leaps of thinking and action, and taking decisions to make changes in the face of good reasons (but probably not as compelling as those of New York City) — are part and parcel of approaching a liquid-logistics project. As we look at historical New York, it is easy to see the logistics progression related to water, but as we look at the logistics related to the liquids that are either consumed in or produced by our own operations, those leaps and those changes are much less clear and certainly not easy to see. As an aside, for the thumpers among us, we can get biblical backing for this transition sequence. The Song of Songs, although not at the top of most logisticians' lists of resources, puts this whole development process in a single succinct phrase — "a fountain of gardens, a well of living waters, and streams" (Chapter 4, Verse 15) — following exactly the same fountain/well/stream sequence we just described.

Another mass-movement liquid-logistics method, that of railroad tank cars, helps us make the transition from very high quantities to intermediate quantities of liquids. With a standard tank car capacity of 20,000 to 30,000 gallons, it is not difficult to string together a flow of several hundred thousand gallons or up toward one million gallons of liquid for a single train. Railroad tank cars are like a pipeline in that they support the movement of large quantities of liquids, and they are like supertankers in that they actually move with the product. They also offer another logistically interesting capability: when disengaged from the "flow" of the train as a whole, an individual tank car sitting on a siding can serve a local requirement (a factory or production facility, for example) as a reservoir, that is, a form for holding inventory. Unlike either a pipeline or a supertanker, the railroad tank car's colossal size (when it is part of a train) does not work against it for individual needs (when it is detached from the train and located at a facility). Like the pipeline-supertanker combination, a railroad tank car has different characteristics that can be applied at different points in the logistics stream as appropriate. This flexibility, which we can think of as a sort of self-contained intermodality that creates a methodology that can be applied in different ways, has logistics advantages and implications that we will want to take into account as we look at our liquid-logistics techniques.

For liquid products, a railroad tank car can serve a transport as well as a stocking function, and can also lead us toward other important logistics principles as shown in Exhibit 1.2. Just as tank cars have fittings on the top to load liquids into the tank and bottom outlet valves for unloading the liquids, hopper cars that carry certain types of solids have similar fittings for loading and unloading the products. Hopper cars typically carry dry bulk commodities such as plastic pellets, grain, or coal, and have an opening (or are open-topped) for loading these products and sloped bottoms leading to outlet gates for unloading the products. The loading of these products from silos into a hopper car looks very much like loading liquids from a storage tank into a tank car; the car opening is positioned under an outlet, a valve is opened, and the product flows into the car. Unloading the product can also be done in a similar way into a storage cell beneath the car. In seeing this, we understand that logistics principles that we define for liquids can also be applied to certain other products, particularly granular products that flow under gravity and can be handled in mass quantities as opposed to individual units.

Exhibit 1.2   Several Useful Liquid-Logistics Principles Are Embodied in a Railroad Tank Car

We cannot go past silos without paying tribute to silo thinking, that much-maligned characteristic that deserves better than what it is getting. Silos have been a source of creative, interdisciplinary thinking since they were first known nearly 10,000 years ago. Silos were originally pits dug in the ground, in which corn or other produce was stored for later use as feed. The word "silo" comes from the Greek *siros* for pit, according to its original meaning of an underground, airtight feed store. Even back then, the need to seal the silo to prevent the produce from rotting was known by interdisciplinary agriculturalists who were well familiar with principles of chemistry (or "whole-system people" from a Supply Chain for Liquids perspective). It took until the late 1800s until silo thinking truly became robust. First, the age-old practice of digging silo holes was replaced with the practice of building aboveground silos — truly a revolution in thinking. Following this move, the development of silo thinking was rapid and exciting. The pioneering Wisconsinite F. H. King, for example, not only changed the shape of silos from rectangular to round as a way to resolve issues of corner rot and sagging sides, but he actually built a round silo inside a round barn for maximum efficiency in the distribution of feed to the livestock. This combination of form and function is rarely seen, and certainly speaks highly of silo thinking. Vertical thinking continued when a farmer saw a glass-lined tank that had been built for a brewery, and commented to the manufacturer that if it was set on end it would make a great silo. So it was done, and glass-lined silos became known for their quality due to their resistance to silage acids and spoilage. For creative logistical approaches, silo thinking is clearly quite special and particularly desirable.

We started our journey by talking about the most massive upstream liquid flows, and quickly discovered many principles that we will be able to apply to more immediate liquid-logistics situations. These principles will also be important as we develop the liquids-based Supply Chain for Liquids approach. The principles we have discovered include:

- Packaging has an impact on the efficient use of space.
- The efficiency of product movement depends on the methods of loading and unloading, and packaging also affects product movement.
- Liquids should be viewed and handled as a flow rather than as individual, identifiable units.
- The characteristics of liquids, versus those of discrete products, should be utilized to the advantage of the logistics flow.
- It is important to focus on the movement of the liquid rather than the movement of the package, and to identify the largest form of "packaging" possible.
- A supply stream can include two or more forms of logistics based on the characteristics of the different segments of the stream.
- Revolutionary rather than evolutionary thinking may be needed to move to the next level of logistics effectiveness.
- The motivations for advances in liquid logistics may come from "must do" requirements, or they may come from internal or competitive motivations.
- Logistics methods can incorporate multiple capabilities that can be used in different ways, such as with railroad tank cars.
- Liquid-logistics principles can be applied to certain types of non-liquid materials that have flow and other characteristics similar to liquids.
- Silo thinking — the continual creative upgrading of logistics techniques to address an ongoing operational need — is a great thing.

Now that we have looked at the first segment of liquid logistics — the handling of large-quantity upstream/source liquids — let us go with the flow and take a look at current liquid-logistics practices in the B2B (business to business) segment.

Business-to-Business Practices

The topic of B2B liquid logistics covers a lot of turf, including the industries listed in Chapter 4 and more. At this stage in the logistics flow, products are still moving in large quantities, but the supply river of liquid product coming from upstream is being split into separate supply streams directed to different customers for use in their own businesses. As described above, railroad tank cars are one logistics method with interesting characteristics that are appropriate to the B2B flow, and we can take a look at several more methods and see what advantages and disadvantages we can see in working with them.

The most conspicuous form of B2B movement of liquid products is in relatively small packages of various types: bottles, jugs, pails, and so on up to 55-gallon drums. This way of handling liquids is convenient because it fits right in with the way we handle non-liquid products. If we have forklifts and pallets and racks and shelves that we use to move and store the discrete materials we work with, then the exact same methods and systems apply to all of the products. We translate this sameness between liquid and discrete products as ease of use, even though we lose any benefits or advantages that liquid products may hold over discrete products from a logistics perspective. In any case, the ease of use of the liquid is an important issue, and as we consider different liquid-logistics methods or design our own method, the ease of use is an important factor.

Another advantage of these types of containers is that they provide flexibility in the quantity of the liquid used, with the remainder staying in the container until needed. For example, as cutting fluid is needed during the production process, the machine operator may pour fluid into the reservoir to maintain its level and leave the container nearby for future use. A groundskeeper can use as much pesticide as is needed for a particular spraying, and the remainder stays in the container until needed.

Although many types of liquid containers are "passive" in that they do not offer any particular liquid-related features, some are constructed in such a way as to provide increased functionality during usage. Pressurized containers; containers with special spouts, valves, or control mechanisms; containers with fittings to attach directly to a piece of equipment or dispense mechanism; and containers with other special adaptations make a standard bottle or jug much more useful. An example that combines several of these types of features is a beer barrel that a brewery or beer distributor provides to a pub. A beer barrel goes beyond being just a container; it includes a number of specifically liquid-oriented capabilities that we can examine in more detail to get an idea of its contribution to liquid logistics.

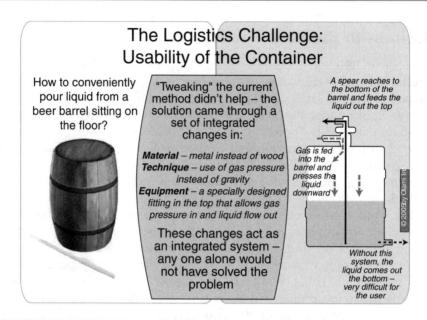

Exhibit 1.3   Changing Needs Lead to Changes in Liquid-Logistics Configuration

Beer kegs have come a long way since beer wagon drivers had to wear leather aprons to protect themselves from the rough wood of the barrel and from the beer that would spill out when the barrel broke open. Both the kegs themselves and the beer taps from those days have been completely redesigned for the purpose of improved logistics. For example, wooden kegs had to be physically inverted for the beer to flow out, which demanded difficult and time-consuming handling at the pub. To overcome this, a design was needed that would allow beer to be easily extracted from the top of the barrel so that it could be used "as it set."

The resolution to this logistics problem came through a completely different way of thinking and a subsequent change in the configuration of the equipment. The key to the solution is found in a fitting with two openings that is placed in the top of the barrel, as shown in principle in Exhibit 1.3. One opening is for the entry of gas, which feeds into the barrel. Pressure is applied from an external source through this opening, and this presses downward on the surface of the liquid inside the barrel, as shown by the dashed gray lines. Under normal circumstances and driven only by gravity, the liquid in the barrel would remain in the barrel. However, the second opening at the top of the barrel is attached to a "spear," a tube that extends from the opening at the top of the barrel down to near the bottom of the barrel. As the gas pressure pushes the liquid down, the liquid's only escape path is through the spear, which actually leads the liquid up through the second opening at the top of the barrel and out through a line exiting the barrel, as shown by the solid black line. The net result is that gas applied through the top of the barrel leads to the liquid exiting through a tube also at the top of the barrel, leading to the result we sought to begin with. Other features, such as the addition of a collar to protect the top fixtures, rounded out the complete design.

This "leap," though, is not just in the design of the fixtures within the barrel, but in the design of the barrel itself. To support this under-pressure technique, the prior barrel construction, from wood, would not be suffi-cient. A wooden barrel would not hold the pressure needed to drive the liquid up through the top opening and would immediately start to leak. So an attempt to find a solution with a wooden barrel would come to naught; the solution had to come from looking at the whole system. Without the ability to pressurize, the only solution available is bottom-exit, as shown by the dotted black line, which does not meet the objective of the specific application. The revised design, construction, and materials for the barrel, plus the design of the fixtures, together were necessary to come up with the optimal logistics approach. That sounds like another important characteristic to add to our list in considering approaches to liquid-logistics systems.

No sooner do we come up with a great solution than another issue pops up, following the general principle that solving any problem only lets the problems beneath it rise to the surface. To avoid having to swap a barrel each time one empties out, we string together several barrels in daisy-chain fashion, each connected to the next, with the pressure source at the opposite end of the flow from the dispense line. Using the top-exit technique and connections between the openings, the gas pressure continually presses against the liquid at the far end of the system so that the liquid constantly flows into the dispense line. The drawback of such a one-after-the-other approach, though, is that if the system is disrupted at any point — a gas or liquid line leaks, a barrel becomes faulty, or any other problem in the system — the whole system ceases working, and the user will not be able to dispense the liquid. Like a serial connection between light bulbs as opposed to a parallel connection, one failure stops the entire system from working. This is unacceptable, so we must specify that the system be constructed in such a way that there is no disruption of service, even during product replenishment or system servicing. We need the liquid version of a parallel connection, as opposed to a serial connection, between the containers holding the liquids.

The drawbacks of using containers to hold liquids are many, including forgoing the logistics advantages of liquids; the need to transport, handle, and dispose of the containers themselves; and a number of other disad-vantages as described in Chapter 5. The force of habit may be leading us to continue to use these types of containers, even when other logistics methods are more appropriate. However, in considering any other logistics method, we want to make sure that we meet or surpass the advantages that liquid containers do offer.

An enlarged version of a container is a tote, or intermediate bulk container (IBC). It is similar to the relatively smaller containers described above in that it holds a fixed amount of liquid and is portable, so that it can be moved to the most appropriate location for usage. It differs from the smaller containers in two ways. The most obvious difference is that it is larger and holds more liquid, which has several effects. First, because one container holds a larger amount of liquid, the container itself needs to be handled less often. Whereas five-gallon pails need to be retrieved and replaced each time one becomes empty, a 200- to 300-gallon tote can service the liquid requirement for a longer period of time and thus needs to be moved less frequently. Let us note that, as a point of value, we prefer a system that reduces the frequency and effort of handling the container. The flip side of this advantage is the relative difficulty of moving the container. Although an employee can easily pick up and move a two-gallon or five-gallon container from a storeroom to the point of usage, a mechanized method (forklift, hand truck, hoist, etc.) must be used to move a tote or IBC. We need to select the type of container and the container movement method that are practical for the work environment, and to make sure that the size/difficulty-of-movement equation works to our advantage.

The next level of containers used for liquid products is tanks. Tanks for liquids come in all shapes and sizes, and are made out of all types of materials including plastic and steel. Regulatory requirements influence tank design and construction, including single-wall/double-wall, edible or flammable contents, and the like. We are particularly interested in exploring the non-standard characteristics of tanks, that is, ways in which tanks are something other than enlarged bottles or jugs.

Tanks take on additional logistics capabilities when they are used in combination with liners. Tank liners are large bags that fit inside the tank and actually contain the liquid. When the tank is used with a liner, it is actually the bag that is filled and holds the liquid, as illustrated in Exhibit 1.4. Tank liners offer several logistics features:

- Because the liquid comes into contact only with the liner and not the tank, there is more flexibility as to the construction material for the tank itself. Sanitary and other requirements may be easier to meet with the liner than with the tank.
- The interior of the tank does not require cleaning because it does not come into contact with the liquid. The liner may be filled and emptied repeatedly, or it may be replaced after each usage or a

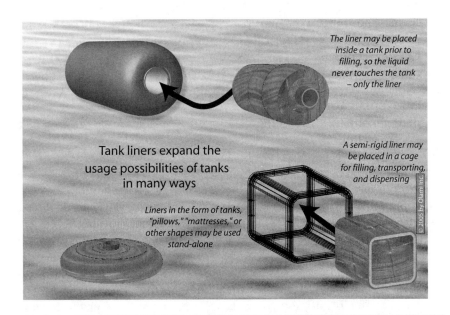

The liner may be placed inside a tank prior to filling, so the liquid never touches the tank – only the liner

Tank liners expand the usage possibilities of tanks in many ways

A semi-rigid liner may be placed in a cage for filling, transporting, and dispensing

Liners in the form of tanks, "pillows," "mattresses," or other shapes may be used stand-alone

© 2005 by Olam Inc.

Exhibit 1.4   Features Such as Tank Liners Extend Liquid-Logistics Capabilities

number of usages, depending on the needs of the system. This not only impacts the manual activities required for cleaning, but there are also environmental issues involved with cleaning a tank and flushing residues into the drainage system.

■ Liners address the air-exposure issue for sensitive liquids. Because the liner contracts as liquid flows out of it, there is no space created for air to enter, thus eliminating the need for a gas blanket. This is in contrast to a tank without a liner, where the space that is formed as the liquid drains must be filled with air or gas to prevent formation of a vacuum.

■ Liners offer an additional level of protection from leakage. In the event a liner does leak, the tank itself serves as a natural second layer of containment against the liquid exiting the system.

■ Tank/liner combinations offer additional options for liquid propulsion. Rather than having gas press directly on the liquid (in the style of beer barrels, as described earlier), the tank-liner configuration allows expansion of the space between the tank and the liner to create pressure on the liquid. That is, air can be pumped into the tank but outside of the liner, which would serve to contract the liner and thus press the liquid out the dispense line. Because the air presses on the liner and does not come into direct contact with the liquid, the liquid is not exposed directly to the air, and so no special gases are needed to perform this task.

Liners, like tanks, come in many sizes and configurations. A bag-in-box is actually a liner in a cardboard carton rather than a tank, and liners are available for virtually any size tank. The variety of tanks available, and the variety of liners, shows us the importance of flexibility in the physical configuration and functionality that is included in a liquid-logistics system.

Taking liners out of the tanks and using them as stand-alone liquid containers is the next liquid-logistics technique. Often referred to as flexible tanks, these bags, like liners, come in many sizes, shapes, and materials, and they are often built to contain certain types of liquid products. Like plastic bags or balloons, they start out deflated and so may easily be inserted into a tank and connected to the tubing. As can be expected of bags, they are very flexible in terms of their physical dimension. As they are filled, they take up more space; as they are emptied, they use less space; and before they are filled they take up very little space, and the same after they are emptied out. They conform to the space in which they are placed, constrained by their own shape. Because they are not fixed into any particular placement, they offer the flexibility of being placed or moved based on the needs at any particular time. This flexibility as to the size/shape/placement of the flexible tanks is a useful characteristic from a logistics perspective. Let us mark it as a capability to consider related to liquid logistics.

We have been referring to the B2B supply stream in a figurative sense, but we can also learn from it in quite a literal sense. Liquid logistics takes on a new meaning when considering James Brindley's construction of the Bridgewater Canal. Two liquids were involved in this project in very different ways: the liquids that would be carried in the boats on the canal, and the canal water itself. Although Brindley was a mechanic with strong engineering skills, he had never built a canal before and had never actually seen a canal, and he turned this ignorance to his advantage by not being limited by "conventional thinking" about canals. Although canals had been built in Europe, the Bridgewater Canal is considered the first canal built in England in the modern period, so its design and construction are truly an example of the power of starting a logistics analysis with a clean slate.

The Duke of Bridgewater needed to get the coal from his mines to the factories in Manchester, and he hired Brindley to do it. From a logistics perspective there was already revolutionary thinking at work. Up to that point, early in the Industrial Revolution and at the beginning of massive factory development, most transportation was done using horse-drawn wagons over poorly developed roads. This slow, difficult approach could not just be tweaked; a completely different solution, such as water transportation, was needed. The obvious solution was to make the Worsley Brook navigable, and with some adjustments and extensions, this could have been a workable solution. During the course of their planning, the Duke told Brindley about his visit to the Canal du Midi in France, and they also talked about the problems that would result from the periodic flooding of the Worsley Brook. Based on these inputs and a complete understanding of the Duke's needs, Brindley "cut through it" and determined that the best solution was to build a canal that would be completely separate from the brook. In addition, Brindley determined that the canal would be level for its entire length, thus avoiding elevation changes that would require locks in the canal, which would have disrupted the efficient flow of goods on the canal.

The easy part of Brindley's problem was the occasional hill that stood along the path of the canal. He was able to cut through or tunnel under them to achieve his objective. Much more problematic was that the canal's path crossed the Irwell River. How can you think about putting a canal across a river, and one with steep banks on both sides at that?

Not bowing to conventional thinking, Brindley determined to "do the impossible" and build the canal over the river. Although water-carrying aqueducts were reasonably common, a traffic-carrying waterway crossing over a river was, for many, unthinkable. Issues of weight, size, height, leakage, safety of those crossing both over and under — there was no end to the reasons given that Brindley's vision could not be accomplished.

Working in his own peculiar way, Brindley planned the multiarch bridge (shown in Exhibit 1.5) that would carry the canal as well as the materials that would be used for the bridge. Brindley was illiterate; it is certain that he never learned to write, although he may have been able to read some simple texts. (That puts a pin in some of our standard assumptions: that the man who designed what is today called "the forerunner of all modern canals" not only did not have a college degree, he could not even write his own name!) His habit was to work out problems in his head, and he would often stay at home, and even in bed, for days at a time as he worked through a particular problem. As proved by the results, his engineering sense overcame his lack of formal education; not one of his engineering efforts was ever known to fail.

Brindley continued to use uncommon techniques throughout the building of the bridge and other canals. Because building a canal over a river was unprecedented, the material for lining the bridge over the Irwell River had to be worked out. In the end, Brindley settled on a mixture of clay, water, and sand that proved impermeable. His techniques and methods were always adapted to the realities of the situation rather than simple repetition of existing methods, even his own. To speed and simplify the building of a canal tunnel, for example, he avoided sizing it to allow the pull-animals to walk alongside the canal within the tunnel. Rather, he made it much smaller by having the boat operator lie on his back and

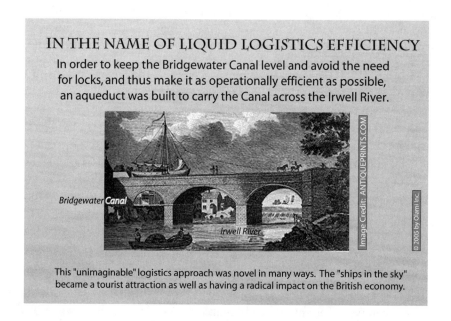

IN THE NAME OF LIQUID LOGISTICS EFFICIENCY

In order to keep the Bridgewater Canal level and avoid the need for locks, and thus make it as operationally efficient as possible, an aqueduct was built to carry the Canal across the Irwell River.

This "unimaginable" logistics approach was novel in many ways. The "ships in the sky" became a tourist attraction as well as having a radical impact on the British economy.

Exhibit 1.5   The Bridgewater Canal Shattered Many Barriers to Achieve Its Logistics Objective

push the boat through the tunnel by "walking" on the ceiling. Meanwhile, the pull-animal was brought around the hill to the other end of the tunnel.

Watching Brindley work, even from this distance of time, place, and world-view, is an act of joy. It is not enough that he blew everyone's socks off by building a waterway hung in the air, with boats, pull-animals, and attendants passing overhead while boats sailed by on the river below ("perhaps the greatest artificial curiosity in the world," according to one local writer). Brindley goes back and rechecks himself and the goal of the project. Remembering that the goal of his effort is not to build a leading-edge bridge — the goal is to move coal from the mine to the factory — Brindley decides that it is not enough to bring the canal to the mine entrance, but rather it would be most effective to *bring it right into the mine itself.* Talk about an optimal Supply Chain for Liquids! The canal was eventually extended to over 40 miles of tunnels within the mine, so the coal could go directly from the vein to the boat to the factory — a truly astonishing conception, execution, and achievement.

From a financial perspective, the project reduced the cost of coal by about half, but its business impact is often seen as much wider. The Bridgewater Canal has been marked as the beginning of the widespread use of canals throughout England, and the canal system is seen as a key component that supported the Industrial Revolution. On all levels — concept, design, technique, execution, utilization, results — James Brindley and the Bridgewater Canal left their mark on industry in the past and serve as a beacon for Supply Chain for Liquids thinking today.

This overview of current B2B liquid-logistics practices has not been an exhaustive survey of industry practices in intercompany logistics movement, but it has identified and highlighted a series of characteristics and capabilities that lead toward efficient liquid operations. The discussion has emphasized the importance of:

- Ease of handling and use of the system by the user with a readily acceptable method of operation
- Flexibility in the quantity of product used at any given time, without affecting the remainder of the product
- Minimizing the frequency of handling of the product and the amount of effort required when the product is handled
- A systemwide view of the logistics flow, including the use of the most appropriate equipment and maximum utilization of the capabilities of that equipment
- Continual flow of liquid for operational purposes without disruption of service during replenishment or maintenance
- Flexibility of the physical configuration and functionality of the system to meet specific user needs
- Flexibility in the location, shape, and placement of the liquid-logistics system components

This list of preferred liquid-logistics functionalities, together with the list developed earlier related to upstream/source liquids, begins to provide a guideline that we can use (1) to evaluate our current logistics operations and (2) to design a Supply Chain for Liquids system. Next, we will look at B2C (business to consumer) liquid-logistics practices to see what currently exists and how these practices can contribute to our thinking.

Business-to-Consumer Practices

Having looked at current upstream and B2B liquid-logistics techniques, we can now turn to B2C flows to see what we can learn from them. We use the phrase "learn from them" in a logistics sense, but even this phrase calls to mind that fantastic chapter in *Siddhartha*, the one about the Ferryman but which should have been called "Ode to a River." Now *that* is learning from a liquid flow. No matter what you think of *Siddhartha*, that chapter speaks to the liquids person in you. Some of the passages

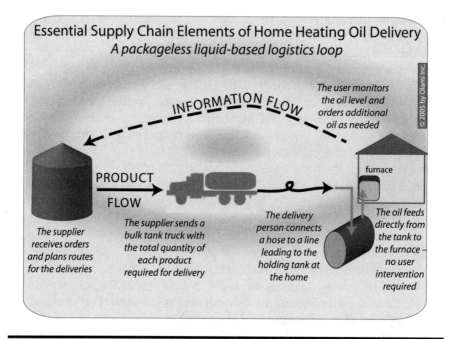

Exhibit 1.6   A Common Activity Offers Interesting Liquid-Logistics Capabilities

even have Supply Chain for Liquids flowing through them: "But out of all secrets of the river, he today only saw one, this one touched his soul. He saw: this water ran and ran, incessantly it ran, and was nevertheless always there, was always and at all times the same and yet new in every moment!" Herman Hesse was halfway to developing the marketing collateral for Supply Chain for Liquids.

Perhaps the most obvious home-delivery liquid flow is heating oil that is delivered from tank trucks. The truck arrives at the house, and the delivery person attaches a hose from the truck to a pipe that is connected to the oil tank. The delivery person delivers the requested quantity, retracts the hose, provides a receipt to the homeowner, and departs. To use the liquid, there is no action required on the part of the homeowner; when the furnace is turned on, the liquid flows directly from the tank to the furnace, with no interim activity by the homeowner. The major elements of this cycle are shown in Exhibit 1.6. In a sense, we take this approach to home heating oil for granted; it is useful, however, to consider what this process would be like if it used 55-gallon drums or some other form of container that the homeowner had to move, store, and dispose of or return.

One of the difficulties typically encountered during this process is for the homeowner to know how much oil remains in the tank. For aboveground tanks, a sight-glass makes this relatively simple, but for in-ground tanks this becomes very difficult. The homeowner has to periodically open the access cover to the tank, insert a dipstick, read it, and return the access cover to identify how much oil is in the tank and whether a replenishment order is required.

From this brief review of a B2C liquid flow, we can already derive several principles for effective liquid logistics. The first is that, if possible, the user should not handle the liquid at all; it should flow directly from the holding equipment to where it is needed. We would take this even farther and say the user should not necessarily be involved in the delivery process. In our case, after the homeowner orders the oil, there should be no further action required on the part of the homeowner. Finally, it should be very easy for the user to identify how much liquid remains in the system and know when to place a replenishment order; even better is for the on-hand balance information to be fed directly to the supplier, who under arrangement with the homeowner makes the delivery with zero involvement by the user other than updating/confirmation of deliveries made.

Several other liquid-logistics flows lead from business to the user/consumer. We can think of these basically as on-premise and off-premise streams within B2C. The on-premise stream refers to use of the liquid product by the consumer at the point at which it passes from the business to the consumer, and the off-premise stream means that the consumer receives the product at one time/location and actually uses it at a different time/location.

On-premise streams include fountain dispense of beverages at a restaurant, dispense of motor oil at an automobile repair facility or quick-lube station, of hand cleaners or other cleaning materials that are immediately used, of machine lubricants or other production-related fluids in a factory, etc. On-premise means "get and use" for the user or consumer and generally involves some sort of dispense equipment. Tank-to-dispense arrangements are relatively rare in on-premise logistics flows, with a much more common approach requiring the user to attach or place a container of liquid on the line leading to the dispense equipment. Examples of this are bag-in-box beverage syrup containers attached to the lines to the beverage dispense unit in a restaurant or jars of hand cleaner onto a line for individual dispense to users who need to wash their hands. Even with the drawbacks of having to manually move the packaging to the point of attachment and going through the process of attaching the container to the line, there are clearly benefits to consummating the liquid flow in user-friendly dispense equipment. The use of appropriate dispense equipment, and the flow of product into such equipment, becomes an additional point of benefit against which we can evaluate our current liquid-logistics flow and to use as a standard for our definition of an optimal liquid-logistics system.

Another characteristic of the on-premise liquid-logistics flow is the tracking and control capability it offers regarding liquid usage. In addition to recording quantity used in greater detail, an on-premise logistics system can be used to gather additional information that is useful for logistics or other purposes. Let us take a look at a specific example to clarify this point. In a vehicle maintenance facility, motor oil is issued to the work area in 55-gallon drums. A tap is inserted into the drum, allowing a mechanic to pour as much oil as needed into a jug that is then taken to the point of usage. Under this method, the company knows in total how much oil is used and how much oil remains on hand, but it loses visibility into the logistics flow at the point at which the drum leaves the storage area. By attaching the 55-gallon drums to a dispense unit, a whole new set of useful information becomes available. The dispense unit allows additional information to be captured at the point of dispense: the employee who is using the liquid, the job number/customer number that it is being used for, and any other special information that would allow analysis and tuning of the logistics flow or proper charging for the work performed. In addition to this information-gathering facility, a control element becomes available. The dispense system can be set up such that liquids cannot be dispensed without entering required information such as that described earlier, or cannot be dispensed without an approval code of the inventory-control person or work supervisor.

Another technique used in on-premise liquid logistics is more limited in usage than what it would seem to deserve, given the benefits that it provides. The technique relates to downstream production processes. When a carbonated beverage is dispensed from a fountain machine, for example, it is not the end of the flow of the carbonated beverage from the original supplier. In fact, up to the point of dispense, the carbonated beverage does not even exist. The beverage actually consists of a syrup, water, and carbonation that are combined within the dispense unit or, in some cases, even right in the cup. The logistics system did not handle the beverage; it handled the components along three different streams. In many cases, the syrup is contained in bag-in-box containers, the water is filtered from the tap, and the carbonation is delivered from a tank truck into a tank in the facility. Each component/ingredient of the product is handled logistically according to the most efficient method for that ingredient — carton, pipe, tank — and the actual "production" is carried out way downstream, practically at the last step before the final product finds its way into the consumer's mouth, as illustrated in Exhibit 1.7. Contrast this with the difficulties and complexities of having to transport carbonated beverage for the length of the supply stream. It would be something like the handling of beer in barrels, only much less effective because a carbonated beverage contains on the order of 80 percent water, so most

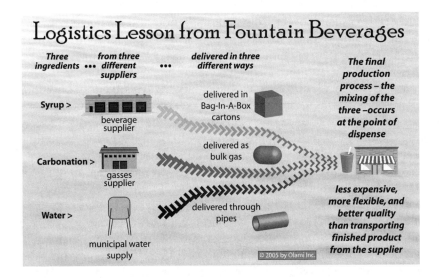

Logistics Lesson from Fountain Beverages

| Three ingredients ••• | from three different suppliers ••• | delivered in three different ways | The final production process – the mixing of the three –occurs at the point of dispense |

Syrup > beverage supplier — delivered in Bag-In-A-Box cartons

Carbonation > gasses supplier — delivered as bulk gas

Water > municipal water supply — delivered through pipes

less expensive, more flexible, and better quality than transporting finished product from the supplier

© 2005 by Olami Inc.

Exhibit 1.7   Moving Production Steps as Far Downstream as Possible Provides Many Benefits

of what would be flowing through the stream would be the water. Another factor is the flexibility this approach provides. The same water and carbonation can be used for any beverage, and they are not "committed" until the last moment, thus enhancing their flexibility as product ingredients. The idea of moving production out of the factory and into the supply stream is a valuable aspect of existing liquid-logistics practice. We will put it on the list of techniques we want to consider going forward.

Although we have laid out some common issues and techniques related to liquid logistics in on-premise establishments, a different issue arises because of the differences between the various types of on-premise operations. A large automotive service center, for example, has a relatively regular flow of a predictable set of automotive maintenance fluids. This is especially true for a fleet service facility, in which a large portion of the services are preventive maintenance performed according to a predefined schedule. In contrast, the same supplier or distributor may need to provide product to a small neighborhood service station with very limited space for inventory and sudden surges in demand that lead to low inventory levels. An even more dramatic example relates to beverages. The day-in and day-out activities of a diner, for example, are relatively regular and predictable, although there are peaks in times and days of demand. Another on-premise beverage channel such as a sports stadium is very different logistically. At such a location, large quantities of beverage are served in a very short span of time, usually within a matter of a few hours. In some cases, suppliers/distributors handle the two channels in a similar manner, simply throwing larger quantities of the on-premise equipment at a venue such as the sports stadium. Other alternatives exist, however. Whereas a supplier might use small tanks of syrup or bag-in-box arrangements in a diner, large mobile tanks are available for conditions such as a sports stadium. Such mobile tanks can be filled, pulled to the stadium, utilized to dispense the beverage, and then removed following the event. A liquid-logistics configuration should be able to service multiple channels within the different logistical parameters of each channel.

In addition to these on-premise streams, off-premise streams show us other characteristics that are important for the liquid-logistics flow. The first characteristic reveals a particularly telling distinction between the two environments, on-premise and off-premise. With on-premise liquids, we saw the value of providing the customer/user with exactly the quantity of liquid desired, often a quantity much smaller than the quantity of liquid contained in whatever package or container the liquid came in. At the point of consumption, the customer/user wants to be able to get just the quantity needed. We find that the popularity of warehouse stores with their megasized containers demonstrates the exact opposite for off-premise: the willingness of consumers to invest extra effort within the logistics flow to obtain the convenience of ready availability of product at home, together with some cost savings that result from this extra effort. In other words, to achieve the goal of convenience at the point of usage, the user is willing to make an additional investment earlier in the logistics flow that will contribute to that goal. With this observation, we can ask whether we have serviced the point of usage as much as possible, even at the cost of some additional effort at other points in the logistics flow, and we can take this concept into account as we lay out our projected liquid-logistics program.

Another logistics issue that we observe downstream is the need for flexibility and nimbleness in product placement. Although the hype about giving customers a product "any way they want it" is pretty well overblown, there is a diversity of product configurations that the logistics system must be able to handle. These different configurations are not just in package size, but extend into variations of other differentiating characteristics — flavors, colors, additives, sizzle, and whatever other hooks the marketing people can figure out to put in the product. The logistics system must be able to handle all of the variations of the product and, even more so, be nimble enough to deal with extraordinary timing issues — market tests, new-product introductions, seasonal shifts in demand, and all the other demands that make logistics conditions so dynamic. Viewing the range of any particular product in a store reveals just how broad product variation has become. There seem to be enough different types of tea to stretch from here to the Dry Tortugas. Speaking of the Dry Tortugas, they are quite a liquid puzzlement of their own; when you look at them, you see almost nothing but pristine blue water, which is a little strange for a place called "dry." They do teach us, though, how bad it is to be good at the wrong thing. Construction of the big half-finished fort on the Dry Tortugas was stopped when rifled artillery was invented that could fly right past the fort and hit the real target behind it, rendering the fort unable to fulfill its protective mission. The fort represents a system that is great for some purposes but with very little usefulness for the one for which it was built, a situation that any logistics person wants to be very careful to avoid.

We have run through the downstream segment of the logistics flow to learn of different techniques that are available for handling liquid products. As with the earlier segments, there is no lack of options and alternatives for how liquids are moved through the system, or for that matter for what the system itself might look like. Some of the techniques and characteristics we discovered are:

- The liquid should flow directly to the point at which it is to be used, with no need for additional effort by the user.
- Information regarding inventory balances should be readily available to the user or, better, be transmitted directly to the supplier for replenishment action.
- The inventory-holding system should feed directly into dispense equipment in on-premise B2C environments.
- Close control and reporting over usage, including quantity and other meaningful user/usage data, should emanate from as close to the point of usage as possible.
- Convenience at the point of usage is critical, even if it entails additional effort earlier in the logistics flow.
- Moving "production" steps as far downstream as possible increases logistics efficiency and flexibility.
- Flexibility in the logistics flow allows the flow to be configured at any particular location to meet the needs of that location.
- Nimbleness in product placement and configuration enables the supplier to service a diverse and demanding customer base.

In this section, we have identified a variety of techniques and elements of current liquid-logistics practices in different segments of the inter-entity logistics flow. Our final step in this survey will be to look at liquid-logistics activities within a company, as reflected in process-engineering techniques related to liquids.

Process-Engineering Practices

We have been looking at liquid-logistics techniques in different segments of the supply stream to get a picture of current practices, provide insight into alternative approaches that may be appropriate to our own operations, and establish guidelines to direct our development of an advanced liquid-logistics approach. We examined some of the practices in the upstream/source area that dealt with the largest quantities of liquids, and then moved downstream to view the B2B flow of intermediate quantities of liquid products to a broader diversity of destinations. This led to the B2C flow at the retail level of quantities and number/diversity of customers. All of the flows we have reviewed thus far have been inter-entity — between companies or between a company and a consumer.

Another area with highly developed liquid-logistics practices, from which we can learn much and gain concepts and guidelines, is within a specific company. The use of liquids within a facility, whether as components/ingredients in a product, as part of the production process itself, or within a support or maintenance function, could be considered a localized supply stream. Many of the issues of control, movement, and handling that occur within a company can provide valuable instruction for overall liquid logistics. Although the transportation element is, for the most part, removed from the process flow of liquids within a facility, there are still a number of logistics issues that are valuable for us to review.

One of the most visually striking elements of the logistics flow within a production facility is the presence of a human-machine interface, or HMI. HMI is often part of an overall method for controlling processes that is referred to as a SCADA (Supervisory Control and Data Acquisition) system. HMI generally refers to the point at which a person interacts with technology, and this occurs on several levels that are important from a logistics perspective.

The first point of HMI is informational, that is, the presentation of process information to a human. HMI systems display graphically, usually on a computer screen, the physical conditions present in the logistics flow. The physical conditions in the flow are measured using sensors based on the specific attributes being monitored or controlled: the temperature of a machine, the cooling-water flow rate, the amount of liquid in a tank, or whatever other physical action is important to the manufacturing or logistics system. These sensors are placed at the appropriate points in the logistics flow and are connected to programmable logic controllers (PLCs) or other types of data-gathering and control devices. These devices convert the electronic signals received from the sensors into a logistics reading, for example converting the speed with which a turbine flowmeter is rotating into the rate of flow of a liquid through a pipe. The PLC gathers the data from all of the sensors that are connected

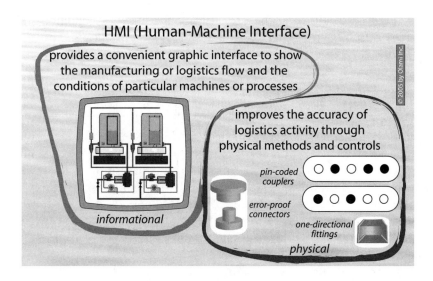

Exhibit 1.8   Humans Interface with Machines/Equipment Both Informationally and Physically

to it, converts/processes the data, and transmits the resulting information to the HMI system. HMI then presents the information to the user, as illustrated in Exhibit 1.8.

HMI displays often consist of a graphical layout of the production process or whatever process is being monitored. This layout shows the machines, tanks, pipes, and other elements of the internal supply stream according to the physical flow between them, that is, the flow of product is fully represented on the screen, although in a simplified way. The user sees a representation of the entire flow of the process being monitored and can zoom in on any particular part of the flow, such as a particular production machine.

HMI often goes further than this, displaying graphically the relevant data associated with the flow. For example, HMI may receive data from the sensor/PLC that a certain tank is currently three-quarters full. To show the user that the tank is three-quarters full, the HMI display shows a tank as if in cutaway view, and this view shows liquid that has filled the tank up to the three-quarters level. Thus the user receives a readily understood picture of the logistics conditions within the process at any given time. The use of graphic images is exploited as much as possible. For example, the temperature in a certain tank or machine is shown as a thermometer reading, with the temperature levels divided into green, yellow, and red zones to reflect normal, warning, or dangerous temperature levels, respectively, for the operation. Thus the user not only sees current conditions, but also where the current reading is within the range of possible readings for that item.

In addition to allowing the user to monitor logistics conditions, HMI provides a number of other capabilities. The system allows the user to control the flow using the same graphic interface. A valve may be shown on the computer screen, for example, and by clicking on the valve using the computer mouse, the valve can be opened or closed. This is done through a reverse flow of information from that of data monitoring. In the control function, the HMI interprets the mouse click as a command to close the valve. HMI sends this signal to the PLC, which interprets it into the appropriate action for the appropriate valve. The PLC sends a signal to the valve, activating the motor or mechanism to actually close the valve. When the valve is actually closed, the open/closed valve sensor sends a signal reflecting this to the PLC, which sends it on to the HMI for display on the screen. A very simple action on the part of the user, therefore, results in an entire sequence of events and physical actions within the logistics control system.

In addition to monitor and control functions, HMI contains an alert capability. As HMI receives information regarding conditions in the flow, it continually evaluates these conditions against parameters that have been input by the user. These parameters include ranges of acceptable values, time constraints on various activities, and so on. When HMI identifies that a condition falls outside of a normal parameter, it issues an alert to the user, even if the user may not be monitoring that particular part of the system at the moment. The alert may be in the form of displaying a window or screen highlighting the problem area, using sounds or red images to draw the user's attention to the problem, showing warning messages on the screen, or other methods to communicate these alerts as defined by the user. These alerts are especially useful because they are exception-based; if the logistics flow is working as it should, then HMI is "quiet," and the HMI system notifies the user only when a condition has occurred that requires user attention and action.

Another characteristic of HMI that is important from a liquid-logistics perspective is that it can take a large amount of data and present it in a very specific way to very specific users. The user does not have to be physically near the equipment or logistics process to have a complete view of and control over the process. The familiar picture of telephone company technicians viewing huge screens that display nationwide activity in the telephone system demonstrate very clearly HMI's ability to bring massive systems into very centralized monitoring and control. This capability can be used for virtually anything, from sewage systems to hydro-electric networks, but we want to view it specifically in light of its impact on liquid logistics.

HMI capabilities as described can be valuable additions to a logistics system. Specifically, the capabilities we have seen in the information area include gathering data directly from the logistics process and presenting the flow to the user in a graphically effective way, controlling the equipment along the logistics flow, providing alerts to exception conditions that occur in the flow and bringing them to the user's attention, and the ability to perform all of these tasks remotely without physical proximity to the logistics system. These capabilities are enhanced because we are focused on logistics systems specifically for liquids, which lend themselves to the kinds of sensors, monitors, and controls that make the most of an HMI system. We will list HMI as a capability to consider that is related to the information aspects of our current logistics system as well as the liquid-specific system we will design.

Another aspect of the HMI concept, in addition to the information interface, is the physical human-equipment interface. In cases where humans touch, move, or in other ways handle equipment or machinery, the physical nature of the contact can be built in such a way as to improve the success of the logistics flow. A mission-critical example of this is the shape of the controls in an airplane cockpit. The control for flaps is shaped like flaps, the landing gear control is round like a wheel, and each of the different controls that the pilots work with has a distinctive shape. This allows the user to mentally confirm that the correct control is being moved without having to look at the control. Much less critical is the small bump on the letters F and J on a keyboard, a form of HMI that allows the typist to confirm proper positioning of the fingers for typing without looking at the keyboard each time.

In a liquid-logistics environment, the physical aspect of the HMI takes on several forms. Valve handles for liquids versus gases are shaped differently to warn the user of which type of valve is being opened. Connectors for different types of liquids have different shapes, making it impossible to connect the hose for one type of liquid to the line for a different type of liquid. Many types of piping have the contents of the piping, and direction of the liquid flow, attached in large letters and with large directional arrows. These protections decrease the likelihood of error during the logistics process and make for a more secure and more effective logistics flow. For these reasons, we take them into account as we review our existing logistics system and plan a focused liquids-based system.

A characteristic methodology related to process engineering is the high degree of planning that goes into the creation of operational flows. In fact, planning new flows or changes to existing flows is a large part of the process-engineering function. Process engineering has whole methodologies and sets of tools that it uses to perform this planning function. For example, CAD (computer-aided design) is a tool that allows a very high degree of precision for a very detailed level of planning. CAD allows the user to not only plan an operational flow in advance, but also to evaluate how closely the actual implementation corresponds to the planned configuration. It is common to hear practitioners say that once they start using a CAD system, they would not want to do their job without it. This is testimonial to the power of high-quality planning and the importance of a strong planning methodology and proper planning tools. It is important that we take this into account in reviewing our own logistics methods and include it as an integral part of the liquid-logistics system we will design. This may seem self-evident, but it is not. Disciplined planning is not necessarily a characteristic that is shared at all levels and departments within an organization.

Although process engineering applies to any type of process and any type of product, process engineering related to liquids is especially applicable to our focus on liquid logistics. The process engineer in a liquid-oriented environment is familiar with and takes into account all aspects of the liquids and their behavior within the process. This includes knowledge of chemical engineering for the interaction of each liquid with other liquids, other materials, and its environments; mechanical engineering, including hydraulics for the behavior of the flow of the liquids and the behavior of the equipment as the production or logistics processes are in progress; materials engineering to specify the equipment to be used in the process based on demands of the process and operating parameters of the system; electrical engineering for all the power requirements and the PLC/HMI system described earlier; and the other engineering disciplines required for a logistics system. We can say that the engineering aspects of liquid logistics are important, so that at the end of the day the system does what we want it to do, but that would not be doing the engineering functions full justice. Engineers identify what is needed for a system to work as required, but the marbles can also roll in the other direction; engineers can tell the company about capabilities that the company might otherwise miss out on. Given this, we can say that detailed knowledge of liquid behavior is only the starting point for engineering's role in the liquid-logistics process.

In crossing paths with process engineering, there is always a high likelihood that the topics of safety, quality control, and environmental impact will arise. Happily, it seems to be almost embedded in the function for these issues to be evaluated as part of any planning or review activity. Beyond their sensitivity to these issues, we can learn something else from process engineers. Safety, quality control, and environmental impact are essentially very "dry" topics, that is, the requirements for each of these areas are usually defined very clearly and in a very detailed manner, and the engineering person makes the matchup to ensure conformance to each regulation or standard. This requires an extraordinarily deep degree of knowledge and concentration. But sometimes the engineering person goes beyond the black-and-white evaluation to identify aspects of the regulations that can work in the company's favor. In reviewing safety regulations, for example, the engineer may discover a way of reducing the company's insurance premium. An aspect of quality may be so high that it can serve as a competitive advantage in the marketplace. It is like hearing the singer singing "The Star Spangled Banner" before the game; there is not much flexibility in what you can do with the song, so the best thing you can do is belt it out with all your heart to come up with the biggest effect. We can use the process engineers' concern for safety/quality/environment as a guide to how we should relate to these topics, and beyond this, we can value the idea of going beyond the basics to gain business benefit from these topics.

Besides being deeply familiar with all of these different issues, process engineers are often very sensitive to the interconnectivity between different issues. They can usually distinguish between bogus issues and real issues that may be contributing to a certain condition or problem. It is far too easy to fall into the trap of looking in the wrong place for the problem, much less the solution. This brings to mind the extraordinary scene in *Catch-22* in which Yossarian is so proud of the neat, tidy bandage he made to dress the wound in Snowden's leg, only to discover that a piece of shrapnel had penetrated Snowden's flak jacket and ripped apart most of Snowden's insides. The process-engineering mind helps us make sure we identify the real condition or problem and not get distracted by lesser situations that may be more obvious but are actually of lesser priority.

Perhaps the most important lesson we can learn from process engineering is the essence of what the function is all about — continuous productivity and process improvement. As much as the physical laws of liquid dynamics are unlikely to change over the near term, the business and operating environment in which the liquid-logistics system is operating is certain to change over the even nearer term, and with it the demands on the system. Like the caterpillar that is built to change into a butterfly, we can learn from process engineering that any system we build should have the seeds and mechanisms of change built right into it. Process engineering is like the little hormone that makes these things happen, and having the right amount of the hormone is essential to the health of the system.

We have learned a lot about liquid logistics from the world of process engineering. Specifically, we have learned the importance of:

- Exploiting the capabilities of the information side of HMI, including monitoring and controlling the liquid-logistics flow, receiving alerts regarding exception conditions in the flow, and having the ability to monitor and control the logistics system remotely

- Utilizing the benefits offered by the physical side of HMI to decrease the likelihood of error during the liquid-logistics process and increase the effectiveness of the liquid-logistics flow
- Integrating a strong planning methodology into the liquid-logistics function to plan the logistics system in advance, to evaluate its design against the actual implementation, and to support ongoing enhancements and improvements to the liquid-logistics flow
- Providing full engineering support for the liquid-logistics function, both for the broad array of engineering issues that arise from the liquid-logistics flow and the contribution that engineering can make to enhance system functionality
- Taking into account the safety, quality, and environmental angles of each aspect of the system to ensure compliance and to provide for the area beyond compliance that will have a true business impact
- Learning to distinguish the important from the less important when planning systems functionality and evaluating problems and conditions in a system
- Building the liquid-logistics system to accommodate future processes change and adaptation to keep it continually current

In addition to the intercompany liquid logistics we looked at earlier, the process-engineering function within a company has a great deal to tell us as we consider the operation of our logistics flow.

Summary of Lessons Learned from Current Liquid-Logistics Techniques

We started this chapter thinking we would take a brief look at current liquid-logistics practices, but when we started listening to what those practices were telling us, we learned a lot. Let us summarize what we have found, but let us mix them together slightly differently than we did as we were developing these observations. We came by these concepts by floating along with the flow of liquid logistics and examining each segment: upstream, B2B, B2C, and process engineering. We definitely believe in the "one system" concept and do not want to divide our findings into seemingly separate "pieces" that are in fact much more effectively viewed as a unity. With that caveat, let us list our findings in terms of three perspectives on the liquid-logistics flow: planning, product/product usage, and process.

Planning refers to global issues that are taken into account in liquid-logistics planning; *product/product usage* sensitizes us to product-based aspects of the system; and *process* relates to characteristics of the flow of the liquids as they move through the supply stream. Looking at the findings in this way allows us to consider them across all types of applications and industries, independent of the one from which we extracted the principle.

Planning

- Revolutionary rather than evolutionary thinking may be needed to move to the next level of logistics effectiveness.
- The motivations for advances in liquid logistics may come from "must do" requirements, or they may come from internal or competitive motivations.
- Silo thinking — the continual creative upgrading of logistics techniques to address an ongoing operational need — is a great thing.
- It is important to have a systemwide view of the logistics flow to select the most appropriate equipment and to maximize utilization of the capabilities of that equipment.
- The capabilities of the information side of HMI should be exploited, including monitoring and controlling the liquid-logistics flow, receiving alerts regarding exception conditions in the flow, and ability to monitor and control the logistics system remotely.
- A strong planning methodology should be integrated into the liquid-logistics function to plan the logistics system in advance, to evaluate its design against the actual implementation, and to support ongoing enhancements and improvements to the liquid-logistics flow.
- It is important to provide full engineering support for the liquid-logistics function, both for the broad array of engineering issues that arise from the liquid-logistics flow and the contribution that engineering can make in enhancing system functionality.
- System designers must take into account the safety, quality, and environmental angles of each aspect of the system to ensure compliance and, additionally, to provide for the area beyond compliance that will have a true business impact.
- System designers must learn to distinguish the important from the less important when planning system functionality and evaluating problems and conditions in a system.

Product/Product Usage

- Packaging has an impact on the efficient use of space.
- Effective product movement depends on the strategies for loading and unloading as well as the nature of the packaging.

- The characteristics of liquids, versus those of discrete products, can be utilized to the advantage of the logistics flow.
- Liquid-logistics principles can be applied to certain types of non-liquid materials that have flow and other characteristics similar to liquids.
- It is important to facilitate ease of handling and use of the system by the user with a readily acceptable method of operation.
- A system should provide flexibility in the quantity of product used at any given time without affecting the remainder of the product.
- Efficiency is increased by minimizing the frequency of handling of the product as well as the amount of effort required to handle the product.
- An optimal system provides continual flow of liquid for operational purposes without disruption of service during replenishment or maintenance.
- The liquid should flow directly to the point at which it is to be used, with no need for additional effort by the user.
- The inventory-holding system should feed directly into dispensing equipment in on-premise B2C environments.
- Efficiency is increased through close control over and reporting on usage, including quantity and other meaningful user/usage data, and such control should emanate from as close to the point of usage as possible.
- Convenience at the point of usage is critical, even if it entails additional effort earlier in the logistics flow.
- Nimbleness in product placement and configuration will enable the system to service a diverse and demanding customer base.

Process

- Liquids should be viewed and handled as a flow rather than as individual, identifiable units.
- Focus on the movement of the liquid rather than the movement of the package, and identify the largest form of "packaging" possible.
- A supply stream may include two or more forms of logistics based on the characteristics of the different segments of the stream.
- Logistics methods can incorporate multiple capabilities that can be used in different ways, such as railroad tank cars.
- The physical configuration and functionality of the system should be flexible to meet specific user needs.
- Provide flexibility in the location, shape, and placement of the liquid-logistics system components.

- Information regarding inventory balances should be readily available to the user or, better, transmitted directly to the supplier for replenishment action.
- Logistics efficiency and customer flexibility are enhanced by moving "production" steps as far downstream as possible.
- A system should have the flexibility to configure the logistics flow at any particular location to meet the needs of that location.
- Utilize the benefits offered by the physical side of HMI to decrease the likelihood of error during the liquid-logistics process and increase the effectiveness of the liquid-logistics flow.
- Design the liquid-logistics system to accommodate process changes and adaptation to keep it continually current.

To the degree to which our current systems reflect these lessons, or to which we can create a system that utilizes and exploits these lessons, our liquid-logistics system will be that much more effective. With this survey completed, we are now ready to put these factors together into a unified flow, into a true Supply Chain for Liquids.

Chapter 2

Supply Chain and Supply Chain for Liquids

This book is called *Supply Chain for Liquids* only because "supply chain" is the popular terminology today, not because it is necessarily a good description of how liquids-based companies do or should operate. The phrase "Supply Pipe^{SM}" offers a better image of what the Supply Chain for Liquids® is all about, although it loses all of the associations — many of them quite valuable — we currently have with "supply chain." Words can sometimes get in the way and cloud our thinking as much as they help us clarify and understand, and this is the case related to the phrase "supply chain."

The phrase "supply chain," as it is generally applied, is a lot like the phrase "TQM/Total Quality Management"; it can mean pretty much whatever the person using it wants it to mean at any given moment. "Supply chain" is often used simply as another word for a company's logistics or operations, but it provides a spin for hipness that people often like to have. In other cases, it extends to other players along the logistics path, and sometimes to what would be considered the full supply chain — everything that happens from the original supplier through the entire flow to the final consumer.

In addition to being subject to hazy usage, the term "supply chain" has another drawback as related to liquids. The word "chain" evokes discrete segments, composed of pieces and units. The name itself leads us to think in terms of units of solids rather than the flow of liquids. A major portion of creating an effective Supply Chain for Liquids is Thinking Liquid[SM]. It will help us to change our current thinking if we change our current image of the process and vision of how it works. Therefore, in this book we picture the Supply Chain for Liquids as a stream, a supply stream through which liquid products flow. The flow of liquids in a stream is vastly different from the movement of solids from link to link in a chain; and a Supply Chain for Liquids is vastly different from a supply chain. An optimal Supply Chain for Liquids is not just an adaptation of a supply chain; as described in Chapter 5, it is an integrated system all of whose elements take advantage of the liquid nature of the product it carries in ways that solid products simply cannot.

Definitions and Terminology

Clear definitions are the basis of clear thinking. The four types of systems that we will be referring to throughout this book are defined in Exhibit 2.1. These four types of systems are arranged hierarchically, with each successive level representing a higher degree of efficiency, lower costs, a greater opportunity for revenue, and additional business advantages beyond the previous level. A company can identify its current position in the hierarchy of Exhibit 2.1 and define a path for advancing to the next level. The Liquid Lens[SM] method (defined in Chapter 3) suggests that the most effective approach is to define the long-term objective (that is, the optimal Supply Chain for Liquids) and then to build a structure that advances through a series of steps to achieve that overall objective. Knowing the final objective creates a single unified framework for all of the steps and activities along the way.

Supply Chain

Supply chain is the movement of products and information based on traditional logistics methods. Liquid products in a supply chain are often put into a container such as a bottle and then, for all intents and purposes, treated as a solid until the user pours the liquid out of the container and uses it. For example, a supplier sending automotive lubricants to a chain of quick-lube centers in two-gallon jugs can be considered as a supply-chain configuration. In this situation the product is transported, delivered, and maintained on-site in traditional units (jugs) that are more appropriate to their transportation than to their usage or to the liquid nature of the product. The entire logistics operation is based on the conversion of the liquid (lubricant) to a solid (jug), with all handling, inventorying, transporting, and issuing done by jugs of lubricant.

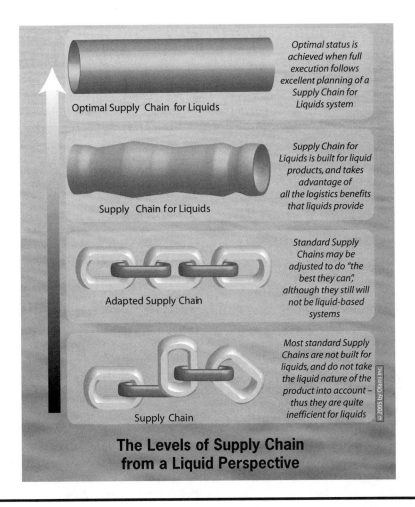

Optimal Supply Chain for Liquids — *Optimal status is achieved when full execution follows excellent planning of a Supply Chain for Liquids system*

Supply Chain for Liquids — *Supply Chain for Liquids is built for liquid products, and takes advantage of all the logistics benefits that liquids provide*

Adapted Supply Chain — *Standard Supply Chains may be adjusted to do "the best they can", although they still will not be liquid-based systems*

Supply Chain — *Most standard Supply Chains are not built for liquids, and do not take the liquid nature of the product into account – thus they are quite inefficient for liquids*

© 2005 by Olani Inc.

The Levels of Supply Chain from a Liquid Perspective

Exhibit 2.1 The Four Levels of Supply Chain in Terms of Liquid Logistics

The supply chain approach to logistics is in many cases excellent, and companies worldwide are using and benefiting from supply chain techniques that are constantly undergoing development and refinement. But for companies that deal with liquids, the continual advancement of standard supply chain misses an important part of their business. The situation is comparable with continuous improvements in automobiles. The automobile industry is constantly finding ways to make cars better — better safety, improved gas mileage, more comfortable interior, and the like. That is great for people who buy cars, but what about people who buy trucks? Yes, some of the improvements made to cars can have a carryover effect and be applied to trucks as well. But if the automotive industry did not separately focus on improvements to trucks, then truck buyers would not be getting all they could out of their trucks. Trucks are vehicles, as are cars, but on the other hand, trucks are different and have special characteristics that cars do not have. The size of and access to the bed, regular and extended cabs, options related to cargo units, hauling capability, internal workings such as the engine and transmission, and off-road options, all of these are functions that need to be attended to apart from and in addition to all of the functions in which a truck is similar to a car. The common functions — design of controls, interior materials and fabrics, air conditioning — apply to both cars and trucks. But a truck that uses only the design elements of a car, and not design elements that take into account its special nature and uses as a truck, is not a full-capability truck.

Similarly, basic supply chain principles work for both discrete and liquid products. The problem arises because, in many cases, we design trucks using only the design principles of cars. Similarly, we design the Supply Chain for liquids products using only discrete-based thinking. This is why the next three stages of liquid-logistics functionality are needed — to build a liquid-specific system beyond what a discrete-based system can provide, and thus achieve a "full-capability vehicle."

It is important to emphasize that Supply Chain for Liquids does not in any way impact or detract from the value of supply chain principles. Just because the bed of a truck is designed in a certain way, that is not a reflection on how cars are designed. There is a set of elements that applies to trucks that simply does not apply to cars. In the same way, this book does not assert that there is anything wrong or defective with supply chain thinking for discrete products. Indeed, Supply Chain for Liquids addresses issues that do not even arise with discrete products. There may be some principles of Supply Chain for Liquids that could be interpreted or adapted to discrete products, as described in Chapter 12, but these are ancillary to the objectives of this book. The point here is that what is great in one place may be bad in another place. Corn is a weed in a bean field, and just because something is good for supply chain for discrete items does not necessarily mean that it is good for supply chain for liquid items.

Adapted Supply Chain

Adapted Supply Chain considers the liquid nature of the product while still working within the supply chain framework. The supplier in the automotive lubricants example above may start using intermediate bulk containers (IBC) to deliver product, attaching the IBCs directly to the dispense system at the user site to complete the flow of product to the end user. The supply chain has moved to some degree toward recognizing that it is supporting a liquid product rather than discrete solids, although it is still in the business of moving containers rather than moving product. For example, automotive maintenance fluids such as antifreeze and windshield washer fluid can be supplied to an automotive repair facility in 300-gallon IBCs rather than in one-gallon jugs. Except for the fact that the IBCs must be moved with a forklift, while a one-gallon jug can be handled manually, the processes related to the IBCs are the same as those for the jugs. The fundamental thought process has not changed: an IBC is still being thought of and treated as a large jug. Specific operational efficiencies may result from use of IBCs, both in handling and in dispense, and so IBCs are in many cases an attractive operational improvement over smaller stock-keeping units. However, this benefit should not distract us from the fact that the liquid (for example, antifreeze) is being treated logistically as a solid (the IBC container), and so this approach is not a true liquids-based solution.

Adapted Supply Chain is not the final stage of liquid logistics, but from a supply stream perspective, it is an improvement over a standard supply chain approach. As described in Chapter 5, the path to Supply Chain for Liquids does not demand a "great leap forward" from whatever level a company is at now to its ultimate destination. Rather, such factors as cost, organizational issues, customers and suppliers, and operational conditions are taken into account to develop a step-based incremental approach to achieving the ultimate goal. As such, Adapted Supply Chain may be a productive first step from basic Supply Chain and toward the desired configuration. If handled properly, Adapted Supply Chain can be achieved with relatively little cost or effort while achieving meaningful benefits. Any time a change is undertaken it is important to get an early "win" to counterbalance the negatively perceived aspects of the change and to provide a foundation on which to build ongoing changes. Because Adapted Supply Chain is a variation on the Supply Chain theme but not a paradigm shift, it can serve a useful role in this overall process.

Supply Chain for Liquids

Supply Chain for Liquids is a paradigm shift in thinking. The user looks at the entire logistics flow of liquid products and designs a Supply Chain for Liquids built on the liquid nature of the product, using techniques described in this book. An integrated approach brings all the elements in the design together into one synergistic system in which the whole is greater than the sum of the parts. In our example, the lubricant may stay in bulk form during transport and then be maintained in bulk or semi-bulk form at the user site, right through to the point of dispense. The entire process is oriented toward the liquid nature of the product and its form at the beginning and end of the flow; packaging is unnecessary and is therefore not introduced at any point in the flow. This scenario shows that Supply Chain for Liquids is part thinking and part doing. The company has broken through to Supply Chain for Liquids thinking and has laid a plan for implementing a true Supply Chain for Liquids system.

Because this step is out of the ordinary in terms of everyday business activities, let us look at it more closely. The move to a Supply Chain for Liquids mind-set means that we are "wiping the slate clean" to design the best liquid-logistics system for our products, filtering that design for reality, and then going through all of the steps to implement that design. This parallels any paradigm-shift development. Take, for example, the transition from propellers to jet engines. Airplane propellers and the engines that turn them have been developed extensively since the early days of flight. In fact, it is not commonly appreciated how much the Wright brothers' engine-propeller arrangement was a paradigm shift of its own from earlier attempts to build heavier-than-air craft. The Wright brothers chose a more energy-efficient, high-speed, thin-propeller design as opposed to the lower-speed, heavier propeller designs that had been common up to then. Moreover, they set the two propellers on their first airplane in counterrotational directions to eliminate gyroscopic forces that would have made control more difficult. Since that time and even up until now, there have been constant improvements to engine-propeller design, including materials, blade faces and angles, geometry, and positioning. However, all of the improvements taken together do not total the paradigm shift of the jet engine, which uses a completely different approach to the propulsion of aircraft. The jet engine is not a "tweak" of a propeller engine; it is a fundamental rethinking of the objective and how to achieve it. There is no value judgment related to propeller engines and jet engines; each is appropriate to its own environment and each has value, and both represent large industries today. The point is that all of the fine-tuning in the world cannot achieve what a completely different approach can achieve. Just ask the makers of the most advanced slide rules or the best steam engines how their improved techniques are doing. In both cases, these advances were blown away by the new methods that came along.

Like the jet engine versus the propeller, Supply Chain for Liquids involves a fundamental rethinking of the objective and how to achieve it. For Sir Frank Whittle in the United Kingdom and Dr. Hans von Ohain in Germany, who independently but concurrently developed jet engine designs, the objective was not a better propeller but a different way of propelling an aircraft. For us, the objective is not to have the lightest, strongest containers or the most efficient warehouse rack design. Our objective is to flow liquid product as efficiently as possible from the point of origin to the point of consumption.

Supply Chain for Liquids says that standard supply chain thinking is limited in its ability to service the needs of liquid products and the companies that deal with them, just like propellers and propeller aircraft are limited in their ability to service high-speed, large-volume transportation needs. Just as jet engines are not an extension of propeller engines, you cannot get to Supply Chain for Liquids by adjusting the supply chain. We should approach Supply Chain for Liquids with the same mind-set that led aviation people to develop the jet engine.

Optimal Supply Chain for Liquids

Optimal Supply Chain for Liquids (OSCFL) means that a company has brought all elements of the material and information flow into alignment with the product's liquid nature, using the approaches and techniques described in this book. In our example, the information flow would have been introduced to optimize the entire process, making it as efficient as possible given the nature of the product, its production, and its usage. You can tweak a supply chain to create an adapted supply chain, but a Supply Chain for Liquids or Optimal Supply Chain for Liquids is designed (and functions) as a fully integrated unit that takes full advantage of the properties of liquids.

This brings up the question: What is the difference between Supply Chain for Liquids and Optimal Supply Chain for Liquids? The difference lies in the completeness of planning and the completeness of execution. A company may undertake the Liquid Lens process (see Chapter 3) and achieve Supply Chain for Liquids status with all the benefits of the system. In doing so, however, either the planning or execution may include "holes" for any number of legitimate reasons. In other words, the company works to achieve the Supply Chain for Liquids as opposed to the supply chain, but some pieces of the Supply Chain for Liquids are missing or incomplete. With Optimal Supply Chain for Liquids, the company can demonstrate that its planning process was comprehensive and inclusive, and that it was executed according to the plan that it developed. The activities involved in achieving Optimal Supply Chain for Liquids are described in more detail in Chapter 11.

Like Total Quality Management (TQM), there is no one configuration for Optimal Supply Chain for Liquids. This configuration involves the integrated use of equipment, techniques, and technology to create the most efficient flow of liquid product and information among the players in a particular logistics relationship. The effective approach to Supply Chain for Liquids is to lay out all the elements in the relationship and then to design the complete Optimal Supply Chain for Liquids together with a staged implementation approach for achieving it. This is much different from the common situation companies face of being dragged into a piecemeal flow based on diverse perspectives and practices that are assembled in bits and pieces. As described in Chapter 5, the interim steps of developing a Supply Chain for Liquids are likely needed before a company can achieve Optimal Supply Chain for Liquids.

Optimal Supply Chain for Liquids should be the ultimate in simplicity and functionality, but even so, there may be some room for allowances. On the one hand, we can take the Diogenes model for absolute simplicity, functionality, and frugality. Diogenes wandered around Athens and made it clear he did not believe in any of it — not government, not indications of wealth, nothing above the barest requirements for doing what needs doing. Diogenes would have been a great guy to have on the Supply Chain for Liquids planning and implementation team; he was all about cutting out the extraneous. On the other hand, perhaps we can take a leaf from Sir Christopher Wren, the brilliant Brit whose architectural approach was to design in the clean classic style and concentrate all of the flourishes in one particular part of a building, such as the dome. We should design and build our Supply Chain for Liquids systems according to the cleanest style we are able to achieve and tightly control the points, if any, in which we add extraneous ornamental touches.

These four stages have not been defined with the goal of assigning "grades" to a company in terms of where their operations stand. Rather, they are a measuring stick for a company to assess its operations relative to liquid products and establish an overall objective for where the company wants to be in the continuum between Supply Chain and Optimal Supply Chain for Liquids. After a company maps out its current position along this continuum as well as its target position, it can begin the process of defining an action plan for moving from where it is to where it wants to be. The four stages also serve as identifiable milestones along the course of liquid-logistics development. Like knowing which floor you're passing as the elevator is going up, the four stages serve as benchmarks that tell you when you have gone up to the next level on your journey.

Key Drivers of Supply Chain versus Supply Chain for Liquids

One of the key aspects of switching from Supply Chain thinking to Supply Chain for Liquids thinking is in understanding the drivers of liquid logistics. Under Supply Chain thinking, it is frequently the movers of liquids — the transportation and distribution functions — that determine the design of the logistics process. Bottles, cartons, pallets, and other forms of packaging may be the "automatic" form of the product for a number of reasons. The force of habit is incredibly powerful. Once some liquid products are put in containers, the natural process is to put all of that product, and all other products, into containers. "Packaging" becomes an automatic part of the production process. For some companies producing liquid products, it may have never occurred to them *not* to put their products in containers. For other producers, the internal focus may be so strong that they never learn how the product is ultimately used. Even if they have a salesperson in the field making the rounds and speaking with the customer's purchasing person, the idea of a different form of the product does not even come up. The producer does not offer it, and the purchasing person is not tuned into possible usage efficiencies, so the current packaging is the assumed form of the product. Many of these trappings of a company's operations are the business equivalent of "the whole catastrophe" that Zorba the Greek defined on the domestic side — the normal things in life that come with a price that can get pretty heavy as they accumulate over time.

In fact, given the usage methods that are currently in place at the customer's location, it may be that bottles, jugs, or drums are the most effective form of the product. In some instances, industry standards and common practice may formally or informally dictate the form of the liquid, but these are usually nonbinding and irrelevant if a more effective form (for the producer, the distributor, and the user) can be found. In many cases, the jug/carton/pallet configuration is seen as a particularly effective form of holding liquid products, fitting well into racks and storage space as well as on trucks. In other words, both the producer and the consumer pay the price of making life easier for the logistics function. Because so much of the industrial transportation infrastructure is built around movement of solids — semi-trailer trucks, railroad boxcars, etc. — it is often a "given" that these modes will be used to transport most liquids. The supplier therefore goes through the process of converting the liquid into a solid by putting it in a jug, bottle, drum, etc., and the user/consumer receives the liquid in this form.

The Supply Chain for Liquids world, on the other hand, looks at logistics through the Liquid Lens. The Supply Chain for Liquids is designed from the ends toward the middle, and if there is a conflict between the two ends (the producer and the consumer), then it is designed from the consumer to the producer. Supply Chain for Liquids has the appealing attribute of being not only more fully consumer-oriented than Supply Chain, but also in many cases more flexible and cost-effective than Supply Chain, as we shall see in Chapter 5.

What does it mean to design the Supply Chain for Liquids from the ends toward the middle? First, it means removing all our prior conceptions about liquid products and looking at them with a completely different set of priorities. The "ends" are the producer at the beginning of the stream and the consumer at the end of the stream. From the producer's perspective, what is the most effective way to produce the product? Effectiveness takes into account all the factors involved in production — timing, quantities, production rotation between products, equipment utilization, etc. In addition, it takes into account the characteristics of the product itself. Perhaps the most famous example of this orientation is the Model-T that was available in any color as long as it was black. And why were they all black? Because Ford discovered that black paint dries faster than other colors and thus makes for the shortest and most efficient production process. In other words, the nature of the product itself was determined by the design of the production process.

Of course in today's world in which consumers are demanding and getting ever more specialized products, the principle needs to be adapted appropriately. In Chapter 8 we discuss the consumer end of the process, focusing in particular on the methods the consumer uses for product dispense and usage. The key point is that it is the matching of an effective form for production with an effective form for consumption that drives Supply Chain for Liquids design. The "middle" of the supply pipe, the logistics and distribution elements, is then designed around and in support of the ends.

As an example of the form of consumption driving the form of the packaging, let us take a look at a different field, that of consumer foods. For a long time, food came basically in either a bag or a box in many different sizes. The combination of demographic/lifestyle changes together with the development of highly sophisticated materials such as plastics has led to broad diversity in the way foods are packaged. Some cereals and snacks come already in a bowl with a spoon included, cheeses come in push-tubes that serve as both the package and the dispense method, meals come in fully self-contained heat-and-eat containers. These are just some of the many examples in which the way the consumer uses the product dictates the form of the package. In many of these cases, the packaging has become as much of a differentiator, if not more so, than the product itself. Interestingly, the opposite trend in food packaging is also evident. Foods sold in warehouse or shopper's clubs are often near-bulk in dimension (gallon jugs of salsa, for example) and are intended to serve customers' needs in a different way — not measured by immediate consumption needs, but by purchase-pattern needs for consumption at home. In both cases, the usage/consumption pattern by the user has dictated the form of the package/delivery method. This B2C example has not been fully extended to B2B liquid products, and this is the Supply Chain for Liquids perspective of the consumption activity driving the form of the product.

It is important to note that Supply Chain for Liquids does not necessarily mean "bulk" handling of liquids. If the source of the product and the end-use configuration indicate that bulk is the most effective manner for holding the liquid, then the Supply Chain for Liquids should be designed around a bulk approach. On the other hand, the user may not be in a bulk environment. Lubricants for sale at retail, for example, have to be packaged to take into account that the user is going to take a relatively small quantity of the product home for use in a private vehicle. In this case, the Supply Chain for Liquids should be built around the source and target requirements of the liquid, with the form of the liquid/packaging defined as appropriate. In many industries, the Supply Chain for Liquids approach is best built to operate alongside package-based channels. Interestingly, for companies in several industries, the ratio of package-based usage need to bulk-based usage opportunity is about four to one, that is, Supply Chain for Liquids can add value across about 20 percent of a producer's distribution channels. This may apply to fountain syrup versus bottled/canned product for a soft drink producer, or do-it-for-me automobile lubrication garages versus do-it-yourself jugs for a motor oil producer. In any case, the portion of the business for which Supply Chain for Liquids is appropriate is identified during the Supply Chain for Liquids planning process, and the cost-benefit evaluation is performed while focusing on that portion of the process.

Additional factors may also come into play in the Supply Chain for Liquids/package evaluation. For example, those channels in which Supply Chain for Liquids is appropriate may be higher-visibility channels, leading to a strategic/marketing advantage to using Supply Chain for Liquids to penetrate these channels, which will then provide support to the package-based channels. Supply Chain for Liquids–oriented channels may also be higher-margin channels, so that improved performance through use of the Supply Chain for Liquids system may have even further positive impact on a company's overall financial performance. As described in Chapter 11, the interplay between Supply Chain for Liquids–based channels and container-based channels may also be expressed in Supply Chain for Liquids' ability to create channel extensions or channel derivatives that provide support for channel-based marketing and sales.

As a concrete example let us take a common usage of Supply Chain practice and see how it might be converted to Supply Chain for Liquids. Carbonated beverages for fountain sale, such as at restaurants, are typically produced in bulk as syrup that is transported to the retail location and mixed with filtered water and carbonation to produce the consumable beverage. In the earliest days of fountain beverages, syrups were frequently transported through the logistics chain and to the retail site in stainless steel drums, not unlike the steel beer kegs that are used today. This required extensive drum handling both for delivery and for return, cleaning, and reuse. This is a classic Supply Chain approach to a liquid product, that is, that Supply Chain is actually a process of distributing the packaging rather than distributing the product itself.

Adapted Supply Chain enhancement to this approach was the development of the bag-in-box (BIB) technique. Because the product is in fact a liquid, it can be filled into a sterile, disposable plastic pouch that is placed inside a carton for easy handling. The BIBs are palletized and stored in various warehouses along the logistics path, and when they reach the restaurant they are placed in the storeroom. For usage, a BIB carton is moved from the storage area and placed on a rack that contains BIBs for each beverage as well as connections to the lines to the dispense area. A dispense line is fitted onto a nozzle in the BIB pouch, and product is passed to the dispense system, where the user once again sees the product in liquid form. On the one hand, this is still a Supply Chain discrete-handling-based approach, with BIB packages being handled as units throughout the entire process. BIB-fill is a production operation, and the quantity of syrup is measured in the number of BIB cartons on order or in inventory. Restaurant employees handle the BIB packages as individual units and must do inventory counting, movement, hook-up, and package disposal just as with any discrete product. On the other hand, the BIB process does recognize the liquid nature of the product. The BIB package acts as a "disposable steel drum" and thus simplifies the logistics process by eliminating the return, cleaning, and refilling of the drums from the usage cycle. Although heavy, BIBs are easier to handle than steel drums. In traditional Supply Chain terms, the rectangular BIB carton is much more efficient for storage, transport, and handling than steel drums. From a product perspective, the collapsible pouch inside the BIB unit prevents contact between the liquid and air or gas and thus is oriented toward the quality of the product. Clearly, Adapted Supply Chain as defined here is an improvement over Supply Chain, with a series of benefits in the operational, financial, quality, and environmental areas. It is, however, an improvement on the existing method, rather than a fundamental shift in the method of getting syrup from the producer to the consumer. Adapted Supply Chain does better what is already being done, but it does not consider doing it differently.

A Supply Chain for Liquids approach to this scenario would not be based on the existing system, but would start out by focusing on the ends of the process. The logistics flow is seen in the light of the end-consumption point — the user actually dispensing the product at the restaurant

— and not the delivery person moving the product into the restaurant, so that internal activity in the restaurant is within the scope of the flow. The approach would identify that the product is in liquid form when it is produced and liquid form when it is consumed. Containerization is not part of either of these ends and does not add benefit or value to either end.

Having determined that containers do not add value at either end, alternatives related to the logistics process that connect the two ends are raised and considered. The first-pass list of these alternatives would include what is possible rather than what ultimately would be the most effective. For example, the alternatives may include large inflatable bags at the customer site that could be filled by tank trucks that would include a collapsible lining offering the benefits of a BIB, fixed tanks at the site that could be filled through an external port, and other liquid-logistics methods. A Supply Chain for Liquids technique in current usage is to place large syrup tanks in a restaurant and have a tank truck feed the on-site tanks through a hose that is pulled from the truck into the back room or basement of the restaurant to fill the tanks. The packaging no longer moves; the syrup remains in bulk form from the point of production to the tanks held in the restaurant. This is a breakthrough in thinking and operating that begins to truly take advantage of the liquid nature of the product. In current practice, however, the breakthrough is not complete. The level of syrup in the tanks is monitored manually through a metered tube on the side of the tank, replenishment orders are placed manually, and there are other limitations to the completeness of the logistics flow.

What is important to note is that these alternatives are raised and evaluated without packaging being a "given" as part of the logistics process. The Supply Chain for Liquids process is described in greater detail in Chapter 5, but this example shows some of its fundamental aspects, in particular the focus on the "ends" of the logistics flow. As we undertake the Supply Chain for Liquids planning process, we fully examine (and question) all aspects of logistics activity, both from a logistics and a business perspective. After our own initial evaluation, we go further with the customer in exploring the dispense process. In the customer's business strategy, how would the customer (the restaurant) like to relate to *its* customers (the patrons)? What dispense/customer experience capabilities would it like to be able to offer? Will dispense always occur in restaurants, or are there other locations at which it would like to dispense? Does the customer have in mind other products to dispense that might affect the logistics flow, such as the at-dispense combination of multiple products? What other liquids are involved in the customer's current business, and are there other businesses that the customer is currently engaged in or contemplating that would involve liquids as part of its products or part of its processes? Because the input on these issues is an important driver in the design of the logistics system, we lay out a clear process for gathering, confirming, and evaluating this information as we transition from Adapted Supply Chain to Supply Chain for Liquids.

Optimal Supply Chain for Liquids is the next stage of logistics development. To some degree, Optimal Supply Chain for Liquids is to Supply Chain for Liquids as Adapted Supply Chain is to Supply Chain. We have already taken the quantum leap to get to Supply Chain for Liquids, so we enter a process of continuous improvement at the Supply Chain for Liquids level. In all likelihood there are aspects of our overall design that we have not yet put in place or peripheral aspects of the system for which the planning may yet be open. We continually use customer feedback, advances in technology, analysis of data, and improvements in technique and equipment to refine the Supply Chain for Liquids system. Optimal Supply Chain for Liquids means that we have done a great job of planning our logistics system and have built on that planning with excellent execution. As anyone who has been involved in a business-improvement project knows, however, the day on which you say "we have reached all of our objectives" is the day when you also say "look at all these new opportunities that we have created for ourselves." Over the course of time, we continue with this stable state until the day arrives in which we realize that, relatively speaking, we have slipped back from Supply Chain for Liquids to Supply Chain — or more likely, the world has advanced to the point where we need to undergo another paradigm shift to achieve optimum operation.

In the restaurant example, it is possible to see operations at each of the levels of liquid logistics. In one advanced system, liquids are delivered to the restaurant through an external port in the restaurant wall. The liquids are held in bulk containers in the restaurant, and they are continuously monitored, and replenishment orders are placed automatically. These and a series of other steps described later in this book come together to provide a fully synergetic system in which all pieces contribute to the efficient flow of the whole: efficient movement of product is maximized; costs are minimized; and techniques, technology, and equipment are deployed in such a way that each contributes to achieving Optimal Supply Chain for Liquids status.

Why Supply Chain for Liquids?

Now that we have dug a little deeper into Supply Chain and Supply Chain for Liquids and the variations on these themes, let us go back and check ourselves (as we should do periodically in any venture). Should you be interested in Supply Chain for Liquids?

Each individual has to answer that question based on his or her own situation, company, vision, and motivations. The last thing you should do is try to approach a Supply Chain for Liquids project because it smells like the latest fad or you think it sounds impressive. You should do it if you recognize that liquids play a significant role in your company, if the methodology used for a Supply Chain for Liquids project — the Liquid Lens process described in Chapter 3 — appeals to you, and if you and your company are forward-looking and can envision Supply Chain for Liquids techniques as powerful weapons for your marketplace battles. In a sense, any company with significant involvement in liquids — for its products, its processes, or its position — is already on the road toward Supply Chain for Liquids, probably without even knowing it. Many companies involved with liquids are like a driver whose car has cruise control but who has never learned to use it. The capability is there; once the process is learned, the desire to use it is there ("the appetite comes with the food" according to the old saw); and after it is used, it is hard to imagine being without it. Such it is with many advances, and such it is for companies whose product base puts them in the exclusive club of companies who are in a position to take advantage of Supply Chain for Liquids principles.

You may recognize another value of Supply Chain for Liquids that would lead you to pursue it. The fundamental Supply Chain for Liquids approach is to strip away complexity and cost from the entire system. Like a Rube Goldberg machine that has simply gotten too complex to function properly, it is in the nature of business systems to "gain weight" over the course of time. The Liquid Lens process within Supply Chain for Liquids is an opportunity to do more than go on this diet or that diet; it is an opportunity for a change in lifestyle. This is not easy to do, and certainly cannot be done in a scattershot approach. The Liquid Lens approach provides a framework for pursuing an effort such as this with a comprehensive focus on all aspects of a company's logistics processes. Alternatively, your company may be in a position in which one of your logistics partners (either a supplier or a customer) has dictated, or one of your competitors has made essential, that you undertake a process to make your company more competitive. Supply Chain for Liquids does this in the many areas it covers — cost saving, revenue enhancement, and customer satisfaction, among others.

If you have reached this point and meet the criteria of recognizing the use of liquids in your business as well as seeing that the Supply Chain for Liquids approach may potentially apply to you, then you should definitely continue this journey and explore Supply Chain for Liquids further. After a brief discussion of process industries, our next step will be to look at the methodology involved in Supply Chain for Liquids —

the Liquid Lens—a different sort of methodology designed to lead to a different sort of result.

Supply Chain for Liquids and Process Industries

With the overview of Supply Chain for Liquids that we have covered thus far, we should make a sharp distinction between Supply Chain for Liquids and "process industries." The relationship between the two could cause confusion from a number of directions. For somebody within a process industry, the thought might be, "Why do I need to think about Supply Chain for Liquids? I am already working with liquids." The reverse of this position may come from someone outside of a process industry, who says, "I don't need to consider Supply Chain for Liquids. I don't work in a process industry." Both of these positions miss the point of Supply Chain for Liquids, which addresses a different set of issues than process industries.

Let us start by clarifying the view that somebody working in a process industry is "already there" when it comes to Supply Chain for Liquids. There are several misunderstandings contained within this statement. First, the concept "process industries" often refers to the production side of the logistics flow, in the sense of production methodologies that occur in a continuous process or result in a continuous flow of product. This is distinguished from a discrete industry in which the process and product are separately identifiable units. Several other characteristics of process industries are identifiably different from discrete industries, such as the production planning and control approach and the way materials are handled during the production process. Because process industries often are involved in the production of liquids or materials with liquidlike characteristics, there is naturally more of an affinity between process industries and Supply Chain for Liquids in terms of *products* than between discrete industries and Supply Chain for Liquids. That is, Supply Chain for Liquids is applicable to liquids that serve as ingredients to production in process industries as well as to the liquid products that result from process industry production.

Process industries are generally considered to be the upstream end of the entire logistics flow: the production process and possibly the initial movement of large quantities of product as raw materials to another producer or production operation. This is typical, for example, of petroleum refining, petrochemicals, and many types of chemical products. At some point in the logistics flow, however, these processes cease to be identifiable as "process industries" and become discrete, as we have defined this term earlier: products are broken down into smaller quantities for whatever usage they are directed toward. In most cases, this involves placing the products in discrete containers without considering creation of an extension of the process flow. This is where Supply Chain for Liquids kicks in. It covers the entire flow of the product from the point of initial production, through the various stages of the supply stream, and to the point of dispense and usage by the end consumer. Supply Chain for Liquids also includes the raw-material liquids used in the production operation. Thus there may be some overlap of process industries and Supply Chain for Liquids at one stage of the entire process, but in mathematical terms, process industries could be considered a subset of Supply Chain for Liquids. The actual manufacturing aspect of process industries addresses detailed production considerations that Supply Chain for Liquids does not focus on, but Supply Chain for Liquids covers the entire flow of product that is lost to process industries. However, they both cover the movement of liquid products at a certain stage of the logistics flow. In summary, process industries and Supply Chain for Liquids are related but not identical, and certainly a company in a process industry will extend its reach and improve its competitive position by adding a Supply Chain for Liquids orientation to the flow of its products to the point at which they reach the consumer.

Apart from the *product* aspect of process industries, there is the *process* aspect of process production in the sense of the equipment, facilities, and transportation used during the production process. Independent of the fact that the products produced may be liquid, there are many liquids required to facilitate production for which Supply Chain for Liquids is applicable. Lubricants for the production equipment, cleaning fluids and materials, and facility upkeep and maintenance liquids are all used by a process-industry company and should be viewed in terms of Supply Chain for Liquids.

This last point addresses the second challenge that was presented above: "I don't need to consider Supply Chain for Liquids because I don't work in a process industry." For people who equate Supply Chain for Liquids with process industries and who do not work in a process industry, the value of the Supply Chain for Liquids approach will be missed. As described earlier, the liquid element of discrete industries is often extensive but hidden. Once you go through the mental process of taking all the liquids you use out of their containers and understanding the types and volumes of liquids that are used throughout your operation, you will see the degree to which Supply Chain for Liquids is not only appropriate, but also could be valuable to your company. Each type of liquid you use has a complete set of potential benefits with Supply Chain for Liquids — economic benefits in terms of cost savings, environmental benefits, competitive benefits, opportunity benefits either in terms of increased opportunities for efficiency or increased opportunities for revenue, efficiency benefits in working with suppliers and with customers, and more. Viewing these benefits across the multiple types of liquids that are used in many companies allows the overall benefit of Supply Chain for Liquids to become evident. The major liquids used by companies often include liquids to run the operation, such as machine lubricants, hydraulic fluid; cleaning solutions; liquids used in the transportation process such as automotive lubricants and coolants; maintenance liquids such as cleaning fluids and paints; and liquids used as components of products such as colorings, adhesives, or other component materials. Thus producers of discrete products, as well as service companies and others, can benefit from an evaluation of implementation of Supply Chain for Liquids for the liquids in their operations.

Process industries and Supply Chain for Liquids — we have looked at both sides of the coin. For companies in a process industry, Supply Chain for Liquids acts as an extension and an enhancer of liquids-based operations. For companies in a discrete industry, the distance from a process industry does not affect the value that Supply Chain for Liquids can have in all aspects of the operation.

Chapter 3

The Liquid Lens

The Liquid Lens[SM] is a way of seeing, a way of thinking, and a way of acting as related to liquid logistics. We cannot expect the system we develop to be better than the thought process we use to develop it; therefore, it is necessary first of all to organize how we think about liquid logistics. Having done this, Supply Chain for Liquids® will be a powerful tool that we can use to go out and destroy the competition. Without this, Supply Chain for Liquids becomes just another flash that comes and goes with very little value.

We can get into the spirit of the Liquid Lens by reflecting on how it has been used in the past.

Archimedes, the Eureka! man, would have had a lot to say about the Liquid Lens. Besides his famous moment in the tub (and Einstein said his best thinking came in the shower — could there be more to our slogan Thinking Liquid[SM] than we realize?), he was almost habitual about breakthrough approaches to liquids. Starting with the gold crown, for us to imagine that the answer to the question of whether the crown was pure gold or not would be answered by how much water spilled out of a tub is, well, astonishing. We can assume that it was this enlightenment, and not the thought that he had discovered a way to keep his head connected to his shoulders in the face of King Hiero II's demand to find out if the crown contained cheap metals, that led to Archimedes' outcry.

"Liquid logistics" is written all over Archimedes screw, another of his major discoveries. Standard thinking had it that you could raise water by pushing it or pulling it, but Archimedes determined that you could raise water by turning it. This was literally outside-the-box thinking. The existing methods at that time involved some sort of container — pushing pans or containers on a waterwheel from a lower level to a higher level, or pulling buckets using ropes and pulleys — while Archimedes' invention utilized a tube with an endless spiral in it. How much farther out of the box can you get than that? What kind of a slap does that give us about broadening our thinking to achieve our desired result?

Like many technological developments, Archimedes screw found plenty of business applications. Although the Nile flooded its delta regularly, there were periods in which the floods did not come as usual or did not extend as far as normally. Archimedes screw was used to irrigate the area along the Nile and thus support the areas that were normally flooded and extend the acreage in which crops could be grown. Spanish copper, lead, and zinc mines yielded more minerals because water was removed from deep in the shafts by the use of Archimedes screws. This method was so successful that a series of screws were placed one after the other from the bottom of the mine to its entrance. Water was removed from the bottom interior portions of ships using an Archimedes screw, a method that was very popular because one person could remove a large quantity of water.

Archimedes' many other discoveries and inventions are only marginally related to liquids, but one of his most famous quotes characterizes the spirit of Supply Chain for Liquids. "Give me a place to stand and I will move the earth." Our objective is to make the Liquid Lens the lever that will let companies move the worlds they live in.

Liquid Lens adds the liquid dimension to a standard project-management/change-management process. It is not intended to be a completely self-contained methodology, but rather a method that augments and must be included in a project-management approach when it is applied to a Supply Chain for Liquids initiative. Liquid Lens is the perspective that differentiates a Supply Chain for Liquids project from a standard logistics project or any other type of project. It sees things in liquid terms, as shown in Exhibit 3.1. The Liquid Lens can be added to whatever technique a company normally uses for identifying, evaluating, and implementing changes to business processes while ensuring that the elements of the Liquid Lens are fully integrated into that technique.

Why do we need the Liquid Lens? We need it because the methods define the results, and because we are looking for liquid-oriented results, we should use liquid-oriented methods. A saw is the right tool for some jobs, but not to turn a screw. Or more precisely, if you want to cut wood, then a saw will do you just fine, but if you want to build a house, you will need a saw and a screwdriver. The Liquid Lens does not come in place of standard supply chain and business practices; it adapts them and enhances them to suit the needs of a liquids-oriented environment. Because

The Liquid Lens provides a liquids-based perspective on both products and processes – to exploit the logistics capabilities that liquids offer

© 2005 by Olana Inc.

Exhibit 3.1   When You Look through the Liquid Lens, You See Things Differently

adaptation means survival and flourishing, and we adapt better to our environment the more we are sensitive to it, the Liquid Lens is an approach that helps us "see" and exploit liquid-specific aspects of our operations. Like any other tool, with practice you can learn how to use it effectively; you can learn to adapt it to different situations you face and different people you come into contact with; you can wield it when you want to drive home a point but the wood is a little hard and the nail is not going in so well.

We refer to this tool as a "lens" because it, by itself, does not change anything, but it very much changes the way things appear and how we relate to them. It allows you to focus on specific parts of your organization and filter or highlight elements that otherwise might well get lost within the overall activity. Like a lens, it is widely applicable; you can look at any part of your operation through the Liquid Lens and discover interesting things. When you look at something through a lens, you see it in a way that you have not seen it before, even if you have been looking at it for many years. Most importantly, like a lens, you can share it with others, look through it together with others, compare thoughts about what different people see when looking through it, and thus come up with an even sharper and more complete picture.

The Liquid Lens takes a liquids-oriented business and looks at it in a very special way. The main issues that the Liquid Lens deals with are:

■ What are the implications of the fact that we are working with a liquid product, and how do we take full advantage of that fact?
■ Are all the parts of our systems fully integrated and oriented toward our products?

- How can the capabilities offered by the Supply Chain for Liquids be used to create new opportunities, both logistical and from a wider business perspective?
- What will the Supply Chain for Liquids world look like for our company, both in terms of internal impact and external/competitive impact?
- What are the caution points related to the liquids that we need to be aware of throughout the process?
- How can we simplify? Supply Chain for Liquids is all about removing layers rather than adding layers to the logistics system.

We can examine each of these in detail to develop a Liquid Lens for looking at our own business. A good process may well lead to a good result, but it is difficult to find situations in which a bad process consistently leads to good results. The Liquid Lens is a good process that helps us develop good liquid-logistics results.

Logistics Characteristics of Liquid Products

Woody Allen was determined to rob a bank. Even though the bakery his girlfriend had started as a cover for the robbery was wildly successful and they had all the money they could ever want, the con man in *Small Time Crooks* was determined to stick to his ways. Allen declares that he still wants to hit that bank, sticking to his original plan despite completely changed circumstances.

Liquid distribution as used by most companies sticks to a standard methodology despite circumstances that direct otherwise. Ignoring the nature of the product, companies jam the square peg of liquids into the round hole of discrete products in their distribution and dispensing processes. They actually convert the liquids into a "solid" by placing it in bottles, jugs, drums, or other package, then ship it using cumbersome and expensive distribution methods, and finally get it to the end user. The user removes the liquid from the packaging and uses it — in its original liquid form. *In fact, liquid distribution is often not driven by the liquid at all; it is driven by the packaging that contains the liquid.*

In addition, the "brainlock" that treats liquid products like solid products also prevents consideration of the tremendous opportunities for efficient distribution of liquids. When we try to think about beverages and lubricants and chemicals, other things get in the way, things like car tires and bird cages and television sets. The habit of looking at logistics systems from a discrete-based perspective is so powerful that it is easy to never step back and think about these systems from a liquid perspective.

Even when we get a glimpse of what the opportunities are, there are many forces at work in life that keep us to the status quo rather than moving us toward revolutionary acts. Like the legendary story of the early focus groups for mobile telephones that nixed the idea because participants could not think of any reason that people would want such things, "the way things are" is often a much more powerful influence than "the way things might be."

We use the Liquid Lens to shatter this locked view of logistics. When we look through the Liquid Lens, we continually ask the question, "Are we fully taking into account the fact that we are talking about liquids and not about discrete items?" We are constantly on the lookout to prevent ourselves from backsliding into solids-based thinking in every discussion about every aspect of our product. We bring in new inputs that are oriented toward liquids to draw us — like a sponge, so to speak — toward liquid thinking. These inputs may come from liquid-oriented industries outside our own, from an individual or group within the organization who is tasked to be the source of positive energy when it comes to instilling liquid thought processes, or from our own efforts to break through traditional thinking and truly absorb a liquids-based orientation. Our internal processes take on the elements required for this effort. We enlist the whole group to monitor itself the way we enlist the whole family to let us know if we have eaten something that is not on our diet. We slip not because we want to or because it is good for us, but because old habits and old desires become part of our bone marrow, and it is hard to clean out. We surround ourselves with examples that we have created or that have come from elsewhere of the differences between liquids-based thinking and discrete-based thinking. Having instances of this distinction readily at hand helps keep it "in our face" rather than having it slip out of sight and out of mind.

Having symbols of liquid-oriented thinking constantly present is also important for anti-groupthink purposes. Even in an environment in which we are encouraging change or at least adaptation, it is often difficult for an individual to raise an idea that is non-mainstream. Even after a person overcomes self-censorship, the power of the group to pour cold water on the hot sparks of ideas serves to dampen the generation and development of these ideas. Having physical symbols of innovative liquid-logistics methods or equipment obviously displayed is a powerful way to overcome this resistance. A person trying to raise ideas has these icons available for support: "Do you remember the initial reaction to the U-Mix Restaurant Salad Dressing Dispenser? We spent most of our efforts getting by the reactives, and only when we put our mind to it did it start to take off." Anytime something new or different comes up, it is easy to visualize that some of the people impacted quickly take out a virtual shotgun and

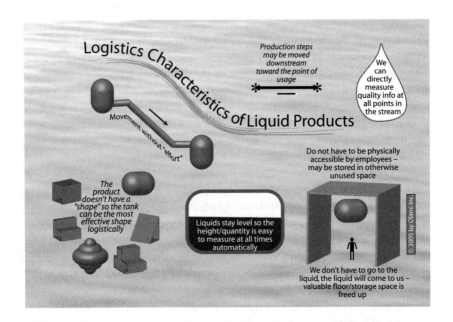

Exhibit 3.2   Liquids Have Logistics Characteristics That Discrete Products Cannot Offer

sit with it on the sidelines, waiting for the opportunity to take aim and start shooting. With proper management of the process, these people could be identified and converted to scouts patrolling ahead of the idea to help nurture it, or at least to ensure that their virtual shotguns are loaded with equally virtual blanks.

What are some of the characteristics of liquid products that become important to us as we start looking at our operations through the Liquid Lens? Different characteristics will be more or less important based on the specific liquid and the logistics system involved, but we can identify some of the major characteristics that will be important to us, and these are summarized in Exhibit 3.2.

The first is how liquids move. Under most circumstances liquids, if left alone, will flow from a higher level to a lower level. All we need to do is to provide the channel in which we want them to flow. Let us be careful to understand exactly what we are talking about. It is not just that liquids flow down a pipe. If the liquids are in a tank at the top, and the pipe is hooked to another tank of some type at the bottom, the liquids will flow without any human or mechanical intervention. For liquids, the process of moving the product can take place without anyone physically "moving" the product at all. The quantity of product we want moved can travel from Point A to Point B without investing additional effort in the process. If we think that this is trivial, let us try putting television sets at the top of a big tube and see what shape they are in after they have tumbled down to the bottom. Certainly, conveyor belts can be used to "flow" discrete products from one point to another, but unlike liquids, they have to be moved onto the conveyor belt on one end and off the conveyor belt at the other end. More to our point, quart bottles of motor oil are in a discrete form — bottles. To get the bottles or cartons containing the bottles from a truck into a storage area, even if we could put a conveyor belt in place, someone would have to move the bottles or cartons from the truck onto the belt, and someone on the other end would have to take them off and put them away. For delivery to a customer site, a conveyor belt is unlikely to be used, but rather a forklift or an even more labor-intensive hand truck. The same concept applies within a facility, for example moving liquids from a storage rack to the point of usage. In these examples, imagine the differences between moving 500 gallons of motor oil in liquid form (through a pipe) versus moving the same 500 gallons in discrete form. We will quantify this difference in financial terms in Chapter 11, but for now, this is a good exercise in looking at this process through a Liquid Lens.

Let us use the Liquid Lens to look at this point even more closely. We say that liquids can move by themselves without additional effort. That means that we can move the product without moving the container or packaging: *in liquid form, we can move only the product without moving the container or packaging at all*. The truck is outside the quick-lube facility, and the product can flow in from there *all by itself.* We are not yet painting a full picture of the target process, but we are beginning to understand that there may be opportunities for tremendous logistical efficiencies here.

The fact that liquids flow leads to another important logistical characteristic: we do not have to access the liquids, the liquids can come to us. What does this mean? Perhaps it can most easily be illustrated by comparing access to liquid products versus discrete products. In order for a mechanic at a quick-lube shop to get to a two-gallon jug of motor oil, the jug must be accessible. It must be at floor level, or on a rack, or in some other position in which the mechanic can take it for use. In terms of the facility, the product is taking up valuable space that is being used for storage. Liquid in a tank, on the other hand, will always flow down. So if the tank is higher than the user, the user can get to the liquid simply by opening a dispense pipe that is connected to the tank. The tank may be placed in any position as long as it is higher than the user. We can think of this as the water-tower principle. A town has to flow water to all the houses and businesses in its domain. It could pump the water to each house, but that would require a huge investment in equipment and effort. A much more efficient method is to have one set of pumps to pump water to a high point — a water tower — and then let gravity do the hard work of getting the water out to all the houses. This is a very powerful approach that is very widely implemented. One part of the Liquid Lens is to utilize liquid-oriented techniques, such as the water-tower technique if appropriate. Another alternative is to have the tanks lower than the user, such as in a basement, and have a pump propel the liquids from the lowest point in the tank arrangement up to the user/dispense level. We will see the full value of these approaches shortly.

Another characteristic of liquids that is important to us from a logistics perspective is that they are in many ways completely flexible in terms of the shape and size of the container. Generally speaking, the liquid does not care how big a container is or how the container is shaped, although for quality purposes it may be significant what material the interior of the container is made of or what gas fills the part of the container that the liquid does not fill. The flexibility of container shape provides a great deal of flexibility in thinking through the containers or packaging in which the liquid may be placed at various points throughout the Supply Chain for Liquids. This flexibility does not exist with discrete products. The shape of the product has a large impact on the way it is handled. Brooms or coffins or lampshades each have specific requirements as to the type of container or shipping packaging in which it will be placed, and the shape of each item (complete or broken down for shipping or storage) cannot be changed or modified.

Again, let us use the Liquid Lens to go beyond this base fact to consider its logistical significance. The importance of the flexibility of containers/packaging for liquid products goes far beyond the design of the containers themselves. The containers in which the liquids are held will affect the nature of the facility in which the goods will be stored. Or, more properly for looking at containers and storage through the Liquid Lens, the container and the facility can be designed together for maximum efficiency of the Supply Chain for Liquids. The implication goes even farther than this: assuming that the facility already exists (such as a quick-lube garage), the design and shape of the container can be adapted to utilize otherwise unused space. Combining the flexibility of container design and shape with the accessibility characteristic described previously, we realize that the nature of the liquid product will allow us to gain large logistical benefits in terms of facility layout. Liquid products can be stored in containers/tanks in previously unused areas of the facility — overhead, on the walls, above the ceiling, etc. These tanks are filled from lines running from the fill point, and they are accessed by running a dispense line to the spot at which the liquid is needed. Logistically we win twice: first, inventory essentially takes up no (usable) space, and second, this approach is more convenient to the user because it brings the product to the point of use.

This approach is comparable with other unused-space storage solutions. Those plastic under-bed storage boxes convert the wasted space under the bed into useful extensions of closet space. Obviously, the closet will not fit under the bed, so the storage container is adapted to the physical dimensions of the unused space that is available to create "free" storage space. A refrigerator shelf that has suspended beneath it a rack to hold a horizontal bottle, but that leaves room for items to be stored under the rack on the next shelf below, is using space that often goes empty — that just beneath each shelf. The space is there, so if we use unutilized space wisely for products that can be put into that space, then we are ahead of the game. Perhaps the most efficient use of very limited, very valuable, but unused space is that of fuel storage in a passenger aircraft. Not only is there fuel storage in the fuselage, just as passengers, luggage, and cargo are contained in the fuselage, but inside the wings and in the horizontal stabilizer at the tail of an aircraft as well. On a Boeing 747, for example, the horizontal stabilizer tanks alone hold 3300 gallons of fuel. A 747's fuel consumption is measured in gpm (gallons per mile) rather than mpg (miles per gallon), and runs at about five gpm under standard conditions. At that rate, "finding" the space for the extra fuel in the horizontal stabilizer adds 660 miles to the range of the aircraft, about the distance from Boston to Cleveland. We can learn from the fuel-storage layout of an aircraft (Exhibit 3.3) that our ability to "find" space for liquid products adds value to our overall liquid-logistics system in a very similar way.

Compare this liquids-based approach to that used for a discrete product, such as motor oil in a jug. As described earlier, the jugs must be placed in an accessible and thus valuable area of the facility so that the user can easily obtain the jug for use. Motor-oil jugs, bag-in-box cartons in a restaurant, and other liquid containers in the facility storage area are typically placed on the floor or on a rack that is no higher than convenient reaching height for an employee. This puts a premium on floor space and storage space up to a level of five feet or so and ignores virtually completely all of the space from that level and higher, possibly half of all available space in the storage area. In addition to the inefficient use of space, standard methods lead to an inefficient use of time. The user has to go to the storage area and retrieve the jugs and bring them to the point of use, an inefficient use of time resulting from an inefficient use of space. We have looked at the use of space in the storage area, but certainly there are many other unused spaces in most facilities. Some beverages are currently placed in under-bar tanks to exploit that unutilized space, but the same limitations of accessibility apply to those tanks. A

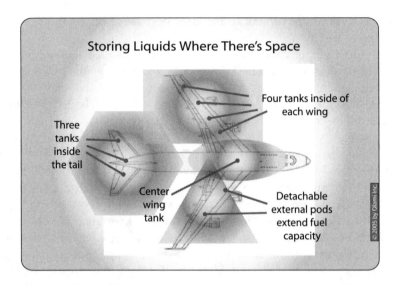

Storing Liquids Where There's Space

Four tanks inside of each wing

Three tanks inside the tail

Center wing tank

Detachable external pods extend fuel capacity

© 2005 by Olami Inc.

Exhibit 3.3   The Possibilities of Liquid Logistics Become Most Evident When Space Availability Is Limited

user still has to physically remove and replace them as they become empty. Using the Liquid Lens approach, we can explore the facility and identify almost any unused space, at any level and independent of ready accessibility, as potential storage space. Because we are looking at the facility through the Liquid Lens, we will not make the mistake of looking for storage space as we traditionally think of it, that is, as a single block of space that is vertically oriented and readily accessible to place and remove items.

Of course there are issues that come into play — building codes/regulations, safety, ambient conditions such as temperature, exposure to potentially dangerous conditions such as electrical junctions and wires, and so on — but at least we are eliminating the logistics constraint that had previously put so much of the facility "out of bounds" for storage purposes. We will examine the financial impact of this liquids-based approach in Chapter 11; for now, we are learning to use the Liquid Lens to discover these opportunities and capabilities.

Combining several of the characteristics of liquids described previously leads to another important differentiator for liquids versus discrete products. We used the water-tower principle related to liquids' tendency to flow from higher to lower levels, and said that the container a liquid is held in can be virtually any shape. Within the container, the water-tower principle also applies: a liquid will always fill up the bottom of the container first and reach an equilibrium level. Given that we know the size and shape of the container, we can always calculate the amount of liquid within the container if we know the height of the equilibrium level at any point in time. That is, we can use the uniformity of the level of a liquid to our advantage by identifying the level and then converting that to the quantity of liquid that is in the container at that point in time. Because the measurement can be done automatically and continuously using liquid-level sensors as described in Chapter 8, this characteristic of liquids allows us to constantly know the on-hand balance of liquid in a tank. This ability to inventory our liquid product without counting it is a huge advantage that we will explore in greater detail in Chapter 5.

For clarity let us compare this characteristic of liquids with the corresponding characteristic of discrete products. When you have a number of units of discrete products, can you know how many there are without counting them? There are actually several techniques available, such as pallets that include scales to take the total weight of product on the pallet from which the number of units can be derived based on the per-unit weight. For most discrete products, we do not even try to count the on-hand balance, but rather rely on our recording of inventory additions and removals to give us an accurate picture of the on-hand balance. Of course, currently the most prominent method of tracking on-hand inventory of discrete items is to attach a tag to each unit and then keep track of the tags using an RFID (radio frequency identification) system. We compare RFID for discrete products with Supply Chain for Liquids for liquid products in Chapter 5, but we can summarize the comparison by saying that Supply Chain for Liquids offers virtually all of the advantages of RFID more cheaply, simply, and with broader distribution of benefits along the logistics flow than the corresponding system for discrete products. Perhaps the biggest difference between RFID for discrete items and Supply Chain for Liquids is that RFID is just beginning what appears will be a massive, time-consuming, and complex process of introduction and penetration into the logistics world, while all of the equipment required to gain a corresponding benefit for liquid products is already available. By taking into account the liquid nature of our product, we can put together a system with massive benefits that would not be available, or would be available only at much greater expense and difficulty, than what we are able to achieve with a liquids-based system.

Another characteristic of liquid products relative to discrete products is how the quality of the product is defined and how it is measured. Liquids are dynamic; they react to their environment and change their characteristics based on their environment. In many ways, we can determine the current status of the quality of a liquid by measuring specific characteristics of the liquid. For some liquids, exposure to air leads to impaired quality that is identified through the presence of certain gases in the liquid. For others, the color, opacity, viscosity, or other characteristics change and serve as an indicator of reduced quality. Any of these characteristics of liquids can be monitored through sensors and the results reported at a frequency defined by the user, so that information about product quality, like data about product quantity, is available in real or near-real time.

Other quality-impacting factors may relate to the environment that the liquid is in, such as temperature or pressure. For example, temperatures beyond a set range of limits may impair quality, and it may be simpler or more effective to measure temperature than to detect the resulting change in the liquid. These types of environmental monitors can also be put into place, either inside the tanks or related to ambient conditions such as the storage area.

Comparing the approach to quality that is available for liquids with quality issues related to discrete items, there are a completely different set of issues for discrete items. "Quality" for a discrete item often relates to physical damage such as a dent, breakage, mechanical damage from having been dropped or bumped, water damage, or some other physical impact on the item. Either damage to the product itself or damage to the packaging may render the individual unit unsellable as is. This entire set of "damage" issues is eliminated for liquids within the Supply Chain for Liquids system, as liquids themselves are not "damageable" in the physical sense, and the packaging to which the damage often occurs is eliminated. Most discrete items do not change in a measurable way as some liquids do, so techniques for monitoring quality and identifying quality exceptions that can be used for liquids are not available for discrete products.

An interesting distinction between liquids and discrete products has to do with bringing the product to its final configuration. Although most production activities for liquids take place in production facilities, some processes may take place downstream and, in so doing, significantly improve the efficiency of the production process. Several obvious examples have to do with food products. Carbonated soft drinks from fountain service are in the form of a syrup from the point of production to the point of dispense, where they are combined with water and carbonation to form the consumable beverage. Some types of ice cream are shipped as liquid and then frozen within the dispense unit, thus taking their final form only immediately prior to consumption. Tap water becomes filtered water as it passes through the filter on the way to the water bottle or the customer's glass in the restaurant. For wine and many alcoholic beverages, of course, the changes that take place during product storage and transportation are an inherent part of the nature of the product itself. For nonconsumable liquids, several types of soaps are shipped as concentrates and diluted at the point of dispense for usage. Glues and other adhesives are in liquid form up to the point of application and serve their purpose as they dry; in contrast, gels and urethanes solidify as they are exposed to air or are combined with certain chemicals and become solids. From a logistics perspective, liquids offer the opportunity for a production step far outside the confines of the production facility, as far as the point of dispense and even beyond. This capability is taken into account when looking at our logistics systems through the Liquid Lens.

Discrete products in some cases offer self-changing capabilities, although in a much different sense than with liquid products. Assembly of a product usually requires manual intervention, and it could be argued that product changes such as ripening of fruits or vegetables constitute a change in the product between the point of origination and the point of consumption. For the vast majority of discrete products, however, the form in which they are manufactured is the same as the form in which they are purchased, with conversion to their final usable form requiring some form of external intervention.

We have seen here ways of using the Liquid Lens to look at the characteristics of liquids and the processes they undergo in relation to each other. In each case, we started with the nature of liquids and then moved from there to the logistical implications and methodologies that might be used with liquid products. This is just the opposite of basing our thinking on standard logistical processes and then trying to tweak them for our own purposes. Some of the major characteristics of liquid products that impact their logistical handling are listed as follows:

- Liquids flow from a higher level to a lower level, so they can be moved without mechanical propulsion or manual intervention.
- Liquids adapt to the shape of their container, which provides a great deal of flexibility in the design of storage systems and enables the use of dead space for storage.
- Liquids settle to a uniform level in a tank, so volumes can be automatically and continuously measured.
- Changes in liquid characteristics can be monitored via sensors, and these data can be translated into measures of the quality of the liquid.
- In some cases, liquids can be processed well downstream from the original production facility, thus offering the opportunity for improved efficiencies throughout the supply stream together with greater flexibility as to the nature of the product at the point of final usage.

Starting with a liquid focus allows us to throw off all kinds of presumptions that would have otherwise impaired our thinking. Of course, each company must start with the specific characteristics of the particular liquid products with which it deals, and then proceed to look through the Liquid Lens. In any case, the basic fact is that we are dealing with liquid products. Let us start with that and then develop our thinking to gain maximum benefit of this great advantage. Going back to Woody Allen and his bakery, we may discover that approaches and methods that we had not thought of, or that were considered only secondary to our main way of doing business, lead to far more productive results than trying to improve on the original methods. Perhaps that is the best way to turn small efforts into big successes.

All Parts of the System Work Together

The first area that the Liquid Lens brings into focus, as described previously, is the interplay between liquids and logistics. The second area that the Liquid Lens focuses on is the interplay between the pieces of the logistics system and the system as a whole, within the context of the liquid products in the system. In this sense, it is almost a reverse-lens, putting together the whole picture rather than viewing any single part of it.

We can enlist the help of a 1950s movie, *Creature from the Black Lagoon*, to examine this second principle of the Liquid Lens in greater detail. Whatever the merits or demerits of this movie, it left several environmental and artistic messages that should not be ignored, and we can learn a lesson from a logistics perspective as well. The movie was produced during the height of the 3-D (three dimensional) movie craze, and in some quarters, it is considered to be the finest of the lot. (Indeed, the "Jaws"-style scene of the attractive swimmer being attacked from below is drawn from this movie.) Our interest in the movie, however, relates to the glasses that were needed to watch it. We can think of the Liquid Lens as acting like a pair of 3-D glasses, the ones with one red lens and one blue lens. On the piece of paper on which a 3-D image is printed, or on the movie screen on which it is being viewed, there are two distinct sets of images — one in red and one in blue. Looking at the raw images without the glasses gives you a general idea of what the picture is about, but putting the glasses on provides an even better view than is seen in a regular image. The glasses go beyond the completion of the two-dimensional image; indeed, they provides the fullness of a three-dimensional image with a depth that is not available in a regular view.

As described in Chapter 8, the Supply Chain for Liquids involves many management-level issues as well as many technical/operational-level issues. We can think of the management-level issues as the blue lines on the page and the technical-level issues as the red lines on the page, as illustrated in Exhibit 3.4. If we pursue the design of the Supply Chain

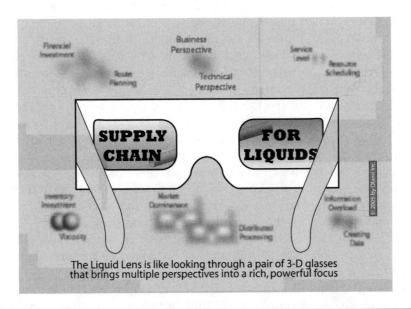

The Liquid Lens is like looking through a pair of 3-D glasses that brings multiple perspectives into a rich, powerful focus

Exhibit 3.4   The Liquid Lens Is a Tool for Bringing Diverse Topics into a Single Focus

with just the blue lens and then pass a decision to the technical people for implementation, we will get some sort of a system. Similarly, we will get some sort of a system if we design the Supply Chain while looking through just the red lens, that is, the Supply Chain is viewed as a technical issue with minimal management implications. Neither one will be as complete a system as we would see by looking through the dual-view red/blue glasses. Indeed, it is impossible to achieve the status of Supply Chain for Liquids or of Optimal Supply Chain for Liquids by using either a management approach or a technical approach separately. Using the Liquid Lens, we can put together these two approaches to create a truly exciting and magnificent picture. It is the dynamic interplay between management-level and technical-level thinking that truly creates a Supply Chain for Liquids. The ability to bring these two modes together, and to switch back and forth between these modes, is an important part of the Liquid Lens approach.

This approach is unusual in that it involves an iterative process within different organizational functions that frequently take an arm's-length view of each other. It is not at all unusual for management to hand out directives and leave it up to the technical side to execute, with the thinking that "we don't want to get involved in all those technical details." On the other hand, technical people often receive instructions that are not fully defined or, more importantly, where the business thinking behind the instructions is not evident. When this happens, the line of thinking is, "Here comes another order from above; let's stop thinking and move forward." From a Liquid Lens point of view, each side is exactly half right. Each group has its own function to perform, and neither function can take on the role of the other. Management cannot get lost in the details, and detail-focused groups cannot see the full breadth of the broad picture. On the other hand, powerful results are obtained when each side invests the effort to understand the other side. Management need not get involved in the technical details, but understanding the technical issues from a management perspective can yield new views, both technically and managerially. By the same token, technical people who carry out directives mechanically often have ideas that would impact the business applicability of technical issues, but they have neither the vocabulary nor the forum to express their ideas. The Liquid Lens approach creates a middle ground for the two perspectives to mix and, in so doing, to nurture a unified view of the logistics process.

Indeed, the Liquid Lens approach can lead to new insights that neither side would have discovered alone. Consider the example of pouring milk into a cup of tea. A common tea-making technique is to put hot water into a cup, bathe a teabag in the water, put in some sugar, and stir. At the beginning, you can see the whirlpool of the tea around the center, but shortly thereafter, the tea seems to settle, and no movement is apparent. As the last step, you pour in a little milk, and what was invisible a moment ago now becomes delightfully obvious. The milk swirls and twirls as it spreads through the tea, which, as has become apparent, is still roiling and full of eddies. Similarly, although the management and technical sides may have a "calm" view of each other on the surface, placing the relationship in the right environment allows the dynamics of each side to become evident to the other. And out of those dynamics — the swirls and twirls that make up the thinking of each side — a new "brew" can be created, to the benefit of each of the sides and to the benefit of the company as a whole as well.

Let us look at a specific example to understand exactly what this means. Earlier, we discussed the power of using a liquids-based versus a discrete approach in the delivery process. We described how liquid can flow from a delivery truck through a tube into a facility much more effectively than moving the same quantity of liquids in jugs or bottles. The concept of using a liquids-based approach to delivery is a management-level direction, as there are many issues of marketing and customer relationships involved, but there are also many technical factors involved. For example, the technical side may identify that putting monitors in the on-site tanks proposed by management will help control the flow of liquids into the tanks. When the technical side begins to speak about monitors, this idea can flow back to a systemwide method of planning and monitoring inventory usage, which is again a management-level issue. Thus a true Supply Chain for Liquids conversation is a nurturing of ideas through two aspects — management level and technical level — toward an optimal solution for the specific flow. This process requires either a special set of skills in a few people — the ability to work at both management level and technical level — or a special process in which management and technical personnel work together to develop a plan for their Optimal Supply Chain for Liquids.

In any case, following the thought step of the Liquid Lens must come the action step — implementation according to some plan. The thought process does not do any good unless it leads to action, although many companies have found what they consider to be an acceptable alternative to action. As a management consultant for many years, I always pictured two imaginary piles in the corners of the meeting rooms of the companies where I worked — one a pile of results, and the other a pile of excuses. Any company can find an excuse not to move forward with any project, and Supply Chain for Liquids/Optimal Supply Chain for Liquids is no different. It is a useful exercise to check the corners of your meeting room and examine the relative height of the results pile versus the excuses pile. If your results pile is good and high, then the Supply Chain for Liquids process will be powerfully beneficial to your company.

It is important to note that there need not be any "black boxes" related to Supply Chain for Liquids, and no secret or highly complex technologies need to be purchased or developed to make it work. In fact, every "piece" of the process mentioned in this book is already operational and readily available commercially. The trick is to make the whole come out greater than the sum of the parts by using and integrating the pieces in such a way that the whole system works far better than it would based on any of the individual pieces. Just as excellence has been defined as nothing more than the right combination of hard work and common sense, so Supply Chain for Liquids is nothing more than the intelligent combination of the right factors — most, if not all, of which already exist — to produce a result that, for the most part, does not currently exist in the marketplace.

An adjunct of this integrated approach is the injunction to "know your goal," that is, to develop a vision for what the end result is going to look like prior to setting out on the effort. There may be adjustments to the vision along the way, but having an ongoing idea of the target end-result always provides a framework for the different "pieces" that will be addressed along the way. "Know your goal," in operations and in life, is an exercise in self-discipline that is well worth the effort. Once you know what it is you are trying to achieve over a period of time, you will be surprised to realize how frequently your tactical actions actually run counter to your longer-term objectives. More than once, a person has gotten caught up in a battle that turns into an all-consuming distraction, never to see the objective again. There are people for whom fighting the battle *is* the objective. That is what they enjoy doing, and it does not really matter what the battle is. For others, though, there is a goal out there, although it may be hard to keep in sight. The single most important sentence I read in two years of MBA school was tucked away inside one of those endless case studies and really had nothing to do with the subject of the case study. The author apparently decided to throw it in as a point of philosophy to anyone who would value it. We have the luxury here of including it as being very relevant to the Liquid Lens: "In a world based on competition, you may find yourself at the top of a mountain you never would have climbed." The Liquid Lens helps us draw a complete picture, creating the framework for many detailed actions and ensuring that the detailed actions are all contributing to our goal of a highly effective liquid-logistics system.

Finding New Opportunities through the Liquid Lens

So far, we have seen how the Liquid Lens can help us focus on the liquid aspects of our products and show us the process for building a highly integrated liquids-based system. The third aspect of the Liquid Lens approach has the lens serving as a crystal ball, allowing us to see the opportunities that are not available in the absence of Supply Chain for Liquids capabilities.

We will also learn about the advantages that the Supply Chain for Liquids approach offers both operationally and from a businesswide perspective, but we will need the Liquid Lens to help us take full advantage of it. Sticky notes are a good example to illustrate this point. The inventor of the nonsticky adhesive used in this product did not have a "sticky lens" to help him fully appreciate the value of the invention. Only six years later, when one of his coworkers was having trouble keeping the book-marks in his hymnal, did the idea of applying the adhesive to small paper slips occur to the inventor. Using the Liquid Lens, we can shortcut that birthing process and exploit the advantages of Supply Chain for Liquids as it is implemented. We need a Liquid Lens mind-set to help us explore and discover all the value offered by the Supply Chain for Liquids.

How does the Liquid Lens work in this regard? As described in Chapter 10, part of the Supply Chain for Liquids process is to strip away the extraneous logistics processes and map out the producer-user relationship based only on the liquid itself; that is, what form is the liquid in when it is produced, and what form is it in when it is used? Using these two anchor points for the entire process, the optimal logistics that "connect" the points can be defined. The Supply Chain for Liquids approach uses the existing production method and the existing uses of the product as a starting point. Within that starting point, however, we have "wiped the slate clean" in terms of logistics so that we can take a greenfield look at logistics based on the proposed starting and ending points.

The Liquid Lens "new opportunities" function capitalizes on that process and takes it one step further. If we are going through the process of freeing ourselves from the constraints of logistics for the purpose of that exercise, let us see what happens when we free ourselves from the constraints of current usage methods as part of a Liquid Lens exercise. Let us break the vicious circle of form and usage where a person uses a product in a certain way because that is the way it is presented, and where it is presented that way because that is the way it is used. We can see an example of this in the struggle that the wine industry is currently going through related to corks. The big question in the wine industry today is whether corks are the best way to seal a bottle of wine. In listening to the arguments on the various sides (natural cork, synthetic cork, screw-off tops), it is clear that not far below the surface lies a very entrenched method of form and usage. The fact that natural cork can be bad for the wine — up to 5 percent of wine is ruined by "cork taint" — is lost in the perception that opening the bottle with a corkscrew adds to the value of the wine experience. Wine bottles are opened with a corkscrew because that is how they come; bottles of wine have been sealed with corks for millennia. The standard form-usage approach is quite strong here, although there has been some breakout from the standard approach recently. The Liquid Lens wants to go two steps beyond this. Not only does it ask the question, "What are the ways in which wine is currently consumed?" but beyond that, "What are the ways that wine could be used/consumed if we completely put aside the constraints we are currently working under?" In short, what new opportunities can we create once we get rid of the old limitations?

This is not to suggest that the old ways are necessarily wrong or bad, or are even likely to go away. For example, even in the epitome of high-speed instantaneous communication — e-mail — remnants of the communicationally obsolete remain. As you write an e-mail, you can send it to specific addressees, and then you can "carbon copy" (cc) it to others. Even when carbon paper was the only alternative available to create multiple copies of a message, the technique was clumsy and prone to error — getting out a sheet of carbon paper; checking to see whether there was still enough carbon on the sheet to produce a legible copy; putting together a "carbon sandwich," with the carbon inserted between

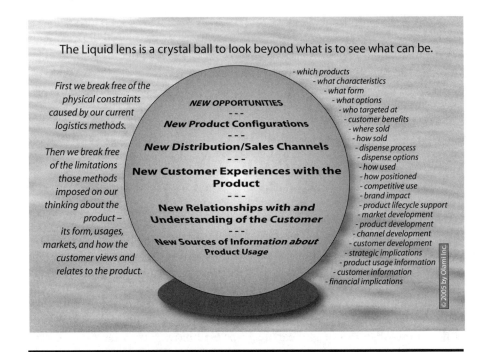

The Liquid lens is a crystal ball to look beyond what is to see what can be.

First we break free of the physical constraints caused by our current logistics methods.

Then we break free of the limitations those methods imposed on our thinking about the product – its form, usages, markets, and how the customer views and relates to the product.

NEW OPPORTUNITIES
- - -
New Product Configurations
- - -
New Distribution/Sales Channels
- - -
New Customer Experiences with the Product
- - -
New Relationships with and Understanding of the *Customer*
- - -
New Sources of Information *about* Product Usage

- which products
- what characteristics
- what form
- what options
- who targeted at
- customer benefits
- where sold
- how sold
- dispense process
- dispense options
- how used
- how positioned
- competitive use
- brand impact
- product lifecycle support
- market development
- product development
- channel development
- customer development
- strategic implications
- product usage information
- customer information
- financial implications

© 2005 by Olami Inc.

Exhibit 3.5   The Liquid Lens Opens the Doors on New Marketing Opportunities

two pieces of paper; and occasionally being dismayed to find that you had put the carbon paper in backward, so one sheet had the typing on both sides while the other was blank. Although the method of creating copies is certainly easier now — you just throw as many addresses as you want in the "cc" line — we see that the "carbon copy" terminology holds out, against all odds, in today's hyper-electronic-instantaneous-communications world.

It is important to remember that using the Liquid Lens to support the objective of finding new opportunities for a product is not a logistical issue. Instead, the Liquid Lens uses logistics in the service of the broader marketing and strategic needs of the company. Normally, the marketing effort drives logistics requirements; the Liquid Lens says that logistics can open doors that marketing did not know were there. Exhibit 3.5 illustrates the true value of opportunity creation using the Liquid Lens.

Let us focus the Liquid Lens on the restaurant example we used previously. We would feel very productive and successful if we were able to say that we had planned, implemented, or were operating a much more efficient method for getting beverage syrups into our restaurants. But the Liquid Lens approach instructs us to take another look at the situation, like a seer with a crystal ball, to discover aspects and directions that are not readily apparent. The Liquid Lens asks us to step back and define exactly what we have achieved. Thus far we have installed a personnel-free methodology for delivering liquid and having it reach the point of dispense. The next step is to explore what else we can build on top of that foundation. If we can get the liquid to the dispense point without "effort," then we have created flexibility in the positioning of the dispense point. It does not necessarily have to be behind the counter; it can be in front of the counter, as it currently is in some restaurants. But the Supply Chain for Liquids lets us think about putting it outside the restaurant. Let us create a kiosk outside the restaurant for customers who want to buy something to drink but are not necessarily hungry. Provide a self-operating dispense system combined with a payment system and a few picnic tables, and now we have given the customer a pleasant experience and added a customer to the restaurant who might otherwise have gone to a conventional vending machine to buy a can of soda at lower margin. This is the "opportunity development" approach that the Liquid Lens guides us to.

In addition to the development of business-level opportunities, the Supply Chain for Liquids offers operational-level advantages that we may discover using the Liquid Lens. For example, we can repeat the above Liquid Lens statement from an operational perspective. We have installed a personnel-free methodology for delivering liquid and having it reach the point of dispense. What does that means operationally? If we do not need restaurant personnel to accept the delivery, then we are no longer limited to restaurant operating hours to perform the delivery. We can schedule deliveries to achieve operational efficiency, such as overnight, when traffic would be much lighter and delays on the route far fewer. The Liquid Lens approach tells us that it is not enough to achieve improved processes; we must always step back and see how the improved processes can create new realities that will work in our favor.

The following example from antiquity illustrates how new realities created by improved processes can lead to unexpected benefits. The Egyptians were getting very good at making jars to hold water and other liquids, and the water was used mainly for drinking in the days before home plumbing. The improved process of constructing water jars included a hole at the bottom that would allow easy draining of the water into a cup. With such a system in place, some Egyptian noticed that as water dripped out of the bottom of the jar, the level of the water in the jar seemed to go down at a steady rate. The unknown jar watcher took advantage of the improved process for storing drinking water to create a method for using water to tell time. A few regularly spaced marks on the inside of the jar, and suddenly it was possible to measure the passage of time anywhere, day or night, a completely unexpected benefit from an improved technological capability.

The ability to push the logistics system farther in terms of creating new consumer-interface points and new revenue opportunities moves the producer's position an additional step forward. As described in Chapter 6, with the package-free flexibility that the producer (or distributor) gains from the Supply Chain for Liquids approach, the producer can approach the customer and make the creation of new distribution channels and new user/consumer experiences a joint effort between the producer and the customer. This interaction is not only productive in itself, but also more likely to lead to an even more comprehensive exploration of new business opportunities based on the products involved.

Wider Impact of Supply Chain for Liquids

The main focus of the Liquid Lens is the logistics process in particular and operations in general, while also taking into account the interactions between these areas and the rest of the company, such as finance, marketing, environmental compliance, and others. The Liquid Lens recognizes, however, that there is another ring of impact of the Supply Chain for Liquids system that will affect the company, and that in fact the Supply Chain for Liquids world will look different than it does using conventional approaches. Anticipating these additional issues will both mitigate those with potential negative impact and exploit the ones that have a positive impact on the company.

Any situation involving change will lead to a set of "people" issues involving those who feel threatened and those whose position will either change or be eliminated when moving to Supply Chain for Liquids. The detailed handling of these issues is beyond the scope of this book, but the overall approach must be included in the Liquid Lens process to get a fuller view of the impact of the implementation and operation of the Supply Chain for Liquids system. Although Supply Chain for Liquids is not reengineering for the sake of reengineering, its utilization of the characteristics of liquids to streamline the liquid-logistics flow and make it more efficient is likely to change the tasks performed by some people along the flow and eliminate other tasks altogether. The degree of impact and how this is handled is determined within the context of each individual company.

Another wide-scope issue that the Liquid Lens covers is the competitive situation and, in particular, the likely competitive response to a Supply Chain for Liquids initiative. Although this is a general business issue, it is of particular interest within the Liquid Lens methodology because there are steps that can be taken to dampen the opportunities that competitors have to respond to the introduction of Supply Chain for Liquids. To put

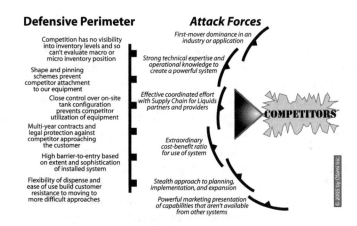

Exhibit 3.6   The Liquid Lens Arrays a Battle Plan for Combating the Competition

it in Sun Tzu's terms as he writes in *The Art of War*, "Hence to fight and conquer in all your battles is not supreme excellence; supreme excellence consists in breaking the enemy's resistance without fighting." The planning and implementation of Supply Chain for Liquids is as much a part of the battle as is the actual operation of the system, as shown in Exhibit 3.6, and if properly handled, it can overwhelm the competition and forestall any meaningful response.

There are several aspects of Supply Chain for Liquids that the Liquid Lens can focus on to achieve this level of competitive advantage. The first is the use of a stealth approach that keeps Supply Chain for Liquids under the radar screen until its implementation is committed to or becomes widespread. This can be done through the use of a limited number of pilot sites followed by commitment for broad implementation by the customer across a wider range of sites. A surprise attack accompanied by a maximum display of weaponry is a powerful competitive combination.

Even having said this, though, Sun Tzu reminds us that "the principles of warfare are: Do not depend on the enemy not coming, but depend on our readiness against him. Do not depend on the enemy not attacking, but depend on our position that cannot be attacked." We can create a situation that makes any move by a competitor more difficult. It is common with some liquid products such as soaps that the dispense equipment that the supplier installs is only compatible with the replenishment jars sold by that supplier, thus precluding a competing supplier from selling a different product while using the supplier's dispense system. Supply Chain for Liquids provides for even broader capability to ensure that "our position cannot be attacked" by closing off the entire logistics flow with proprietary elements of the equipment such as external ports. Further, only the producer/distributor has access to information regarding the customer's inventory balances and when replenishment might be needed; there is no physical access for competitors to the locked external port through which product is delivered; connectability to the external port/pin system for attaching the delivery hose to the customer site can be proprietary; and the configuration of the on-site tanking system represents an unknown and uncontrollable element for the competition. These multiple lines of defense provide the physical barriers to competitor attack. Multiyear contracts and first-mover domination of Supply Chain for Liquids application to a particular marketplace provide the legal barriers. Technical expertise, effective utilization of logistics-related resources, and effective marketing of Supply Chain for Liquids capabilities also serve as the business barriers to competitive counterattack.

Another wider-impact issue that the Liquid Lens examines as part of a Supply Chain for Liquids project is that of partnering or outsourcing. Again, this is a standard issue for many business-related initiatives, but there are certain characteristics to which the Liquid Lens pays particular attention. The entire Supply Chain for Liquids flow can be divided into several areas of expertise that can be considered as components of the system. These include:

- The production of the product itself
- The trucking capability to transport or deliver the product
- The physical equipment such as the tanks and pipes at the producer/distributor/customer locations
- The electronic equipment such as the sensors, PLCs, and data communications equipment at the various sites
- The central computer system that performs the processing to support the replenishment cycle as well as the analysis of the data that pass through the system
- The procedural elements, such as the work of a dispatcher, to guide and monitor the entire process

The Liquid Lens helps us correlate between the essential elements of the Supply Chain for Liquids system and the core competencies of the company initiating it, and it distinguishes these from activities that are essential to the proper operation of the system but that may be more effectively handled by another entity. The Liquid Lens examines each of the components of the overall system and determines which can be most effectively handled in-house and which can be outsourced to another company to perform. A company would likely perform those activities that fall within the strengths or competencies of the company, or in the extreme case a company could outsource all of the components other than its own role in the supply stream and serve an overall control function over the outsource suppliers.

We have seen that in addition to focusing directly on the logistics flow and the business functions associated with or impacted by the flow, the Liquid Lens examines several additional elements. These include:

- The "people" issues related to the impact of implementing Supply Chain for Liquids on the internal organization and processes of the company
- The handling of competitive considerations and maximizing the competitive advantage that results from implementing and operating a Supply Chain for Liquids system
- The idea of outsourcing those elements of the Supply Chain for Liquids system that fall outside the company's core competency, capability, or desired investment of time and resources

These issues represent an incremental set beyond the essential elements of the Liquid Lens.

The whole set of business and project issues that apply to any business investment should be applied to a Supply Chain for Liquids project as well, but these are not enumerated here. In addition, all of the issues laid out related to the Liquid Lens process should be examined in greater depth than they have been described here. For example, while examining the issue of utilizing the liquid nature of the product to logistical advantage, the characteristics of the product in its liquid state are laid out and analyzed from a logistics perspective. The examination should go further than this, however. The product itself should be examined to see in what ways it might be altered, and then what impact the altered product would have on the logistics process. Does the product actually consist of several ingredients, such that allowing the proportions to be altered at the point of dispense would provide greater benefit to the customer? If so, the company might consider using the Supply Chain for Liquids system to hold the ingredients at the customer location and have the dispense unit perform the mixing process. Could the product be partially dehydrated and shipped as a concentrate, with water or other diluter added at the point of dispense? Conversely, is there benefit to the customer if the product is shipped as is with additives included in the Supply Chain for Liquids flow that would provide greater flexibility for the customer in the usage of the product? In the case of consumables, these additives might consist of colorings or flavorings, with corresponding additives for other types of products. Similarly, are there chemicals that could be transported with the product through the Supply Chain for Liquids system and be added to it by the user that would change the behavior or characteristics of the product to best suit the user's needs — viscosity, boiling point, acidity, and so on? These are the types of thought processes that are carried out with each element covered by the Liquid Lens process.

Potential Leaks in a Supply Chain for Liquids System

The Liquid Lens looks closely at the present and the future to see a Supply Chain for Liquids system working along a particular logistics flow. Although the design of the system and its potential benefits are a big part of the Liquid Lens approach, it is also important to look at potential downsides or problems that would limit the system's effectiveness. Knowing where these "leaks" are likely to occur can help a company avoid them during the planning and implementation of a Supply Chain for Liquids system. We are looking here at certain problems that can be anticipated, but it is important to remember that evolution is based on permutations, so that just because something looks out of line does not necessarily mean the result will be bad. We can use a multi-ocean example to illustrate the point. When Frédéric-Auguste Bartholdi designed the statue "Egypt Carrying the Light to Asia" to be on the grand scale of the Pyramids and as a gigantic lighthouse at the entrance to the massive canal that his friend Count Ferdinand-Marie de Lesseps wanted to build from the Mediterranean to the Red Sea, he had a specific plan in mind. That project was never commissioned, so Bartholdi had to change his plan — and thus the Statue of Liberty came to be carrying the torch of liberty in New York Harbor. The problem that prevented the execution of Bartholdi's first plan led to an even more visible and more dramatic result on his second try.

Several potential leakage points are shown in Exhibit 3.7, and the first relates to government regulation in all its forms. Many companies know that one of the major snares that lies in wait around many corners is regulatory — dealing with and meeting the requirements of the many agencies that control how commerce is conducted. Regulations related to food products and consumables are very stringent, as are statutes related to safety, environment, transportation, consumer protection, and many other issues connected to a myriad of products. Regulatory issues require special attention in the context of Supply Chain for Liquids because activities within the same sector may fall into completely different regulatory frameworks, with the difference in methodology leading to a difference in regulatory authority.

An example of regulatory requirements can be found in transitioning to the Supply Chain for Liquids method for petroleum products such as motor oil. Motor oil that is held at a quick-lube station in jugs or drums may fall under one set of regulatory requirements, whereas the exact same

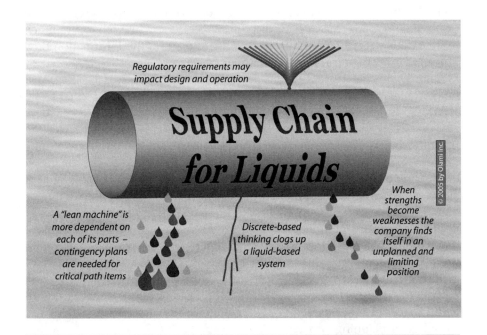

Regulatory requirements may
impact design and operation

Supply Chain
for Liquids

© 2005 by Olami Inc.

A "lean machine" is
more dependent on
each of its parts –
contingency plans
are needed for
critical path items

Discrete-based
thinking clogs up
a liquid-based
system

When
strengths
become
weaknesses the
company finds
itself in an
unplanned and
limiting
position

**Exhibit 3.7   The Liquid Lens Identifies Where the System Might "Leak" and Plugs
the Holes before They Open**

liquid held in tanks touch on a different set of regulatory requirements.
The tank requirements come in many forms, not only related to the nature
of the tanks themselves (requirements for single-wall/double-wall construction, venting, etc.), but also related to catchment systems in the event
of leakage, fire protection, drainage, dispense, and many other equipment-
centered standards. On top of regulating the specifications of the equipment itself, building permits may be required at several levels of legislative
authority such as state, county, district, or city for the construction of the
system. Many types of Supply Chain for Liquids installations in many
industries each have their own regulatory issues, and these should be
explored as part of the Supply Chain for Liquids planning process.

Related to legislative constraints, a legal issue that should be examined
prior to implementing a Supply Chain for Liquids system is the existence
of patents for Supply Chain for Liquids–like systems. Patents have been
issued and are in force for logistics flows related to specific liquids, and
these describe functionality that is highly specific to the characteristics
and usage of those liquids. Other patents have been issued for the logistics
loop and various types of liquid-logistics flows, and these do not specify
or address any particular liquid but, rather, apply to liquids in general.

Some of these patents cover specific aspects of the supply stream, such as holding, sensing, moving, or dispensing product, while others are much more extensive and cover both the product flow and the information flow in a global and comprehensive manner.

Like legislative issues, patent issues may in some cases be clear-cut, but in other cases they may require the work of an attorney to sort out. What constitutes infringement, what are the risks and rewards of pursuing any particular path related to an approach that resembles an existing patent, what other systems are currently in place and how have they addressed the patent issue — unfortunately, all of these can be time-consuming and expensive questions that can result in only best-judgment answers. Because there are many patents related to Supply Chain for Liquids–like processes, and each patent relates differently to the plans or operations of any particular company, we will not describe or explore the specific patents here. We raise the alert because common thinking considers patents as related only to physical products or features of products rather than processes or business models. This is not accurate; patents can relate to processes that include no unique products or equipment whatsoever. Consideration of patent issues should be part of the Liquid Lens planning process.

Another caution point that the Liquid Lens searches for are the dependencies along the Supply Chain for Liquids flow. This point requires an examination as to which elements must perform properly in order for the entire system to work correctly, and for this purpose it also calls for consideration of the converse question: looking at each element, what would happen to the entire system if that element were to fail? Failure does not necessarily mean that a part of the system ceases to function, just that it does not function in the way required by the system. For each element, the possible failure modes are listed together with the likelihood of each failure mode. Based on this listing, the highest-likelihood failure modes are selected and addressed. For example, for the data-communications aspect of the system, the most likely failure point may be identified as the communications equipment at a site. If the data-communication system is set up to communicate data from the sites to the central computer system once per hour, what happens if the communications equipment at a particular site fails, thus preventing the transmissions? There are many results that may fall out of this type of analysis, such as increasing the reliability of the most-failure-prone equipment, setting up redundant systems at critical points, establishing service capabilities within the critical time period for each failure point identified, or identifying secondary approaches to continue operation for a specific period. Care is taken so that the solution to potential problems does not reverse the positive impact of the Supply Chain for Liquids system and lead to precisely the wrong conditions. For example, in a quick-lube facility, the pressurization system may be identified as a high-likelihood failure point that would prevent the mechanics from dispensing maintenance fluids into the vehicles. It might be determined that the packaged motor oil that is maintained at the facility for retail sales is sufficient for emergency purposes to allow the facility to keep operating should system pressurization fail, and that this is the most effective contingent strategy compatible with the Supply Chain for Liquids approach given the limited likelihood of this fault occurring and the avoidance of adding inventory or other complexities/mechanisms to the basic Supply Chain for Liquids system.

The Liquid Lens seeks another potential trouble spot in locating where a Supply Chain for Liquids strength might turn into a weakness. A strength can turn into a weakness in several ways. Focusing one's power in one area, and bringing massive force into play to accomplish a single purpose, can be a tremendous strength. Sun Tzu's description of this concept is that "the impact of your army may be like a grindstone dashed against an egg — this is effected by the science of weak points and strong." Even a weaker opponent can have advantage over a stronger opponent if the weaker side focuses its forces, thus having a relative advantage at a particular spot selected by the weaker contender. This strength turns into a weakness when the concentration of forces limits flexibility and in effect ties the hands of the side focusing its forces. Having choices means having power, while certainty can be a weakness. In the case of Supply Chain for Liquids, this is translated into a situation in which a company has committed itself in a certain area to accomplish a certain advantage, but the commitment also serves to lock it into that specific method. An example of this situation would be a producer that works with a distributor to implement a Supply Chain for Liquids system. The distributor may do an excellent job of executing the Supply Chain for Liquids methodology to the advantage of the producer, the distributor, and the customer. At the same time, the fact that the producer is working with that distributor limits the producer in terms of bringing other distributors into the flow, at least in that particular geographic region or product line. Although exclusive territories are common in producer-distributor relationships, it is often balanced by the fact that when the term of the exclusive agreement ends, the producer may choose to work with a different distributor. To the degree to which Supply Chain for Liquids allows less flexibility to a producer in operating with multiple distributors, or "locks in" a producer to a specific distributor more than occurs in a different Supply Chain scenario, this strength of Supply Chain for Liquids threatens to become a weakness. This is a common conundrum related to outsourcing in general, in that where a company gains effectiveness it also loses control and flexibility. In many cases this is worth it, but the Liquid Lens ensures that we recognize this potentially limiting aspect of a Supply Chain for Liquids system.

Another strength that is liable to turn into a weakness, and which the Liquid Lens method watches for, is the extensive marketing and distribution opportunities that Supply Chain for Liquids creates. As described in Chapter 8, Supply Chain for Liquids not only streamlines the entire liquid supply stream, but it goes much further and opens new customer-facing channels that do not exist in a package-based process. These are oriented toward B2C applications, but they also occur in some B2B contexts as well. Some of these formats in the B2C arena include drive-up liquid dispense kiosks and refillable mugs for use on college campuses or other high-density locations. The strength of the Supply Chain for Liquids method is that it makes these configurations technically feasible as well as financially attractive, and it opens the door for many other innovative customer experiences.

Because the capabilities that Supply Chain for Liquids supports are beyond the boundaries of customary techniques, the risk arises that the strength of "what is possible" will not be properly addressed by a process of "what makes sense," or put differently, the "can I do it" is not properly balanced by the "should I do it." That is, Supply Chain for Liquids is capable of taking the marketing effort to places that have not yet been proved in terms of customer acceptance. This is not a new concept; there are plenty of examples of technology overreaching the marketplace's acceptance of what is technically possible. A big part of the Internet bubble consisted of big ideas with little applicability, at least at that period of time. An example that echoes Supply Chain for Liquids capability is the concept of Internet shopping, that customers would log on and do massive amounts of shopping from Internet sites. This spawned creation of techniques for all aspects of the shopping process, from the slickest Web sites imaginable to delivery companies for Internet purchases. These were all visionary ideas that made a lot of sense when viewed from a future-looking perspective, but made very little sense when viewed from an average-customer perspective. These failures demonstrate quite clearly how the strength of innovation can turn into the weakness of over-innovation, providing a product or service that the marketplace does not accept. Too good is no good in business as well as in life. As it happens, some of these innovations are being reincarnated several years later in a much more disciplined and reserved fashion, much more closely matching technological capability to market receptiveness. The Liquid Lens focuses on utilizing the capabilities that Supply Chain for Liquids offers in such a way that its strength leads to penetration and expansion of the market-place instead of turning into the weakness of overshooting and missing the marketplace.

A final weakness that the Liquid Lens constantly watches for is the one that is most ubiquitous and most natural: the constant tendency to slip back from liquids-based thinking to discrete-based thinking. Supply Chain for Liquids' power comes from its maximum exploitation of the logistics opportunities offered by liquid products as described earlier in this chapter, and slippage from a liquids-based outlook is liable to decrease the completeness of the opportunity created by the Supply Chain for Liquids system.

In addition to helping design the most effective Supply Chain for Liquids system, the Liquid Lens helps us avoid potential pitfalls in the process. As described previously, these pitfalls include:

- Regulatory requirements, especially in light of the differences in regulatory demands for different systems holding the same products, as well as other legal requirements such as patents
- The creation of dependencies on different parts of the system that may lead to inability to perform should there be a failure in a single part of the system
- The potential that the strengths of a Supply Chain for Liquids design/operation will change into weaknesses based on changing circumstances or the lack of an ongoing adaptation process
- The infiltration of discrete-based thinking or action into the liquids-based foundation of Supply Chain for Liquids

It is important to keep the Liquid Lens close at hand to help avoid the negative as well as to create the positive.

Simplify — Snatch Simplicity from the Jaws of Complexity

The Liquid Lens inverts our usual way of looking at logistics systems or, for that matter, any system. Generally, when we examine a system and want to improve it, we enhance it. We put more operational or control processes in place; we add another position; we grow the process because we think that is the corresponding and appropriate response to addressing the needs of a problematic system. The Liquid Lens has us do the exact opposite. The Liquid Lens comes to simplify and strip away complexity rather than add to existing systems or structures. The Liquid Lens has us look at the essential elements of the overall process and drive the process toward those essential elements. Working with the Liquid Lens we question any addition to the core process, and we work to keep the entire integrated process true to its fundamental purpose. As described in Chapter 11, we measure our success in terms of stripping away steps together with their costs and non-value-added activity, measuring the number of "touch points" as it is described there, that is, the number of times that somebody or something does any sort of act related to the liquid. This indeed runs counter to common thinking — the advertising tagline of a major supply chain consulting firm, for example, says that "Supply chain execution has entered a whole new world of complexity." Complexity is good for big, expensive consulting engagements, but is it good for operational effectiveness or for a successful company? Supply Chain for Liquids takes the exact opposite approach, asking what is the simplest combination of components we can put together to get the job done in an excellent way.

The Liquid Lens does not take this approach simply because it is a good hypothetical concept, but because the nature of liquid logistics lends itself to simplification, and we are here to fully exploit the benefits available to liquid logistics that are unavailable, or less available, from logistics for discrete products. Throughout this book, many points of differentiation between liquid and discrete logistics are described, and we can use one of these points to illuminate the idea of simplicity in liquid logistics. If we want to move a discrete product from one place to another within a warehouse, for example, we have to undertake a series of steps to carry out this movement. We need to go to the place where the discrete product is kept, identify that it is the product we want, get access to it such as removing other products that may be sitting on top or in front of it, physically take it (with a forklift, by hand, by crane, or by whatever method is appropriate), physically move with the product to the destination location, and then reverse the process — arrange the position in which it is to be placed such as by moving other products, physically placing the product, and then returning to our home location. The number of steps, complexity, and time requirement for moving a specific quantity of a discrete product from one place to another contrasts with the simplicity of a system that is built for liquids. Assuming that the liquids are being treated as liquids and thus are held in tanks, and they are being moved as liquids and thus there are pipes connecting the tanks, moving liquids from one place to another can be as simple as opening a valve that connects two tanks and letting the liquid flow from one tank to the other. The nature of specific logistics operations can be significantly simplified under a liquids-based approach as opposed to under a discrete-based approach.

We can contrast our approach with two examples from the world of music. Richard Wagner composed orchestrations of such complexity that a listener is simply incapable of hearing all the nuances he built into them; only someone reading the score, not listening to the music, can truly appreciate the work that Wagner had done. Similarly, some sound systems are so good that they can generate distinctions in sounds that the human ear is incapable of hearing; only a good electrical engineer, looking at the diagrams for the systems, can truly appreciate their capabilities. This complexity for the sake of complexity is the antithesis of what Supply Chain for Liquids is all about. We prefer the story of the Japanese samurai who was famous for his beautiful, extensive orchid garden. The emperor decided to visit the samurai to see the garden, and when he arrived he was stunned to see that the samurai had cut down all the orchids save one. "All of the beauty you want can be found in this one orchid," explained the samurai, declaring the appeal of a solitary flower over a whole gardenful, of quality over quantity.

Simplicity, or reduction in complexity, is not an easy goal to achieve, and it is particularly difficult from the inside. Someone who is involved in the systems being examined, who knows what all the systems are, why they exist, the history of their evolution, and their justifications will have a very difficult time figuring out how to remove those processes. That is why the Liquid Lens does not use the existing systems and conditions as its starting point, but rather starts off with a greenfield view of company needs and processes. As described in Chapter 10, the user first draws a picture of the start and end of the logistics process, and then goes about filling in the middle. The result of that process, which shows the "ideal" situation as clearly as it can be envisioned, is then married back to the actual situation, and thus the target configuration and the path to achieving it are defined. This is a far more effective method than trying to clean up a system as it exists, in which inertia works against the success of the project.

In a broader sense, an example of how the Supply Chain for Liquids approach differs from standard supply chain thinking is in the area of data and information. One of the highly touted aspects of Supply Chain is CPFR® (Voluntary Interindustry Commerce Standards Association, Lawrenceville, NJ) — Collaborative Planning, Forecasting, and Replenishment. CPFR is a method by which different companies coordinate their various planning processes to reach some ideal result. *Logistics Management* magazine, however, in surveying the status of CPFR at the start of 2004, says bluntly that CPFR is "not working," and goes on to say that "comprehensive collaborative programs like CPFR have yet to appear on the radar screens of most logistics professionals … visibility over shipments in the pipeline remains an elusive goal for most companies." The Liquid Lens has us look at the issue of coordination differently. As described above, the liquid nature of products in the Supply Chain for Liquids means that the quantity of product can be directly measured at and disseminated from any point in the system. This approach gives direct and continuous visibility to anyone authorized to see it. The Supply Chain for Liquids approach holds that this visibility and its appropriate response are sufficient and suggests a much simpler visibility-based approach, CPVR^SM (Coordinated Procedures for Visibility Response^SM), that is described in detail in Chapter 10. The CPVR approach says that companies working together along a Supply Chain for Liquids coordinate their separate procedures to respond to the different situations that will become visible through the Supply Chain for Liquids process, such as "bulges" of product at specific points in the Supply Chain for Liquids. Because all players are working off the same data, however, there is no need for a complex and often unsuccessful effort to integrate the entire planning process. Each company works with a relatively small, simple local piece of processing to support the CPVR approach, as described in Chapter 10.

Whether simplifying the actual logistics processes, the logistics planning and control processes, the information flow related to logistics, the points of manual intervention, the configuration of the product and its packaging, or any other aspect of liquid logistics, Supply Chain for Liquids sees its success in what it can remove, streamline, and simplify. The Liquid Lens helps us look at our processes and build/rebuild them as "skinny" and as effective as possible. The concept of simplicity and complexity is of itself quite extraordinary, as described in chaos theory and other places. The places where these concepts show up are also quite astonishing. The tragic case of Kitty Genovese, who was murdered while 38 people knew what was happening but did nothing to stop it, illustrates this point. As psychologist Robert Cialdini explains the theories of Bibb Latané and John Darley in the book *Influence: The Psychology of Persuasion*, it was exactly *because* there were so many people involved that nobody did anything. Within the dynamic of this number of people, each thought someone else would act, and in the end no one did. It is like answering the phone at home. When you are at home alone, there is a high likelihood that you will answer the phone when it rings because you know that if you do not, the phone will not get answered — a situation characterized by simplicity. On the other hand, if there are six people in the house, each assumes someone else will answer it, and the chances of it going unanswered go way up — a situation characterized by complexity. As counterintuitive as it is, there is less chance of the phone getting answered with six people in the house than with one person in the house. The very fact of complexity introduces conditions and behaviors that may be counterproductive to the objective, leading to the value we have placed on simplicity as an overall approach within the Liquid Lens.

We have laid out here the major methodological principles of Liquid Lens, which support the process of approaching, planning, and implementing Supply Chain for Liquids. The principles described here involve:

- Recognizing the logistical characteristics of liquids and exploiting them in the design of the logistics process
- Building a whole system in which the parts are cross-integrated and drive the entire system toward its overall objective
- Using the Liquid Lens as a crystal ball to look at demand-side opportunities that may not yet exist or be viable
- Going beyond the direct and secondary activities of the logistics system to take into account the broader impact of Supply Chain for Liquids operation
- Checking for possible "leaks" in the system, issues that could potentially impair the Supply Chain for Liquids's ability to function properly
- Bringing the logistics process to its fundamental form and stripping off unnecessary complexities and costs

By adding these thought processes and activities to the logistics planning and development processes that are already in place in a company, the soil is prepared for planting the seeds of Supply Chain for Liquids and the subsequent growth of the tremendous benefits that Supply Chain for Liquids has to offer.

Liquids: A Primer

Before we jump into the details of adapted Supply Chain and of Supply Chain for Liquids, it is useful for us to become acquainted with some of the major attributes of the object of our attention: liquids. Like any courtship, our relationship with liquids will be more productive the better we get to know them. This overview is intended to get us "into the spirit" and move us toward an understanding that liquid products behave differently, have different characteristics, and are fundamentally different from discrete products. This section is a summary; for any particular application of adapted Supply Chain or of Supply Chain for Liquids, the specifications of the exact liquid we are working with must be taken into account.

Let us look at some of the specific characteristics of liquids that impact the logistics of working with them.

Flow

The most obvious characteristic of liquids is that they flow, which enables the entire tanks/pipes methodology used in the Supply Chain for Liquids approach as opposed to discrete-based approaches using containers, cartons, and pallets. This fundamental characteristic lays the foundation for the flow-based approach and many of the special and useful capabilities of flow-based systems.

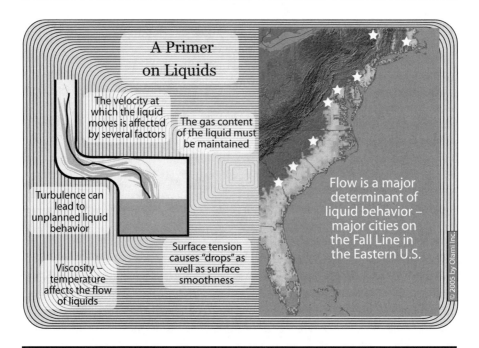

A Primer
on Liquids

The velocity at which the liquid moves is affected by several factors

The gas content of the liquid must be maintained

Turbulence can lead to unplanned liquid behavior

Viscosity – temperature affects the flow of liquids

Surface tension causes "drops" as well as surface smoothness

Flow is a major determinant of liquid behavior – major cities on the Fall Line in the Eastern U.S.

© 2005 by Olami Inc.

Exhibit 3.8   The More Familiar We Are with Liquids, the Better We Can Exploit Their Behavior

We should never underestimate the power or influence of the simple fact that liquids flow. Far from being trivial, the more we are aware of the potential of falling liquids, the more we will be able to take advantage of this characteristic. For example, on a broad scale, the fall line marks a geological ridge that separates the lowland hills from the coastal plain down the East Coast of the United States, from the northeast to the southeast, with important implications on American history and business. The availability of energy from falling water and the commercial significance of flowing rivers influenced the development of many cities along the line, including Lowell, MA; Pawtucket, RI; Troy, NY; Trenton, NJ; Georgetown/Washington, DC; Richmond, VA; Raleigh, NC; Columbia, SC; and Augusta, GA, as shown in Exhibit 3.8. The proximity of these cities parallel to cities on the coast further increased their importance, but the fall line — the flow of liquids — was their lifeblood. The distribution of electricity from hydroelectric power generators and dams spread the influence of falling water even further. The fall line served as a double booster for economic and political development. The sharp drop in the rivers provided power and also prevented upstream shipping, making those points all the more important. We do not expect the flow from our liquids to generate electricity, but we should always be aware of the importance and capabilities of liquid flow.

Viscosity

The flowability of a liquid is measured by its viscosity. Viscosity has several logistical implications. A highly viscous liquid is very thick and does not flow well. As it is held in tanks or moves through pipes, it may not flow as quickly as needed, resulting in a dispense rate that is slower than required for a very viscous liquid. This slow flow also results in a residue of the liquid in the tank, so that the shape of a tank might be determined by taking the viscosity of the liquid into account. For example, a tank with an angled bottom enhances the effect of gravity on the liquid more than a tank with a flat bottom, thus reducing the amount of residue that remains in a tank.

If a viscous liquid must be moved more quickly, we have several choices. The fluidity of a viscous liquid increases as it is heated, so the temperature of the liquid becomes more important for viscous products. In some cases, controlling the ambient temperature — the temperature of the room or storage area in which the tanks are held — is sufficient to provide the needed level of fluidity. In other cases, there may be a need to heat the tanks or pipes to ensure proper flow of liquid. This heating does not necessarily need to be significant; directing the heat generated by surrounding equipment toward the tanks and pipes in an on-site facility, or heat generated by a truck's engine for on-truck tanks, may be enough to achieve the fluidity objective. Heating of liquids has its own implications, however, such as increasing the vapor pressure of the liquid, as well as possible safety and quality implications. In solving one problem, we may be causing others. That is why the Liquid Lens looks at the entire system in all its technical, logistical, and business aspects to reach the most productive balance between all of the factors.

Viscous liquids can also be moved more quickly by applying pressure to them. Like squeezing the ketchup or maple syrup jar, many liquids can be pushed to increase their rate of flow. The use of pressure to propel viscous liquids means that the design of the equipment must support this approach. Gas (or air) pressure as a supplement to gravity means that the gas must be introduced from the top of the system, with the liquid flowing out of the bottom of the system (for example, to a pipe to the dispense area). If a different design is used, such as direct interconnectivity between tanks, the result may be no flow instead of a better flow. Gas under pressure will find its easiest natural path from the source of the gas to the outlet, and this path will not be through the liquid if the system is not designed properly. With the wrong design, gas will come out of the dispense lines and the liquids will remain in the tanks. Because the flexibility of tank design and placement is one of the strengths of a Supply Chain for Liquids strategy, the design of the system must be scrutinized carefully to ensure proper results.

Another way to move viscous liquids through the system more quickly is to provide larger openings for liquid passage. This relates to the piping more than to the tanks. The larger the pipes, the greater is the amount of liquid that can pass through them. This strategy also increases the quantity of slower-moving liquids that arrive at the dispense point. The material from which the pipes are made, and especially any coating on the inner surface of the pipe, can also enhance the movement of liquids.

In terms of liquid logistics, viscosity may appear as a serious drawback, but in fact the application of proper liquid-logistics principles can go a long way toward addressing viscosity issues. For example, some liquids such as grape juice concentrate are very thick. The usual method of holding such liquids in steel drums leads to a great deal of waste, particularly the concentrate that is difficult to remove from the corners and edges of the drum. Even with a highly viscous liquid, a bulk approach can reduce waste and significantly increase worker productivity in handling and utilizing these liquids.

Turbulence

The effective movement of liquids is impeded as turbulence increases, but our systems can be designed to limit turbulence. We are particularly concerned about turbulence in (a) the hose from the supplier's tank to the delivery truck, (b) the hose from the delivery truck to the on-site system, and to a lesser extent (c) the tubing to the dispense system. Although a completely laminar flow, that is, a flow without turbulence, is not possible, we can minimize the amount of turbulence in a flow by taking into account a number of factors that increase turbulence. These factors include liquid velocity, the number and severity of curves or joints along the length of a pipe, any obstructions or irregularities within the pipe along the course of the flow, and the liquid and pipe materials.

Turbulence from an external source into the tanks is of greater concern than turbulence within the internal system. The reason is that liquids are likely to move faster during the fill/replenishment process, and there is likely a longer distance and a larger number of turns or curves from the external source into the system rather than within the on-site system. Thus turbulence is more likely to affect the flow during the fill process, increasing the amount of time required for the delivery person during each refill operation and directly impacting the entire logistics process.

Some liquids are particularly affected by turbulence, such as carbonated liquids or those that are subject to foaming, and so systems for these types of liquids must be designed with particular care. With relatively low velocity, straight pipes, a pressure blanket, and other design factors, turbulence problems can be avoided or at least reduced. Under the Liquid

Lens approach, it is preferable to invest in effective design rather than later fixing a problem caused by poor design. Turbulence in the on-site system is further reduced, for example, if bags or liners are used within the tanks, as described in Chapter 1. Such liners provide an additional level of control over the liquid flow and dampen the creation and impact of turbulence. The need to add antifoaming agents or other turbulence-related fixes leads to unnecessary and unproductive complexity in the system, exactly what Supply Chain for Liquids seeks to avoid.

Volume and Velocity

Volume and velocity are important to us when we are moving liquids, such as when we are delivering liquids from a tank truck to an on-site tank. We want the delivery to be completed as quickly as possible so that we can maximize delivery efficiency. Our inclination might be to make the delivery hose as large as possible, which would lead to the greatest delivered volume at a standard pressure. However, there are several factors that must be taken into account in hose size. First, the weight of the hose increases proportionally as its diameter increases and the hose holds more product. Taking into account the length of delivery hose required, we must make sure that the hose will not be too heavy for the delivery person to pull. Second, characteristics of the delivery hose must be coordinated with the size and configuration of the tubes and tanks to which the liquid is being delivered. Trying to ram too much liquid through the delivery hose and into the holding system will cause turbulence and backflow, reducing delivery efficiency. Third, there are advantages to grouping the delivery hoses into a single bundle or into a set of bundled hoses, and as the size of each hose increases, the number of hoses that can be effectively bundled decreases. Bundling several hoses together allows the delivery person to attach multiple hoses/multiple liquids from the delivery truck to the external port at the site simultaneously, thus saving time during the delivery process. The net volume and velocity of the delivery are affected by these factors and others such as viscosity (as described previously), and all of these factors are combined and evaluated against the logistics objectives during the system-design process.

A related factor that can have a significant impact on the physical performance of the system is the phenomenon of "water hammer," which many of us are familiar with as sounds that are emitted from lines holding liquids, such as steam pipes. Hammer is caused by the sudden start or stop of liquids in a pipe, such as when they hit a turn in the pipe, a valve, or other obstruction. The shock wave of several pounds or more of liquids hitting such an obstruction reverberates back down the pipe, possibly causing physical damage to the pipes and equipment in the pipe as well as generating the familiar hammering sounds. Several techniques for preventing or minimizing the impact of hammer are available, and these are well worth investigating.

Part of the system design might call for the introduction of flowmeters at various points in the system, both on the truck and in the on-site system, to measure the flow of liquids at specific points. A variety of flowmeters are available that use different techniques to measure liquid volumes, as described in Chapter 8. However, each of these techniques affect the flow in a different way. The impact on the flow of liquids is among the factors taken into account in selecting the type of flowmeter to be used at each point in the system.

Surface Tension

Every liquid forms a "skin" on its surface as a result of surface tension. Droplets of liquid are formed and display cohesiveness due to the surface tension that develops on the external edge of the droplet. Put simply, the pull of the molecules within the droplet, and of the molecules on the surface of the droplet, are not balanced by the pull of other molecules outside the droplet, so the surface molecules behave as if they are adhering to each other and to the droplet itself.

Surface tension comes into play in liquid logistics in several ways. First, surface tension affects the degree to which some types of liquid-level sensors can detect the exact height of liquid in a tank, thus affecting the accuracy of these types of sensors and limiting the selection of appropriate flowmeters for certain types of liquids (see the discussion of liquid level sensors in Chapter 8). Low surface tension can also lead to the release of vapors from liquids, which could interfere with the operation of some types of liquid-level sensors. Second, surface tension affects how easily a liquid can be cleaned from inside a tank and thus the nature of the cleaning process that should be used. Some cleaners work by reducing surface tension, allowing the cleaning fluid to penetrate the target liquid more easily. Cleaning systems are described in greater detail in Chapter 9.

Gas Content or Carbonation

Liquids can contain different levels of gases for different purposes, and there are several processes by which the gases appear in the liquids. Carbonated beverages require carbon dioxide for their sparkle or fizz, and carbonation results from carbon dioxide gas being added to a water-based liquid, leading to a chemical reaction with the water molecules to form carbonic acid. For beverages such as beer, fermentation occurs when a bacterium (yeast) breaks down sugar into alcohol and a biogas (carbon dioxide). A permeation process can use brute-force pressure to achieve the objective of introducing a gas into a liquid.

For the purpose of liquid logistics, the gas content of a liquid requires several sensitivities. If we want to propel a liquid through a system using gas or air pressure, we must be aware that the gas used for propulsion may actually penetrate and change the liquid's properties. In many cases, this is not an issue because the level of pressure used for propulsion is less than the level that actually affects the liquid. For liquids that already contain gas, such as beverages or beverage syrups, a gas blanket might be used to enhance quality (to prevent contact with oxygen), propulsion (to move the liquid), and maintenance (to maintain the proper levels of gas in the beverage or syrup). The amount, type, and pressure of gas used in a system for this type of liquid must be defined according to the combined needs of the liquid and the logistics of the liquid.

Because there are several different activities that impact the pressure within a Supply Chain for Liquids system, they must all be considered to ensure that the proper pressure is maintained at all times. During normal operation, the pressure applied on the liquid is affected by the dispense process, with multiple dispensers affecting the system pressure to different degrees as more or fewer dispensers are activated. During the filling process, pressure from outside the on-site system (that is, from the delivery truck) propels liquid into the system at a higher pressure than system equilibrium. A vent is set to allow gas to escape from the on-site system to avoid increasing system pressure and to allow the liquids to flow from the truck into the system. Each of these pressure-affecting activities is taken into account in the design of the system.

Capillary Action

Capillary action can force a liquid to behave in surprising ways. It causes water to rise in a tube, against the force of gravity, because of the attraction of water molecules to the material from which the tube is made. When you spill red wine on that beautiful white rug, you end up with a larger stain because the capillary action of the material causes the wine to spread. On the other hand, capillary action also moves the wine to the cloth you use to clean up the mess. The walls of your house may even be damp because capillary action draws water from the wet ground up into the walls. Capillary action is powerful. It is what pulls water and sap from the roots of a sequoia tree nearly 300 feet straight up to be evaporated through the leaves. For logistics purposes, we need to be aware of the impact of forces such as capillary action and ensure that we do not end up with some puzzling situation that leaves the system working less than optimally.

Acidity

The amount of acid in a liquid is measured in terms of pH, with pH <7 indicating acidity and lower numbers representing higher levels of acidity. Acidity is the source of several colorful tales about the destructive power of liquids. Widely disseminated stories describe the ability of certain soda beverages to dissolve objects (flies, baby teeth, nails, the steps of the U.S. Capitol, etc.) in a very short period of time. These stories have been proved false, but this does not lessen the need to be concerned about this issue from a logistics perspective. Many beverages contain acidic ingredients, but these are only a small part of the total liquid volume, and because the beverage moves over the teeth and is swallowed quickly, the acidity does not affect a person's teeth. Holding a beverage or other liquid in a bulk container over a period of time, however, allows the liquid to interact with the container material, with possibly deleterious effects on the container. For this reason, we need to consider not only whether the material of a container can withstand the acidity of a given liquid, but whether it can do so for an extensive period of time.

Liquid Characteristics: A Summary

These are just a few of the characteristics that affect the performance of liquids within a closed system. These liquid characteristics may seem technical or unimportant, but only to those who are not viewing them through the Liquid Lens. The Liquid Lens shows us that:

- Viscosity affects the speed of liquid flow, which has a direct effect on the speed of the delivery process.
- Turbulence affects the movement of liquids, which has a direct effect on the design of the piping and the tanks.
- Volume and velocity dictate the relationship between the physical sizing of system elements and their operational usage, and impact whether logistics needs will be met during delivery and during liquid dispense.
- Surface tension affects the choice of methods that can be used in sensing the height and thus the quantity of liquid in a tank.
- Gas content or carbonation of the liquid dictates special handling in terms of the amount and type of pressurization that is used in the system.
- Capillary action allows liquids to flow in unexpected ways and can affect sensor measurements.
- Acidity determines the kinds of material that will be used for tanks, piping, and connections.

The Liquid Lens tells us to look at the whole package. The technical side affects the application side, which affects the performance side, which affects the sales side. Although we may not understand each of these in detail, in every case we need to verify that each of these issues is addressed and understand the impact/opportunity that each issue presents for the system as a whole.

Chapter 4

Industry and Product Applications of Supply Chain for Liquids

Supply Chain for Liquids® applies to the largest industries in the world. In this section, we identify these major industries and highlight the main usages of liquids in each industry. In doing so, we examine the scope of liquids that are candidates for use in the Supply Chain for Liquids system.

During this overview of liquids in different industries we will "break down the walls" between seemingly completely disparate industries. We will see similar liquids popping up in different industries, similar needs for liquid usage, and similar operational requirements. As this happens, we begin to get a feel for the liquids industry, and we begin to understand that a logistics person in an airplane-parts factory in the West has much in common with an operations manager of a hospital complex in the South. They are tied together, and can benefit each other, in ways they might not yet have imagined.

The scale of liquid usage in these industries is so large that even modest use of Supply Chain for Liquids principles yields huge benefits to the participating companies. Supply Chain for Liquids is not an all-or-nothing methodology. As laid out in Chapter 5, there are incremental steps that can lead to operational, financial, and marketing benefits, even though they are only partial implementations of Supply Chain for Liquids capabilities. Because of the size of each of these industries and the companies within the industries — and given the significant role that liquids play in them, as described in each section below — the "butterfly effect" comes into play, where a small change can lead to a very large result.

Another characteristic that becomes apparent from this review is that liquid usage has a web effect, that is, it is not isolated within a single area but, rather, goes through the many touch points in business to impact neighboring industries and companies. The major industries that can use Supply Chain for Liquids directly — petroleum products, beverages, personal care products, cleaning and maintenance products, chemicals, etc. — interact with other industries, thus expanding the range of industries that can benefit from Supply Chain for Liquids, including automotive, entertainment, hospitality, manufacturing, and many others. These expansions are caused by the fact that we are looking at liquid usage not only in terms of the products themselves, but also in terms of the processes surrounding the products — liquids consumed during manufacturing, distribution, and facility maintenance activities, among others, and by employees during ancillary activities.

As we view these industries, we will also understand that liquids correspond more to nondurable goods than to durable goods, as defined for discrete products. Many liquids are very nondurable; beverages, for example, are intended to be consumed as quickly as possible. Soaps and cleaning products are equally as perishable in terms of their useful life. Some liquids have a longer lifespan in terms of their usage. Hydraulic fluids and machine lubricants are intended for use over a period of weeks, months, or even years, but even so, they are periodically replaced as their useful life comes to an end. Of course, there are also liquids that are used in small quantities as components/ingredients in other products and at other points in the production and logistics processes. In general, though, the velocity with which liquids move through the logistics processes makes their handling in many cases even more sensitive than that of discrete products.

Industry Applications

Some of the major U.S. industries and their liquid components are surveyed below, together with some sample volumes as indicators of the scope of liquid usage in these industries. This is a selected list; many other large-scale industries use liquids extensively. For example, construction (one and a half billion gallons of paints and coating per year and six billion gallons of formaldehyde, of which about half is used for resins and glues), food preparation, pharmaceuticals, and many other industries have large liquid components that only serve to reinforce the understanding of the ubiquitous nature and constant presence of liquid products.

For the most part, the applications described here represent the down-stream segments of each of these industries. The downstream part of the logistics flow usually involves taking very large quantities of liquids, such as tens or hundreds of thousands of gallons that result from production runs, and converting them into smaller quantities to channel them toward their end users. For example, petroleum refining is an upstream activity that produces large quantities of initial petrochemical products that are held in mass-storage facilities, while the downstream activities convert these into end-user products and then into the form and quantity needed for each distribution channel and customer. Supply Chain for Liquids is certainly applicable in the upstream, but it is in the downstream where the most common and visible applications can be found.

Food Service/Hospitality

The food-service/hospitality industry is huge, the largest employer in the country outside of the federal government. It covers many familiar and some unfamiliar types of establishments. Of course, the 52,000 hotels and nearly 900,000 restaurants in the United States are part of this industry. Also included are cafeterias in production plants, office buildings, and hospitals, as well as other mass-residence facilities such as university dormitories, prisons, military bases, and other housing providers.

The size of this industry is reflected in the magnitude of the liquids it uses, and it uses a lot of liquids. Liquid consumption in the food-service/hospitality industry and other industries is described in Exhibit 4.1. Let us set the context of food service/hospitality against total beverage consumption in the United States. Soft drinks are the highest-volume beverage consumed, at a rate of 15 billion gallons per year. The next tier of beverages, consisting of water, beer, milk, and coffee, moves at a rate of five to six billion gallons each annually, followed by juices and teas at about two to three billion gallons each. With roughly a quarter of these quantities consumed in the food-service/hospitality industry, the figure of ten billion gallons gives us the order of magnitude of beverages consumed each year in this industry. Ten billion gallons of beverage products each year — let us think about what that means. As an illustration, ten billion gallons is as much water as needed by a population the size of Cincinnati in a year. In terms of familiar logistics, the food-service/hospitality industry is moving over 9500 trucks (each with an assumed capacity of 22 pallets) worth of beverages every workday of the year. That is a heck of a fleet. If our tastes run more to the recreational, we could fill over 22,000 Olympic-sized pools with this quantity — over 1000 pools full of tea alone! The lesser categories of liquids used in the food-service/hospitality industry are also massive, including soaps and detergents as part of the

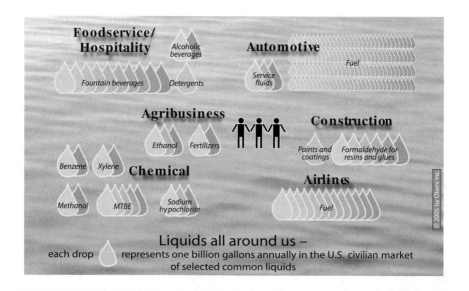

Exhibit 4.1 Massive Quantities of Liquids Are Flowing; the Issue Is, How Efficient Are the Flows?

one billion gallon per year liquid detergents flow, pool chemicals, dishwasher soaps, and condiments. Even what seem to be minor components of the liquid flow, such as sauces, are moved in sizable quantities. Over 30 million gallons of barbecue sauce, for example, are sold in bulk containers (not those little foil pouches that are so hard to open when your hands are even slightly greasy). Nearly 50 million gallons of salsa, over 12 million gallons of cheese sauce — with the large population and broad eating habits of Americans, the flow of liquids for food service and hospitality is a large river indeed.

Now that we have seen the dimension of beverages in the foodservice/hospitality industry, let us characterize the usage of these liquids so we can learn the potential benefit that the Supply Chain for Liquids approach might have for this industry. In most customer-facing beverage situations in this industry, beverages are served by the glass, cup, or pitcher rather than from a can. Similarly, dispense of cleaning chemicals is not dependent on small quantities or small packages. These environments already use dispense systems rather than packages, and so they are particularly appropriate targets for Supply Chain for Liquids systems. Given this, it is fair to classify the food-service/hospitality industry as a liquids industry, moving over ten billion gallons of liquid products each year in a manner that makes them candidates for Supply Chain for Liquids processing.

Specifically, then, where are the points at which Supply Chain for Liquids provides benefits to the food-service/hospitality industry? The major applications are as follows:

- *Fountain beverages*: Syrups, concentrates, and beverages that are dispensed per serving. The syrup is moved from the producer to the restaurant using Supply Chain for Liquids, and the Supply Chain for Liquids tanks are hooked directly into the existing dispense system.
- *Cooking oils, ice cream mixes, condiments, and sauces*: Cooking oils and ice cream mixes are used behind the counter, while condiments and sauces are used in front of the counter. Supply Chain for Liquids eliminates virtually all of the manual handling of these items, both directly at the point of usage as well as receiving, inventorying, and handling these liquids.
- *Cleaning fluids*: Restaurants and food-service establishments utilize several types of cleaning liquids, including personal-hygiene soaps, equipment cleaners, laundry soaps, and floor cleaners and waxes. All of these liquids are maintained in Supply Chain for Liquids tanks and dispensed either into cleaning units, such as hand-soap dispenser jars, or directly into the bucket used by the cleaning person. In addition to those used by food-service establishments, many hospitality establishments have adopted the use of liquid soaps for guests using in-room dispensing units. Supply Chain for Liquids fits into this approach fully and eliminates packaging throughout the entire process. Liquid soaps move from the tanks into units on the housekeeping carts, and from there are dispensed directly into the in-room soap units.

It should be noted that a broader definition of food service/hospitality — such as to include airlines, ships, and trains — represents untapped opportunity for implementation of Supply Chain for Liquids. At 27 million gallons of in-flight beverages served per year, for example, the volume is comparatively small versus ground service. But there are powerful logistics reasons why the on-site mini-tank system characteristic of Supply Chain for Liquids would provide large benefits in these types of mobile, limited-space environments. Airplanes require weight-reducing, space-exploiting, high-convenience methods to hold their beverages as well as other liquids, all characteristics of an onboard Supply Chain for Liquids system. Ships and trains are less weight-sensitive, but the Supply Chain for Liquids system meets their needs in the areas of space utilization, flexibility, and ease of use.

Automotive Transportation

The automotive transportation industry refers to the use of vehicles for transportation of people and goods, not the automobile manufacturing industry. The automotive transportation industry uses liquids in several major segments: fuels, lubricants, and maintenance fluids. Fuels are sold largely at service stations, and lubricants and other fluids are used in fleet-maintenance facilities, quick-lube centers, service and repair stations, and automobile dealerships. Petroleum products as a whole move at a rate that is on the order of five billion barrel-miles per day, which by way of comparison is about twice the flow rate of the Mississippi River. Making this process more efficient by just one penny per barrel-mile yields savings of $50 million per day, or nearly $20 billion per year. This efficiency can be realized in many ways: improving the physical transportation method used, reducing overhead costs throughout the process, reducing the quantity of fuel in the overall pipeline and thus the financial investment in product in the pipeline, and many other ways.

Virtually all of the 120+ billion gallons of fuel used each year in America's road vehicles is dispensed through bulk systems, from large gasoline tanks into vehicle fuel tanks. The fuel Supply Chain, though, does not operate according to Supply Chain for Liquids principles — the complete loop of product and information — and thus is open to large efficiency improvements. In most cases, the physical side of the Supply Chain — bulk trucks delivering fuel into large tanks, and from there the fuel being dispensed into vehicle fuel tanks — is in place in parallel to a Supply Chain for Liquids approach, but the information side of the flow is significantly lacking.

Similarly, automotive lubricants used for vehicle servicing, currently often sold in small containers such as quart jugs, are ripe for adaptation to a Supply Chain for Liquids system. Although the three billion gallons of lubricants used each year is a small quantity relative to fuel usage, the logistics and economics of the lubricants industry makes Supply Chain for Liquids a very attractive approach, offering large savings in both product costs and distribution costs. For example, the quick-lube industry operates in many ways according to principles similar to those of a quick-serve restaurant. The principles include the need for employees to focus on service and to move customers (vehicles) through an oil-change facility with maximum efficiency, the use of a standard but limited set of liquid products, limited space and need for best utilization of available space, and a set of overhead activities that are eliminated when the Supply Chain for Liquids system is used. The DIFM (do-it-for-me) approach represented by the quick-lube industry is growing relative to the DIY (do-it-yourself) segment of vehicle owners who change the oil in their vehicles themselves, and has in fact exceeded DIY on a volume basis. Even with this, longer oil-change intervals are becoming more common and putting pressure on the quick-lube industry, so the efficiencies and savings offered by the Supply Chain for Liquids approach are attractive or even necessary for some companies.

The many fleet-maintenance facilities in the country have a somewhat different focus, but many of the same principles apply, and the volumes of these operations are also quite large. The U.S. Postal Service (USPS), for example, services about 220,000 vehicles at 350 vehicle maintenance facilities across the country, including all of the fluids required for regular maintenance of these vehicles. At the federal government level, the General Services Administration uses something more than half the quantity of vehicle lubricants that the USPS does, and the Department of Defense uses over four times the USPS quantity. Vehicle service entails massive quantities at all levels; Hertz's fleet consists of over 500,000 vehicles, and Avis performs 700,000 periodic vehicle services per year. At the point at which automotive transportation meets the product-transport aspect of Supply Chain — the trucking industry — we can get an idea of the scale of lubrication requirements for trucks. There are over four million tractor-trailers operating in the United States, and cumulatively they travel over 170 billion miles per year. At an average of about six miles per gallon, the tractor-trailer segment of the automotive transportation industry consumes over 40 billion gallons of diesel fuel per year, in addition to motor oil and all of the other vehicle maintenance fluids such as brake and hydraulic fluids, windshield-washing fluid, antifreeze, suspension fluids, gear oil, and others. Given these volumes of motor oil and other maintenance fluids, we can easily begin to see the liquid element of the automotive transportation industry, with all of the operational benefits and cost savings that result from the use of the Supply Chain for Liquids system.

Peripheral benefits and savings are also significant. For example, total lubricant sales volume equates to nearly 55 million 55-gallon drums, with the cost, handling, and environmental problems associated with those drums. Extrapolate lubricant usage even further to the smaller plastic containers, and the cost and environmental issues surrounding liquid logistics are even exponentially higher.

Manufacturing

Despite the well-publicized difficulties facing American manufacturers, manufacturing remains the largest single sector in the economy in terms of contribution to gross domestic product, leading the finance, retail, and service sectors by significant margins. The five largest U.S. industries in terms of percentage of gross domestic product are chemicals, industrial machinery and equipment, electronics and electronic equipment, food, and motor vehicles. The scale of manufacturing in the United States sets the stage for the quantity of materials both used in and produced by manufacturing companies.

Manufacturing encompasses huge amounts of liquids of many types. We can categorize manufacturing liquids into two types: product and process. Product liquids are those used as components or ingredients in the manufacturing process, or the liquids that are produced during manufacturing.

Product liquids come in more forms than can be counted — cough syrup to formaldehyde, furniture stain to beaker cleaner. There are many billion-gallon-per-year products in this country: chemicals, food products, additives, and liquids described throughout this section.

Process liquids are those that are used to support all aspects of manufacturing — in facilities, equipment, transport, and all the other contributors to the production process. Machine lubricants and cleaning fluids are needed for virtually every type of production facility, and each type of manufacturing has its own needs. Printing plants use inks, pharmaceutical companies use chemicals, food manufacturers use flavorings, and on and on. A sampling of a few specific types of liquids provides insight into the quantities involved. American industry consumes over 700 million gallons of industrial lubricants annually; 160 million gallons of various types of inks are used each year by the printing industry, which then uses 120 million gallons of solvents to clean the printing equipment; over 40 million gallons of transformer oil are used each year. Every manufacturing facility is awash in liquids to make the production processes work. This does not even take into account the liquids used during the transportation of products to and from the industrial plants, the beverages consumed by employees, or materials used to clean the facility, as described elsewhere in this section.

The facilities in which all of this production activity takes place are found in virtually every community and geographic area in the country. The chemical industry, for example, encompasses over 12,000 production facilities. Each of these facilities has its own liquid-logistics pattern, but common to all of them are the product liquids and the process liquids. Given the order of magnitude of potential cost savings and revenue enhancements (as described in Chapter 11) and the size of this industry, the opportunities for the chemical industry alone are extraordinary. Specifically, some of the points of cost savings under the Supply Chain for Liquids system within a manufacturing environment include the following:

- *Component and ingredient fluids* upstream from the manufacturer, that is, ingredient liquids coming in from suppliers and held at the manufacturer's site. For manufacturers of discrete products, these can include dyes and other coloring agents; chemicals such as reactants, glues, or binders; flame retardants; flavorings or fragrances; coatings or rust inhibitors; or other liquids that are included in the production process as part of the product.
- *Product liquids* downstream from the manufacturer, that is, liquids produced by the manufacturer and their flow through the distribution process, to the customer, and through the dispense process to the consumer/user.
- *Process liquids* used during the manufacturing process. These include liquids that are used to support the manufacturing process, although not directly a part of the product being produced, such as machine lubricants and cleaners, catalysts, rinses, coatings or protective layers, and the many other liquids that play a role in the manufacture of various products. To the degree to which transport and distribution are also a part of the company's operation, this includes vehicle-related liquids such as lubricants and other maintenance fluids, waxes, etc. The internal transport method, such as forklifts or conveyor systems, can also require liquids that can be included in the Supply Chain for Liquids system.
- *Maintenance and overhead liquids* related to the manufacturing facility, although indirectly related to the manufacturing process. These include janitorial liquids, cleaners, lawn-care products, beverages for employee consumption, and other liquids consumed within the company.

For any particular manufacturing operation and product, the specific list of liquids involved will be different. In addition, the relative role of liquids in the manufacturing process will be different in different companies, from negligible to primary. What frequently occurs, however, is that the significant role of liquids in the manufacturing process is often overlooked because the liquids are not even thought of as liquids, they are thought of in terms of their containers, which are discrete items. Given the volumes of liquids used in and produced by manufacturers across American industries, and the opportunities for cost savings under Supply Chain for Liquids as described in Chapter 11, the total savings available is quite large. It is up to each company in each industry to identify and partake in the savings opportunity that is available to it. Applying these opportunities to the industries listed above, and to the many other industries that make up the U.S. manufacturing sector, shows the power of the Supply Chain for Liquids system for American producers.

Entertainment/Leisure

Large congregations of people for entertainment or leisure are frequently accompanied by expanded liquid usage. For example, the amusement-park experience and the sports-stadium experience frequently include beverage consumption, as do visits to movie theaters and health and sports clubs. Going to a shopping mall can be considered a leisure-time activity, with beverage consumption at the extensive restaurant centers frequently found at shopping malls.

To get an idea of the magnitude of liquid consumption at amusement parks and the benefit available from Supply Chain for Liquids, let us take a quick look at liquids used at Disneyland in California. Visitors consume 1.2 million gallons of soda per year, while 1400 gallons of disinfectant and nearly 10,000 gallons of degreaser are used in the restrooms those same visitors use on an average of three times per day to off-load the soda. More than 20,000 gallons of paint are used each year to keep the park ever new. Additional liquids are used for the large amount of equipment that is used to make things happen in the park. Despite rumors of a giant piping system that moves all the liquids used in the park from a central location to each dispense point, this is not so. However, the park is an example of an excellent candidate application of a Supply Chain for Liquids–type method, such as a dispense cart that circulates each night to replenish the liquids required, freeing up the beverage-dispense system to operate virtually independently. The benefits to the amusement park are clear. A patron who moves through a refreshment line more quickly has a more pleasurable experience, and not incidentally has more time to spend money in other places, in addition to the many other benefits of Supply Chain for Liquids in this environment, such as reduction in trash and simplicity of operation.

Sports stadiums and movie theaters are also highly concentrated users of beverages, although they are significantly different from a Supply Chain for Liquids perspective. As an example of beverage usage at a stadium, the Metrodome in Minnesota averages about 750,000 gallons of beverages served per year. Movie theaters have a more ongoing pattern of beverage dispense, so the design of the Supply Chain for Liquids for each type of entertainment facility would be different, but the principles of Supply Chain for Liquids apply extensively to each type.

Health Care

The health-care industry delivers its services in a variety of venues, including hospitals, convalescent centers, long-term-care facilities, and geriatric centers. The scale of the health-care industry is shown by the

5,000 registered hospitals serving over 35 million inpatients and 15,000 nursing homes with 1.8 million patients across the United States, in addition to other types of facilities such as assisted-living residences, community clinics, emergency centers, and hospices. The types of liquids used in health-care facilities include:

- Liquids used in the food-service aspects of the health-care industry, such as kitchens and dining facilities
- Cleaning fluids and disinfectants, which are used extensively to maintain proper hygienic conditions in the facility
- Laundry detergents, softeners, and fresheners used in ongoing laundry operations
- Personal-cleanliness products, such as soaps and lotions both for patients and for professional staff usage

The business approach to health care in the United States puts issues of cost savings, employee utilization, and effective use of facilities and resources high on the agenda of health-care operators. These are the cost-side benefits that Supply Chain for Liquids offers to the health-care industry, in addition to administrative relief from the process of ordering, receiving, inventorying, and maintaining all of these liquid products. In addition, the Supply Chain for Liquids approach opens opportunities for more effective dispense methods than bottle- or jug-based liquid usage, such as point-of-usage dispense stations that can be placed at the appropriate locations for each type of liquid. These opportunities for operational efficiencies, on top of the cost-reduction and utilization-enhancement benefits described above, provide a complete set of advantages for health-care companies from the Supply Chain for Liquids system.

Case Study: Supply Chain during Military Operations

It is usually a given that the conditions under which a Supply Chain operates will in some ways be fairly stable — a fixed set of players operating from fixed locations working in a fixed way. These rules, and many others, go out the window when the Supply Chain is operating in a combat zone, and halfway around the world at that. This was the situation faced by Colonel Joseph Walden as he contemplated the monumental task of supplying American troops during Operation Iraqi Freedom. But Col. Walden came personally armed with a set of powerful weapons: a strong background of over 25 years in leading-edge logistics activity, an ability to analyze and act that would lead to his being named "Practitioner of the Year" by *Supply & Demand Chain Executive* among other accolades, and the vision provided by being a disciple of Sun Tzu, which has also led him to write and speak extensively on *The Art of War* as applied to Supply Chain. As the old axiom has it, amateurs talk tactics, professionals talk logistics. Colonel Walden is director of the School of Command Preparation at the U.S. Army Command and General Staff College.

The logistics system for which Col. Walden was responsible involved all military and basic personal needs for the 130,000 American troops in Iraq as well as their equipment. This system ran in parallel to the AAFES (Army and Air Force Exchange Service) system, formerly the Px, which made additional items available for military personnel. Colonel Walden was tasked to plan, implement, and operate this system to support all U.S. military units in Iraq and Kuwait.

Some of the supplies were prepositioned or presourced in the area around Iraq, including on ships and at land sites in neighboring countries, and the troops that would need the supplies were deployed at known initial locations during the run-up to the war. As a central logistics site, Col. Walden established a theater distribution center (TDC) on 4.2 million square feet of desert in Kuwait. All shipments would be made to the TDC, and from there distributed to the troops.

From a liquids perspective, the major products that were handled in the logistics system were water and vehicle fluids, including fuels and lubricants. For water, which is of course critical in a desert environment with temperatures well over 100°F and soldiers arrayed in full battle gear, the strategy was essentially to outsource until production could be achieved, that is, to bring into the area of operation a sufficient quantity of water until reverse-osmosis water purification systems could be put in place. Bulk water was provided by the Kuwaiti government from local water sources, and from there it was transferred to smaller containers — 300- or 500-gallon tanks, 1000- to 3000-gallon fabric pillows or collapsible tanks, or 5000-gallon water trailers. Bottled water was also supplied to the troops in 1.0- or 1.5-liter bottles, which was sourced from seven suppliers in the Middle East region. As a precautionary step, each shipment was sampled to ensure that it would be safe for human consumption.

From the TDC, water was distributed to the troops, usually combined in a shipment of repair parts, rations, or other material to make the distribution process most efficient. Tactical water pipelines, similar to the RIFTS system (Rapidly Installed Fuel-Transfer System) described in Chapter 7, were used to supplement the distribution process. To ensure that water distribution would be done in a highly effective manner, tactical water-distribution teams were created to focus on executing the water logistics plan. This allowed the development of groups focused on water logistics and also avoided having the entire organization become enmeshed in this critical activity.

The handling of fuel paralleled that of water, but lubricants utilized different logistical arrangements. Fuels were delivered in large bags of up to 50,000-gallon capacity, with the Kuwaiti pipeline being used as a possible source of fuel. As fuel moved through the Supply Chain, temporary tactical pipelines were used, as they were with water. In addition, 5000-gallon tank trucks, specially built to allow them to traverse the difficult terrain, were used to transport fuel. Lubricants were held in containers from one-quart jugs to 55-gallon drums, but not in containers larger than 55 gallons.

The Army was faced with the task of planning the quantities of these liquids required during operations. Rather than seeing the war as a "once-off" occurrence, the Army planning staff — the 3rd Army Sustainment Cell and the Distribution Management Center — and Col. Walden found several precedents that helped to define the quantities required. The Army's National Training Center at Ft. Irwin, CA, has an extensive desert-training capability and provided information regarding liquid requirements for soldiers in desert-combat situations. In evaluating data from Operation Desert Storm, it became apparent that there were relatively stable consumption rates of liquids based on miles moved or hours spent in the desert, thus providing an additional foundation for planning liquid requirements during Operation Iraqi Freedom.

Not satisfied to receive reports from the field regarding liquid requirements, the planning staff used the historic-miles/day consumption patterns to project requirements and actually have the product on the way to the field units before the field units ordered it. By tracking reports of the movements of the different units, the supply chain system was able to translate this into usage and thus into future needs. Better than real-time tracking of actual usage, this was truly anticipatory supply chain management based on conditions and activities in the field.

Although this proactive approach was a remarkable achievement, as Col. Walden points out, the difficulty of the conditions would have made anything less completely chaotic. American forces covered the same distance in 14 days that Allied forces covered in nearly nine months of World War II when they moved from Omaha Beach to the Rhine River. The logistics system had to hit a moving target in much the same way that the soldiers themselves did.

The information flow used to support this enormous effort was based on the existing Army logistics and replenishment infrastructure, with tweaking as required to meet the special needs of the situation. As such, the logistics operation during Operation Iraqi Freedom can serve as a model for subsequent military operations of such scope and scale.

Colonel Walden's vision for future logistics incorporates some of the aspects of his Operation Iraqi Freedom experience and takes them much further. Some of the supplies for Operation Iraqi Freedom had been prepositioned on ships, which made it easier to bring them in, off-load them, and move the goods to the TDC. Although this scenario was productive, it includes several drawbacks. First, the materials had been placed in large containers, and so several different types of products were included in each container. Colonel Walden envisions more widespread use of smaller containers, of a size on the order and magnitude of a carton of copying-machine paper, that would hold one product each. With each such container tagged, there would be no need to break down the larger containers and recontainerize the products in them. Similarly, Col. Walden emphasizes the importance of RFID (radio frequency identification) tags for material tracking. Tagging and physical documentation for containers is a problem that the military began addressing nearly ten years ago, spurred on by an incident in which 27,500 containers were unloaded onto a dock during Operation Desert Storm and nobody knew what was in them. Each container had to be opened and the contents manually inventoried and handled, a task that proved how much easier it is to do it right the first time. The RFID system that is currently in place in the military uses mobile interrogators and handheld units that contain several functionalities that particularly suit the military's needs, such as the ability to locate critical material from within a group of material and the ability to rewrite tags, such as during the repalletization process.

Colonel Walden's work is extraordinary, and it is based on a crystal clear focus. When asked who his customers are, Col. Walden responded without hesitation, "every single soldier." The Supply Chain that is focused from the top on its end results will succeed even under the most difficult conditions, even in the midst of military operations.

Retailing and Residential

The use of Supply Chain for Liquids techniques in retail or residential environments is largely unexploited. For the most part, liquids sold in retail environments are package-based, although the popularity of larger-sized containers for beverages, cleaning products, and other liquids at warehouse stores is an indicator that consumers want to purchase and hold liquids in larger quantities. In fact, consumers are taking the largest-sized packages offered; it may be lack of ability to properly think through logistics issues, that is, lack of Supply Chain for Liquids thinking, that is the constraint in liquids-based retail sales, not the lack of demand.

Taking the convenience-oriented approach to its logical conclusion would extend the Supply Chain for Liquids right into the home. The closest example of this type of activity in common practice is the delivery of heating oil to individual homes, where a tank truck hooks up to an external pipe and transfers the oil into a tank inside the house. The ability to deliver product right into the consumer's home represents the next generation of positioning in the marketplace and a powerful competitive tool for the company that uses this approach.

The concepts behind retailing and residential use of the Supply Chain for Liquids can be applied to related methods as well. Corresponding to retail Supply Chain for Liquids would be the establishment of liquids-based kiosks, a sort of liqui-mart mini-mart for liquids, at which the consumer purchases many types of liquid products by dispensing them into containers. Similarly, residential use of Supply Chain for Liquids could be replicated in offices and other facilities in which the end user actually consumes the product. These concepts are described in more detail in the B2C (Business to Consumer) Applications section later in this chapter.

Additional Industries

The benefits of Supply Chain for Liquids are applicable to many other industries, depending on the breadth of liquid products they use or produce. A brief description of several of these industries follows.

- *Agriculture*: Bulk handling of liquids has been characteristic of some agricultural applications for a long time due to the large scale of some agricultural activities. Application of chemicals, fertilizers, pesticides, soil fumigants, poisons, or other agrochemicals to crops is commonly accomplished through spraying directly from bulk tanks onto the fields or groves. In addition, the large quantities of farm equipment used in agriculture use motor oil, hydraulic fuel, and other automotive maintenance fluids.

- *Education*: University campuses use liquids in many forms. Dormitories have many of the same liquid needs as the food-service/hospitality industry, the stadiums and sports events parallel the liquid consumption of the entertainment industry, and the classrooms and laboratories consume large quantities of chemicals as well as cleaning liquids.

- *Paper and printing*: The comparison of a roll of paper in a web-press operation to the flow of liquids is an interesting one, but there are many more direct usages of Supply Chain for Liquids related to paper manufacture and the printing industries. Liquids are used throughout the entire papermaking and printing flow, from the chemicals used to cook the chips at the beginning through the inks used for printing at the end.

- *Construction and furnishings*: The building and decorating industries each use a set of liquids for the materials used in the industry, and in addition have several types of liquids in common. The architectural coatings used in construction correspond to polishes and finishes used during furniture manufacturing, and there are many types of adhesives used in the two industries. Construction materials and furnishings are both manufactured in production facilities and thus can utilize a typical Supply Chain for Liquids arrangement, whereas construction-site activity and furnishing renewal take place remotely, and take advantage of mobile forms of Supply Chain for Liquids.

■ *Waste management*: The Supply Chain for Liquids system can be used in a reverse-logistics sense as a collection system rather than as a distribution system. Used motor oil is among the most commonly collected liquids, but many other contaminants are also collected for recycling or protected disposal. The use of the collection truck, corresponding to the use of the delivery truck in the case of distribution, can be made much more effective by knowing the locations that require pickup during any given run and even being able to plan the truck tank configuration should multiple liquids be involved that require segregation. These efficiencies would be gained by a monitoring system on the on-site collection tanks, but because the need for ongoing quantity readings may be much less critical, the sensing and data transmission configuration can likely be less complex than under normal Supply Chain for Liquids.

The implementation of Supply Chain for Liquids is adjusted for the needs of each industry in which it is applied, but in all of the industries, the fundamental principles and processes of Supply Chain for Liquids remain the same. The Liquid Lens^{SM} approach is valuable across all industries, and will help create a Supply Chain for Liquids configuration that is most beneficial in each environment. The Liquid Lens serves as a filter to identify which products/customers are legitimate candidates for inclusion in a Supply Chain for Liquids system, and for which the system is not appropriate. As described in Chapter 10, there are several threshold measures for determining the applicability of Supply Chain for Liquids to a specific environment, and these should be evaluated in particular for industries that meet the requirements only marginally. The volumes of the liquids involved, the complexity and cost of the equipment configuration, the costs eliminated and revenue opportunities gained, and the need for add-on investments such as in new or modified dispense equipment come together in the evaluation of the appropriateness of the system. The Liquid Lens guides us to adapt the Supply Chain for Liquids design to the needs of the application, including cost-reduction measures such as smaller trucks as appropriate, and will also inform us whether the total projected benefit gained from Supply Chain for Liquids is worth the investment.

B2C (Business to Consumer) Applications

The applications of Supply Chain for Liquids listed above are based on B2B (business to business) relationships. Supply Chain for Liquids also has extensive applicability to the B2C world. These applications are described in the following three subsections.

Home Delivery

Adapting the classic model of home heating oil to other liquids represents an untapped application of Supply Chain for Liquids concepts. Liquids such as home-care, personal-care, or automobile-care products make particularly attractive targets for the system; consumables such as beverages and juices require additional quality-assurance capabilities. Home delivery of liquids through a Supply Chain for Liquids setup represents the next consumer step beyond warehouse clubs. Warehouse clubs show that consumers are willing to purchase larger quantities to achieve savings and convenience. Under a Supply Chain for Liquids approach, the convenience would be further increased, as the customer would not need to actually purchase and haul the liquids from the store to the home. The economics of Supply Chain for Liquids would allow competitive pricing, but the advantages such as home delivery and auto-replenishment might even allow a premium to be charged for these products. Certainly, capturing the consumer and having the product delivered directly to the consumer's home is a marketing prize that any company would value.

The logistics of residential Supply Chain for Liquids is a parallel but simplified version of a B2B Supply Chain for Liquids. The major elements — external-port access and in-home tanks — remain, providing the ability to deliver product without disrupting activity in the home or requiring that anybody be at home. Several elements that are simplified for B2C versus B2B Supply Chain for Liquids include the following:

- The sensor system, which uses one or a set of relatively inexpensive need-to-replenish point sensors rather than a continuous-monitoring sensor (see Chapter 8 for a description of sensor types).
- The communications device that is connected to existing equipment in the home, such as a home computer. Such a system replaces the PLC (programmable logic controller) or RTU (remote telemetry unit) of an industrial system (see Chapter 8) and is activated

whenever the home computer is used. The system allows the user to approve, adjust, or cancel a suggested replenishment order prior to its transmission to the supplier or distributor.

■ The liquid propulsion system, in which a small pump is used rather than pressurized gas to ensure the safety of the system and eliminate any risk of gas leakage to the homeowner.

The efficiency of the delivery routing in residential neighborhoods maintains the cost-effectiveness of the system. The sizing of the trucks and tanks on the trucks is adapted to the volumes of the delivery runs and limitations of the environments in which they will operate, that is, residential areas. Unlike industrial deliveries, however, home delivery in some areas is more effective during the workday, when residents are away and traffic is at a minimum.

Office/Shopping Center

Similar to home delivery, but with a variation in logistical details, is the application of the Supply Chain for Liquids approach to office complexes and shopping centers. Office complexes are highly concentrated consumers of high volumes of specific liquids — beverages for employees and cleaning products for the facilities, among others. Office complexes frequently include eating facilities for individual offices as well as restaurants and refreshment stands throughout the facilities. The Supply Chain for Liquids concept might be applied collectively, with a central holding point from which the individual customers acquire these products, or directly to each customer site, depending on the logistics configuration.

Additional B2C Channels

The Supply Chain for Liquids concept permits development of new marketing, distribution, and sales channels. Some of these are:

■ *Kiosks*: Stand-alone kiosks in any of several formats provide an opportunity for producers or distributors to sell consumer liquids directly. The concept of a kiosk is a structure with a set of tanks, replenished by a Supply Chain for Liquids system, that dispenses liquids to consumers. A kiosk might be attended, or it could be unattended with a payment system and protected dispense system. Small kiosks that dispense beverages might be placed around a university campus, for example, and students would use mugs that they carry with them to dispense the liquid using any of a number of payment schemes. More comprehensive walk-up kiosks that dispense beverages as well as household and personal-care products might be placed at certain types of stores, such as do-it-yourself centers, to allow customers who are oriented toward self-activation to purchase bulk liquids for home consumption. Still larger drive-up kiosks, such as in shopping center parking lots, would allow the customer to drive up, purchase various types of home-consumption liquids, have the bulk containers such as one- to five-gallon jugs placed in the vehicle, and take the liquids home. The bulk basis and automated replenishment systems of each of these Supply Chain for Liquids–based configurations allow effective operation of each type of kiosk.

▪ *Customer-filled beverage containers*: A concept that has appeared using various methodologies is that of having consumers fill their own containers with liquids in supermarkets. An in-store tank holding system, combined with a dispense and payment system, makes this operationally feasible, and the Supply Chain for Liquids approach handles many of the logistical aspects of such an arrangement. The in-store system could be a version of the kiosks described above, or more oriented toward a shelf-based approach.

▪ *Lawn care*: A more sophisticated use of Supply Chain for Liquids involves two-directional communications between the site and the central computer system. Standard Supply Chain for Liquids involves only sensors reporting liquid level or quality readings to the central computer system. An expansion of Supply Chain for Liquids is for the central computer system to be able to send control signals back to the site. PLCs are built with both monitoring and control capabilities, so this is not a technical issue. An example of this type of application would be use of a Supply Chain for Liquids system in conjunction with a lawn-care system, be it at a residence, office park, public park, golf course, or any other area that receives regular care. The on-site tank system contains different types of fertilizers and pesticides, and it is hooked into the pipes that carry water to the spray heads. The central computer system is fed information regarding conditions in each local area, such as the amount of rainfall, daily temperature, infestations of insects or other damaging factors, and other variables that affect the growth of a lawn. Based on this information, the central computer system sends signals to each site as to the mix of chemicals to be introduced into the watering flow, and the quantity of each chemical. These signals adjust valves attached to the on-site tank system and thus allow the correct amount of chemicals to be released to the sprinkler system. This illustrative example shows the potential of a bidirectional communications flow between the on-site controller and the central computer system. Many other situations in which it could be useful come readily to mind, for example, to feed quality signals from the site to the central computer system, which in turn sends adjusting signals back to the site. Should the temperature at the site exceed acceptable limits, for example, the central computer system could instruct the site to increase the speed of a fan or take other predefined steps to correct the exception condition.

The B2C applications of Supply Chain for Liquids create an additional set of marketing opportunities for a company, as described in Chapter 11. Although the applications are slightly different from B2B Supply Chain for Liquids, the basic structures and systems follow all of the standard Supply Chain for Liquids approaches.

For either B2B or B2C applications, the Supply Chain for Liquids concept is most powerful when implemented for the entire length of the logistics flow, from the raw-material supplier through the end user. However, it may not always be possible, practical, or beneficial to implement the system along the entire flow. This could be for any of several reasons: upstream logistics might already be using large-scale bulk principles, downstream players might be limited in their ability to implement the system, etc. However, applying the Supply Chain for Liquids to a limited portion of the logistics flow can still have tremendous benefits, and the implementation of even a limited-flow system should be considered, even if all of the parts of the supply stream cannot be involved.

Nonliquid Applications of Supply Chain for Liquids

Adapted Supply Chain and Supply Chain for Liquids naturally focus on liquids, as it is the behavior of liquids versus discrete products that provides the huge logistics advantages that these approaches offer. Once we understand Supply Chain for Liquids principles, however, we can see that there are nonliquid products to which these approaches can be applied. Certain types of nonliquids behave in a way that is similar enough to liquids that they could be processed through a Supply Chain for Liquids–type system. These products include powders, pellets, seeds, grains, pills/capsules/tablets, or other materials whose physical characteristics match the requirements of the Supply Chain for Liquids flow. These requirements in general are the ability to be held in containers of different sizes and shapes and to be moved through pipes, the ability to be leveled so that quantity can be measured by the height of the material within a container or alternatively by weight, and a dispense methodology that lends itself to being held in bulk prior to the point of dispense. Nonliquid products that meet these requirements are candidates for inclusion in a Supply Chain for Liquids–like system with most of the benefits that are available for liquid products.

Certain Supply Chain for Liquids principles can also be utilized for discrete products with the use of the appropriate techniques and equipment. For example, Supply Chain for Liquids operates by knowing what liquid is in a specific tank, and then constantly measuring the height of the liquid in the tank and converting the level into a quantity. A corresponding approach for discrete products would be to "know" what products are sitting on a certain pallet or at a certain storage position by utilizing a pallet that can measure and transmit the weight of product on the pallet, and then convert the weight of product on the pallet into the number of units of the product at that location. Many obvious differences arise between the two situations. With a Supply Chain for Liquids system, the "wrong" liquid is physically prevented from entering a tank because of the design of the system and the physical connections between the tanks, whereas a method would need to be defined to ensure that only the specified product is placed on a single pallet. Depending on the unit weight of the product on the pallet, the total weight reading may or may not be accurate enough to define the exact quantity of product on the pallet. Although weight-reading scales do exist, the technological portion of the discrete approach is not nearly as developed as the liquid level sensor/flowmeter technology used in the Supply Chain for Liquids approach for liquid products. Other approaches to measuring the presence or absence of discrete items, such as the height of a stack of the item, using a camera that can count how many units are in a particular location, or other methods also exist, but all are problematic.

In addition to discrete products, a Supply Chain for Liquids–type approach could be used for gases in place of delivering gases in containers and removing the empty containers. In the case of gases, the approach to measuring the quantity remaining in the tank is quite different from that for liquids or for the nonliquid products described above, but this is well-developed technology that is readily available. Although there are a number of other adaptations required to utilize the Supply Chain for Liquids methodology for gases, the methodology is more readily applicable to gases than to discrete products. Many of the advantages of Adapted Supply Chain and Supply Chain for Liquids can be realized when these approaches are applied to gas products.

Cross-Fertilizing Supply Chain for Liquids Applications

Cross-fertilizing applications means having two or more applications of the system and having each benefit the other, leading to a greater benefit than each of the systems gains alone. Supply Chain for Liquids applications can be cross-fertilized in two ways. First, a company can use liquids in several different areas, such as ingredients for its products and for facility-maintenance fluids (floor cleaners and waxes). By installing the system in one area, it can fine-tune its usage before installing it in the other area. Further, some of the equipment, such as the PLC/RTU and the data-communications equipment, can be used for both applications, thus decreasing the total cost and complexity of applying the system to the two areas separately. Having an operating example of a Supply Chain for Liquids system at work in one area will also support the development and implementation of a corresponding system in another area.

The second opportunity for cross-fertilization relates to visibility outside of the company. As we have seen in this section, liquid-logistics and Supply Chain for Liquids applications cross the boundaries of traditionally defined industries. Such seemingly different industries as automotive and entertainment both use liquid products, albeit different liquids and in different ways. However, viewing logistics systems from a liquid perspective offers an opportunity for benefit for users in all liquid-using industries. The Supply Chain for Liquids Society provides an opportunity for such cross-industry perspective, with companies able to interact with each other without competitive issues that sometime inhibit the open exchange of ideas. Chapter 11 provides more information about the Supply Chain for Liquids Society, how it functions, and the benefits it offers across different industries. The Internet site for Supply Chain for Liquids provides information and resources for both cross-industry liquid logistics and the Supply Chain for Liquids Society (www.SupplyChainForLiquids.com).

Chapter 5

Operational Configurations of Supply Chain and Supply Chain for Liquids

Before we go through a detailed evaluation of the major stages of the supply stream — production, distribution, and usage — in Chapter 6 to Chapter 8, respectively, this chapter defines in detail the four types of operational configurations we will be referring to: Supply Chain, Adapted Supply Chain, Supply Chain for Liquids®, and Optimal Supply Chain for Liquids. Although certain liquids have special logistical characteristics, the configurations we will define are generalized operational overviews that apply to many types of liquids in many industries, as described in Chapter 4. These configurations demonstrate the advantages available from viewing liquids as liquids (instead of as discrete products), as well as the process of moving from the most basic to the most advanced logistics configuration.

In this chapter, the four types of configurations are presented here sequentially in the order that they would occur in a company that is evolving its logistics systems for liquid products from Supply Chain to Optimal Supply Chain for Liquids. It is important to note that this is not the order in which the configurations would be planned. For many companies, a configuration similar to that shown in Supply Chain represents current practice. The Liquid Lens℠ tells us to plan for the ultimate objective, Optimal Supply Chain for Liquids, together with transition stages of reaching Optimal Supply Chain for Liquids status — Adapted Supply Chain and Supply Chain for Liquids — before entering into transition activities. This is a much more effective approach than planning each configuration step one at a time after the prior step has been achieved. An interim step so planned may run contrary to achieving the overall goal as described in Chapter 3.

Each configuration is described in terms of its complete loop, that is, the product flow from producer through consumer and information flow back from consumer through to the producer. Even the most basic configuration, Supply Chain, assumes that a company recognizes that it is part of a flow of goods and information and has relationships with its suppliers and its customers on both these levels. The nature, extent, and impact of those relationships evolve as we move from Supply Chain to Optimal Supply Chain for Liquids.

Before we launch into these ideas, perhaps it is useful to reset our thinking, clear our minds, and take ourselves back to basics. We could make the argument that the most instructive example for Supply Chain for Liquids is the Bindibu tribe in Australia. Although they live in an arid landscape in which few of us could survive, their culture does not include either storage jars to hold liquids or cups to drink them from. When they want to drink, they get down on all fours and drink directly from whatever puddle they find, and they return the liquid to the earth in a similar natural fashion. This represents the complete absence of a supply chain, the logistics equivalent of zero-based budgeting. This is also the first step of Supply Chain for Liquids thinking — in what state is the liquid at its point of origin, in what state at its point of use, and how close can we keep it to those states in between? Organizations, including supply chains, most often tend to add complexity and functionality to themselves, growing and expanding over time, so that anyone starting to design a Supply Chain for Liquids already has a full (and perhaps overfull) logistics operation in place. It is a real trick to take a cue from the Bindibu and go back to basics — what would be the most direct way to get the liquid from the source to the destination?

A brief review of the development of personal liquid usage gives us insight into liquid thinking that we now take for granted, but at the time was innovative at each step along the way. The earliest people lived near rivers and springs: "we need to go to where the water is." This would have been the rule of the game as long as the technology of the time limited water usage to direct consumption. Two technological advances led to revolutionary thoughts in some unknown primitives' brains. The first was the ability to make vessels that could carry things, be they made out of animal skins, wood, stone, or grasses, and later of pottery or more advanced materials. This stage would be the birth of liquid logistics as we know it — the ability to move or manipulate liquids so that we set the rules for them rather than them setting the rules for us. In all likelihood, it would have been only a few ounces of water to begin with, and the distance would have been the few feet from the river to a big shady tree, but the idea was extraordinary and revolutionary. Everything else we will do with liquid logistics is simply a fine-tuning of that original idea of moving water from one spot to another.

The other technological advance, besides "let's move water," was "let's get water here." This was accomplished in several ways, again based on what the technology of the times permitted. By moving a little dirt from a spot of ground, rainwater would have collected and been available for a few days after a rainstorm. Some sharp-eyed primitive may have even spotted a bowl-shaped indent in a rock formation and realized that the water that gathers there would be available for a few days after a rainstorm. When digging techniques progressed — the use of stones and later metals — our ancestors discovered that there was water under the ground, first at very shallow levels and later much deeper.

In order for us to gain value from this story, we have to remember a couple of things. First, people naturally would do things in a way that the available technology allowed, and as technology advanced, it would sooner or later lead to different ways of doing things. Nonapplied technology creates a vacuum that is filled at some point with something we refer to as "progress." It is the ability to marry existing/new technological abilities with new/changing personal or commercial needs that results in business advance. This is what Supply Chain for Liquids is all about. Second, over the course of time, people learned to relate to the nontechnical issues involved with these advances. Given the central role that both earth and water play in so many religions and belief systems, we can easily imagine the conflicts that arose the first time someone dug a hole in the ground and started taking out water to drink. Heresy! You are violating mother earth and stealing father water! Certainly a bird dropping will fall on you soon, the harshest sign of a curse that can be imagined! For every step in the process, there were forces at work, based on the thought patterns of the previous processes, that took a certain period of time to adjust to new techniques. The clashes created from these situations were in some cases dramatic and well-known — Galileo and the Catholic Church, for example — but for the most part such conflicts would have been much more limited and subtle. As a combination of continually advancing technology and business needs, it can be expected that any effort to pursue Supply Chain for Liquids will run into some forms of this resistance, which if properly handled should affect the progress of such a project only in a most limited way.

Supply Chain

Supply Chain is the traditional operational configuration for companies that do not distinguish liquid from nonliquid products. Each step is carried out as if the product is a solid, with no exploitation of the product's liquid nature. The steps in the standard configuration are shown in Exhibit 5.1 and described below, together with specific characteristics of each step that will be evaluated subsequently. After we establish this as a common baseline approach, we will be able to re-view it in terms of the other more advanced types of configurations: Adapted Supply Chain, Supply Chain for Liquids, and Optimal Supply Chain for Liquids. To draw a sight-line on where we are heading with this analysis (or put more crudely, to throw out a teaser), out of the 14 "standard" steps we are about to list, we will find ways to get rid of at least nine of them as we move from Supply Chain through to Optimal Supply Chain for Liquids.

Step 1: Production

Unlike discrete goods, liquid products are often produced using recipes rather than bills of material and using ingredients rather than components. Corresponding to discrete goods, in which an exact number of components are used to make an exact number of end-product units, liquid recipes are usually proportional. For each X quantity of end product required, the production person should include Y quantity of a specific ingredient in the batch. In other cases, ranges of end product are used to produce a batch within a specific quantity range, a set quantity Z of an ingredient suffices for the batch size.

It is not uncommon in production companies that operate according to simple logistical principles to utilize a min/max inventory and production scheme, especially when they have no visibility into demand at their customers and at their customers' customers. That is, they produce to meet target inventory levels that are set internally based on historical demand but are independent of actual current demand. In cases such as this, the inventory levels themselves are designed to be large enough to buffer the ongoing rises and falls in demand. For this type of company, raw-material inventory is maintained in a similar way. An internal min/max system drives what the level of each raw material should be, independent of actual current or future needs for the raw material. For both sales orders and purchase orders, the order itself is the link with the customer or supplier. There is little if any ongoing contact between the company and its customers or suppliers that provides visibility into factors that will affect future production or inventory needs.

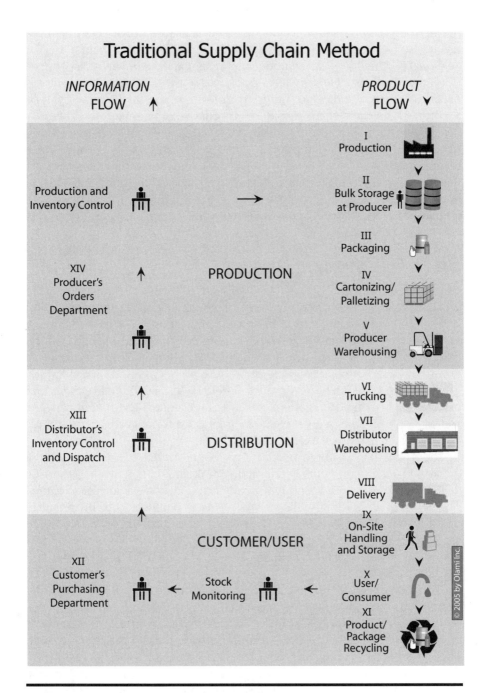

Exhibit 5.1 A Typical Supply Chain Configuration

The min/max system represents, in some ways, one level of disconnect between the company and its customers, in that production and inventory levels are set based on internal calculations instead of actual needs. Standard production-order quantities represent another level of disconnect. When the on-hand inventory level decreases to the minimum, a production order is entered either to bring inventory to the maximum level or according to some standard production-order size. In either case, this may be the wrong response to the true situation. It may not trigger sufficient production/inventory to support a peak in demand, or the product may be produced and sit in inventory for an extensive period in the event there is a trough in demand. Again, the lack of visibility into future requirements costs the company in terms of production activity and inventory levels that are out of sync with the company's true needs.

Step 2: Bulk Storage at Producer

Unless the production process feeds directly into the packaging line, the producer will hold a certain amount of liquid in bulk at the production facility. This is advantageous to the producer, as it provides more flexibility as to the exact form and size of packaging in which the product will be placed (one-gallon jugs, two-gallon jugs, fifty-five–gallon drums, etc.). From our perspective, this is one of the few points in the standard Supply Chain process in which the product is held in its native environment and under liquid-oriented conditions. Bulk storage generally consists of some sort of holding tanks with capacities ranging from hundreds to thousands of gallons. In some cases, the production tanks and holding tanks may be the same. For a simple production operation that consists of flowing the appropriate ingredients into a mixing tank and then activating a stirring device to mix the liquid, enough mixing tanks may be available that they can be used as holding tanks as well. This is particularly appropriate in cases in which the holding tank also serves a production function. In cases where the product must ferment, set, or otherwise process for a period of time, this tank actually serves a combined production and holding function.

The presence of such a bulk-storage tank at the production site provides the first hint of advantages that will be available in later configurations, such as Supply Chain for Liquids. No manual effort is required to physically move the product from the mixing tank to the holding tank. This is done by passing the liquid product through pipes between the tanks. The tanks are very space efficient. A full tank uses virtually 100 percent of its volume for the product, unlike packaged product on a rack, which uses a much lower percentage of the space taken for actual product. It is also very easy to see how much liquid is in the tank. With a sight gauge — a clear vertical tube on the side of the tank that shows the height of the liquid in the tank against an incremented scale marked with the number of gallons — an operator can see at a glance how much product is present. This is in contrast to the process of manually counting packages or cartons to determine how much of a discrete product, or liquid product held in containers, is present. These are some of the areas that we will explore later as we move from Supply Chain to Adapted Supply Chain and then on to Supply Chain for Liquids.

Step 3: Packaging

The packaging line often consists of several stages such as filling, capping, sealing, and labeling. In the case of liquid products, the packaging line may be more complex than the production of the product itself. The packaging line is both an operation within the production process and an entire process on its own. Indeed, the packaging materials themselves must be planned, ordered, inventoried, and issued to the production line. Moreover, the packaging line must be balanced with the company's overall production capability to avoid its becoming a constraint to production or an excess cost through overcapacity. In this sense, the packaging line serves as another link in the Supply Chain that must be coordinated with the link before it (production) and the links after it (cartonizing/palletizing and warehousing).

The packaging process amplifies the negative effects of a min/max inventory-planning and -control system in a standard Supply Chain company. As described previously, the min/max approach to the product itself is liable to lead to shortages during periods of rising demand or to excess inventory during the reduced-demand phase of the sales cycle. A min/max system for packaging material is twice removed from external/customer demand, and so it is even more disconnected from actual demand. Whether packaging material is produced at the production facility, such as bottles, or is procured from an outside supplier, the "ideal" quantity of packaging material exactly corresponds to the amount of product produced rather than the quantity reflected by a min/max planning approach. This "ideal" quantity is intentionally put in quotes, as we shall see when we discuss the Supply Chain for Liquids configuration. Giving ourselves the opportunity to eliminate the packaging process and packaging materials altogether holds great benefits for the effectiveness of the logistics operations and for the business as a whole.

In a standard Supply Chain, the liquid product loses its identity at the packaging point, where it becomes a solid, that is, it assumes the identity of the package in which it is placed. Putting the liquid in a bottle, jugs, or barrel eliminates all of the logistics advantages that the product has in its liquid form. The next time the product is handled as a liquid is at the end of the Supply Chain, when the end user removes the product from the package.

Step 4: Cartonizing/Palletizing

Placing packages such as jugs in cartons may be a relatively standard process, but palletizing includes a number of complexities. If a standard pallet configuration with a full pallet load of a specific product is used, then palletizing is relatively simple. On the other hand, a pallet may be assembled according to a specific standard or for a specific customer, in which case cartons of different products must be assembled and arranged on a pallet. Thus what will ultimately become a multiproduct delivery to a customer becomes a multiproduct logistical complexity already at the palletizing point.

Like packaging, both cartonizing and palletizing have operational requirements of their own. Both involve material that must be planned, purchased, and inventoried, both require storeroom or warehouse space to hold the material, and both are more than likely overstocked to avoid their becoming a constraint that holds up production or delays a shipment.

The cartonizing/palletizing operation can be seen in an interesting light from a Supply Chain perspective. For discrete items, palletized product is the closest the logistics system can come to creating a "bulk" status for the product. A pallet of a product is easier to move, count, handle, identify, and control than cartons of the product, and cartons are easier than individual units of the product such as bottles or jugs. Thus a pallet is the discrete approximation of a tank of a liquid product, that is, product in bulk form. Putting a liquid in containers, and then putting the containers in cartons on pallets, could be considered a "double reverse" situation — trying to recover for the liquid as much as possible its original state, which we lost when we put it in packaging in the first place. Again, this gives us a hint of the advantages we can gain and the benefits that are available as we move toward the Supply Chain for Liquids configuration.

Step 5: Producer Warehousing

Under a standard Supply Chain approach, the producer warehouse serves as the first of a set of buffers that are set up all along the logistics flow. These buffers protect the system from:

- Uncertainty regarding actual product demand
- Inaccuracy of forecasts or of inventory-balance information
- Risk of stock depletion and the resulting loss of sales
- Fear of being the weak link in getting product from the company to the customer
- Lack of communication between the downstream customer-facing end of the logistics flow and the upstream production end of the flow
- Inflexibility that limits coordination of manufacturing capabilities to customer requirements

In short, inventory sitting in a warehouse is the great rug under which business maladies of every sort are swept. Unfortunately, it is both a very expensive rug and a very thick, heavy rug for which it is often difficult to lift even a corner, much less throw off and sweep out the accumulated piles beneath it.

The holding of product in warehouses entails a whole set of activities with their associated complexities and costs. The disease that is oddly called "inventory shrink" (it does not shrink, it disappears) sets in, and covers damage, theft, expiration or contamination, miscounting, misplacement, and other acts of man (not to mention acts of God) that affect the world of the warehouse. The corresponding disease of "inventory bloat" is also exacting its toll — the set of costs that pile on top of each carton of inventory in the warehouse, including racking, forklift trucks and drivers, counters, pickers, warehouse management and all the associated overhead, and on and on.

Warehouse utilization in this environment is also governed by a standard set of constraints. The packaging/cartons/pallets have limitations related to stack height, rack configuration, forklift reach and capacity, and other factors that define how and how well the warehouse space can be utilized. In short, because this standard approach treats liquid product as solids, they must be directly, physically accessible for put away and picking in the warehouse.

Step 6: Trucking

In a standard Supply Chain configuration, liquid products are treated as solids from a logistics point of view — it is the packaging that is handled, not the product itself — and this is reflected in the trucking/transportation methodology. There are two parts to the trucking step of a standard Supply Chain configuration. The first has to do with getting the product on and off the truck — loading and unloading — and the second is the actual movement of the truck from location to location. Looking at each of these parts, we can see that there are questions that can be asked related to each of them.

Anyone who has been involved in loading trucks knows that, although it may seem to be a simple task, it is often actually quite complex. The complexity has several sources:

- A truck has to be loaded in consideration of how it is going to be unloaded, especially semi-trailers that are accessed only from one end. The product should be loaded strictly according to the LIFO (last in, first out) principle (or FILO if you like to think in terms of first-things-first). The first product loaded on the truck and placed at the far end will be the last product off-loaded, and the last product in will be the first product out. If the shipment is to multiple locations, this implies a staging process. Not all of a given product is loaded together, but rather all of the product for a given delivery location is loaded together, so the product for each delivery location must be staged near the truck before the loading process begins. This of course adds another layer of activity and complexity to the process.

- Some types of trucks such as side-loaders contain racking to hold the product; other types of trucks enclose what is essentially an open space where the product is subject to shifting and thus requires bracing. Depending on the physical attributes of the product, the process of bracing may be a very quick act, or it may take more time and effort on the part of the driver or warehouse personnel to perform properly.

Complexity in this case relates to resources: how much time does it take to load the truck, how many people, how much equipment such as forklifts or stabilizing equipment are needed, how much is the truck's/driver's utilization impacted by the time it takes for loading and unloading, what effect does the time a truck spends at a dock have on the flow of product by preventing other trucks from being loaded or unloaded, etc. Each of these resources represents costs that are incurred by the company.

The second part of the trucking step is the actual transportation from point to point. There is no way to change the laws of physics and make two points closer together, but how you get from here to there is certainly open to many options. For liquids that are treated as discrete products, transportation methods are generally oriented toward semi-trailers or rail. Looking ahead to the Supply Chain for Liquids configuration, the options will widen greatly and provide flexibilities that are unavailable under the standard Supply Chain approach.

Step 7: Distributor Warehousing

The issues related to the distribution center or distributor's warehouse are similar to those of the producer's warehouse as described in step 5. In addition, because the scale of the warehousing operation might be larger than that of the producer (if the warehouse is handling the products of multiple production facilities or multiple producers), complexities such as space utilization and consolidation of a producer's products come into play. For example, seasonal products take up much more space in-season and less in the off-season, creating shifts in the space to be used for the product. During the high-volume season for a product, an incoming shipment of that product might be divided and put away in a number of different locations. Thus the effort required to both put away and to retrieve the product is increased. Over the course of time, a phenomenon akin to disk fragmentation on a computer, in which parts of a single file are stored in multiple locations on the computer disk, sets in — different quantities of the same product are stored in different parts of the ware-house. In addition to the movement issues this creates, it also impacts other efforts such as product rotation, which could lead to degradation of product quality.

Another significant activity that is carried out in the warehouse is staging, the assembly of products by delivery order or delivery route for the next day's deliveries. In what is often a fairly large space near the shipping docks, rows of products are lined up according to the truck on which they are to be delivered. When a truck returns from the current day's run, the products remaining on it are off-loaded, and the products for the next day are loaded. The staging process is like a nerve ending hanging out waiting to be trampled on. Any one of a number of problems can make it go wrong, and because this is the final step prior to delivering product to the customer, the level of performance in the marketplace is dependent on productive staging. If the quantity of product is not where it is supposed to be, if the product is in the right place but has been damaged in some way, if a forklift is not working properly so there are not enough machines to do the staging — these and similar factors will determine whether, at the end of the day, this company meets the customers' expectations or not.

The corresponding activity on the product-receiving side, although less complex, also requires significant resources. One set of unloaders/forklifts might be dedicated to truck unloading and placing the material in a receiving area, while a different set of machines moves the product from the receiving area to the racks after it has been counted and approved.

Step 8: Delivery

The delivery step begins with planning, establishing a route for each truck for the delivery run. Under standard Supply Chain procedures, the delivery process comes in several flavors, each of which requires its own form of planning. On the one hand, product deliveries might be completely unplanned, in the sense that the truck is sent out on a standard route with a standard set of products, and the driver clarifies at each stop what products are needed. This approach is most common in a very stable environment with a high percentage of regular, repeat customers and steady demand for regular products. The other extreme is a completely preordered delivery process, in which only products that have actually been ordered by customers are loaded onto the trucks and delivered. A third, very common approach is a hybrid of these two, in which trucks are loaded with customer orders and then filled out with standard product to meet the on-the-spot requests that arise during the delivery process. The difference between these approaches is information. To the degree that the specific quantities and products that customers need are known in advance, truck loading and the whole delivery process can be more effective. This points us toward a functionality that will be important to us under the Supply Chain for Liquids configuration, that of maximizing the level of knowledge available about product requirements for each customer and in total during the planning for a delivery run.

Each delivery involves traveling to the delivery site and then moving the product into the delivery site. Each of these acts has its own considerations. Travel time between sites is affected by traffic conditions, whether the delivery run is done during heavy traffic hours or during off-hours when transit time can be reduced to a great degree. Moving the product into the site depends on the receiving hours that are allowed at each customer site, delays caused by other deliveries to the same customer, the time that the delivery person needs to physically move the products into the customer site, and interaction time between the delivery person and customer personnel both formally (such as to clarify/confirm delivery products, invoice signing) and informally. Again, this points us toward functionality: the ability to cut down the actual act of delivery as close as possible to the essential act of product flowing into the customer site, and eliminating all other activities surrounding the delivery. If we are able to achieve these two functionalities — reducing travel time between delivery locations as much as possible and reducing the amount of time the delivery person spends at each site — we will make significant improvements in the delivery process. These improvements mean that fewer trucks can deliver more product while better meeting customer needs.

Step 9: On-Site Handling and Storage

On-site handling and storage involves a number of steps and players. First, the delivery person brings the product into the warehouse or storage area as part of the delivery process as described in previous steps. Either prior to the delivery person's arrival, or following the delivery of the products, the warehouse person or store employee arranges the containers for access and proper product rotation. For small containers, this can be done by hand, but for larger quantities a forklift or other equipment is required.

The way the product is moved for usage depends on its packaging. Large containers such as 55-gallon drums are moved to their location of usage, but for products in bottles or jugs, this is usually done by taking a carton from the pallet, removing the bottles from the carton, and taking the bottles to the location of usage. Many handling/storage/usage scenarios are much more involved, such as in quick-serve restaurants. When a bag-in-box container of beverage syrup has been emptied, the employee disconnects, removes, and disposes of the empty container and then places the full container in its position and connects it to the system. Even with seemingly small packages, this is not an easy task. For example, five-gallon bag-in-box cartons are surprisingly heavy, and lifting them into position on a rack is beyond the capability of many employees. Other types of handling in quick-serve restaurants are equally difficult. For example, the ice cream machine is often filled through an opening at the top of the unit, which may be higher than the employee is tall. The contortions the employee has to go through to open the bag of mix, open the ice cream unit, and guide the bag to the opening would be humorous if the task were not so difficult, time-consuming, and possibly dangerous.

On-site storage takes space, and for most companies space means money. For product that must be manually handled for storage and retrieval, the space that can be used for storage is even more limited. A person can only reach to a maximum height of six feet or so to retrieve a package from a stack or rack, so the usable space for storage is only the first six feet above floor level. This limits the area in which product can be stored, and the space higher than six feet up to ceiling level is wasted space in terms of product storage. Although other storage areas are used as much as possible, such as under-counter storage, these play only a limited role in making usable storage space available to the operation.

An additional aspect of managing the on-site inventory is the physical conditions related to the inventory. This includes monitoring stock rotation, accounting for damage or other adjustments required to inventory, ensuring that quality-related and safety-related conditions are in place, and setting and enforcing procedures related to inventory receipts, issues, and usage. In addition, management of the product includes maintaining inventory-related equipment such as racks, the condition of the storeroom or storage area, disposal of inventory-related refuse such as packaging or used/unusable product by trash or recycling, etc. For sites that have a dispense system associated with the flow of the product, the dispense system must also be properly maintained and utilized.

A factor common to many storage and handling situations is the location of storage relative to the location of usage. There is often a significant distance between the two. In retail establishments, accessing the product may involve going to the basement or climbing on a rack. For larger containers such as 55-gallon drums or IBCs (intermediate bulk containers), a forklift driver may need to move the product. On-site handling adds no value to the final product, but it does have plenty of downsides in terms of the personnel and equipment costs to move product, risks to employees involved in product movement, damage to the product that occurs as it is being handled, and other drawbacks to many storage/handling scenarios. Given this situation, it becomes clear that reduction (or, better, elimination) of on-site handling would be beneficial — yet another reason why we are looking at alternative approaches to the conventional supply stream.

Step 10: User/Consumer

The user is focused on getting the liquid where it is needed, when it is needed, and how it is needed. For example, a restaurant wants to get the beverage to the dispense point so that the customer can drink it; at an automotive service facility, the goal is to get the lubricant to the vehicle; in a hospital, the goal might be to get the disinfectant cleaner to the cleaning cart of the wing that requires cleaning; for a factory, the goal might be to get the machine lubricants to the area where the machinery is maintained.

The typical Supply Chain scenario can thwart the user's best interests. In a car repair shop, for example, the mechanic has to identify the type of motor oil required, go to the storeroom window, requisition the proper quantity of oil, return to the repair bay, open each of the bottles, pour them in, and then dispose of the empty containers. This is clearly a much more cumbersome and costly process than having a set of retractable dispensers over the repair bay from which the mechanic selects the appropriate fluid, pulls the hose to dispense directly into the vehicle, releases the hose, and continues the maintenance work.

The user's efforts to obtain and use a liquid product differs with each usage environment. But the ultimate measure of success for a logistics flow — from the user's perspective — is the amount of time it takes the user to do the job versus the cost of overhead or ancillary logistics tasks that need to be done to support that job. There are thousands of jobs: serving customers at a restaurant counter, changing a car's oil at a quick-lube shop, running production machines at a factory, sanitizing the facilities at a hospital, cleaning rooms at a hotel, maintaining manufacturing machines at a production facility, preparing food at a club, doing laundry at a resort. In each of these job situations, the liquid-logistics system can provide added value by reducing the nonproductive time spent while the user chases down the right materials to get the job done.

The time saved by giving the user direct accessibility to the product is a major source of cost reductions. However, costs are also reduced by minimizing (1) insurance premiums for injured employees (e.g., while lifting or moving heavy containers) and (2) involvement with regulatory or labor organizations regarding safety-related working conditions for the employees. Beyond this, the ready accessibility of product addresses several fundamental job-satisfaction issues: that the "customer service" message is real and is taken seriously by the company, that the employee has access to the tools that are needed to do the job right, and that the focus is on the quality of the employee's work. The employee might reasonably consider ancillary logistics activities to work against the focus on customer satisfaction. For example, quick-serve restaurant employees often complain that the need to swap beverage syrup containers during periods of high customer activity runs counter to the high priority placed on customer service. Employees could easily interpret this to mean that backroom activities are interfering with the quality of customer service.

Step 11: Product/Package Recycling

The recycling of used product or empty packaging can be time-consuming and expensive. The recycling of automotive fluids is a typical example. All fluids must be collected and deposited into some type of holding container, and the recycling company is periodically contacted and requested to remove the waste liquid. In some cases, the containers in which the fluids were originally delivered, such as 55-gallon drums, must be cut up before they are sent for disposal if they are not to be reused.

Even more burdensome, from a logistics perspective, are returnable containers. In a B2B (business to business) environment, these can include beer kegs, gas cylinders, some IBCs and other types of bulk drums, as well as the pallets that are typically used to ship containers. The empties must be stored at the user site until the time of pickup; transported back to the supplier; accounted for in the supplier's inventory; cleaned, repaired, or refurbished; and then inventoried at the supplier site until they are refilled and put back into the distribution stream. The container-return process is a sub-business unto itself, requiring logistics and overhead resources in line with the main production/distribution business of which it is a part. In a B2C environment, container disposal is an entire industry, with massive resources invested in recycling, trash collection, and processing.

With many materials, there is no good disposal/recycling solution in a typical Supply Chain situation. Disposal or recycling of the used liquids/packaging costs money and requires a certain amount of employee activity. Moreover, both alternatives have environmental implications. Container and packaging waste — estimated at 57 million tons per year — is the largest single component in the country's waste stream. Eliminating packaging from the entire logistics process — from the original packaging operation during production through disposal of the packaging material after the use of the product — is the principal benefit of Supply Chain for Liquids.

Step 12: Customer/User Planning and Control Activities

Having described each of the steps in the flow of product from the producer to the user, we now look at the remaining part of the logistics loop, the flow of information from the user back to the producer. This is truly a loop; the product flow generates information that measures activity along the flow, and the information flow generates activities that trigger the product flow. We will look at each of the information-related steps under a Supply Chain configuration, and then using this baseline we will later be able to see how it is changed as we move to a Supply Chain for Liquids configuration. The first step in the information flow relates to information at the user site.

There are numerous activities at the customer/user site related to gathering and transmitting liquid-related data. Employees at customer/user sites commonly perform the following:

■ Manually count the number of containers or amount of product that is currently in on-hand inventory, or monitor inventory levels if a system is in place to do so. Depending on the days-on-hand inventory kept at the site, this counting may be done periodically. For locations in which space constrictions or other constraints limit the amount of inventory that can be held, or in which ease of theft or other considerations require close tracking of inventory balances, inventory counting may be performed every one or two days. Counting inventory involves the physical counting of product containers, reconciling the count to the previous count and interim activity, investigating discrepancies between the actual and calculated quantities, and updating records to reflect the actual balance.

■ Calculate the amount of product required for replenishment if this is performed manually. The calculation takes into account current inventory, the amount of time between deliveries and the depletion rate for each product, the total space available for current on-hand product plus product being ordered, and minimum order quantity or other constraints defined by the supplier.

■ Communicate the replenishment order to the distributor. In addition, all of the overhead activities relating to purchasing — purchase-order tracking, the inventory-receiving function, matching a receiver to the purchase order and the invoice, etc. — are carried out by the customer company.

These activities also assume that the tools and support required for effective performance are available, such as a computer, communications device, inventory-monitoring system (manual or automated), personnel trained to perform these activities, and management attention that the activities are being performed completely and properly.

Step 13: Distributor Planning and Control Activities

The distributor/distribution center handles both sides of the information process. On the demand side, it gathers order information from customers and compares inventory requirements with current and incoming inventory. On the supply side, it translates these demand-side requirements into supply side orders on the producer. All the overhead activities related to both sides — order tracking, matching shipments/receipts against orders, missed or inaccurate orders, etc. — are carried out related to sales or purchase orders.

In addition to the information flow in which the distributor acts as the connection between the customer and the producer, an entire internal information flow is required. Recording incoming shipments, tracking inventory quantities and locations within the facility, performing periodic inventory counts and dealing with inventory adjustments, preparing pick lists and routings for outgoing shipments, and planning and recording delivery runs are all internal informational activities for the distributor. For most distributors the internal information flow is automated at least to a basic extent and often with quite sophisticated data collection, processing, and reporting capabilities. Looked at in isolation, this is a very positive condition. Looked at in the context of the flow of product from the producer to the user, we will see other possible configurations that change the set of activities that the distributor performs to fit into a different product/information flow than that described here.

Step 14: Producer Planning and Control Activities

The product/information loop is closed when demand information comes back to the producer. The producer first evaluates demand against on-hand inventory quantities and planned production orders, and if demand can be satisfied by current or projected inventory, then that will be used to fulfill the demand. If not, the producer enters or adjusts production orders as needed to meet the demand.

Once the producer is able to fulfill demand, the final connection is made. The demand information is converted into a replenishment order, and product is prepared and shipped. In this way, information is converted into action, and the flow begins its cycle over again.

We have seen the limitations of the standard Supply Chain way of operating at each step of the way, and there are limitations at this step also. One of the major ones is that in this methodology, the producer's horizon extends only as far as the next player, the distributor. The producer knows the demand coming in from the distributor, and ships product to the distributor. This is the universe the producer is operating in, and it does not include the entire flow of the producer's product or the return of information from the user several steps away. The issues related to a min/max approach to operation are described above, and even a producer using an MRP (material requirements planning) system that is more closely tuned into customer demand is still missing the total picture related to the demand pattern.

Supply Chain as Baseline

We have worked through the entire cycle of operation of a standard Supply Chain configuration for a producer of liquid products. This flow is our "baseline", that is, the basic configuration against which we will compare other concepts and approaches related to liquid logistics. Although we have pointed out drawbacks to the standard Supply Chain configuration, these are not viewed as a value judgment; many companies are extraordinarily successful using the standard Supply Chain configuration, and for others they have achieved the degree of success that is possible given the constraints of the world they are operating in. Having viewed this way of operating, however, our next step is to see how the fact that the product we are working with is liquid can affect, and in fact enhance, this flow. The next step is not to jump forward revolutionarily, but rather to consider the liquid nature of our product and see what evolutionary advances we can make based on the standard Supply Chain configuration.

Adapted Supply Chain

Now that we have laid out a baseline flow of product and information associated with a Supply Chain in the previous section, we can take the next step of seeing how it might be moved toward an Adapted Supply Chain. A useful exercise, though, would be for you to spend a moment evaluating your own operations related to liquids against this baseline flow. Out of the steps described for Supply Chain, how many of them do your liquid products go through during the logistics flow? If you recognize a good deal of your current method of operation in this baseline configuration, the following configurations — Adapted Supply Chain, Supply Chain for Liquids, and Optimal Supply Chain for Liquids — represent improvements that you can make to your operations and your company.

If you feel that your liquid logistics is perhaps not all that it could be, you are in very good company, you might say company of biblical proportions. The Bible provides us insight into liquid logistics in several ways, one of which could be called "do-it-yourself" Supply Chain. In Genesis 24, Rebekah offers to water all ten of Eliezer's camels, thirsty after a long journey. A thirsty camel can slurp 25 gallons at a rate of five gallons per minute, so assuming Rebekah was hefting a ten-gallon jug on her shoulder, she trotted down to the well 25 times in as close to five minutes as she could. Put in logistics terms, satisfying a total of 250 gallons of demand from ten customers was constrained by the delivery container and method: one water-carrier with one jug. It may be that Rebekah did not even have the time or the energy to stop and think about a better way to run this logistics activity.

The goal of the Adapted Supply Chain stage is to achieve some incremental benefit for relatively low effort. Remember that according to the Liquid Lens technique, this stage is not being taken haphazardly or independently, but as part of an overall plan toward an optimal Supply Chain for Liquids. This will neither maximize the benefit nor gain the most efficiencies that are available, but it will provide a "proof of design and implementation" for improvements in the Supply Chain. This step is evolutionary rather than revolutionary; its approach is to ask the question, "Within what we are doing now, how can we tweak or improve the system while minimizing effort or disruption?" This step should be designed such that the results of this step will build toward the ultimate goal while minimizing throw-away activities that will later be abandoned in favor of further improvements.

This type of change can be done at a number of points in the Supply Chain baseline, but for the purpose of this illustration we will use the simple exercise of moving from relatively small liquid containers to larger bulk or semibulk containers. That is, the shipping containers will be increased in volume, and some associated peripheral changes will be made, but the basic methodology used will remain the same. This change is mapped into the baseline flow in Exhibit 5.2.

The easiest situation to execute is that in which we undertake a "size upgrading" project, in which we review customer sales history over a specific period (for example, per month over the past year) and move the customer from smaller container sizes to larger container sizes. For example, if the customer's purchases of a product average eight five-gallon jugs per month, the Adapted Supply Chain upgrade may be that the customer accepts a 55-gallon drum with less frequent deliveries, along with a shift in how customer personnel use/dispense the liquid. This step helps both sides exercise "muscles" that they may not have known they had, with the goal of helping build strength as they move toward the Optimal Supply Chain for Liquids.

Producer/Distributor

The distribution system thinks in terms of the trade-off of packaging and delivery efficiency rather than being tied to "whatever the customer orders." In fact, under Optimal Supply Chain for Liquids, a vendor-managed inventory-type situation occurs in which the supplier initiates the replenishment cycle. The move to consider the trade-off of packaging and delivery efficiency is the first step toward introducing the manner of thinking that could lead to acceptance of a vendor-managed replenishment cycle. Creating the opportunity for a reduced number of deliveries with the corresponding reduction in expenses while increasing the per-delivery quantity also builds in the direction of the Supply Chain for Liquids. It is, of course, preferable to develop this approach within the framework of package-size "upgrading," as described above. However, companies have introduced the use of IBCs to accomplish a similar purpose. In any case, some reduction in pricing as reflected in lower per-unit price in larger packaging may be put in place and will be a partial trade-off for reduced distribution costs.

Customer

Like the supplier, the customer can also take some modest incremental steps toward Supply Chain for Liquids during this stage. For example, in an environment where employees carry two-gallon jugs to different points

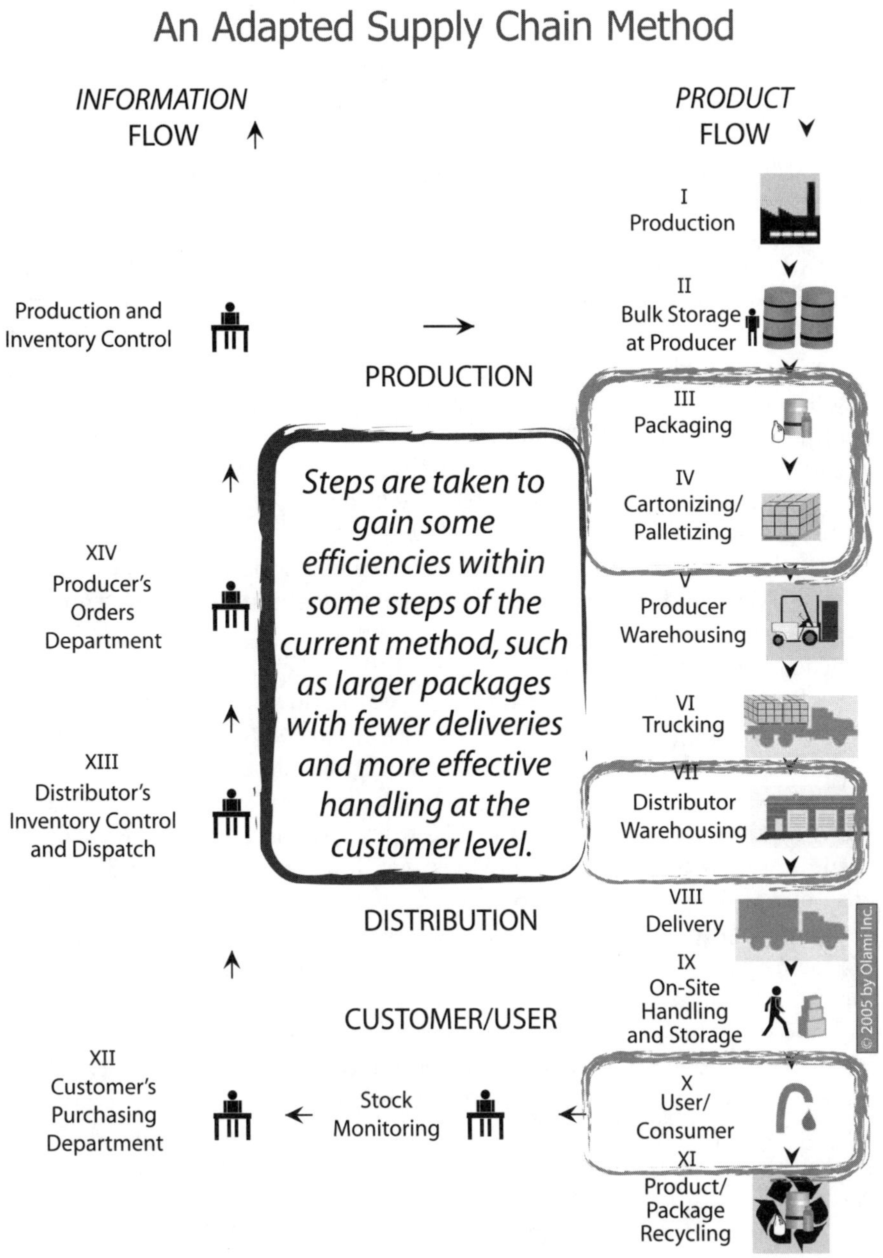

An Adapted Supply Chain Method

INFORMATION
FLOW ↑

PRODUCT
FLOW ∨

I
Production

Production and
Inventory Control ⟶

II
Bulk Storage
at Producer

PRODUCTION

III
Packaging

> *Steps are taken to gain some efficiencies within some steps of the current method, such as larger packages with fewer deliveries and more effective handling at the customer level.*

IV
Cartonizing/
Palletizing

XIV
Producer's
Orders
Department

V
Producer
Warehousing

VI
Trucking

XIII
Distributor's
Inventory Control
and Dispatch

VII
Distributor
Warehousing

DISTRIBUTION

VIII
Delivery

IX
On-Site
Handling
and Storage

CUSTOMER/USER

XII
Customer's
Purchasing
Department

Stock
Monitoring

X
User/
Consumer

XI
Product/
Package
Recycling

© 2005 by Olami Inc.

Exhibit 5.2   Adapted Supply Chain Improves upon Specific Points of a Supply Chain Configuration

in the user facility, the introduction of larger containers could support the introduction of a dispense system that would make the employees' work more efficient. In an automobile-service garage with several bays, tubing that draws motor oil from a central drum and allows dispense at each bay can be a more efficient system than one in which an employee takes jugs from a central storeroom. Such an internal distribution/dispense system will also hold good throughout the upgrade process to the Optimal Supply Chain for Liquids level, and so it can truly be considered a step forward toward the goal that has been established. Again, in a true Liquid Lens approach, planning for the Adapted Supply Chain step does not follow implementation of the Supply Chain step. Rather, Optimal Supply Chain for Liquids planning has already been undertaken to define the ultimate target in the "know your goal" fashion described previously. Adapted Supply Chain comes as an interim step in moving from the Supply Chain toward the Optimal Supply Chain for Liquids. Thus any steps taken within the Adapted Supply Chain framework will already have been defined in terms of how they fit into the overall logistics enhancement plan. This is a much more productive approach than having the players in the logistics flow sit down and design the next step each time a logistics-flow enhancement is made.

The exact technique used to approach the Adapted Supply Chain stage will of course depend on the industry, the product, and the relationships between the supplier and the customer. It might be to use larger package sizes and adapt the customer's internal distribution/dispense system, as described in the previous scenario, or it might involve some other incremental movement toward Supply Chain for Liquids. The Adapted Supply Chain stage represents an improvement for the supplier and for the customer, but it is not a departure from the basic thinking used by a company to run a standard Supply Chain operation. It is an improvement that gains operational efficiencies and cost reductions, but more important for the longer-term success of the company, it is the in-the-trenches beginning of the journey that can lead to extraordinary gains and effectiveness in the marketplace. Successful movement from Supply Chain thinking to Adapted Supply Chain thinking means that the key capabilities for the remainder of the effort have been proved, such as the ability to execute, coordination among the different players in the supply stream, and the leadership to envision and execute such a movement.

Supply Chain for Liquids

Moving to the Supply Chain for Liquids configuration represents the point where the logistics paradigm changes. Although this stage is fully planned out in advance on the path to Optimal Supply Chain for Liquids, this is the phase in which "change management" is most critical. Not only are the physical aspects of product logistics altered, along with a change in the functions performed by various individuals along the process, but the basic method of doing business is changed. The replenishment process is still driven by a "pull" approach based on customer requirements, but instead of the customer initiating the order, the replenishment order is issued directly from the supplier based on data received from the customer site. The Supply Chain for Liquids stage, as with all the stages, is carefully planned in advance, including the equipment, procedure, personnel, process, and information-flow elements. It is no longer packaging that is being moved, but product. The transportation method, the way liquids are held and used on-site, the information flow — all are altered during this stage.

Before we get into the details of how the Supply Chain for Liquids system works, we can look at an historical example of people in a similar situation. The Romans had a very strong knowledge of liquids and their uses. This knowledge extended to many areas — their baths with extraordinary water-heating systems; cisterns with extensive local water-collection systems; and jars for transporting and storing oils, wine, water, and other consumables. In their engineering brilliance, they realized that container-based liquid logistics was highly constrained by the container. This became most clear to them as the population of the city of Rome grew and the local water supplies were unable to keep up with the demand. Pulling water out of the ground and moving it in buckets or barrels was not an efficient process. Thus the issue of discrete-based versus liquids-based approaches to liquid logistics is not at all new, but has been around for thousands of years.

We can look to Sextus Julius Frontinus as an example of how the Romans addressed their water issues. Frontinus was the first Commissioner of Aqueducts for Rome, and in truest Roman form, he was entirely focused on the practicalities of the situation — the need for Rome to have a sufficient water supply. In his writings Frontinus bad-mouths both the Pyramids and famous Greek structures as being "useless," that is, although they were important from an engineering perspective they were misdirected because they did not serve a function that benefits the state. Frontinus tells us all about the aqueducts — how they were built and how they worked — with a clear level of enthusiasm.

Discrete logisticians find the Appian Way interesting as an overland road used heavily for commerce, but liquid logisticians will find the Aqua Appia more to their liking. The Aqua Appia was the first of 11 aqueduct systems built in Rome that would eventually amount to over 300 miles in total length and serve the daily needs of over one million people with

300 million gallons of water. Like many of the aqueducts, most of Aqua Appia ran underground, with only certain portions running over the stone-arch structures we normally associate with aqueducts. The builders of the aqueducts did not believe in interim inventory, and for the most part, water flowed from the source to the endpoints continually without large cisterns in the middle or at the end of the flow. They also built the aqueduct systems to require minimal operational effort; almost all of them are downhill from source to end and operate based on the flow caused by gravity. Because different aqueducts had different sources, their names often reflected the character of the water they carried. For example, Aqua Tepula delivered tepid water, and others were known for carrying clear water or for low-quality water that was used for gardens. Today's positioning of bottled waters would not have been lost on the Romans and their "positioning" of aqueducts.

Vetruvius wrote an excellent description of the Roman aqueduct system that explains the three construction methods used. The first of these called for the use of walled conduits. Upon reaching the city, the water passed through a channeling station that directed it to its final destination. Some of it went to baths, some to fountains, and the rest to private houses. This division was done in an interesting way. The aqueduct water flowed into a channel with three inlet pipes, one above the other. The lowest inlet pipe went to the public fountains so that the general public would have access to it. Above it was the inlet to the baths, and the highest inlet pipe was to the system that fed to private houses. Should the flow of water slow down and the level drop, private consumption would be the first to be reduced or stop altogether.

The second system used lead pipes to transport water. As can be well understood, a virtual army of workers was required to keep the system in repair and to fix the leaks that occurred. It is the lead in the pipes that echoes down to us today as a remnant of that activity. "Lead" in Latin is *plumbum*, and the workers who toiled so hard to keep the system going were "plumbers." That also explains lead's symbol in the periodic table, Pb.

The third, and most economical, method was the use of earthenware pipes. They were no less than two inches thick and joined together. The earthenware pipes had several advantages. They were very easy to repair, and the water was not contaminated by lead. As a result, the flavor of the water was better, and the workers were much less affected by the use of clay than by using lead. Matching the material used in the system to the product carried by the system was an important consideration in Roman times, as it is today.

The proliferation of a new technology often creates a need for regulation, as we see even today. Not surprising, then, along with the aqueducts came many laws and procedures. Theodosius, for example, issued a proclamation in the fifth century that dealt with landowners who had aqueducts pass through their lands. If a landowner had aqueducts on his property, he was exempted from large taxes and other burdens so that he could concentrate on keeping the aqueduct clean and in good working order. But if the landowner neglected this duty, he was subject to forfeiture of his lands. Effective liquid logistics was not just a "nice-to-have"; it was a civic obligation that entailed both rewards for success and punishment for improper fulfillment. The engineering writings that describe the technical aspects of the Romans' liquids-based methods make fascinating reading not despite, but perhaps because of, the two millennia that separate us and them.

The Roman environment combined the characteristics that are necessary for the success of a Supply Chain for Liquids project: awareness of and desire to utilize the most appropriate techniques and technology available, a need for effective liquid-logistics processes, and the leadership to make it happen. Being aware of and using these aspects of the Roman approach can only help us as we approach similar projects. We should also be careful not to take too lightly the Roman accomplishments with the aqueducts. Before the Romans built the aqueducts so extensively, they were a rarely used method for carrying water, and after the fall of the Roman empire, more than 1000 years would pass before anyone built aqueducts in any significant degree. The aqueducts were a liquid-logistics phenomenon that required boldness, vision, and a lot of thought, which we should not lose sight of as we view the magnificence of their results.

The Roman approach that integrated methods, materials, objectives, and leadership/rules serves to reinforce the Liquid Lens method of looking at the entire system rather than the individual parts. Let us look at an example of how focusing on one piece of the flow is completely unsatisfactory. When setting thresholds, be they time or quantity, it is natural to "fudge" a little and throw in a bit of extra padding. So the sales department could quote as a standard that there is a three-day lead time for customer deliveries, even though the process of delivering — picking, loading, and delivering — is closer to a one-day process. In this case, it would be erroneous to pick out this single element — the quoted delivery lead time — and try to reduce it simply by quoting one-day delivery time to the customer. The systems are not in place to support that sort of commitment; the time frame for executing the process has been set at three days, and that is how the mechanisms are working. Given that there is probably a three-day backlog in the process, a one-day promise will lead to some customers not getting their deliveries within the time promised to them.

On the other hand, if we put the systems in place to execute next-day deliveries with a high degree of certainty, the next-day delivery quote would be beneficial for many reasons: improved competitive position in the marketplace, higher inventory velocity, improved cash flow from order to payment, etc. The point is that although you can make "spot" fixes to some problems, many logistics situations require a solution that encompasses a broader scope. Similarly, you tweak interim improvements to move from Supply Chain to Adapted Supply Chain, but moving to Supply Chain for Liquids requires integrated, coordinated, systemwide action.

As another example, companies frequently go on campaigns to reduce inventory levels. Inventory is often held because each step along the process wants to protect itself by establishing something of an inventory buffer, a little extra on-hand quantity to cover exception conditions and ensure the required level of customer service. With the system built to plump up inventory, an inventory-reduction campaign is like going on a quick-fix diet. You may temporarily see some reduction, but it will all come back and possibly more because you have not done anything to change the fundamentals. On the other hand, once you change the fundamentals, the resulting savings (such as reduced inventory levels) become a natural outgrowth. It is this changing of the fundamentals, not the quick fix, that Supply Chain for Liquids is all about.

Such a fundamental change is not easy within an organization, and it is even more difficult between organizations. This is why the Adapted Supply Chain configuration that precedes the Supply Chain for Liquids configuration is so important. The example given earlier about moving to Adapted Supply Chain is not random, but rather involved a coordinated change between the supplier and the customer. The supplier switches to a different type of delivery container, and the customer adjusts the liquid flow/dispense system within the on-site facility. Such an exercise allows a change to be planned and executed with relatively little investment or risk, and it will prove that the capability for coordinated change is in place. With this foundation, the more extensive changes required by Supply Chain for Liquids are more likely to be accomplished successfully. Even companies that share a common vision as to how the logistics flow between them should ultimately work should develop incremental steps to ensure the success of the ultimate objective.

This emphasis on planning is an important differentiator between true Supply Chain for Liquids systems and systems that have evolved to include some of the elements of Supply Chain for Liquids. Intention is an important part of achievement; indeed, it usually drives achievement. We should not be misled into thinking that implementation of some part of the system, such as sensors, is the same as running a fully integrated Supply Chain for Liquids system. Sometimes things can be achieved without full intention, but they are most notable as exceptions. For example, as the crowd looked with riotous anger at the Bastille in Paris, with its ten-foot-thick walls and towers soaring over 90 feet high, they knew what they wanted but did not have a specific plan for getting inside the structure. The Marquis de Launay, the governor of the Bastille, was ready to fight with plenty of men and ammunition, so the situation looked formidable. The crowd made little progress until de Launay lowered a drawbridge to admit some artillery of the Royal Guard, at which point the crowd rushed in and history was made. This is a case in which the objective was achieved from a general idea rather than a specific plan; in running our business, we should not rely on a de Launay to show up one day to let down the drawbridge that will lead us to our next logistical success.

In transitioning from Adapted Supply Chain to Supply Chain for Liquids, we look at our entire operational process through the Liquid Lens and evaluate it based on Liquid Lens principles. As part of this review we work with our customers to identify the liquids that would be more effectively used in bulk-dispense form rather than in bottles or other containers, and we then define the processes needed to convert and operate the logistics cycle from package-based to liquids-based operation.

In the Supply Chain for Liquids scenario diagrammed in Exhibit 5.3, we have moved from package-based distribution to a liquids-based distribution method. The liquid is held in bulk tanks at the production site and transferred to compartmentalized bulk trucks for transport. At the customer site, the liquids are not delivered as in a standard discrete-based method — with containers physically transferred into the customer facility — but rather passed directly from the delivery truck through a port in the facility wall and into mini-bulk tanks on the customer site. From the mini-bulk tanks, the liquids are fed directly to the dispense point, so the first nonbulk handling of the liquid since production is when the end user actually dispenses the liquid and is ready to use it. The on-site mini-bulk system includes liquid-level sensors that read and report product quantity-on-hand information at the frequency defined for the system. This entire system has been built as a flow, and none of the individual parts would work as effectively (or in some cases, work at all) if the entire flow did not "fit together" from a product-flow and information-flow perspective.

Let us break down the transition elements and compare them with the steps we defined for our Supply Chain "baseline" system so that we can fully understand them and their impact on the overall process.

Step 1: Production

Under a Supply Chain for Liquids configuration, a number of tools become available beyond the previously described min/max or MRP systems to help the producer plan production more effectively. Using data supplied

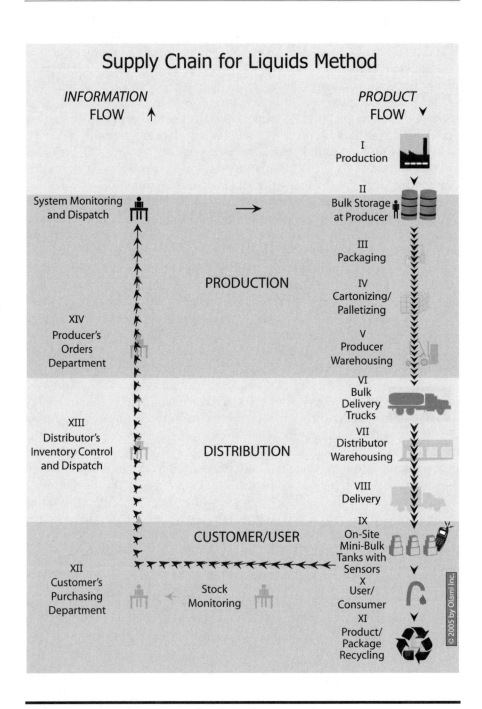

Exhibit 5.3   A Supply Chain for Liquids Configuration

by the RFID for Liquids® (Radio Frequency Identification for Liquids®) system and channeled through the CPVR^SM (Coordinated Procedures for Visibility Response^SM) relationships with other players along the supply stream (as described in Chapter 10), the producer gets advance warning about spikes and troughs in the demand pattern. It is like a child playing in the waves at the beach. The child who is scared and closes her eyes waits to jump until she feels the wave is getting high, so she jumps as the wave is passing and is still in the air well into the following trough. She lost twice; she was hit by the wave and also did not take advantage of the trough to rest. The child who keeps her eyes open and has visibility into what is coming sees the waves and knows when to jump; she also avoids overreaction by knowing of the trough that follows. Instead of responding to the spike separately and then the trough separately, as occurs using a min/max approach or even an MRP approach based on internal data, the producer has the information needed to develop an effective production and inventory plan that takes into account both spikes and troughs. In turn, this longer view allows the producer to better utilize production resources and work in planning mode rather than firefighting mode to meet customers' requirements.

Step 2: Bulk Storage at Producer

The bulk storage of product at the producer takes on a much greater role under the Supply Chain for Liquids configuration. For any product that will be maintained in liquid form throughout the logistics flow, it is of course maintained in bulk form at the producer. To the degree to which products stop moving through the subsequent steps of packaging and cartonizing/palletizing, that capacity is moved to bulk storage at the producer.

The expansion of bulk-storage capability under the Supply Chain for Liquids configuration includes replacement of racks with tanks, placement of tanks on racks, or some other transition from discrete-based to tank-based storage for the liquids involved. This is done using an approach that meets the ultimate objective. Because tanks can hold double or more of the volume of liquid as the same amount of rack space, the expansion of bulk-storage capacity does not necessarily mean that more warehouse space is going to be used. Changing storage from a package-based to a liquids-based methodology will actually require less warehouse space for the same amount of liquid.

However, the tanks holding the liquids are not the only focus of the Supply Chain for Liquids approach. The goal is to take full advantage of the liquid nature of the product, so the arrangement of the tanks; the piping from the production area to the tanks, between the tanks, and from the tanks to the truck-fill area; the method of propelling the liquids in the pipes and tanks; and the method used to continuously monitor the quantity of liquids in the system are all part of the bulk-storage design. As described in Chapter 8, the planning for the sizes of the tanks and the ability to swap liquids between the tanks are important factors to maintain flexibility as demand shifts between different liquid products. As the supply source for the entire logistics stream, the producer bulk tanks are set up to move liquid products quickly and effectively into the Supply Pipe^{SM}.

Step 3: Packaging

Eliminating packaging eliminates the whole set of activities described earlier in the packaging step of Supply Chain (step 3). The packaging equipment used in the postproduction process, the packaging material and the warehouse space it requires, and the manpower related to packaging (such as purchasing, line attendants, maintenance crew, inventory people, the packaging planning function) — these all are eliminated when the packaging step is eliminated from the process. In place of individual packages, the liquid product is held in bulk or semi-bulk tanks. These may be the same tanks in which the liquid is held at the end of production and before packaging, or they may be separate holding tanks. Unlike packaging, these tanks do not move, are not handled as part of the distribution logistics, and do not require disposal or recycling. They are an investment whose cost can be measured on a per-gallon basis across the total number of gallons of liquid that are projected to flow through them for the lifetime of the equipment. Also unlike individual containers, these tanks can be made of the same material as that used for the production equipment, thus preserving the liquid in its native environment beyond the production process. In fact, this is true for the remainder of the equipment throughout the logistics process — the on-truck tanks and the on-site tanks — so that the liquid remains in its optimal environment until the point of dispense.

The packaging step can be used as a specific example of a general question that comes up during planning for Supply Chain for Liquids implementation. In most situations, moving to Supply Chain for Liquids is a valid and attractive option for some of a producer's liquids, but the usage of other liquids requires that they be in some type of package or container. For example, an automotive lubricant producer may determine, together with its vehicle-repair and -maintenance customers, that it is preferable to use a Supply Chain for Liquids configuration rather than selling to these customers in packages. On the other hand, the same producer may need to sell the same products to retail stores in quart or gallon containers, as they will be purchased individually by consumers and must be conveniently carried from the store. In this case, the packaging line will not disappear; rather, it will continue to be used but less frequently than when all products passed through it. In terms of performance measurement or financial analysis, the utilization of the equipment is likely to drop based on this change. The same might be said, for example, of the delivery trucks, as discussed below. If I am sending a delivery truck that contains not only packaged liquids but also discrete products to a customer anyway, is it not a duplication of effort to send both a tank truck and a delivery truck to the same customer? If my warehouse space is fixed, what is my benefit if I use my storage space more efficiently only to create more empty space?

There are many factors to take into account in evaluating this issue, and of course the results of the evaluation should feed into the design of the Optimal Supply Chain for Liquids. These issues are discussed in detail in Chapter 11. Apart from the analysis presented there, we can present the question in a different light, a light that is useful in evaluating many types of questions. Let us ask the question, "What decision would my competitor like to see me make?" Although the purely objective/financial analysis is useful to have and understand, there are marketplace and competitive elements that we should take into account as well. If our decision makes our competitors happy, it is likely that we should rethink that decision.

Step 4: Cartonizing/Palletizing

The cartonizing/palletizing step is viewed very similarly to the packaging step within a Supply Chain for Liquids operation. Within pure Supply Chain for Liquids, it is completely eliminated for those liquids flowing through the system. There are no bottles or jugs, so there is nothing to cartonize or palletize.

Step 5: Producer Warehousing

Because the liquids are held in bulk tanks, there is no need for all of the usual means of moving and holding them when they are in packages — hand trucks, forklifts, racking systems, and the like. Within the warehouse, they may be moved between tanks as required using a pressure or pumping method without any manual effort. In this sense, they can be moved without being moved. The sizes of the bulk tanks can be set based on the storage quantities of the different liquids, taking into account required segregation (nonconsumable versus consumable liquids, for example), optimal tank material in which to hold each liquid, etc. Larger tanks can be compartmentalized to provide further flexibility in the capacity available and the ability to shift the capacity among different liquids.

Such standard warehouse functions as picking, pulling, staging, and loading become irrelevant as the entire mind-set of storing and shipping changes. The process of picking-pulling-staging-loading is replaced by a single flow as the liquid is pumped directly from the storage tank to the appropriate tank truck for transport and delivery. This is not to say that this stage does not require planning and thought. For example, the piping from the tanks to the truck-filling area must conform to all the operational requirements: fill rate, pumping method, etc. In addition, if liquids are intermixable, then fewer pipes are required, corresponding to the number of liquids that are to be carried in the tank truck during delivery runs so that multiple liquids can be filled onto the truck simultaneously. If use of common pipes would cause contamination of the liquids, then each liquid should have its own pipe so that cleaning the pipes will not be required, with each pipe carrying a specific type of liquid. The truck-filling area should be planned for maximum efficiency. For example, rather than moving trucks to a single filling position, it is more time-efficient to have the trucks park in a filling area and allow the piping to be moved from truck to truck for the filling operation, or to have sufficient piping to fill multiple trucks at the same time.

Moreover, inventory counting becomes irrelevant, as liquid-level sensors in each tank provide virtually continuous information about the exact quantity of each liquid present in the system. The value of this capability should not be underestimated. The manual effort associated with inputting and processing stock transactions is often extensive. The warehouse person often records a stock transaction manually and passes it for data input, or a radio-frequency or similar device might be used to directly input the stock transaction data. In either case, these transactions are subject to error, failure, overlooking, or duplication. Any of these anomalies will cause inaccurate inventory information in the information-processing system. The immediate availability of direct inventory information can also address other causes of inventory shrink or inventory bloat. For example, theft can be readily detected by simply closing the loop on automatic inventory transactions. After a filling operation, if the in-tank balance of a liquid does not equal the starting balance less the quantities recorded as having been used to fill the trucks, then liquid has been siphoned off outside of the fill process. Similarly, detection of reduction in the in-tank balance during off-hours, when trucks are not being filled and there is no other reason for taking liquid from a tank, points to activity that should be investigated.

Space utilization in the warehouse or storage area is radically improved under a tank versus a package approach. As described in Chapter 11, bottles in cartons on pallets contain an amount of liquid that is equivalent to something on the order of 50 to 60 percent of the space taken by the pallet and cartons. In other words, liquids held in tanks take about half the space as the same amount of liquids held in packages. Thus you can use a much smaller facility to hold the same amount of liquids in tanks as you do in packages, or inversely, you will need a much larger warehouse to hold packaged liquids than tanked liquids. Add to this the aisles needed for forklift access to pallets and packages, the limitations on height imposed by forklift reach, and other space requirements for packaged goods that do not exist for bulk-held liquids, and the net savings in space can reach the 70 to 80 percent level.

Quality issues are also addressed by the tank-versus-package approach to warehousing and inventory movement. In a bay-type warehousing system, in which cartons of a product are stacked in a bay or area of floor space, the picker naturally tends toward a LIFO system, where the newest cartons to arrive are placed at the front of the bay, and these are also the first ones to be picked to be loaded onto the trucks. From a quality perspective, this runs counter to a FIFO system, which promotes stock rotation and takes the oldest product first. Proper FIFO operation in a bay-based warehouse with front-only access requires that the forklift driver move the existing stock to the side, put away the new stock in the back of the bay, and then return the older stock to the front of the bay — a mission that is at odds with working as quickly as possible and getting the put-away process done in as short a period as possible.

Step 6: Trucking, Step 7: Distributor Warehousing, and Step 8: Delivery

This is one of the areas in which the integration and efficiency of a Supply Chain for Liquids design come to full fruition. A combination of factors lets us think in terms that are unthinkable in a standard Supply Chain environment. Extraordinary visibility into inventory balances all along the Supply Chain for Liquids, including that being held at the customer site; elimination of the need to guard against inaccuracy and uncertainty that usually leads to holding of stock at points along the Supply Chain; physical techniques that make the transportation and delivery processes far more efficient than is possible using discrete-based approaches; and range-extending delivery methods as described in Chapter 7 — all of these are characteristics of Supply Chain for Liquids that let us break the barrier and create a new dynamic for transportation and delivery of liquid products.

Let us walk through this process and see exactly how it works. We have complete visibility into current inventory at all of our customers as well as the most recent usage history — even up to the last several hours based on the sensor-reporting frequency that has been defined — and can readily identify the customers and products that are "must deliver" at current inventory and usage levels. For all noncritical customers/products, which will be the vast majority, we use our adaptation of vendor-managed inventory (VMI) to our advantage. We are using VMI in the sense that the supplier, or whichever party has taken the lead in system monitoring and dispatch, is initiating the replenishment process rather than waiting for an order from the customer. This is not VMI in the sense of the vendor setting up and replenishing display racks and other commonly understood VMI activities. Under our system, we have the flexibility to use fixed routes, to adapt to flexible routes for the most effective delivery schemes, to either complete-fill or top-off customers, or to delay what would be a normal delivery based on what makes the most efficient use of *our* delivery capability. Because we can plan the next day's route with a high degree of efficiency, we can get a high degree of utilization of our trucks. We know that what we send out is what will be passed to the customer with neither additions nor reductions.

The high degree of efficiency comes not only from knowing quantities in advance, but also from the Supply Chain for Liquids allowing us to deliver during low-traffic night hours. This is the result of the Supply Chain for Liquids delivery method based on the fact that we are working with liquid products. We deliver through a secured port in an outside wall of the facility, without need to enter the building. The delivery person extends a hose or hoses from the truck and attaches them to a fitting in the port. The fittings include error-proof shaping that prevents the delivery person from attaching the wrong hose to the wrong fitting, or attaching the hose in the wrong way, even if the operation is being carried out in the dark of night. As described in Chapter 10, the delivery person enters the customer number into the data device on the truck, and the required amount of each liquid is metered through the delivery flow, removing quantity error from the amount of product delivered. This predetermined quantity and metering also frees up the delivery person to attach a delivery hose and begin its flow and then move on to the next hose/liquid, so that multiple liquids are delivered simultaneously. Although a multitube bundled hose configuration would be even more efficient, the weight of several tubes bound together and attached to a multiconnector dock makes it impractical in situations in which larger hoses are used to provide greater liquid throughput and faster delivery speed.

Because deliveries are made "through the wall" rather than requiring the delivery person to enter the premises, the driver can make vastly better use of the hours-of-service (HOS) period. Much less time will be spent in traffic, limited by rush-hour restrictions or finding alternative routes to the next destination. At the same time, the delivery itself will be much faster: plug in, pump, and pull out. Physical handling of the product, interaction with customer personnel, recording or printing the transaction — all of these are eliminated, so the per-site delivery time is radically reduced. The extended-range capability described in Chapter 7 and the increased capacity of our trucks (because they are carrying bulk rather than packaged products) at the customer site (again, because it is held in bulk) means that we can consider replacing the warehouse/distribution center with a process that better pinpoints the placement of product where it is needed and when it is needed.

Given the powerful distribution capabilities that Supply Chain for Liquids offers as described previously and detailed later, the concept of eliminating the warehouse/distribution center becomes viable in many cases. As the overall flow is laid out using the Liquid Lens approach, it might become apparent that a small increase in inventory at each customer site could increase the efficiency of the total distribution system by eliminating the need for interim warehousing. An increase in on-site inventory does not have to be to the detriment of the customer, either physically or financially. With a tank-based system, product can be stored in currently "dead" storage space at the customer's location (as described in Chapter 8), and the availability of highly accurate and highly current information makes possible a consignment-type arrangement that provides flexibility in the financial accounting for on-site inventory. In other words, on-site inventory is a very small and painless price to pay for the tremendous efficiencies and savings gained through potential elimination of an interim warehousing arrangement. Excellent information and excellent process combine to change the entire way of thinking of the transportation and delivery function.

Step 9: On-Site Handling and Storage

The customer Supply Chain for Liquids represents a radical step forward in terms of operations. In contrast to the previously described activities and problems for on-site handling and storage under the Supply Chain scenario, the Supply Chain for Liquids user can quite literally "forget about it." There is no more need for the customer to be concerned about activities related to on-site liquids, such as moving jugs, cartons, or drums; replacing empties; inventorying and reordering materials; or disposing of empty packaging. The liquids are delivered directly, maintained and monitored automatically, and are always available at the point of dispense, all without any involvement by (or disruption of) on-site personnel.

Using a tank arrangement on-site does, however, require some setup work and ongoing maintenance, which can be performed by either the Supply Chain for Liquids service provider or the facility personnel. When the tank configuration needs to be changed, for example to shift a tank or tanks from one liquid to another, the valving and connections needed to be altered to meet the new requirements. The tank configuration must be defined to allow proper calculation of on-site balance for each liquid, and all of the mechanical and electrical equipment must be periodically serviced and maintained. While much of this work is manual, responsibility for it may be shifted away from on-site personnel.

Having said this, though, the tank configuration can of itself yield great benefit. For example, in many restaurants, backroom floor space is at a premium, and there just is not enough room to store all of the supplies and products needed to run the restaurant. A standard bag-in-box (BIB) rack, together with the storage area for the BIB cartons, takes up a significant amount of floor space. They must be at floor level, as users must take the BIB units from the storage area and place them in the racks where they are connected to the dispense lines.

Under a tank-based approach, all of this floor space can be completely freed up and used for other purposes. The tanks do not have to be placed on the floor, because they do not have to be accessed regularly by store personnel. They can be affixed to the walls, placed on overhead racks, set into above-ceiling spaces (as long as there is proper temperature control and there are no safety or other issues), or located in other spaces that are not currently used and not necessarily usable for any other purpose. This flexibility derives from the fact that the tanks do not need to be accessed by personnel and from the method used to drive both inflow (fill) and outflow (dispense). Fill can be driven by gravity, gas pressure, or a pump on the truck, and dispense can be driven by gravity or gas to the lowest point in the tank arrangement, and then by gas or a dispense pump from the lower point of the tanks to the point of dispense. In any case, the vertical positioning of the tanks is completely flexible, as the liquid is driven in the most appropriate way within the existing configuration of tanks and piping.

The on-site tanks contain sensors and data-transmission equipment that allow system monitoring virtually continuously without any on-site involvement. There are many alternative approaches to the kinds of sensors that can be used and how they will function in the system, as described in Chapter 8. For the purpose of this overview, the data coming directly out of the tanks ensure that the central site will always be aware of the inventory balance of each liquid at each site, and be in a position to ensure that, from the customer's perspective, the tank is a "bottomless pit" that always supplies the liquid and never runs out. The data guiding all of the processes — whether related to monitoring inventory, creating a replenishment order and dispatching a delivery truck, or filling the tanks through an external port in the facility — are completely invisible to on-site personnel and do not require their involvement at any stage.

Step 10. User/Consumer

Having the liquid readily available at the point of dispense is a much more efficient setup for the user compared with fetching the liquid and bringing it to the point of use. A mechanic in a garage who can pull down a retractable hose and in a matter of seconds put four quarts into the motor is a bigger revenue generator than one who has to go to the storeroom and chew the fat with the storeroom operator for a few minutes before carrying the four quarts back to the bay, open the cans, pour each in, and then go throw away the cans. In environments that need to control or record dispense, such recording devices can be attached to the dispense line, as described in Chapter 8. Interestingly, some companies are going "beyond the user" to get the liquid directly to the end consumer. In some quick-serve restaurants, for example, the consumer pays for a beverage and receives an appropriately sized cup, and goes to the dispense machine and dispenses the beverage directly. This is the kind of thinking that the Liquid Lens encourages, and there are plenty of parallel opportunities to be exploited in other industries.

Step 11: Product/Package Recycling

As far as the package goes, the Supply Chain for Liquids process is clear: no package, no disposal, no recycling. Because many liquids are double-packaged — the container, such as a plastic jug, and the carton it is shipped in — there is a double savings in the elimination of packaging. The haulage required for waste removal and the collection area and cost of removal for cardboard cartons both represent expenses that are eliminated under the tank-based Supply Chain for Liquids approach. Each type of packaging has its own type of removal or recycling expense. Users of 55-gallon drums are sometimes required to remove the top and bottom or cut up the drum prior to disposal, and IBCs must be physically removed and returned to the supplier for refilling. All of these are package-related activities that add only expense but not value to the product itself. Other factors, such as conformance to governmental regulatory guidelines or achievement of an ISO-14001 Environmental Management System, may be drivers in moving to a Supply Chain for Liquids system. The environmental considerations related to Supply Chain for Liquids are discussed further in Chapter 11.

Step 12: Customer/User Planning and Control Activities, Step 13: Distributor Planning and Control Activities, and Step 14: Producer Planning and Control Activities

The overhead associated with inventory management is eliminated for some players and reduced for others in a Supply Chain for Liquids environment. The information flow is an integral part of Supply Chain for Liquids and is designed to integrate with the product flow and with the equipment in both directions. The equipment provides data to feed the information flow, and the information flow triggers actions related to the equipment.

At the user site, in-tank sensors (as described in Chapter 8) monitor liquid levels and transmit this information to the central information system as frequently as defined by the user. The manual user-site inventory-monitoring and -ordering function is completely eliminated and is handled instead by the producer or whichever player is doing the dispatching function based on information provided by the central information system. Depending on the elimination of the distribution center, or a modified role played by the distribution center in any particular application of the Supply Chain for Liquids configuration, the monitoring and ordering of inventory can be eliminated there also. This does not mean that these players lose contact into or control over inventory activity at their locations. In any case, the system can be set up in such a way that all demand information from the sites, as well as all replenishment, delivery, and other supply information, is available to all of the players via the Internet. In addition, the CPVR system (as described in Chapter 10) can be set up in such a way as to give the players as much of a role in the process as they choose to have, and still ensure that their actions are coordinated and that the full benefits of Supply Chain for Liquids become available to the whole system. By removing processes, complexity, and stages from the system, however, Supply Chain for Liquids creates a situation in which a single control function can cover a very large area in terms of the logistics flow. It is not that the control function is so improved or sophisticated, but rather that the elegant simplicity of the Supply Chain for Liquids operation serves to leverage the control function across the widest possible area.

As with the tanks at the supplier site, ongoing sensing of liquid level allows detection of exception conditions — suspiciously high dispense activity during a certain period, product usage when the facility is closed, etc. Under normal conditions in which product shortages are detected only during periodic inventory counts, it is difficult to pinpoint the source of some shortages. Virtually real-time information about abnormal product usage, on the other hand, allows immediate responsiveness and identification of the source of the shortage.

In addition to measuring on-hand balances for replenishment purposes and monitoring product for unusual usages, the Supply Chain for Liquids information flow can reduce or replace other user activities. In situations in which certain measurements are required for quality or other purposes, these can be included in the Supply Chain for Liquids information flow. The temperature of the liquid inside the system or the ambient temperature surrounding the tanks, the pressure of gas within the system, the frequency of tank cleanings, and other measures can be made an integral part of the Supply Chain for Liquids information flow by inserting the corresponding sensors into the system and passing the data to the appropriate recording facility.

Finally, Supply Chain for Liquids sensors can elevate the accuracy of consumption reporting to levels that are otherwise unavailable. Using the example of beverage dispensing by customers in a quick-serve restaurant, the restaurant knows how many cups of each size it sold, but can only infer usages based on periodic replenishment orders. With Supply Chain for Liquids, the restaurant has a high-resolution granular view of usage — detailed data not only regarding quantities of product dispensed and the on-hand balances, but even time stamping that will provide time-of-day and day-of-week data regarding dispensing of each specific beverage. Chapter 8 provides a further description of the customer-site information flow and how it can be constructed.

As data is passed from each site to the central information system, the central system evaluates on-hand balances and recent usage against planned deliveries and creates or adjusts replenishment orders as required. Chapter 10 describes the processing at the central system.

From the supplier's or distributor's point of view, the consolidation of data literally closes the loop in terms of operational planning and execution. As described in Chapter 10, the Supply Chain for Liquids approach provides visibility into product quantities all along the supply stream. Each player along the way can maximize the use of that visibility. For the producer/distributor, the information is used to create the most efficient production and shipping schedules, to set the most effective inventory balance targets, and to obtain the maximum return from every resource that the company has invested in along the length of the process.

Optimal Supply Chain for Liquids

After a company has made the leap from Supply Chain to Supply Chain for Liquids, the next step is to achieve Optimal Supply Chain for Liquids status. We will briefly describe Optimal Supply Chain for Liquids to distinguish it from the three prior statuses we have described. Chapter 11 discusses the concept of Optimal Supply Chain for Liquids in further detail, as well as the formal achievement of Optimal Supply Chain for Liquids status.

There are two aspects to Optimal Supply Chain for Liquids. The first relates to the internal operation of the Supply Chain for Liquids, and the second relates to the external results that have been obtained through achieving Optimal Supply Chain for Liquids. Let us look at each of these aspects.

The internal operation of the Supply Chain for Liquids system refers to the operation and interaction of all the players along the Supply Chain for Liquids flow. Optimal Supply Chain for Liquids means having fulfilled the plan that was originally laid out in looking at the entire logistics flow through the Liquid Lens with whatever adjustments may have been made along the way as the implementation effort unfolded. A company or group of companies operating an Optimal Supply Chain for Liquids system has the full product and information flow working in close synchronization and uses all the elements we have described — equipment, procedures, technology, resources — in one unified system. RFID for Liquids® and CPVR functionality are in place and are being used as was envisioned in the original plan, and the information flow ensures that the status and condition of the physical product is being monitored and responded to appropriately. By nature, a Supply Chain for Liquids system is not a static system, but rather a dynamic system that is able to handle the fluctuations and challenges of the logistics flow while staying within the working methodology of the system. A company that has achieved the Optimal Supply Chain for Liquids level of performance has the internal mechanisms in place to handle all of the variations that occur in the logistics process.

The external element of Optimal Supply Chain for Liquids points out that this entire effort was not undertaken as an academic exercise; it is not efficiency for the sake of efficiency. Rather, Optimal Supply Chain for Liquids creates a new position for the company in the marketplace and its relationships with customers and competitors. As anyone knows who has reached this level of success in any endeavor, it does not feel like the end of the effort, but rather like the beginning. Once you have achieved Optimal Supply Chain for Liquids, you begin to see the tremendous opportunities related to customers, products, and markets that are created by operating at such a high level of effectiveness, and you begin to pursue these opportunities. This is the external measure of having achieved Optimal Supply Chain for Liquids status — that new customer opportunities, revenue-generation opportunities, distribution-channel opportunities, and marketplace competitiveness opportunities have opened to the company based on its Supply Chain for Liquids capabilities. This is the true benefit of the Supply Chain for Liquids effort.

Case Study: Worldwide Liquids

The ability of a company to combine evolutionary and revolutionary thinking is shown in the path followed by Worldwide Liquids, a New York–based company that, through predecessor companies, has gone through the steps from Supply Chain to Supply Chain for Liquids — with a few extra steps included in the process.

Worldwide Liquids's earliest steps were as part of a beer wholesaler in the New York area for a well-known beer producer. As such, it followed Supply Chain principles rigorously, but even within this context it planted seeds of innovation that were unusual for a company in this tightly controlled setting. Two Supply Chain enhancements — (1) empowerment of route delivery personnel beyond the normal definition of their role and into partially autonomous business units, and (2) creation of a proactive customer satisfaction function with personnel dedicated to measuring and enhancing the customer experience — showed that normal Supply Chain practice was too confining for the company. The company took many steps in this direction. For example, during an early restructuring intended to bring its focus entirely onto the customer, the company organized itself into two departments. The sales department included all the direct customer-interacting functions, and the sales support department included all other functions in the company, such as accounting, warehousing, and so on. The entire company consisted only of these two departments, so all of the company's employees thought of their positions in terms of their relationships to the customer, be it direct or indirect.

Expanding beyond the boundaries of traditional business practice, the company widened its line of business — with a twist. Because wines were an extension of, but related to, its core business, the company decided to enter into that world while applying some Adapted Supply Chain principles. Rather than simply moving bottles and cases of wine as it had been moving bottles/cans and cases of beer, the company decided to apply the beer-barreling principle to wine. Supplying wine in barrels made a lot of sense for excellent Liquid Lens reasons. Wine is often consumed by the glass, and at the same time wine is highly sensitive to degradation once a bottle is opened and the wine is exposed to air. So restaurants that open a bottle of wine to serve one or two glasses to a customer may well lose the value of the remainder of the wine in the bottle, as the remaining wine goes bad very quickly.

Wine provided to the restaurant in a barrel with a protective gas layer resolves this problem and saves the restaurant quite a bit of money. The restaurant dispenses a glass of wine from the barrel and maintains the 100 percent quality level of the wine still in the barrel. From a logistics perspective, barrels represented movement toward bulk delivery and holding of the product, and the stainless steel barrels preserved product quality even better than the traditional bottle-and-cork container. (A surprisingly high percentage of wine bottles suffer from "cork taint" that makes the wine go bad.) Altogether, the approach to wine followed the path toward an Adapted Supply Chain configuration.

The geographic location for the wine barreling program was also carefully considered. There was a keen focus on imported wines in the United Kingdom at that time, and the market was more dynamic than that of the United States during the same period. The British were out to show that they had as fine a taste for wine as anyone else, and the rest of the world had identified the United Kingdom as one of the hottest markets for wines from all the corners of the world — Australia, Bulgaria, Chile, and everywhere in between. In addition, something of a break from bottled wines had occurred with the introduction of bag-in-box (BIB) wines. This methodology offered some of the advantages of the barreled-wine approach, although the nature of the coating in the bag and the air-permeable plastic fixtures associated with BIB dispensing supported the view that BIB wines were generally of inferior quality and not appropriate to better restaurants.

Following its introduction in the United Kingdom, the wine-barreling business soon expanded to continental Europe as well as to the East Coast and West Coast of the United States and to Asia, particularly in Japan. The expansion of the business in its Adapted Supply Chain configuration also provided the foundation for its transition to a Supply Chain for Liquids business, with a radically different logistics approach. As it happened, this was triggered by the expansion of the business to Japan.

For the European and American operation of the business, the process was more or less "local." For example, barrels were filled with wine in France and trucked to the United Kingdom, where they were held in a distribution center prior to delivery to individual restaurants. This paradigm worked well enough that there was no particular incentive to seek out a new paradigm. On the other hand, once the new paradigm was developed, it became clear how valuable it would be even as applied to Adapted Supply Chain operations such as these. The need arose, and the new paradigm was developed, as a result of the business in Japan.

Japan is not naturally blessed with the geography and climate needed to grow the grapes for winemaking, so the availability of Japanese-produced wines is limited. With the market available for imported wines and a cost-competitive approach such as barreled wine holding many attractions, the company moved into the Japanese market. From a logistics standpoint, the geographic stretch was quickly felt. Sending barrels of wine from Europe or the United States to Japan, and then returning the empty barrels from Japan to their source for cleaning and refilling, was going to chew up a significant part of the margin from the business as well as requiring a significant logistics infrastructure. Consideration also had to be made for the extraordinarily tight space conditions in Japan, in terms of the restaurants as well as storage facilities. The incentive was in place to search for an enhanced approach to liquid logistics.

Because the distance to Japan was so great, the objective was to find a way to ship the most product and the least packaging from the source to Japan. After consideration of a number of alternatives, a completely different design of the supply stream was developed. What if the barrels were left stationary at the restaurant, and the product was moved in bulk from the producer to the site? This combination of logistics approaches addressed all of the major transit and on-site issues, including the need for a cost-effective solution. In essence, the "packaging" remains on-site, where it serves an inventory holding and dispense function, and there is no packaging, in the traditional sense, from the point of production to the customer site. Thus a Supply Chain for Liquids shift in concept and approach arose out of the necessity of getting good wine to Japan.

The next stage of this development process came from reversing the concept back to its original source. The Japanese wine business had developed based on the European wine business; now was the time to reevaluate the European wine business based on the thought process that had developed in Japan. Lo and behold, it became clear that the European operation could be more effective if it adapted the Japanese logistics model. Like a hurricane gathering energy, though, it was not just the winds of change that were blowing, but truly a more complete paradigm shift in approach. Once the model was applied to Europe, a number of further adaptations and enhancements to the model became apparent:

■ There were physical improvements that could be made to increase the logistical effectiveness of the approach. The interface point between the bulk truck tanks and the on-site tanks were a constraint and, as such, deserved attention to release as many limitations as possible. The needs of the delivery process were examined in detail, resulting in the design of a through-the-wall external port that would eliminate the need for the delivery person to enter the restaurant at all. Other logistical enhancements included multiple tanks on the delivery truck and the approach to interconnections of the on-site tanks.

■ The information-flow side was addressed by integrating sensors and data-transmission equipment into the system, thus allowing the efficiencies of the physical side of the logistics process to be matched by efficiencies in the data side of the logistics process.

■ In perhaps the most productive breakthrough, the application of the entire principle, which had been focused on wine since its inception, was generalized to all liquid products. In the nature of progress, in fact, it was determined that wine is actually a less attractive liquid to be carried in this system than other liquids, for cultural rather than technical reasons. Even though wine has been ordered by the glass, periodically a customer may request to see the bottle or label. That would not be a good moment to start explaining the advantages of bulk wine, and this could lead to unnecessary complications. Given that there are so many more "paths of less resistance" (as listed in Chapter 4) that would enjoy all the benefits of the system without this particular drawback, the company focused on utilizing the system for other liquids. Other applications would view this system as their Optimal Supply Chain for Liquids that would provide the kind of competitive advantage that companies can often only dream of.

Progress does not lead to an end of progress, but rather to discovery of new opportunities, and so, after undergoing this evolutionary process, Worldwide Liquids realized that the creation of this logistics method was itself an asset that was as valuable as running a business using the method. With a patent on the process, the company has focused on running the system for certain liquids but more broadly marketing the system as a whole to a variety of industries. It is the logistical equivalent of "the medium is the message." In this case, the nature of the logistics system is more important than the specific liquid that passes through the system.

Once we have looked at the four stages of liquid logistics and understood what each is about and how the transitions between them occur, the natural next thought is, "What about the numbers?" Of course the financial benefit of implementing a Supply Chain for Liquids system will vary with each application, but there are some general principles that we can apply. A financial analysis is discussed in Chapter 11, including a summary of the financial impact based on a standard set of assumptions. Each stage will have its own costs and cost reductions, but the structure used in Chapter 11 can be useful in assembling and evaluating information regarding the overall benefit of moving to a Supply Chain for Liquids system.

Chapter 6

Producer Activities and the Supply Chain for Liquids

The producer of liquid products may act as the initiator of the Supply Chain for Liquids® approach, or a customer may understand the benefits of Supply Chain for Liquids and request the supplier's participation in the process. Either way, Supply Chain for Liquids is a cooperative process among all the players involved — the producer, the distributor, the retailer, and even the consumer. Even more, Supply Chain for Liquids offers each player a "win" and a motivation for participating in the process, which is crucial to its success. This is in contrast to other situations such as, for example, early efforts to implement RFID (radio frequency identification) systems. In these situations, there were clear winners and losers along the Supply Chain. In general, the suppliers came out the losers. They were mandated to add RFID tags to their products or packaging at considerable cost to themselves, but with very little benefit. The mandate was such that many suppliers added RFID tags at the end of their production process and thus gained little benefit themselves from the tags. Compliance with customer requirements was the motivation, and because of the time frame and cost of introducing RFID as a last-stage item, few manufacturers undertook broader RFID initiatives from which they could have gained benefits in their internal operations. To limit the damage, companies invested in the minimum RFID systems possible — tags and writing devices — rather than more widespread readers and processing needed for their own internal operations.

On the other hand, the customers downstream saw immediate benefits as pallets and cartons began to arrive with RFID tags. They were readily able to reduce their own data capture and tracking efforts by using the RFID tags to track inventory. Supply Chain for Liquids, in clear contrast, lets everyone participate in the benefit from the very beginning of system usage as long as, like RFID, the effort is coordinated all along the logistics flow. The benefits available to each of the players — producer, distributor, and customer/user — are described in each of Chapters 6, 7, and 8, starting with this chapter on the benefits to the producer.

Packaging

Let us examine the efficiencies and cost savings that accrue to the producer in adopting a Supply Chain for Liquids approach as they are shown in Exhibit 6.1. These consist of direct savings — reduction in direct expenses — as well as indirect savings in terms of reduction in support activities and gains in operating efficiencies. In either case, these are not potential savings somewhere in the future, but actual, immediate savings. The first savings occur right at the beginning of the logistics process and continue throughout the entire supply stream.

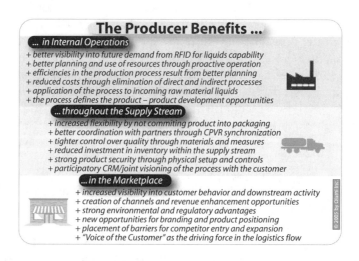

The Producer Benefits ...

... in Internal Operations
+ better visibility into future demand from RFID for liquids capability
+ better planning and use of resources through proactive operation
+ efficiencies in the production process result from better planning
+ reduced costs through elimination of direct and indirect processes
+ application of the process to incoming raw material liquids
+ the process defines the product – product development opportunities

...throughout the Supply Stream
+ increased flexibility by not commiting product into packaging
+ better coordination with partners through CPVR synchronization
+ tighter control over quality through materials and measures
+ reduced investment in inventory within the supply stream
+ strong product security through physical setup and controls
+ participatory CRM/joint visioning of the process with the customer

...in the Marketplace
+ increased visibility into customer behavior and downstream activity
+ creation of channels and revenue enhancement opportunities
+ strong environmental and regulatory advantages
+ new opportunities for branding and product positioning
+ placement of barriers for competitor entry and expansion
+ "Voice of the Customer" as the driving force in the logistics flow

© 2005 by Oلام Inc.

Exhibit 6.1   The Producer Benefits from Supply Chain for Liquids in Many Ways

The most obvious savings under the Supply Chain for Liquids approach are the elimination of entire steps of the production process, particularly those having to do with packaging. Packaging is a many-faceted step, and the Supply Chain for Liquids approach to it is indicative of its overall approach: the best way to improve a process is to get rid of it, or to come as close to doing so as possible. We can use an example from the world of beverages.

For a beverage or beverage syrup producer, the act of transferring the liquid beverage into the BIB (bag in box) package represents the packaging process. The number of steps involved in packaging alone means that this makes up a production process of its own:

■ The actual packaging material needs to be procured, in a manner similar to that of procuring raw materials for the product. In some cases, packaging procurement may be more extensive and more complex than that of the product itself. First, a single product may be sold in a number of different sizes and configurations of packaging, so each of these types of packaging must be planned, procured, and inventoried separately. Even for a single package size of a single liquid, the printing/labeling requirements may differ for different customers or different geographic areas (languages, product name, health and safety labeling, etc.). Each of these variations represents a complexity in packaging that does not necessarily exist with the product itself — complexity of planning, ordering, tracking, multisourcing, and other aspects of the procurement process. A single product that of itself, as a liquid, has none of these complexities can be divided into these different packaging types that have all of these complexities.

■ Like the product itself, packaging material must be stored with all the complexity of inventorying. Storage takes space; it is subject to the usual percentages of damage/theft/error; it requires administrative and physical attention; and it is subject to obsolescence as package sizes and markings shift. Depending on the nature of the packaging, it can be quite space-consuming. Although cartons and BIB containers can be folded, other types of containers such as bottles and jugs take up a large amount of space that is even more pronounced when they are only filled with air and not with the product. Each type of packaging, for example BIB cartons marked for different products, is held in inventory with its own level of safety stock, as the cartons are obviously not interchangeable. In this sense, inventorying the packaging is in many ways more complex than inventorying the product itself.

■ Just as there is a packaging operation, in some companies there is a repackaging operation. Bottles of the producer's product may have been placed in cartons with a specific customer's logo, product number, or other identifying information on it. In the event of a shortage of the product for another customer, the bottles may need to be removed from one customer's cartons and repackaged into cartons with the other customer's information. This further emphasizes the point that for packaged product, the packaging is an integral part of the product, and the wrong packaging means that the liquid has been turned into the wrong product.

■ There is frequently a preparation process with packaging that must be executed as the packaging is picked and issued to the production line. Some types of packaging require unfolding or setup, others require assembly, still others may be preprinted immediately before being issued to the packaging operation. The packaging equipment takes facility space and must be set up, operated, and maintained. This step, like the previous steps, are all preproduction in terms of the product itself: the packaging must be ready at the time and place at which the product is to go through the packaging operation.

Each of these steps represents expenditures of money and effort that do not add value to the product itself. If the liquids are no longer placed in individual packages, then the need for this packaging process is completely eliminated — a direct, immediate benefit to the product producer. In addition, the support activities related to packaging are also relieved. The purchasing effort spent on sourcing the packaging and procuring it; the warehouse effort of receiving, storing, moving, and issuing packaging materials; and the inventory control effort of planning for packaging needs and following up on packaging "emergencies" — all of these are derivative savings to this process. Finally, the inventory investment in packaging materials as well as inventory loss due to theft, damage, and other shrinkage factors are eliminated.

The savings in packaging effort described above include a benefit that has been inferred but deserves to be stated explicitly: the flexibility that it offers the producer. As soon as the producer puts the liquid in a package, the producer is "committed" to that product/package. Taking the same liquid and putting it in another package means undergoing a repackaging operation as described above. Under Supply Chain for Liquids, the producer maintains the liquid in its nominal state, that is, without any packaging, and so can send the product in any number of directions in terms of customers or distribution channels. In this sense, Supply Chain for Liquids works to support product line simplification or SKU (stock-keeping unit) rationalization, that is, a reduction in the number of SKUs that a company produces, maintains, and sells. Selling a liquid in bulk form eliminates however many SKUs are tied up in all the variations of that exact same liquid product — package type, package size, customer-specific packaging, region-specific packaging, etc. The company may still need to issue documentation for some of these variations, but this is much simpler than using the packaging itself as documentation and thus requiring so many different versions of packages.

Although savings in packaging may be the most obvious benefit to the producer of adopting a Supply Chain for Liquids approach, it is not necessarily the most important. Two benefits that are related to each other, Supply Chain for Liquids visibility and production planning/resource utilization, may each yield far greater benefits than the direct savings in packaging material.

Product Demand Visibility

One of the difficulties in implementing Supply Chain processes successfully is the complexity of some of its principles, such as inter-entity collaboration. For example, with discrete goods, to determine how much product is currently on hand or in transit at any point in the Supply Chain, the information systems of the various Supply Chain members must be continuously exchanging information and remain in synchronization. This is because the inventory balances of solid products are normally a computer-based, rather than a product-based, measurement. The computer is keeping track of inventory ins and outs and thus calculating the on-hand balance, rather than having product continually counted and reported. In the best-case scenario, this information is updated reasonably frequently and accurately, but in many real-world cases there are either "black holes" in the Supply Chain from which data is not available or, as is frequently the case, the information stops being available to the producer as soon as product leaves the producer's four walls. The capability of continuous reporting for discrete products is one of the great promises of RFID, which at this writing is still in its formative stage with numerous proponents, promises, standards, and techniques, but with relatively few users.

For liquid products, however, it is a completely different ballgame, which leads to a completely different approach to Supply Chain for Liquids visibility. As described in Chapter 8, liquid-level monitoring and inventory-balance measurement can be a virtually continuous process using common, proven technologies and techniques. These inventory balance measurements are set to whatever time scale is meaningful for the particular product and point in the Supply Chain for Liquids at which the measurement is being taken. For example, at the producer it may be sufficient to measure/report inventory quantities each day, at the distribution points twice per day, and at the retail/dispense point each hour. This is not a computer-based measurement such as occurs in Supply Chain that requires continual update and exchange of information among multiple computer systems. These measurements are being taken directly at the location of the liquids, and as described in Chapter 8, the measurements can be broadcast to multiple points (such as multiple members of the Supply Chain for Liquids) simultaneously. Thus, with a simple Internet connection, all members of the Supply Chain for Liquids can know the exact quantity of liquid at every point in the Supply Chain for Liquids. The difference between the many-to-many (interface of multiple computer systems) information approach required in Supply Chain and the one-to-many (sensors broadcast the same data to multiple computer systems) information approach available in Supply Chain for Liquids has extraordinary implications on the visibility into activity within the Supply Chain for Liquids. Within the predetermined confines of the data-security scheme that has been implemented, the entire Supply Chain for Liquids has constant accurate information regarding the quantity of liquid at each point in the Supply Chain for Liquids. The producer can see all the way down the Supply Chain for Liquids to the point of dispense. Visibility of 100 percent is made simple in the Supply Chain for Liquids configuration.

Visibility (or transparency, as it is sometimes called) is a great thing, but Supply Chain for Liquids takes this concept even further. Even if all the entities along the supply stream have full visibility into product balances at every point in the flow, if they do not have a coordinated method for responding to shifts in inventory along the flow, then the system is not fully effective. The producer in particular is subject to the results of the "whipsaw" effect, whereby each player in the Supply Chain overcompensates for each shift in demand or inventory, resulting in a relatively small impact downstream but a large impact on the variability of demand on the producer. Supply Chain for Liquids resolves this situation by defining a coordinated set of procedures for visibility response — CPVR^SM (Coordinated Procedures for Visibility Response^SM) — as described in Chapter 10. The visibility that is available through RFID for Liquids® within Supply Chain for Liquids tells us what the situation is, and the CPVR technique that is used in Supply Chain for Liquids tells us what to do about it. Although CPVR is described in more detail later, let us look briefly at the additional benefits of visibility and coordination for the producer.

This visibility and coordination are not only valuable for their own sake, but for the benefits they provide to the producer in terms of production planning and resource utilization. The producer not only sees the inventory situation at its direct customer, such as a distribution center, but also at the subsequent points in the Supply Chain for Liquids, including the retail facility. The producer's planning process is thus vastly improved. There may be a bulge of inventory at the distribution center level, for example, at the same time there is a contraction of inventory at the retail level. Whereas the bulge might ordinarily cause the producer to reduce planned production based on slower orders from the distribution center, visibility to the end of the Supply Chain for Liquids allows the producer to assess that the bulge at the distribution center level will soon move down-pipe, and the distribution center will in fact require replenishment. Simultaneous bulges in multiple down-pipe points are an indicator to the producer that short-term production requirements are likely to be reduced. The planning horizon for production moves far beyond the four walls of the production facility and all the way to the point of dispense. Although most companies strive to move from reactive/firefighting mode to proactive mode in terms of their operations, the logistics environment in which they operate often means that the firefighting element remains present. The processes included in the Supply Chain for Liquids approach are another step forward in reducing the need for reactive actions. Many producers supply more than one logistics stream, perhaps with different products or with different sales channels for the same product, so that these producers take multiple "hits" — the reactive activities that result from each of the supply streams the producer serves. Combining all of the Supply Chain for Liquids channels that the producer services provides a powerful tool for production planning and for the efficient and cost-effective use of production resources, including facilities, material, and personnel.

Customer Behavior Visibility

There is a corollary of the product-demand visibility described above that deserves to be described separately, because its importance is often undervalued and its execution even poorer. This is the visibility that the producer has into how the company's products are being used. For a company that produces liquid products and whose day-to-day focus is pumping product into the distribution channel, it is easy to lose sight of where the product is ultimately going and what it is used for. Certainly the marketing and sales departments have the vision of the whole flow of the product, but the internal departments of the company, such as production and logistics, have less immediate knowledge of the outside world. In many cases, it is the anecdotal reports of the sales and marketing people that provide the internal departments with the most information about external activities, particularly those beyond the next stage of the logistics flow, such as the distribution center.

This is of course counterproductive for the company and fosters the kind of provincial thinking that creates barriers where they hurt the company the most. In most companies, the sales-versus-production fissure falls somewhere in the range of uncomfortable tolerance, with each side wondering why the other makes such outlandish statements. ("What do you mean you can't ship it tomorrow? That's when the customer wants it!" is probably heard as often as, "Of course we'll rush those samples — they'll be ready early next month.") We are not interested in exploring this phenomenon here, but what is important is that the Supply Chain for Liquids approach institutionalizes processes that counteract this situation. The RFID for Liquids functionality that is part of Supply Chain for Liquids, and especially when augmented with the CPVR coordinated-response technique, makes the connections among all of the parties to the logistics flow a routine part of the internal thought process and planning activity. With a logistics view into the final stage of the flow at the customer site, the planning personnel at the producer gain a much broader horizon of understanding and can connect with activity much farther downstream than is possible in a four-walls environment.

What does this mean? Let us picture a producer who begins to get insight into the usage patterns of the product two or three steps down the logistics flow, at the end customer's site. As the planning personnel at the producer become familiar with the cycles of usage at the customer — be they daily, weekly, or monthly — they can more closely tune their activity to these cycles, which are what ultimately drive the product flow in any case. This visibility is often denied because of the warehouse layer that buffers the connection between the customer and the producer, with the good intention of assuring product availability for the customer, but with the unintended side effect of disconnecting the producer from the customer. For example, the producer may have shipped product to the distributor, but would not have had insight into the quantity and timing of deliveries to the various customer locations. Producer insight into customer usage patterns from a logistics perspective can help both sides. For example, they might discover that different customer locations would benefit from different on-site tank configurations, which would streamline the delivery process while ensuring proper inventory quantities at each customer location. Differences in usage patterns may indicate misuse of the product. For example, if two similarly sized customer sites use significantly different quantities of a cleaning solution, it may be that one is diluting it in the wrong way and getting subsatisfactory results. The distributor would not be sensitive to this, but personnel from the producer site who saw these patterns could ask the appropriate questions and thus provide better service to the customer. Both sides benefit from increased visibility, and in particular the producer, who learns of product activity after the product has left the producer's facility.

Efficiencies in the Production Process

The three advantages described above — elimination of the packaging operation, improved visibility into future demand, and strengthened connection with the customer — combine to lead to efficiencies in the actual production process for the producer. The production process for liquids is frequently vat-based, with ingredients being added to a large container according to a recipe (the liquid equivalent of a "bill of material" for solids). Recipes are often proportional rather than quantity specific, giving a great deal of flexibility in varying the amount of liquid product produced during any specific production run. The mixing process has its own time constraints, such as an amount of time required for mixing, setting, fermenting, etc., and multiple mixing processes often feed into a single set of packaging lines. Freed from the interim packaging step, the production process can truly become a one-step operation for the producer. The timing that used to go into planning the packaging line can now go into planning the outbound transportation, and product can be fed directly from the mixing vat to the bulk tank trucks. This production efficiency derives from the improved visibility that flows in the reverse direction. Knowing what the customers' needs will be in advance allows delivery runs to be planned in advance, and having delivery runs planned in advance allows production (which feeds directly into delivery because of the elimination of the packaging step) to be planned and executed to directly meet shipping needs. The idea of the mixing tank as combination production and preshipping tank is operationally as attractive as a one-pot dinner. It is efficient, minimizing extra effort and material, and providing maximum flexibility to complete this particular activity and move forward to the next activity. This specific example is one of the keys to successful implementation of Supply Chain for Liquids and achieving Optimal Supply Chain for Liquids status. It shows the need to understand not just the immediate benefit of any particular liquid-oriented process adjustment, but further to understand how that benefit may be combined with all the other revised elements into a totally altered flow that brings about the huge advantages of an Optimal Supply Chain for Liquids system.

This altered flow must take into account all of the factors involved in production and logistics, including efficient batch sizes, the processing time for the product, effective placement of equipment and other infrastructure elements, etc. In considering these factors, it is important to remember the fundamental Liquid Lens[SM] principle that we create complete systems, not fix parts of systems. For example, the initial reaction to the direct-to-truck scenario described above might be to raise several objections that are valid based on current operations: "Our batch sizes are for several days' (or several weeks') operations," or "The physical movement of multiple products in such a short time frame is impossible," etc. These objections are accurate, but they are not valid because they apply the current scenario onto a projected process, and thus do not legitimately address the opportunity for operational improvement. When tying back the benefits of Supply Chain for Liquids to the production process, we must use the same approach as for the remainder of Supply Chain for Liquids: what is the complete "package" that Supply Chain for Liquids is offering, and how will the whole system work in our operation? No assumption should be taken for granted in such a process.

An example of this is the analysis of lead time as a self-fulfilling prophecy. This analysis shows that in many cases, lead time is not determined by what is required to move the product, but by company decision and policy. For example, a company whose order-fulfillment time is one day sets a six-day lead time for its customers. That is, the processes required to actually fill an order take one day, but the company promises six days as a cushion to protect against unforeseen circumstances. Because of this policy, the company has a continuous six-day backlog of orders. Under these conditions, the company cannot do an analysis and suddenly decide to announce a two-day lead time for orders, because it has created a situation that prevents such a step. If the company suddenly announced a two-day lead time, it would never have time to clean up the six-day backlog of orders. Someone looking at this situation would say, "You can't have a two-day lead time; your open backlog is too large, and your information flow is too slow to start shipping orders in two days," and this statement would be correct under the given circumstances. But if the company were to put the processes in place to execute a two-day lead time, it *would* be able to support such a commitment. This example demonstrates that what is considered "not possible" may be so using current assumptions, but when we provide ourselves with the opportunity to change the rules of the game, the "not possible" can turn not only into possible, but even preferable.

Thus far we have been discussing the benefits of Supply Chain for Liquids for the liquid-products producer from the perspective of the producer as being at the back end of the Supply Chain for Liquids. To the degree to which the producer is somewhere within the Supply Chain for Liquids — that is, the producer receives liquid ingredients to feed into the production process — the benefits of Supply Chain for Liquids can also be applied to the producer's purchasing and material-holding methods. The advantages of Supply Chain for Liquids for a customer/user as described in Chapter 8 are fully applicable to the producer in the purchase and holding of liquid ingredients. With sensors in the tanks at the producer's facility and the Supply Chain for Liquids loop extending out to the ingredients providers, the product/information flow includes the producer's suppliers. Depending on the quantities of liquids used in the production process, the timing of production runs, and the availability of just-in-time sourcing from liquid-ingredients suppliers, the ideal liquid-production operation consists of a mixing tank with pipes coming in from the suppliers' delivery trucks and pipes coming out to the producer's delivery trucks. We should be careful not to judge this goal as pie in the sky. It is the liquid-production equivalent of the "cross-docking" discrete-distribution methodology that has set a parallel goal and in some cases is achieving that goal with a great deal of success.

Additional Producer Benefits

Reduced packaging costs and improved production planning and execution are not the only benefits that the producer can reap from the Supply Chain for Liquids. There is a broad range of additional benefits that are available, depending on the nature of the company.

The first relates to quality assurance of the product. Under the Supply Chain approach, once product leaves the producer's facility, the producer has very little insight or control over the conditions in which the product is maintained. The quality of the producer's product is under the control of each set of hands through which it passes until it reaches the end consumer. Under the Supply Chain for Liquids system, both passive and active quality measures can be put in place all along the logistics process. Passive measures include control over the materials that the product comes into contact with all along the logistics flow — the materials of which the tanks and tubes are made in each facility — to ensure that they do not diminish the quality of the product. Although passive, these measures determine the environment in which the liquid is held and the materials the liquid comes into contact with, and thus are an important influence on the quality of the liquid as it reaches the consumer. Active measures include the placement of monitoring devices beyond those required for logistics purposes — monitors that measure such attributes as product temperature, pressure, clarity/color, and other conditions that impact product quality or indications of deviation from optimal quality. The results of these active measures all along the supply stream help the producer in a number of ways, most importantly ensuring that the product received by the consumer meets the quality standards set by the producer. In addition, active measures allow the producer to quickly pinpoint the spot in the logistics flow at which quality conditions have been compromised, a process that otherwise can entail a lengthy and difficult investigative effort. Immediate quality-related information allows the producer to act before a customer-related problem arises, even if that means diverting the suspect product while it is in the supply stream and before it has reached the customer. Finally, all of these capabilities taken together make a strong marketing statement and provide a competitive weapon over other suppliers who do not have this level of quality assurance in place. The benefits of Supply Chain for Liquids in terms of the quality of the product are described in further detail in Chapter 10.

A second benefit of Supply Chain for Liquids for the producer relates to the environmental impact, or lack thereof, of a Supply Chain for Liquids system. For producers facing an array of regulatory requirements related to the environmental effects of their operations and products, Supply Chain for Liquids comes as the proverbial breath of fresh air. The many environmental benefits resulting from elimination of packaging and improved transportation/delivery capabilities are a significant advantage, given the economics of environmental issues. The advantages that Supply Chain for Liquids offers from an environmental perspective are enumerated in detail in Chapter 11, and show that there are benefits to be gained related to each of the producer's activities. The elimination of packages, cartons, and pallets is a huge environmental plus. Beyond that, the more efficient use of warehouse space and equipment decreases the resources need for producer storage, and bulk-transport trucks carry more product per run, thus decreasing pollution as well as congestion. Supply Chain for Liquids is a huge environmental win for the producer.

Lastly, and probably most importantly, Supply Chain for Liquids hits the producer right where the producer enjoys it the most — in the pocketbook. The reduction in product cost from removal of expense items from the logistics process, together with reduction of the quantity of product in the logistics pipeline due to the increased efficiencies of Supply Chain for Liquids, yield a significantly reduced investment in product in the logistics pipeline. The financial benefits of Supply Chain for Liquids are detailed in Chapter 11.

Although reduced costs provide a financial benefit to the producer, we should not overlook the revenue potential created by the Supply Chain for Liquids. This potential comes both from the competitive advantages that accrue to the producer, thus allowing the producer to capture customers from the competition, and from the new distribution and sales channels that open up to the producer using the Supply Chain for Liquids system. The strategic and marketing benefits of Supply Chain for Liquids (detailed in Chapter 11) allow the producer to develop channels that are not possible using a traditional package-based Supply Chain approach.

The following is a summary of the major benefits of the Supply Chain for Liquids system for the producer:

■ Increased operational efficiency and cost reduction through elimination of the packaging operation and its adjunct costs and complexities, such as packaging materials and equipment maintenance

- Better visibility into demand for product along the logistics flow and better coordination with the players along the logistics flow, thus improving planning for production operations
- Strengthened connection with the customer through the information flow and interaction at the logistics level between the producer and the customer
- Improved execution of the production process by supporting direct inflow of ingredients and outflow of product to the distribution system
- Tighter control of product quality throughout the supply stream to the point of sale or dispense by the user
- Strong environmentally friendly characteristics, including reduction in waste generation and reduced consumption of resources for production/warehousing and transport
- Large financial advantages in terms of cost reduction and creation of revenue-enhancement opportunities

Clearly, the producer is the biggest winner from the Supply Chain for Liquids system, but as we shall see in subsequent chapters, the distributor, customer, and consumer also come out ahead in this system. Even so, producers have some common concerns related to the Supply Chain for Liquids system, and these are discussed in the following sections.

Protecting Your Position

As a producer, you see the value of the Supply Chain for Liquids approach for yourself as well as for the partners you work with, be they the distributor or the end customer. However, you may have several concerns about utilizing this approach in the marketplace:

- My brand is as important as my product. If my bottles/jugs/cans/drums with my labels are not there, do I disappear as a brand?
- Once I set up the system along my Supply Chain for Liquids, how do I keep my competitors from moving into the system? Couldn't a competitor come along and fill the customer's on-site tanks just as I would?
- I have an investment in things the way they are — the packaging line, the distribution network, the packaging itself. What happens to these, and why should I consider moving to a Supply Chain for Liquids approach?

One of the reasons these kinds of questions come up is because anyone considering the Supply Chain for Liquids approach is coming at it from the starting point of "the way things are." Applying a set of assumptions or understandings from an existing operation to a completely different way of operating leads to misunderstanding and misevaluation of the new way of operating. This is why the Liquid Lens approach is so important. The process of putting together the whole package in all its aspects helps the user see the system in its entirety with its true implications. The advantages of the Supply Chain for Liquids approach as presented in this book is not an attempt to bully through the system; indeed, the actual case is quite the opposite. It is important that all of the questions about implementation and operation of the system come up during the system planning process, so that they can be addressed before the plan for the system is finalized.

The questions listed above are a few of the many that arise within a company that is considering the Supply Chain for Liquids approach. The questions come from all angles — operations, finance, marketing, etc. — which is why this book covers the system from each of these angles. We address these specific questions in the following subsections in an effort to further understand the system from the producer's perspective.

Brand

Brand and brand perception are critical to products and to companies, and packaging/labeling often serves as an important method of conveying the brand message. The moment the product is left to "stand naked" without its packaging, the advantages of brand may be lost, and with that the advantages that one product enjoys over another. For this reason, the importance of brand cannot be overestimated, and the handling of brand within the Supply Chain for Liquids deserves particular attention.

The fact that Supply Chain for Liquids eliminates traditional packaging does not mean that the brand associated with the product is lost. Rather, it means that new and different opportunities for presenting the brand message are created. A good example of a product in a comparable position is beer. Beer bottles or cans convey the brand message, as does the whole host of branding strategies that accompany the product — glasses, coasters, signage, etc. Does this mean that the brand message is lost when the product moves in other forms, such as beer on tap? The stainless steel barrel that draft beer comes in may give little indication of its contents, but the distribution system is not the point at which the brand message needs to be expressed. For draft beer, the tap serves an important branding function, as do the containers (glasses) into which the beer is poured. This approach has been extended to other liquids. Pump handles in gas stations now frequently include brand logos or messages, and the gas station itself serves as the brand presentation for gas that is delivered in tank trucks. Further, the Supply Chain for Liquids system can offer similar branding opportunities. For example, on-site beverage tanks made of stainless steel or glass have been placed as part of the décor of a restaurant, even to the point of being a central or identifying aspect of the establishment. This combination is the ultimate conjunction of sales and logistics. Like Henry Ford's black Model Ts, the process and the product combine into a single entity, resulting in a solid and virtually unbreakable brand identity.

A variation on the producer concern about brand is whether the producer's product might be substituted with an inferior brand or undergo some other form of adulteration that would detract from the product, the brand, or the company. A common concern among drivers who take their vehicles to quick-lube outlets, for example, is that they do not really know what motor oil has been used during an oil change, despite the fact that a brand name is usually evident and its containers are readily visible. A producer may have a similar concern once the product is disassociated from its standard packaging. However, as described below in the section describing product security, this concern is addressed by the nature of the Supply Chain for Liquids system. The Supply Chain for Liquids is a physically closed system, and it does not offer ready access points where product tampering could occur. On the other hand, bottling is a very vulnerable logistics method. It is easy to inject a foreign substance into a bottled liquid, swap the contents of a bottle for an inferior product, or as more commonly occurs, counterfeit the packaging and fill it with a lower-grade product. For a properly set-up system, a company's brand is better protected within a Supply Chain for Liquids system than it is using a conventional container-based system.

Competitive Entry

No company wants to lay the groundwork for its competitor's success or, as the saying goes, to let someone else eat its lunch. This is especially true in highly competitive markets, where companies battle for every inch of turf. On the one hand, Supply Chain for Liquids could be viewed as a generic approach that another company could easily take over. However, Supply Chain for Liquids offers many layers of security in the sense of barriers to competitor entry once the system has been put in place, primarily by preventing another producer or distributor from using the systems and equipment that have been installed.

The first barrier is the simple physical connection that allows delivery of product to the site. The external port fitting, by which the hose from the truck is physically connected to the pipes in the on-site system, is contained in a locked box on an external wall of the customer site. Barring vandalism, there is no unauthorized access to the port through which products are delivered in the Supply Chain for Liquids system. This is much more secure (in the sense of exclusive to the company that runs it) than a standard delivery system, in which warehouse space or shelf space is readily accessible to any other company that might be selected to deliver product. Physically, a competitor could not deliver product into the Supply Chain for Liquids system without breaking or forcing the lock, or stealing the key, for the access port. Ownership of the external port as well as of the remainder of the Supply Chain for Liquids equipment is established as part of the formal agreement between the producer/distributor/customer.

An extension of this protection is that the external port fitting is built in such a way that an improper hose cannot be physically connected to the external port. This is similar to techniques used for beverages (dispense line connectors) and soap dispensers (bottle/dispenser fitting), among others, that prevent one company from connecting into another company's equipment at installations in the field. Supply Chain for Liquids's external port is set with pins or nonsymmetrical shapes to absolutely prevent cross-contamination of liquids; the hose cannot be physically attached in any way other than the proper way to ensure that each liquid supplied is fed into the appropriate on-site line. This same approach provides first-level protection against unauthorized feeding of product into the lines.

A second barrier is more subtle but no less effective. In a traditional environment with packaged products, the competition can see, count, and actually move the product of another company. This provides an opening for entry should there be a low balance of a company's product, for example, that would invite a competitor to rearrange the product spacing or push its product into the gap. Under the Supply Chain for Liquids system, the entire cycle of product is literally out of sight and thus not available for competitor viewing or manipulation. This is further strengthened by the lack of customer participation in the data flow related to product inventory. Under pure Supply Chain for Liquids, customer personnel do not know either current on-hand inventory balances or ongoing inventory usages. This lack of visibility only complicates a competitor's ability to penetrate the account.

Another barrier to entry is the full-loop nature of the Supply Chain for Liquids system. As a company "sets the bar" at this level of service to the customer, and establishes first-mover dominance of a particular marketplace for particular products, a competitor has a higher hurdle to jump over to gain or regain customers than simply delivering packaged product to a storeroom. The amount of effort required to implement a system offering the Supply Chain for Liquids wealth of functionality serves the first mover and works against a mimicking company.

Finally, Supply Chain for Liquids provides a longer-term view of logistics operations, and is likely to be accompanied by a contractual arrangement for the duration of the operation of the system. In many cases, this is a multiyear contract, with all of the protections needed for each side. As such, it removes immediate competitive considerations and provides for a relationship across a specific period of time, thus reinforcing the competitor lock-out.

Although this last point, that of longer-term commitment between the parties, will always work to the producer's advantage in terms of its competitors, in some cases the producer prefers to have the flexibility to work with several distributors at the same time to gain the advantages of the competition between them. In this case, the producer needs to use the Supply Chain for Liquids planning process to lay out a strategy for maintaining this situation, even with the distinctive requirements and investment required for the system. Definitions of who invests in the equipment required for the Supply Chain for Liquids system, what level of activity is projected that will justify the investment, the methods of coexistence between multiple distributors (such as geographic area, product type, or other approaches), and the rest of the picture regarding the roles of the various players are filled in during the Supply Chain for Liquids planning process.

Changing Methodologies

Every company has an investment in its existing way of doing business that needs to be examined with every prospective change to that way of doing business. Without doubt, Supply Chain for Liquids represents a significant change in logistics approach from a traditional Supply Chain operation. As with any change, it will serve as a benefit to some and a detriment to others.

Quantification of the costs of transitioning to Supply Chain for Liquids is included in the Supply Chain for Liquids planning process. Included in these are the sunk costs, costs that have already been incurred that may become underutilized, such as a packaging operation for which no alternative usage can be created.

The key to this analysis, though, is to phrase the question properly. The issue is not the costs that will be incurred during this process, but rather the net financial result of all aspects of undertaking the Supply Chain for Liquids process. Following the Liquid Lens approach provides for just such an analysis. This analysis also takes into account risks that come in from all sides. What is the risk that a competitor will adopt the Supply Chain for Liquids if you do not, and what will be the impact of the competitor's doing so? Does moving to the Supply Chain for Liquids approach necessarily have to lead to underutilization of the packaging line or other resources, or is this actually an opportunity to use those resources to pursue additional markets that we have not had the capacity or inclination to pursue up to now? It is not always easy to tell whether our current investment and strategy is more like the Great Wall of China that successfully kept the Mongols out for 1000 years, or the Maginot Line that devoured a huge amount of resources and was rendered completely ineffective within a short time after its completion. What is clear is that the fact that we have made one set of investment decisions should not prevent us from considering other investment directions while taking into account the decisions and actions already made.

An important factor that comes into play in these types of analysis, and that may even dominate the analysis, is the source of the motivation for change. There are many dynamics involved in moving to a Supply Chain for Liquids system. In some industries the producer is the driving party, but in other industries the customer more or less dictates the methods used for the logistics flow. In the latter case, the producer may not have much choice, and may engage in a Supply Chain for Liquids project as the result of customer pressure.

It is exactly in a mature industry characterized by stable products, customers, and business relationships that Supply Chain for Liquids holds a great deal of attraction. In such an environment, a producer is not able to differentiate the product based on product characteristics alone. Indeed, in all likelihood the product has become more or less a commodity. With a stable marketplace, the pie is not likely to grow radically, so that will not be a direction for increased profitability. The double-edged sword offered by Supply Chain for Liquids — reduced costs/increased margins from the logistics operation together with a differentiating approach to the distribution process that can be very attractive to customers — can be a key element in maximizing utilization and exploitation of existing position and gaining as much benefit as possible from this part of the business.

A distinction that should be made during the analysis of the value of the Supply Chain for Liquids approach for a company is that the situation is not black and white. A company does not decide that it will operate wholly within the context of Supply Chain for Liquids or not at all. There are very few companies whose entire product line is best used in purely liquid form in every customer usage and application. In virtually all cases, a company will select some of its products, and some of the applications of those products, for possible inclusion in a Supply Chain for Liquids system. Many liquids are used sometimes in a way that is appropriate for Supply Chain for Liquids and sometimes in a way that is not, and the analysis of if, how, and how much of a Supply Chain for Liquids system should be installed in any particular logistics flow should clearly identify the products and channels that are to be included.

As with any business opportunity, the producer has many variables to evaluate when considering a Supply Chain for Liquids initiative, and many alternative configurations of Supply Chain for Liquids should the company decided to pursue a Supply Chain for Liquids opportunity. The evaluation, decision, and implementation involve contacts with the other players in the logistics flow for the producer's products, so that the commutations and permutations of the final configuration are expanded even further. The Liquid Lens principle applies to the whole scope of the Supply Chain for Liquids flow. The entire logistics flow, including both the flow of product in one direction and the flow of information in the other direction, should be defined in advance across all of the players that are to be included in the flow. During this evaluation, all of the companies involved should remember, however, that Supply Chain for Liquids is not a tweaking of a traditional Supply Chain approach, but rather a fundamental shift in the logistics paradigm, with all its accompanying threats and opportunities.

Participatory CRM and the Voice of the Customer

The need to please the customer is as old as business. In the first commercial transaction recorded in the Bible, Ephron uses the approach of trying to convince Abraham that the 400 shekels of silver he is charging Abraham for Sarah's burial place is really a deeply discounted price ("what's that between you and me?") so that Abraham will be a satisfied customer. In our times, we have wrapped various phrases around this activity, such as CRM (customer relationship management), and have learned how to talk a good game about the importance of the customer and the relationship with the customer. With Supply Chain for Liquids, we take this process a generation further — the producer participates with the customer in the operation of the customer's business.

Like vendor-managed inventory (VMI), Supply Chain for Liquids includes active vendor involvement in the customer's inventory activity. As part of Supply Chain for Liquids, a producer or distributor takes over some of the functions that a customer had previously performed related to liquid logistics. These include inventory monitoring and control of liquid products and initiating replenishment orders. The design of the Supply Chain for Liquids system, however, takes this process several steps further. The Supply Chain for Liquids information flow includes quality-related measures where appropriate, so the supplier is taking on part of the quality management of the product even while it is at the customer site. More significantly from a participative perspective, the Supply Chain for

Liquids system extends through the customer's storeroom and on to the dispense system — right through to the point of usage. Supply Chain for Liquids is about more than *quantity* of use; it is about *method* of use. The way the liquid is dispensed by the user is defined in the Liquid Lens as the ultimate driving force in the design and operation of the Supply Chain for Liquids system. As operational needs change, the functionality of the dispense equipment can be adjusted to match the changing requirements. In this way, the supplier is in close contact with the customer on many levels: in relation to the product itself, how the product is held at the customer site, the quantity of product used by the customer, and the method by which the product is used by the customer. Under this scenario, Participatory CRM[SM] goes far beyond standard CRM and puts the supplier almost literally in the customer's shoes. Breaking the arm's length relationship with the customer, Supply Chain for Liquids allows a supplier to achieve an exceptionally strong relationship with the customer that is beneficial to both the supplier and the customer.

In addition to the operational closeness of the customer relationship that Supply Chain for Liquids nurtures, the system supports another type of closeness that is even tougher in this information-drenched age — closeness of mind. Although the producer services the customer's on-site personnel by performing the logistics activity quite literally invisibly, the producer services the customer's management personnel by being quite visible. As described in Chapter 8, there are several levels of information that are generated by the Supply Chain for Liquids system that are of interest to customer management. The system can provide via the Internet a broad range of summary and detail reports and graphs that provide an instantaneous systemwide picture of the flow of liquid products. Key management metrics (described in Chapter 11) are also made available to customer personnel at various levels of management. This information can be combined with information from other sources, such as benchmark figures or other available data, to create an even fuller management-level picture of company activity within the marketplace and compared with competitors. This type of institutionalized customer service provides a strong foundation for the supplier-customer relationship and is a good basis for the objective of keeping the customer happy.

Built into the Liquid Lens/Supply Chain for Liquids approach is yet another level of customer relationship. As described in Chapter 10, the design of the Supply Chain for Liquids system is based in large part from the end of the logistics flow — customer use of the liquid product — back through the distribution process. Thus the voice of the customer is truly a driving force in the creation and operation of the system. It is not enough to view the customer's current methods and build the Supply

Chain for Liquids system around that, because Supply Chain for Liquids offers opportunities that are not available with the current logistics process. Thus an envisioning process with the customer — working with the customer to define what the customer could do with a Supply Chain for Liquids system in place — provides an additional level of interaction with the customer. The producer/distributor works with the customer to develop the customer's business. This level of interaction serves to lock in the customer to the producer both because of the value of the service the producer is offering and also physically, as described in Chapter 10. A customer is less likely to leave a supplier who is not only providing product but working as a strategic partner in the customer's business.

Product Security

A dimension of the supply stream that has taken on heightened importance in an increasingly risk-threatened world is that of product security. The producer of the product in particular, as well as players at all points in the logistics flow, needs to be concerned about the possibility of physical threat based on outside tampering with the product. This threat can take on many forms.

Changes to the Product That Could Make the Product Dangerous to the Public

Product tampering has been in the public consciousness for several decades, but only recently has the potential for a massive attack based on altered product become a realistic possibility. Most product tampering cases have involved packaged consumable products that are readily accessible and thus can be manipulated and returned to store shelves without being noticed. A separate problem is that of contamination, in which a product becomes dangerous for use because of an error in the production process.

Supply Chain for Liquids addresses the security problem of tampering by limiting access to the product from the point of production to the point of dispense. Employees for the companies along the supply stream always have access to the product, but there is far less accessibility to closed tanks than there is to pallets and cartons of product. Depending on the level of concern for a potential threat of tampering, the tanks/piping/valving arrangement can be set up in such as way as to minimize the physical opportunity for ingress to the system. As described in Chapter 10, the external port through which deliveries are made is secured at several levels. First, the external port is inside of a locked box that can be made as strong as necessary to prevent access. Second, the external port utilizes coded patterns or pins to prevent unauthorized connection into the system. Moreover, the addition of liquid to the system would be detected as an unplanned increase in the on-hand balance of the liquid. Finally, for a system that is operating under pressure, any change of pressure that would occur during unauthorized access to the system would be immediately detected, and the cause could be investigated. The most public part of the logistics flow, that of the front-end dispense system, is in most cases virtually tamper-proof in a Supply Chain for Liquids system due to the closed piping leading from the on-site tanks to the actual dispense mechanism.

Facility Attack That Could Lead to Large-Scale Damage

The world has witnessed horrendous attacks on facilities that have led to massive loss of life, although up to now the focus has been on causing direct damage rather than triggering a secondary effect that would result in damage or injury. Facilities that hold many different types of products, and especially liquid products, are subject to this type of threat because of the nature of the products. Petroleum-based products and chemicals used in many industries are incendiary, flammable, or noxious, or may become explosive or toxic if exposed to flame or other types of chemicals. Such dangerous liquids are found universally, and it would be impossible to safeguard against attack in every case.

There are steps that can be taken, however, to decrease this product security risk, and Supply Chain for Liquids incorporates many of these steps. To the degree to which a tank made out of a harder material such as stainless steel is more protective of the liquids than a cardboard carton or plastic bottle, the ability to physically affect the product is reduced. Tank-based facilities that incorporate safety pools or enclosed containment areas are also more controlled than facilities in which leaked or released product flows on the floor/pavement and into the drainage system.

Because of the space-effectiveness of bulk liquids, the Supply Chain for Liquids system offers an additional control mechanism against malicious attack. Storage rooms containing tanks (described in Chapter 11) can hold double or more product than package-based storage facilities, and these can be physically isolated based on their construction. Like compartments in a submarine that can be closed off to limit systemwide impact if one compartment is damaged, tank-based facilities can be compartmentalized to address the physical security issue involved with facility penetration.

Other Security-Related Issues, Such as Product Counterfeiting

Companies need to protect their products from counterfeiting for both terrorist and theft purposes. Forged products could be harmful and cause injury or damage, or they might lead to financial loss by the producer. In either case, the ability to preserve product integrity and reduce the possibility of introducing forged products is to the producer's advantage.

The closed system that Supply Chain for Liquids utilizes significantly limits outside access to the logistics flow and the ability to introduce forgeries. Inasmuch as the flow extends to the point of dispense, there is virtually no opportunity to introduce foreign product into the system. In cases in which exposure to the possibility of forgeries does exist, marking methods for liquid products, such as "taggants," are available. Based on the type of liquid involved and its usage, tiny pellets called taggants can be placed in the liquid to mark its producer or point of origin. The use of a taggant and the type of taggant used are determined based on the characteristics of the liquid — whether it is consumable, whether it undergoes physical or chemical change along the logistics flow or during usage, etc. Taggants are both powerful and flexible. For example, taggants placed in the ink used to print certain documents or materials are scanned and detected to verify the authenticity of the documents. By the same token, taggant powder placed in other liquids can be used to confirm their origin. When the liquid passes near the taggant reader, the reader emits a low level of energy to which the taggants normally respond with an emission of their own, and the lack of a response detected by the reader means that the liquid does not contain the taggants and is counterfeit. Readers placed near the dispense point confirm that the liquid being dispensed is a genuine liquid that the producer fed into the logistics flow. These may be considered covert uses of taggants; in addition, taggants can be placed in such a way as to be overt and used for either security or quality purposes. Overt taggants can be placed so as to change color when certain conditions are met, such as temperatures exceeding a certain level, and so may be an indication of a potential quality problem based on either the use of a taggant reader or visual inspection by the user. In this sense, taggants represent something like the liquid-products equivalent of RFID tags for discrete products, in their passive/active capabilities as well as their ability to detect and respond to environmental conditions. The use of taggants, combined with the use of sensors along the logistics flow, is a powerful combination for assuring both product security and product quality.

In a period when physical security of product is an increasingly important issue, the Supply Chain for Liquids system offers types and levels of security that are not available from package-based liquid-logistics approaches.

The Process Defines the Product

The Liquid Lens tells us that the ends of the logistics flow drive the center, and that the downstream end — how the consumer uses the product — is the critical element in supply stream design. The flexibilities and capabilities that Supply Chain for Liquids provides to realize the benefits of this approach are far beyond those that are available for discrete products. We can provide the most productive user experience with the product and build our whole flow to support this objective. This is already a huge capability, but we can go even further with this concept. Instead of just saying that the product, and the usage of the product, define the process, let us explore the idea that the process defines the product.

What do we mean by the idea that the process defines the product? Let us take a simple, common example that comes close to the concept we are focusing on, and we will explore its implications from there. A beverage sold in a can comes as a final product, a beverage that is ready for the user to drink. It was produced in a production facility and put into the can in its finished, consumable form. When the beverage goes through a different process, however, it essentially amounts to a different product. For the same beverage that is dispensed at a fountain dispenser in a restaurant, it actually only comes into existence as the finished, consumable product when it exits the dispense unit and enters the user's beverage cup. Up until that point, it has been handled as three separate products: syrup, water, and gas. It is handled as these three separate products because that is the process that fountain beverages go through, combining three different products, from three different suppliers, at the point of dispense.

Let us make the final leap and say that once we have the process in place, the actual end product that the user receives could be different. For example, dials on the dispense unit could allow a user to dispense the beverage with more or less fizz or more or less water. In this way, the nature and flexibility of the process define the nature of the final product. For this example, this may seem fairly trivial, because the process and the dispense equipment are already in place and familiar to anyone. The dials mentioned in the example are not a problem technically. But for the vast majority of liquid products, the process is not in place, nor is there a reasonably easy way of adjusting the product once it is in the user's hands.

The producer comes full circle with Supply Chain for Liquids when, going beyond designing the distribution process to fit the product, the producer also designs the product to take advantage of the capabilities of the process. Like the beverage example given above, what other liquid products may be "taken apart" (kept as components) and moved through a Supply Chain for Liquids system as components, and then assembled as a final product at the point of usage? For virtually any liquid product, the characteristics that are added to the product during production can be examined as candidates for inclusion in this process. Fragrances for soaps, additives for oils, colors, flavors, sweeteners, strengtheners, hardeners — whatever the primary variables that lead to an enhanced customer experience with the product, this approach truly allows each customer to get it his or her own way. Moreover, under the Supply Chain for Liquids system, this tremendous flexibility and capability does not have to add any complexity to the logistics system, as all of the liquids required can be included within the Supply Chain for Liquids system flow. Under a package-based system, each of these variables would mean more separately identified products that would have to be handled, moved, inventoried, and controlled through the Supply Chain. All of the advantages of Supply Chain for Liquids are applied to the components, so that the incremental effort is very small relative to the incremental benefit that is made available by this opportunity.

Supply Chain for Liquids points us toward the next area in which technology will play a role in logistics, that of material manipulation and the ability to use the process to enhance the product. Technology's ability to move processing steps downstream will continually improve both the product that is offered to the customer and the efficiency of the distribution process used to get it there.

Chapter 7

Distribution

The distribution system for Supply Chain for Liquids® sits in the middle of the liquid-logistics flow, between the producer and the customer. As described in Chapter 10, the distribution aspect of Supply Chain for Liquids is defined based on the production configuration that precedes it and the customer's requirements that follow it. That is, distribution is seen as the connector between producer and customer, and so it follows the logistics path defined by those two "ends." The distribution method adapts itself to its predecessor and follower rather than itself defining the nature of the logistics stream for the product.

Further, the Supply Chain for Liquids approach tries to minimize the distribution function to the degree possible, as described in Chapter 5. The efficiencies gained by a Supply Chain for Liquids system should allow examination of what level of interim distribution, if any, is necessary to support the supply stream, and the quantity of liquid in the distribution stream should be significantly reduced in any case under the Supply Chain for Liquids method. Some of the factors at work within Supply Chain for Liquids to reduce the quantity of liquid in the pipeline between the producer and the customer are:

- The use of sensors at customer sites reduces the need for buffer inventory along the flow that is often held to protect against the uncertainty caused in part by lack of visibility into current on-hand balances. The sensors provide extensive visibility into activity and product balances for the whole length of the supply stream.

■ Precise delivery quantities, the space advantages of liquids over packaged goods on trucks, and greatly reduced in-transit time and customer-fill duration make delivery runs much more effective and extend the reach of the delivery capability from the production site.

■ Better space utilization based on the use of tanks means that product can be held effectively at the producer and at the customer site, which supports the cost savings resulting from fewer delivery runs and less interim product.

Even with this, geographic or other considerations may dictate the need for interim distribution facilities, such as distributor warehouses or distribution centers, and there is a fundamental approach to distribution within Supply Chain for Liquids that can be adapted to suit the requirements of any particular situation. The major aspects of this basic approach are:

■ The use of a flexible mini-tank system to store liquids at the distribution center
■ Trucks that use a version of the mini-tank system
■ The distribution planning method used to determine the timing and quantities of product movement
■ The information system in place to monitor and control activity throughout the distribution system

We will examine each of these aspects separately, and in doing so draw the picture of the distribution process within Supply Chain for Liquids.

Mini-Tank Storage System at the Distribution Center

One of the key characteristics of the Supply Chain for Liquids system is the flexibility it allows to meet the changes in usage of various liquids. Different liquids such as different types of beverages — regular, diet, caffeine-free, etc. — are each likely to be used in different quantities, and the quantity and thus the storage capacity required for any particular type of liquid may vary based on season, on short-term or medium-term promotional efforts, on long-term trends, or on other factors. The Supply Chain for Liquids system is designed to support these changes without affecting the underlying flow of the system.

Storage of a specific liquid in the Supply Chain for Liquids consists of a series of tanks connected to each other in such a way that any given tank can be disconnected from use for one liquid and reconnected for use with a different liquid. This approach also allows for a very simple isolation procedure for any particular tank for cleaning, as described in Chapter 8. The connections between the tanks are in parallel mode, to borrow a concept from the world of electricity, rather than in serial mode. This means that any individual tank can be closed off from the system without affecting the overall flow of the system, just like an individual light bulb can be changed without affecting the other light bulbs along the same electrical path. Systems that connect multiple tanks in serial mode — one connected to the next in a chain from the first to the last — are much less flexible and more difficult to work with for changeover or cleaning, and thus the parallel approach is used for Supply Chain for Liquids. For example, for tanks in serial mode that are under pressure for propulsion or quality purposes, the pressure must be released from the whole system in order to swap or clean any one tank. This causes disruption of the flow of product to the dispense area, and if the gas blanket is for quality purposes, this could expose the product to air and thus threaten the quality of the product. For tanks in parallel mode, however, one tank can be isolated while the pressure is maintained on the remainder of the system, avoiding disruption to dispense and eliminating the threat to product quality.

The total capacity at a distribution center for any given liquid is the sum of the capacities of the tanks that are dedicated to that liquid at the center. Not only can capacity be switched among liquids by disconnecting and reconnecting a tank from one liquid to another, but overall capacity at the center can be increased or decreased by adding or removing tanks in this parallel fashion. The addition or reduction in capacity, or the swapping of tanks between liquids, does not affect the overall flow within the Supply Chain for Liquids in terms of delivery of product into the system or flow of product out of the system for delivery to the customer or for dispense.

The tanks themselves are configured according to the very specific needs of the distribution center and the liquid, both in terms of size and physical configuration. The sizes of the tanks for each liquid are calculated based on a combination of factors: the frequency of deliveries to and from the center, projected quantity of product receipts at the center and shipments to customers from the center, the cost of the tanks, the likely need to increase or decrease capacity of the liquid, etc. These factors themselves are subject to supporting calculations. For example, the frequency of deliveries from the center will depend on truck capacity and cost, density of delivery locations, and a number of other factors. The maximum benefit of Supply Chain for Liquids is derived from carefully laying out current and projected data for all of these factors, and then optimizing the number or size of tanks for each liquid at each center and site. The approach to sizing the tanks based on the inputs that go into the tank-sizing equation is described in more detail in Chapter 10.

The physical configuration of the tanks can also be used to add flexibility to the system. As described in Chapter 10, Supply Chain for Liquids tanks do not necessarily have to be placed on the floor, but can be located overhead, on walls, etc. The tank can be designed with a cage structure around it that serves as a modular racking system, including all of the piping and connectors necessary. Using this approach, the installation, removal, or reconfiguration of the tanks becomes a relatively trivial process. The systemwide implication of this physical capability is that liquid capacity can be adjusted or shifted relatively easily along the Supply Chain for Liquids. For a distribution center, maximum space utilization might include the installation of tall tanks to exploit the vertical space available in the center. Unlike discrete or packaged products, liquid in a tank does not have to be accessed by a warehouse person or forklift for put-away, picking, or movement, and so the height limitation imposed by racking and forklift reach does not apply to a tank-based storage configuration. In fact, as described in Chapter 3, Supply Chain for Liquids wants to take as much advantage of the liquid nature of the product as possible, so for flow purposes, vertical storage is in many ways better than horizontal storage. This turns traditional thinking about distribution centers and warehouses as very broad, low, many-acre blocks on its head (or at least on its side). The ideal distribution center for liquids is relatively tall and slim, and it can even extend underground with pumps to move the product back up to truck-loading level, just as pumps are used at the customer site to move product from the basement up to the dispense points, as described in Chapter 8. As described below, there are also very significant warehouse storage capacity implications to the use of a tank-based system rather than a rack-based system.

As described in Chapter 8, sensors are used to measure the amount of liquid in each tank and in aggregation at the site as a whole. The addition or removal of tanks with their sensors, or the swapping of tanks between liquids, does not impact the system's ability to track on-hand balances; the additional tanks/sensors or changes to the arrangement are simply configured into the information flow. The tanking system for the physical flow of product in one direction is accompanied by sensors and other information-system elements that support the data flow of information in the other direction, as described below.

The use of a bulk approach in Supply Chain for Liquids versus a packaged approach in standard Supply Chain represents a big win for the distribution system in another way: the physical dimensions and handling of the liquids. If you put a one-gallon jug of a liquid in a carton, only about 62 percent of the internal space of the carton is taken up by the

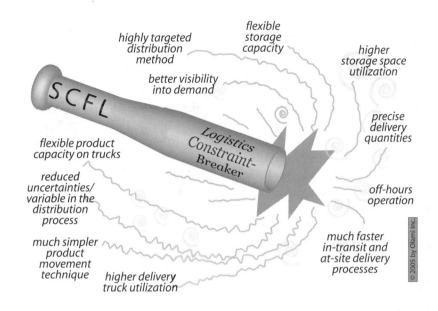

flexible
storage
capacity

highly targeted
distribution
method

higher
storage space
utilization

better visibility
into demand

SCFL

precise
delivery
quantities

*Logistics
Constraint-
Breaker*

flexible product
capacity on trucks

reduced
uncertainties/
variable in the
distribution
process

off-hours
operation

much simpler
product
movement
technique

higher delivery
truck utilization

much faster
in-transit and
at-site delivery
processes

© 2005 by Olami Inc.

Exhibit 7.1   Supply Chain for Liquids (SCFL^SM) Breaks Down Barriers in the Distribution Process

liquid — an automatic loss of 38 percent storage space! Put the other way, moving to a Supply Chain for Liquids system instantly increases your storage and distribution capacity by 30 to 40 percent for the liquids that are included in the system. In fact, the capacity will be increased by much more than this, once you take into account the empty space that is normally left between the top of a package and the rack shelf above it, the space taken by pallets on a shelf, the aisles needed for forklift access to the racks, the empty space between the top of the rack and the ceiling, etc. With Supply Chain for Liquids, you can move much more product using exactly the same amount of space as is available under a standard Supply Chain system. This and other constraint-breaking capabilities of Supply Chain for Liquids are illustrated in Exhibit 7.1.

Moreover, you can move that product much more efficiently. Liquids in cartons or jugs, or pallets of containers of liquids, are usually moved by forklift drivers one pallet (or less) at a time. The pipe approach means you connect one tank to another and move the liquid through the pipes simultaneously for as many liquids at any given time as required, and at the total investment of the pipes and controls involved. What, as they say, is missing from this picture? What is missing are bunches of forklifts, pallets, fuel, insurance, damage, warehouse racks, and on and on. You move much more product much more easily; such is life using Supply Chain for Liquids distribution.

Tank System on the Truck

The functioning of the tank system on the distribution truck is in many ways similar to that of the system in the distribution center. The truck contains compartmentalized tanks that can be connected or reconnected based on the capacity requirements for each transport run. A truck with 6000 gallons of capacity, for example, could be divided into 15 400-gallon compartments or ten 600-gallon compartments, or configurations with different sized tanks to handle products with high usage together with products with low usage. On one run, the 15 tanks might be divided between regular/diet/caffeine-free/lemon-flavor beverage syrups according to 6/3/4/2 tanks, and on the next run 4/4/5/2 based on the quantities of each product to be transported on each run. Like the tanks in the distribution center, the sizes and number of tanks on a truck should be calculated based on the factors that affect or are affected by tank capacity. The number of different liquids that the truck must deliver, the variability of the quantities, "exclusivity" caused by the need to segregate tanks based on the liquids they may contain (for example, some tanks may be designated for consumable liquids and others for nonconsumables, some liquids may leave a residue despite cleaning that prevents specific other liquids from being held in those particular tanks, etc.), the maximum allowable physical dimensions of the truck/tanks, and other factors will be taken into account in designing the truck tanking system.

Distribution Planning and Execution

The benefits of having a distribution system in which you continually know the quantity of product at every point in the system are obvious. Having variable capacity throughout the system also supports more efficient distribution by allowing capacity to be flexed to meet seasonal or irregular changes in distribution quantities.

What Supply Chain for Liquids adds to distribution planning and execution, in addition to the above, is the elimination of many distribution constraints — factors that add cost and complexity to standard distribution systems, or that block efficiency improvements in the planning and execution flow. For example, most delivery schedules are constrained by the hours of operation of the receiving site, be it an interim station such as a warehouse/distribution center or final destination such as a restaurant or factory. For example, receiving hours at a certain customer might be 9:00 to 11:00 A.M. and 2:00 to 4:00 P.M., and delivery scheduling must be done around those limitations. Such a situation adds a great deal of complexity to the distribution/delivery scheduling process, and usually leads to waiting time that lowers the utilization of the truck. This constraint is eliminated under Supply Chain for Liquids. Because product is passed from the tank truck through a secured outlet into the receiving site, there is no limitation to the timing of the delivery. The delivery process takes place the same way whether the receiving site is operating or not, so the trucks can be scheduled based on considerations of distribution effectiveness. For example, a delivery truck working in an urban area will operate much more effectively at night, when street traffic is at a minimum and truck movement is easiest. The truck's most effective delivery period is exactly the time when many receiving sites are closed!

Even in those situations in which deliveries are allowed during the normal working hours of truck operation, truck utilization is often reduced by the waiting time incurred by the driver/delivery person at the receiving site. The receiving person may have other deliveries to process, may be involved with customer activity as well as receiving activity and place a higher priority on customer activity, or for many other reasons require the delivery person to wait and incur a delay during the delivery process. The required interaction between the delivery person and the receiving person is eliminated in the Supply Chain for Liquids approach, as the delivery does not require interaction with on-site personnel.

Another major constraint that Supply Chain for Liquids eliminates is the lack of knowledge regarding exact delivery requirements, in terms of products and quantities, at each site. A truck will frequently make the rounds and discover along the way how much product is needed at each site, or be in a mode of mixed preorders and spot-orders. The loading of the truck reflects the inaccuracies of unknown demand against the actual demand as it occurs along the route. Even with a great deal of experience, a truck often returns with 15 to 25 percent of the outgoing product still on the truck at the end of the run. Supply Chain for Liquids provides highly accurate information regarding product balance and usage at each site, and thus allows the truck to be loaded with close to 100 percent of the correct product that is required for that delivery run. That is, distribution capacity is effectively increased by 15 to 25 percent by knowing exactly what quantity of what product will be delivered at each site, so that the 15 to 25 percent of truck capacity that is used for product that is otherwise not delivered during a run is used for product that is moved to the customer under the Supply Chain for Liquids approach.

A third major constraint that Supply Chain for Liquids eliminates from the delivery process is the physical steps required to perform the delivery.

A standard package-based system may take, for example, 20 minutes to deliver a set of liquids to a site. This includes entering the premises to inquire as to the quantity to be delivered, physically off-loading the product from the truck, moving the product into the facility such as with a hand truck or forklift, rearranging on-site product to make space for the incoming product, counting or sign-off of incoming product by receiving personnel, the put-away of the product in the facility, and any other adjunct activities that can take place during a delivery. A corresponding delivery using Supply Chain for Liquids consists of opening the access point, attaching the delivery pipes to the point, entering the name/number of the receiving location into the flow-control unit so that the correct amount of each product will be delivered to that location, having the liquids flow through their respective pipes into the on-site tanks, and unhooking/recoiling the delivery pipe when delivery is complete. Depending on the flow rate of the liquid in the pipes, this might take on the order of six minutes, or more than three times faster than standard Supply Chain practice. As described in Chapter 7, the exact duration of the delivery process is dependent on a number of physical factors that are taken into account in designing the actual act of delivery. For example, larger tubes to handle the flow of product from the truck to the site means that the product will flow faster and delivery time will be shorter, but this also means that the tubes will be heavier as they are pulled from the truck and attached to the external port. This trade-off is evaluated, and the optimal trade-off is defined during the system planning process. Similarly, bundling multiple tubes into a single unit makes it faster and easier to connect multiple lines from the truck to the site, but this also makes the tubing/bundle heavier and more difficult to work with. The optimal method — single tubes or different configurations of bundled tubes — is defined during system planning.

The steps described above show how the global approach used by Supply Chain for Liquids touches on each aspect of the delivery process, both the in-transit time that is improved by working during low-traffic periods and the actual delivery time through the Supply Chain for Liquids delivery method. The delivery truck moves faster from point to point and completes its work faster at each delivery point, a net win for the entire distribution/delivery process.

Finally, Supply Chain for Liquids breaks through another constraint of a discrete-oriented distribution system, that of the delivery distance that can be achieved from a delivery location. The geographic reach of Supply Chain for Liquids can be extended by enhancing the truck configuration utilized in the process. As described in Chapter 7, double-trailer trucks can be used to pull larger quantities of liquids to a more remote area, at which point the delivery method would follow that used by standard

Supply Chain for Liquids. The filling and travel time of the double-trailer transit cab is coordinated with the delivery schedule of the two delivery cabs that will take the trailers filled with liquid and return the trailers from which the prior deliveries were made. This makes the entire delivery process function as a seamless flow. Although the extended travel time needs to be taken into account in planning for remote deliveries, the Supply Chain for Liquids system allows effective planning and execution for even such extended-reach customers.

These enhancements to the distribution/delivery process, cutting both in-transit and at-site times, help the distribution planning process in two ways. First, they allow for more deliveries during the same period of time or, viewed differently, for fewer trucks to deliver the same quantity of product, thus simplifying the distribution planning process. Second, they add more certainty to the process and thus make it more precise. The variability of travel time (how long the truck will be delayed in traffic), the variability of at-site time (how long the delivery person has to wait at each site today), the variability of required quantities (how much of each product is needed at each site) — all of these variables are drastically reduced or eliminated under the Supply Chain for Liquids system, making distribution planning and execution that much more precise, accurate, and productive.

Even though we believe in the value of making distribution planning more of a science than an art, we are well served to remember that distribution planning, like many aspects of the logistics process, also has an artistic element; some parts simply require the human touch. Perhaps nobody expressed the connection between logistics, liquids, and art with more absolute beauty than the Japanese artisans of Kyoto early in the past millennium. To keep the product transport system in the Kyoto area working well, the owners of oxcarts adopted the habit of soaking the cart wheels in the Kamo River. This kept the wheels from drying out and warping, and so literally kept the wheels of commerce rolling. The sight of the wheels floating in the river caught the local artistic eye, and stylized depictions of the scene became an ongoing motif in Japanese art. Exhibit 7.2 shows a decorative rendering of cart wheels in the beautiful flowing river, one way of expressing the artistic side of the logistics function.

Information System

The entire flow of product within Supply Chain for Liquids is planned, monitored, and controlled by a wide-ranging but surprisingly simple infor-mation-processing scheme. In fact, the elegant simplicity and simple elegance of a Supply Chain for Liquids logistics system — versus a Supply Chain

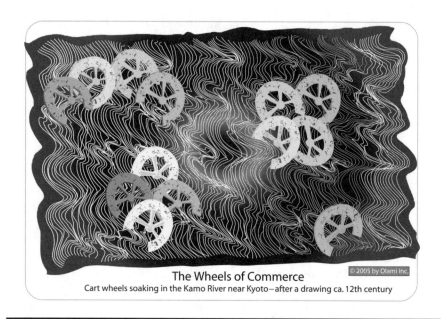

The Wheels of Commerce

© 2005 by Olami Inc.

Cart wheels soaking in the Kamo River near Kyoto – after a drawing ca. 12th century

Exhibit 7.2   The Art of Liquid Logistics — Figuratively and Literally

logistics system that contains more steps, more operations, more activity, and more costs — is matched by the relative simplicity of the information system used to run it. In terms of ongoing daily activity, the information system can be broken down into three major elements: monitoring, processing, and actioning. Each of these elements occurs at a different location and is conducted by a different resource. Monitoring is done by the sensors in the field, processing is done by the main computer system, and actioning is done by the dispatchers who convert the information into action for the following delivery run. All of the elements are integrated and brought together within the single information system to make up the Supply Chain for Liquids information flow.

Monitoring

A foundation stone of the Supply Chain for Liquids approach is the availability of highly current, highly accurate data regarding product quantities throughout the Supply Chain for Liquids. This requires that a comprehensive system of measuring and transmitting quantity data be put in place. Unlike discrete products, whose counting depends on some sort of human interaction (except in those still-rare instances in which RFID [radio frequency identification] systems are operational), liquids lend themselves to measurement directly by sensing/monitoring equipment without any manual action required. Such liquid-level measuring devices are widely used and commonplace, and their installation and usage are relatively simple. Supply Chain for Liquids utilizes liquid-level measurement systems throughout the liquid-logistics flow. Typically, such systems consist of several components. The physical measurement of liquid level or flow quantity is done by a device such as a liquid-level sensor or a flowmeter. Through any of the methods described in Chapter 8, the sensor is able to determine the quantity of liquid in a tank at any given time. Depending on the design of each installation, there may be one such sensor per tank or one sensor/meter per site per liquid. If there is a sensor in each tank, the sensor measures the liquid quantity in the tank based on the height or weight of the liquid. Another technique is to attach all of the tanks for a particular liquid to a liquid column, which will in one place reflect the height of liquid in all of the tanks for that liquid. This method allows one sensor per liquid, with a conversion algorithm to translate the height of the liquid in the column into quantities in the tanks holding that liquid and thus in the system as a whole. In any case, a sensor for the most part detects a condition and sends an electric impulse to a programmable logic controller (PLC), and does not contain much more intelligence than that.

All of the sensors/meters for all of the liquids at a site are attached to a PLC, remote telemetry unit (RTU), or some other device with similar functionality. Usually, one PLC is able to support a number of sensors, that is, receive signals from several sensors, and process them, so that there is one PLC per site. The PLC gathers the raw signals from the measurement devices, and it may do basic calculations such as converting the height of a liquid in a tank to a quantity for the liquid. The PLC also does other housekeeping functions such as placing a date/time and location stamp with each reading that comes in from a sensor, so that the central computer system will know the time and location of each reading that it receives. PLCs also contain intelligence to send control signals. For example, if a sensor shows that a certain tank is too hot, the PLC is able to send a signal to a fan to rotate more quickly to cool the tank. In most Supply Chain for Liquids applications, however, the PLC performs a monitoring function rather than a control functional, so that the signals are usually one-directional, from the sensors to the PLC to the central computer system.

The PLC also logs the data it receives from the sensors, that is, holds the data received from the sensors until it is passed to the central information system. Logging is needed to hold data in case the communication line to the central computer system is temporarily unavailable, to save money in the event that a dial-up line is used to transmit data so that data can be grouped into a single telephone call instead of individual calls, or for other reasons.

The transmission of data from the PLC to the central information system is done using data-transmission equipment. Data transmission can be done using an Internet-based connection, a dial-up telephone connection, a cellular connection, or other communication means. Some PLCs contain the modem/data-transmission equipment, but in other configurations the PLC and the data-transmission device are separate units. There are a number of factors to take into account in determining the most favorable data-communications methods. If the location already has an Internet connection and wiring is readily available to the area of the PLC, the Internet is a very simple and convenient means for passing the data. Remote locations often require telephone connections, and in some cases the locations are so remote that cellular service is unreliable, and a dial-up telephone connection represents the best solution. Although this decision is trivial for any one location, planning data communications across many locations for up to 24 hours per day requires careful analysis to achieve the required information flow while minimizing the expenditure for communications. At the same time, the other end of the communication line must be planned for. If the communications apparatus at the central computer system must be in communication with tens or hundreds of sites multiple times per day, the communications scheme must be a closely organized activity.

The major on-site elements of sensors/meters and PLC/data communications can be supplemented by quality control processing or other specialized processing, such as cleaning-in-place operation, as required. Quality control processing means that, in addition to quantity data being received from liquid-level sensors, quality data is being received from sensors that measure conditions that affect quality: liquid or ambient temperature, contaminants, or other factors. In a manner similar to liquid-level sensors, sensors for quality characteristics transmit data to the PLC for processing, logging, and transmission to the central computer system.

Processing

Data transmitted from the sites is processed in the central information system against a set of predefined parameters. Each site with its configuration (which liquids are held at the site, the site capacity for each liquid, the replenishment scheme based on recent usage data, etc.) is defined in the central system, as are usage data, site location and delivery route, and other basic information. This serves as the base information against which the ongoing activity for each liquid at each site is evaluated and actioned. The central computer system receives streams of data from each site, based on the update frequency that has been defined for transmitting data from each site to the central computer system. The central computer system processes the base data together with the current data and generates a number of results, including management-level reporting of operational information and operational-level reporting of quantities, activity, and exception conditions that require attention. The processing performed by the central computer system is described in more detail in Chapter 10.

Actioning

The Supply Chain for Liquids serves many users at many levels, and management-level and operational-level reporting is available to personnel at each of the players in the logistics flow, such as through secure Internet connections. Each level of reporting is set up to be actionable, that is, to highlight exception-basis conditions that require attention or action.

Operational-Level Actions

The operational actions that are normally generated by the information system relate to either routine daily operational activities or exception conditions that fall beyond the parameters of daily activity. Daily operational activity includes dispatching trucks on delivery runs; dispatching maintenance personnel for installation, repair, or service to Supply Chain for Liquids sites; and handling replenishment activities such as scheduling product loading from supplier locations. Even within these activities, the planning and reporting generated by the system include activity optimization to continually reduce costs and inefficiencies throughout the system. For example, as a truck is routed to a specific customer site to replenish a product at that site, the system examines current balances and recent activity for all products at that site. Based on this examination, the system includes replenishment for each of the products at the site to reduce the number of deliveries required to the site and maximize the period until the next replenishment at the site. Other routine reporting includes any reconfiguration required of the truck tanks so that truck capacity is most closely adapted to the volume of each liquid included in the delivery run being planned. The process of changing the truck tank configuration for each delivery run is described in more detail in Chapter 10.

Exception conditions are identified and flagged by the system and presented to the dispatcher for appropriate action. If recent usage indicates that a product will stock-out at a location prior to the next scheduled replenishment, the dispatcher receives notification and can schedule the delivery to prevent the stock-out. Similarly, an exceptionally high inventory balance resulting from unusually low usage might indicate a sales or other business problem, but from a logistics perspective, it might either indicate or lead to a quality problem. Slow-moving inventory is therefore also flagged by the system.

Among the other types of conditions the central computer system monitors is liquid usage at each site versus the tank configuration at the site. For a variety of reasons, the site tank configuration may need to be adjusted — a tank swapped from one liquid to another, or tanks added to or removed from the overall configuration. The central computer system provides information of this type so that the tank configuration at each site always matches the site's needs.

In addition to standard exception notifications, alerts may also be issued by the system. Alerts identify unusual circumstances that may not be directly related to the daily operational flow, but that do indicate an anomaly at some point in the process. For example, unusually high product usage at a specific site during a concentrated period of time — hours or days — might indicate theft or leakage that should be investigated immediately. A temperature monitor that reports a reading above or below the acceptable range indicates a situation that could adversely affect product quality and should be responded to quickly. Alerts can be directed to any of a number of recipients: to the dispatcher, to an operations person, or to on-site personnel. Often alert-level messages are issued through multiple means, not just displayed on a computer screen, but transmitted as a message to the appropriate person's mobile phone or beeper, and to a chain of individuals if the first target does not respond to the alert. These types of alerts rise quickly to the top of the action list and are addressed immediately by the person responsible, an action that is initiated by appropriate programming within the Supply Chain for Liquids system.

Management-Level Actions

Just as there are notifications appropriate to operational-level personnel, there are notifications that are properly directed to management. The most basic of these are "pulse" reports, specific indicators that are defined by management that allow operational management to keep its finger on the pulse of activity. These are the highest-level measures: total inventory throughout the system, total quantity delivered across all delivery trucks for a given delivery run, etc. Some managers prefer to see the raw numbers each day, while others request that they be notified only when the pulse numbers fall outside of a predefined range. Pulse reporting is most frequently performed daily or weekly and does not represent either immediate-action items or longer-term activity trends.

Exception notifications at the management level are used when unusual but not urgent situations occur. Management is interested in any exceptions that occurred related to the target level of customer service (for example, cases in which inventory ran unusually low while truck utilization was high, indicating that distribution resources are being stretched to meet demand), overtime related to delivery (are the tight delivery patterns slipping?), and other factors such as customer contacts or complaints. These types of reports can be derived from information processed through the central computer system.

Under Supply Chain for Liquids, the producer/distributor is actually losing a touchpoint with the customer, inasmuch as the delivery person who would normally interact with customer personnel is now delivering from outside the facility. Although this is logistically far more efficient, it does lead to a loss of intelligence — the everyday kind of conversation by which the delivery person gains a wide variety of information. This informal information may cover many different topics: customer dissatisfaction, competitive initiatives, comments about the product, or a need that the customer has that is not being fulfilled that could represent a business opportunity. Although some of this feedback relates to operational-level conditions, it is frequently the source of valuable information for management (with the gigantic proviso that management has set up mechanisms to cull this information from the field people, a process that is all too frequently not exploited). Management can compensate for the lost touchpoint in a number of ways, such as developing alternative channels of communication. For example, rather than using an expensive delivery person as the on-site presence (expensive not only because of direct cost, but also because of the delivery resources that are tied up for every minute the delivery person is at a specific customer, such as the truck, lost opportunity for other deliveries, etc.), the company might hire a lower-cost customer-satisfaction representative. Such a representative would be dedicated solely to being the company's presence in the field — schmoozing the customers, watching consumer and competitor activity, and gathering intelligence in all its forms. The customer-satisfaction rep is disconnected from the delivery person; in fact, a rep can cover many more customers than a delivery person because less-frequent visits to each customer are required, albeit for longer duration for each customer.

It should be noted that the relationship between the rep and the delivery person should be carefully constructed. Some companies use a rep-type person as its eyes and ears in the field, not only related to competitor and customer actions, but as a monitor of delivery person action as well. Although this is much less pointed in a Supply Chain for Liquids environment, the relationship between the two functions can be problematic if conflict is built into their relative roles. In any case, the customer-satisfaction rep is a management-level tool. The information, data, and reports generated by the reps are compiled and flow to logistics, sales, and other management personnel. In this way, management is able to keep a critical finger to the wind in the field, in some ways more effectively and at lower cost than can be done by a delivery person while performing delivery rounds.

Like operational-level alerts, management alerts are in place for exception situations requiring immediate attention. Management is the backup in case operational-level alerts are not satisfied. Management is also notified in any "shouldn't happen-couldn't happen" situation that could affect the business, such as a stock-out at a site. In addition, any internal indications of wrongdoing — a rapid drop in inventory balance in a tank at a production, distribution, or customer facility, for example — are channeled to management rather than to the operational-level people directly responsible for the activity.

These are the operational-level and management-level notifications that the Supply Chain for Liquids information system provides to users. In addition, the processing associated with Supply Chain for Liquids may feed information to the company's main computer system to trigger action reporting as appropriate to various functions within the company. These connections are described in more detail in Chapter 10.

These three major aspects of information processing within Supply Chain for Liquids — monitoring, processing, and actioning — cover the flow of information from the customer back to the producer, as highlighted here. Like the flow of product in the opposite direction, which is continually examined and adjusted to maximize efficiency, eliminate any points of waste, and reflect changes in the field that impact the logistics flow, the information flow is adjusted in the same way. Processing is continually fine-tuned, reports and alerts are added as situations arise that require them, and the unity between the product flow and the information flow that is so critical to gaining maximum benefit from Supply Chain for Liquids is continually reviewed and strengthened.

Extended-Distance/Extended-Complexity Supply Chain for Liquids

Many Supply Chain for Liquids products are local in terms of the geographic distance from the producer/distributor to the customer. With the producer or major distribution point within transport driving distance of the customer base, the transportation and delivery trucks can be one and the same vehicles. Obviously this simplifies the Supply Chain for Liquids and reduces the cost and complexity of the entire process. As described previously, the efficiency achieved through the Supply Chain for Liquids approach allows a wider area of coverage for the delivery function, and expands the reach of the delivery capability.

However, many Supply Chain situations are either marginally or decidedly larger than this. The size of the logistics flow is measured in terms of both the geographic distances involved in product movement and in the complexity of the logistics process. Geographic distance can range from intercity to transglobal, and is a function of where production and distribution facilities have been established relative to customer locations, the logistics methods available to move product to the customers within different regions and the resulting constraints on product movement, etc. The complexity of the logistics process is defined in terms of the number of interim touchpoints in the logistics flow (such as warehouses/distribution centers, recontainering operations, cross-docks, etc.), in terms of the intermodal nature of the logistics flow, in terms of special conditions that must be preserved (such as refrigeration of the product), and other complexities of distribution operations. Let us look at several extended-distance/extended-complexity situations to see the Supply Chain for Liquids techniques that are available to address them. First, we discuss a relatively complex short-distance logistics situation and see how Supply Chain for Liquids can reduce the complexity and handle the distribution requirements. We then look at Supply Chain for Liquids alternatives for handling intermediate-distance distribution situations, and finally at alternatives related to extended-distance logistics.

Reducing Supply Chain Complexity

For a distribution system that currently uses warehousing or distribution centers (DCs), the first step is to ask fundamental questions as to whether they are necessary under a Supply Chain for Liquids approach. Although warehouses or DCs may seem to be part of the *solution* related to logistics processes (and are generally created with that in mind), they may in fact actually be part of the *problem* because they serve to hide inefficiencies in the system. Having extra inventory on hand is always a convenient way to cover for operational or data shortfalls, and DCs institutionalize the existence of extra inventory. Having extra inventory allows, or possibly causes, a company to operate with less concern for accurate forecasts, less efficiency in its distribution operations, poorer quality information, less discipline in terms of the use of information, or other shortcomings. Assuming, though, that a company has minimized these inefficiencies, the logistics methodology must still take into account the complexities the company faces in distributing its products.

Supply Chain for Liquids eliminates one of the big deficits common to many companies — the lack of insight into the quantity of product throughout the supply stream as well as lack of precision into delivery quantities required for delivery runs. The visibility into delivery requirements described earlier may create direct-delivery situations in cases that previously required an additional distribution point. Let us use a simple hypothetical illustration to see how the improved data availability from Supply Chain for Liquids can reduce the complexity of the transport/warehousing/delivery process.

United Products produces floor-cleaning fluids and sells them to customers relatively close to the production facility, that is, within delivery distance of the production plant. Smaller customers preorder product, and the truck can thus be loaded with those exact order quantities. However, for competitive reasons, United offers a replenishment service to its larger customers whereby the delivery person makes a weekly stop, inspects the quantity in the storeroom, and replenishes product as necessary. With its product packaged in one-gallon to five-gallon jugs and a total capacity of 3000 gallons per truck, United found that it required ten trucks to service delivery requirements. At 20 minutes per stop and 180 gallons per delivery, and 20 minutes average drive time between stops, each truck was able to make 15 stops per ten-hour operating time per day for a total of 2700 gallons delivered per truck, or 27,000 gallons for the ten trucks per day. The 2700 gallons also represented a natural "limit" in delivery capacity per truck, as United's loading scheme was about 90 percent accurate, and by the end of the delivery route, stock-outs on the truck would start to make the delivery stops relatively ineffective.

United Products decided to expand to a neighboring market, located about 60 minutes rush-hour drive time from the production facility. To support deliveries to these more remote customers and still achieve ten hours of delivery time per day, United applied standard Supply Chain thinking and set up a depot in the neighboring market. This depot was replenished each day by a freight truck and held enough stock to cover normal deliveries for five trucks plus safety stock. The five trucks operating from the depot serviced customers in the neighboring market in the same configuration as the ten trucks in the home market, delivering a total of 13,500 gallons per day. In summary, under standard Supply Chain practice, United used 15 full-time delivery trucks, a freight truck, and a remote depot to support 40,500 gallons to a total of 225 stops per day of delivery.

As United Products adapted Supply Chain for Liquids practices, the company realized that it was able to revisit some of its basic assumptions about how it did business. This was because many of the parameters of business are different under Supply Chain for Liquids. Using mini-bulk tanks at its major customer sites, filled through outside access ports, United changed its entire delivery regime. Instead of the driver having to enter the premises, survey the on-hand goods, go back to the truck, manually transfer the delivery items, and wait for delivery sign-off, delivery became a simple operation of plugging the delivery hose into the port and metering in the correct quantity of each product. This was done during low-traffic off-hours, so average delivery time — including both drive time between customers and transfer time at each customer — dropped from 40 minutes to 25 minutes, even while increasing the customers' on-site capacity from 180 delivery gallons of packaged product to 200 delivery gallons of tank-contained product.

As United Products began to realize the implications of this approach, they understood that off-hours delivery also meant that the 60-minute average drive time to and from the remote customer locations would actually be less than 30 minutes, eliminating the need for the remote depot. Truck capacity would increase, as a tank truck of about the same dimension as the package-delivery truck held 4500 gallons of liquid rather than 3000 packaged gallons. So in a ten-hour shift, less 60 minutes average drive time to and from the delivery area (as a combined figure for all customers, including those that had previously been serviced from the depot), a tank delivery truck could make 22 stops and deliver a total of 4320 gallons. The same 40,500-gallon-per-day delivery capability could be done with just nine trucks, resulting in a savings of six delivery trucks, one freight truck, and the remote depot and its stock.

On one level, this example illustrates the complexities that the Supply Chain for Liquids approach removes from a standard logistics operation, together with the extensive costs associated with those complexities. The next layer of indirect costs is also eliminated — all of the logistics, planning, overhead, and management investment of supporting the remote depot. The margin freed up by this approach is available to be used in the direction selected by the company: to increase market presence and thus build the company, to reduce product prices as a competitive weapon, or to flow to the owners of the company.

A review of this example on a second level, however, reveals our objective in raising it. The cost savings of the Supply Chain for Liquids approach are clear, and they are described in even more detail in Chapter 11. What this illustration shows, however, is that we need to avoid our instinctive response to distribution issues when working under Supply Chain for Liquids. For customers or distribution objectives that seem too far away under standard Supply Chain thinking — and thus lead us to jump to consider solutions such as depots, warehouses, or other interme-diate-distance responses — our first goal must be to strip away the complexities and see if the simplest solutions actually apply, as they do in this case. The intermediate-distance and extended-distance Supply Chain for Liquids approaches described below are appropriate in cases in which the needs of the distribution system extend beyond the capabilities of the simplest approach. However, the simplest approach under Supply Chain for Liquids covers much more ground than a corresponding approach under standard Supply Chain, and we should be careful to

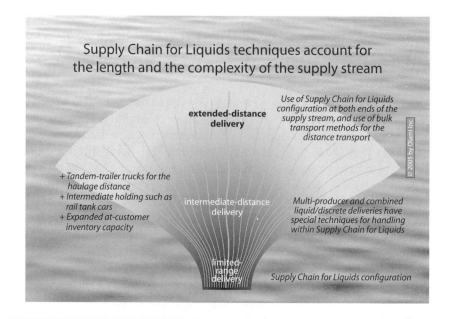

Exhibit 7.3   Supply Chain for Liquids Techniques Are Available for Local and for Widespread Logistics Scenarios

extract all of the benefits that Supply Chain for Liquids offers before considering intermediate- or extended-distance solutions.

Intermediate-Distance Supply Chain for Liquids Techniques

For those Supply Chain for Liquids situations in which delivery cannot be made directly from the source facility, there are still other alternatives besides creation of a remote warehouse or a distribution center. One of the key elements of Supply Chain for Liquids — visibility into demand — allows highly efficient pinpoint placement of product along the logistics flow. Whatever manner that is used to make that placement should be evaluated in terms of its efficiency and cost-effectiveness, as well as appropriateness for the particular products involved. Alternative approaches for extending the length of the Supply Chain for Liquids by creating an intermediate inventory station — other than a warehouse or distribution center — between the producer and the end user are shown in Exhibit 7.3 and include the following:

- *Use of tandem tank trailers*: Even with the highly efficient transport/delivery capability that Supply Chain for Liquids offers, there may be a set of second-ring customers that are just beyond the range of the source facility and too far away to be serviced directly by delivery trucks that are filled at the source facility. These customers are two- to six-hours drive time away — too far to profitably make a delivery run and return to the home plant, and yet barely far enough away to justify a separate warehousing facility. In these cases, the Supply Chain for Liquids approach allows effective use of tandem tank trailers. Instead of using a standard tank truck, tank trailers are used that can be detached from the cab. In this example, each of two tank trailers is filled for remote routes for the next day. One cab pulls the two trailers to a meeting point. At that point, two delivery cabs each take one of the tank trailers to do the delivery route. At the same time, they return the empty tank trailers from the prior day's deliveries, which are pulled in tandem by the first cab back to the central location for cleaning and preparation for subsequent delivery. In this way, the delivery range of the central location is extended without incurring the costs and complexities of an additional warehouse. In the case of a company with multiple production facilities, this approach serves as a low-cost method for providing wide coverage for the company's products. Such a second-ring technique applied to multiple locations around the country quickly covers the major metropolitan areas together with their extended peripheries while minimizing the infrastructure investment required for doing so.

■ *Use of intermediate liquid-holding options such as railroad tank cars*: Many liquids can be shipped by rail using railroad tank cars. The rail cars are cost-effective for long-distance shipment, and in some cases can then be used as the source of liquid for loading delivery vehicles at a remote location. The tank cars can be placed on a protected limited-access siding, and the contents off-loaded directly into the delivery-truck tanks based on the quantity required for each delivery run. Because of the fine-tuned capability to plan demand for each liquid, the rail cars are not serving as an open-ended inventory vehicle, but rather as a method for transporting a specific amount of liquid for a specific period of time.

■ *Expanded capacity at customers, such as on-consignment product*: Another method of extending the delivery range of a production or inventorying facility is to make the deliveries to distant customers more logistically efficient and cost-effective. This can be accomplished by increasing the delivery quantity and decreasing the frequency with which deliveries are made to these customers. Because liquid-holding tanks can be placed at a customer site in such a way as to not take up usable space (see Chapter 8), the additional space required at the user site for such a plan is not an issue in most cases. Similarly, because the supplier is constantly aware of the quantity being held at the user site through the in-tank level sensors, the supplier and the customer can come to a consignmentlike agreement that invoicing for liquids will only be triggered when the excess quantity in a delivery begins to be used. For example, to make deliveries cost-effective, the supplier might make an offer to install Supply Chain for Liquids tanks and deliver 1000 gallons on each delivery rather than the standard 600 gallons, and then replenish the quantity when the level of liquid goes down to 100 gallons. Upon replenishment of 1000 gallons, the supplier invoices the customer for 500 gallons, invoicing the customer for the other 500 gallons only when the on-hand quantity goes down to 600 gallons, at which point the supplier would presumably have made another delivery. In this way, the supplier gains a customer that would otherwise be literally out of reach, while the customer gets the supply of liquid under the same conditions as would otherwise have been available.

These examples provide an idea of how the Supply Chain for Liquids can be extended by adjusting several of the factors related to the supply stream. The examples demonstrate extension of each segment of the distribution flow — allowing the delivery function to travel further, pro-viding alternative product-holding techniques, and increasing on-site inventory in a way that is productive for both the distributor and the customer — while minimizing the addition of complexities and costs. By looking at any particular situation through the Liquid Lens[SM], as described previously, new opportunities present themselves even in the face of seemingly contrary conditions.

Extended-Distance Supply Chain for Liquids

Extended-distance Supply Chain for Liquids involves logistics that cover a large geographic distance, such as cross-country or overseas, from producer to customer. Such a situation does not in any way affect the Supply Chain for Liquids opportunities that are available at either end; both the producer at the beginning of the flow and the customer at the end of the flow can operate according to Supply Chain for Liquids principles, despite the distance between them. The transport phase between the producer and the customer, though, reflects the distance and is adapted to the logistics requirements of the distance. There are multiple opportunities for efficiencies within the long-distance transport phase that support full Supply Chain for Liquids operation for liquids that are trans-ported in bulk. Among the main alternatives available are:

- Intermediate bulk containers (IBCs) are bulk tanks of virtually any size, material, shape, or strength that can be used for transporting liquids. Some come with shipping-ready structures to protect the container itself and to allow fork-lift handling of the container.
- Flexible, collapsible bags made out of special fabrics or other flexible materials can be used either stand-alone or placed within another container, such as a 20-foot trailer. The materials for these containers are often specially treated based on the liquid to be transported in the container, such as drinking water, fuel, chemicals, etc. Many sizes of bags, up to 100,000 gallons or more, are commercially available.
- Pipelines may not be useful for the longest distances, but for certain applications they can provide an effective solution. An example of piping versus containers is the U.S. military's RIFTS (rapidly installed fuel-transfer system). RIFTS is a flexible hose spun off a large coil on the back of a truck that can lay up to 20 miles of fuel pipe per day. After analyzing the cost, capacity, resources required for use, safety, and flexibility of tank versus piping solutions, the military identified specific conditions under which each would be the most appropriate method.
- Beyond these methodologies, large-scale bulk transportation methods such as oceangoing tankers move large quantities of liquids. In some cases, these large-quantity methods are used in the upstream portion of a logistics flow, and Supply Chain for Liquids principles become more applicable in the next stage, during midstream and downstream distribution of the product. This scenario is particularly applicable for some chemicals and petroleum products.

As with any transportation scenario, the issues of safety and regulatory requirements come into play in the analysis and execution of the method. Because long-distance transport often crosses governmental boundaries, it is even more likely that these constraints come into play. However, these limitations do not affect the Supply Chain for Liquids approach of seeking the most effective solution based on the liquid nature of the product involved.

Extended-Distance Case Study: Quaker Chemical

We can look at a model of long-distance liquid logistics by examining the processes used by a company that performs such activities. Quaker Chemical Corp., headquartered in Conshohocken, PA, is a worldwide developer, producer, and marketer of custom-formulated chemical specialty products and a provider of chemical-management services for manufacturers around the globe, primarily in the steel and automotive industries. Quaker Chemical is a particularly appropriate example for us to examine because, over the past several years, it has transformed its operations from a local/regional orientation, in which the logistics of each geographic area essentially operated separately, to a global orientation in which the company has built a system to take advantage of its worldwide presence. All of the processes described in this case study are related to liquid products.

Wilbert Platzer, vice president of worldwide operations, has led the shift in orientation of Quaker Chemical's logistics systems. With responsibility for all manufacturing, logistics, raw material, purchasing, quality, and safety/health/environmental activities, Platzer is intimately familiar with the challenges and opportunities available in broad-range logistics systems. In many ways, the process Platzer describes is akin to the difference between Supply Chain and Supply Chain for Liquids methodologies we described earlier.

Under its former regional orientation, operations on each continent functioned independently in many ways. Raw-material sourcing, facilities planning, research efforts, and inventory policy were set by each region according to its own methods and standards. For both Quaker Chemical and its customers, this situation was suboptimal. Quaker Chemical operated basically as a confederation of cantons from a logistics perspective, and there were many resources that the company was unable to bring to the benefit of customers simply because there was no single point of access to companywide knowledge.

Several years ago, Quaker Chemical undertook to globalize this fragmented structure. From the perspective of our analysis, the company moved from a short-distance logistics system to an extended-distance logistics system. According to Platzer, a key element in this effort was the creation of a central database of information and common methods for all the company's operations. This "one point of information/one system flow" approach is the building block upon which the remainder of the effort was based.

In terms of information, Quaker Chemical viewed its data needs from two perspectives: its own internal perspective and that of its customers. Handling internal information with a global perspective allowed the company to optimize to a level that was not possible in its earlier incarnation:

■ Whereas previously each region dealt with its own vendors, the combined volume of purchases worldwide provided strong leverage with vendors who provide the company's total needs. This leverage is expressed in purchase price, terms, conditions of delivery, and other operational and financial advantages.

- The global view, combined with immediate access to raw-material prices and foreign-currency exchange rates, allows Quaker Chemical to exploit arbitrage opportunities globally. The key to this capability is speed of response — pulling together all the appropriate information in a way that allows fast action before an opportunity slips away. As Platzer points out, even a 1 percent savings in net raw-material costs translates into big money given the volume of purchases the company is performing.
- Through its single combined-inventory system, Quaker Chemical views its inventory position worldwide. After the appropriate analyses, on-hand stock can be moved from one site to another rather than purchasing additional material. For example, esters in China can be loaded into IBCs and shipped to South America to fill a material requirement there if this is shown to be the most cost-effective resolution of the materials need.

These approaches support the Worldwide Operations Business Unit of Quaker Chemical in achieving its prime goal, that of perfect order fulfillment at the lowest possible cost. The availability of a wealth of information and the tools to effectively use the information have provided Quaker Chemical with other innovative capabilities that they did not have previously. The company offers its customers access to its technical resources through an extensive on-line research function. Further, Quaker Chemical creates a "unity of interests" relationship with customers by offering value-proposition pricing in certain circumstances. Under this approach, rather than charging a fixed price for the products it supplies, Quaker Chemical works with the customer to develop a formula whereby the customer's payment to Quaker Chemical is based on the benefit that the customer derives from Quaker Chemical products. Such an approach becomes possible with the company's extensive knowledge base that allows personnel throughout the company to share experiences that apply to different customers. Quaker Chemical has also closed the loop in terms of the information flow related to this process. Everything that field personnel learn about how the company's products perform for the customer is fed back to the product group to use in enhancing existing products and developing new products.

This level of performance is only possible with a single information system and a single operational methodology, and with both halves of the overall flow working completely in sync with each other to the benefit of the company.

From an operational-methods perspective, Quaker Chemical has adopted something of a contrarian approach in certain of its methods. With one major plant in each of North America, South America, Europe, and China, and one smaller support plant in each of North America and Europe, Quaker Chemical has resisted the common practice of building smaller production facilities and warehouses close to customer sites. Rather, the company has focused on tuning its product-transport capability to get product to customers as effectively as possible. With the slight majority of its shipments in bulk deliveries and the remainder in IBCs (250 to 350 gallons), 55-gallon drums, or other small containers, Quaker Chemical has taken steps to make its shipping capability as efficient as possible. Although it operates with multiple shipping companies (albeit as few as possible), it works within Europe and the United States with centralized shipping data that allow the combining of inbound and outbound freight and optimizing between freight (full truckloads), inventory, and the purchase price of raw materials.

The role that the tight relationship between Quaker Chemical and its freight companies plays in effective logistics can be learned from the seamless daily interaction between the entities. The local freight company pulls the appropriate number of empty trailers into Quaker Chemical facilities each day, based on the shipping plan sent to the freight company. Quaker Chemical personnel fill the trailers, and from that point on, the freight company handles the shipment. The treatment of inbound chemicals also exemplifies this close relationship. The global approach to purchasing means that Quaker Chemical buys many of its raw-material chemicals in bulk, which must then be shipped to multiple locations. The freight company provides the bulk-breaking services and directs the appropriate quantity of raw material to each Quaker Chemical location. Platzer points to the strong interaction of Quaker Chemical with its shipping suppliers in terms of both the information flow and on-the-ground logistics as a linchpin of its operational effectiveness.

Quaker Chemical has also added value to its Supply Chain for Liquids through an approach it refers to as product clustering. Previously, certain products had to be produced in certain plants due to special equipment, processes, etc. When the company had ascended to the level of a global perspective, it realized that production costs for certain groups of products were far lower in some locations than others. As a result, the company initiated a planned program of investing in production facilities in such a way as to allow clusters of products to be produced in different locations. This flexibility allows optimized utilization of production facilities and shifting of production runs from overloaded plants to underutilized facilities.

As an additional operational enhancement, Quaker Chemical has boosted its transportation approach to take advantage of intermodal methods. Shipments continue to be done by truck, train, or boat, but the company has now invested in the infrastructure needed to identify the most effective combination of methods for each shipment. Although more complex, intermodal shipping provides cost and timing advantages that Quaker Chemical has learned to exploit.

Being based in Europe while working extensively in the United States, Platzer is sensitive to the differences in logistics approaches between the two regions. Companies must not only work toward the strengths while avoiding the weaknesses related to each region, but they must also handle the issues involved in transporting goods between the two regions. Platzer's education and employment background on both sides of the Atlantic demonstrate the need for a multinational view to properly handle global logistics issues.

Quaker Chemical produces most of its own chemicals, which means that it stands at one end of the Supply Chain for Liquids. Platzer says that Quaker Chemical has bucked common wisdom in this area also; the company has actually in-sourced products that it had previously purchased from contract manufacturers. In Platzer's experience, contract manufacturing is more of a U.S. phenomenon and is not as widespread in the rest of the world.

Having achieved this level of effectiveness in Quaker Chemical's global Supply Chain for Liquids, Platzer knows that the opportunities ahead are even greater than the successes the company has already achieved. He has set up an internal think tank to continuously develop and enhance Quaker Chemical's Supply Chain for Liquids functionality, and is already working on the objectives for the company's next-generation operational enhancements.

European/Asian Supply Chain for Liquids Issues

Although the processes and benefits of the Supply Chain for Liquids approach are universally applicable, some issues are particularly important in different regions of the world. In many ways, these have to do with the level of development of the different areas and the cultural elements that affect their ways of doing business. A closer look at several of these regions shows the particular applicability of Supply Chain for Liquids in those areas. We will first look at Western Europe as an example of a diverse but more-developed economic area, although these conditions are characteristic of some parts of Asia and the rest of the world as well. We then discuss the special applications of Supply Chain for Liquids in less-developed areas, or areas with less-sophisticated logistics infrastructures in place. This also covers a number of geographic areas, including parts of Eastern Europe and Asia and other regions.

Europe/More-Developed Zones

The political and cultural situation in Europe is reflected in its way of doing business. Currently, there is an ongoing tension and balance between each country's nationalistic views and its participation in the European community. Further, within some of the countries, there are strong subdivisions of geographic, ethnic, and cultural regions that reflect a diversity of worldview as wide as the intercountry differences. Although these issues are particularly strong in Europe, they also apply to the more-developed areas of Eastern Asia and Africa. To do business effectively in these areas, the logistical method needs to address a number of issues, as outlined in the following subsections.

National/Regional Focus on Logistics Issues

Supply Chain for Liquids encompasses a direct and highly efficient producer-to-customer flow that allows cost-effective regional operation of the system. The entire system can be sized to meet the needs of logistics relationships with different scales of operation and geographic reach, with corresponding adaptation of the cost of the system and benefits resulting from the system. Thus Supply Chain for Liquids can be applied to regional producer-customer relationships or regional activities within the context of broader multinational relationships. This becomes particularly important when external constraints dictate such a focus. For example, there may be product variations based on national or regional considerations, competitive considerations may dictate a particular zone of operation, or the locations of the producers/distribution points may require a regional approach to the logistics flow. Supply Chain for Liquids supports the creation of a highly effective regional distribution system for liquid products that offers all of the benefits of the system within the context of a focused geographic scope of operation.

One of the major benefits of Supply Chain for Liquids takes on additional meaning when viewed in an interregional context. Chapter 5 discusses the flexibility that Supply Chain for Liquids provides through the elimination of product packaging, in addition to the cost savings. The increased flexibility comes from having the product sold in its raw state, that is, as a liquid alone without the packaging. Packaging adds a great deal of complexity, as different regions may require packaging in different languages, with different types of information, different product names, etc. for the exact same liquid product. Once the liquid is put into a package, it becomes a more specific product — the liquid in that particular package. Supply Chain for Liquids allows a producer or distributor to avoid this level of complexity by maintaining the liquid without packaging throughout the entire supply stream. Any legal/regulatory documentation can be handled separately from the product, and branding issues are handled through nonpackaging techniques as laid out in Chapter 6. Thus Supply Chain for Liquids supports the distribution flow in a diverse regional environment by eliminating the element that most differentiates the liquid product across the region, that being the packaging.

The Need to "Mass Customize" a General Logistics Solution to Local Conditions

The adaptability of Supply Chain for Liquids means that it can operate effectively under many different types of localized conditions. Local terrain and transportation conditions, local relationships and methods, highly specialized selection of liquids to be delivered from certain producers to certain customers — these are all handled within the context of the Supply Chain for Liquids approach. Further, Supply Chain for Liquids serves to remove the need for extensive coordination between players that is required in many Supply Chain and RFID relationships. For example, under Supply Chain for Liquids, different types of sensors can be used in different locations based on the availability of local sales and service, as long as the data transmitted to the central computer system is structured in a uniform way. This contrasts with RFID, in which the types of tags and readers, and the radio frequency at which they operate, must be consistent throughout the entire logistics flow. Supply Chain for Liquids's CPVR[SM] (Coordinated Procedures for Visibility Response[SM]) collaboration approach allows a great deal more coordinated independence than common collaboration techniques, which demand a high degree of communication and integration between players. By providing a structure that allows several degrees of flexibility in how the players coordinate with each other, Supply Chain for Liquids works effectively even within a logistics flow in which the players do not necessarily interrelate with one another extensively. Similarly, Supply Chain for Liquids supports localized behavioral differences at the point of final usage, which is the point of greatest diversity in many supply streams. The Supply Chain for Liquids approach allows the dispense process to be carried out in accordance with local techniques, but the entire flow of product up to the point of dispense is done through the common methodology defined by the system. Thus very different and diverse user experiences may result from a common operational flow that is invisible to the user but supports the full range of user needs.

Environmental Sensitivity

As described in Chapter 11, Supply Chain for Liquids is a highly environmentally favorable methodology. Within Europe, some countries engage in stricter environmental enforcement than others, and Supply Chain for Liquids' environmental advantages address the most critical environmental issues very effectively. Waste is reduced by the elimination of packaging for liquid products. Pollution is decreased as trucks are used more effectively (a tank truck carries more liquid than the same size truck carrying packages) and operate during low-traffic off-hour periods, thus reducing idle run time. Land use is improved by elimination waste/recycling, and tank-based facilities have a smaller footprint for the same liquid capacity than package-based facilities. Waste recovery is improved, as product return (such as used motor oil) is actually built into the distribution process. In any specific application, additional environmental benefits may well be identified as resulting from use of the Supply Chain for Liquids approach. In some cases, the environmental aspect may even be an important motivator to a company to move to a Supply Chain for Liquids system — in addition to all of the operational, financial, and business advantages — as a fast-track way to meet environmental obligations that would be very difficult to achieve using standard Supply Chain methods.

The Need for Off-Hours Logistics

In highly congested urban areas, off-hours logistics represent a significant advantage to the local community. With European cities among the most heavily traffic-bound in the world, removing transport and delivery trucks from both intercity roads and urban streets during high-traffic periods reduces this pressure while working to the benefit of both the distributor and the customer.

Disengaging the producer's/distributor's delivery process from the customer's operational process offers complete flexibility in scheduling delivery activity. This is made possible under Supply Chain for Liquids by the external-port delivery technique that allows the delivery of liquid products to take place without interaction with site personnel and without consideration for whether the site is open/working at the time of delivery or not. Attempts to institute off-hours logistics outside of the Supply Chain for Liquids approach means that the customer incurs extra costs by requiring that a receiving person be available to accept incoming goods during nonworking hours. Off-hours delivery is enabled under Supply Chain for Liquids without incurring such costs. Further, the use of space-effective on-site tanks means that deliveries can occur less frequently while still supporting the same volume of liquid activity at the customer site.

That is, the on-site space limitations that constrain delivery/inventory quantity are relieved under the more space-effective Supply Chain for Liquids approach, thus allowing larger on-site quantity and less-frequent replenishment runs. As described earlier, this does not necessarily demand additional financial investment by the customer. The issue of the physical ability to hold more liquid product can be separated from the issue of the financial investment in the increased amount of pipeline liquid. Such additional inventory can be addressed financially in a consignmentlike (or other) manner.

Although motivated by environmental concerns, off-hours delivery provides many benefits to the distributor, as detailed in Chapter 5. In addition to increasing resource utilization because the truck and delivery person spend more of their time actually delivering rather than sitting in traffic, the higher degree of certainty regarding actual commute and delivery durations supports more precision in the distribution planning process and thus improves distribution efficiency. This is a case in which the environmental impetus can work very much to the benefit of the supply stream, rather than being a barrier or adding additional burden to the process.

The Application of Technology to Operational Problems

Several European countries are recognized leaders in the drive toward the use of technology within ongoing daily and business activity. Among the most notable examples is the widespread application of cellular phone capabilities to any number of operational situations. Supply Chain for Liquids' balance of technology, techniques, and equipment is very much in line with the trend toward properly applied technology used in a cost-effective manner to address operational needs. It is an excellent example of the "click and mortar" combination of the technology side — sensors, PLCs, dispense control, data communications, processing, and Internet usage — with the fundamental operational requirements of moving material from one place to another.

"Silent Commerce" and the Use of Sensors

Supply Chain for Liquids' sensor-based data-generation method serves as a great equalizer among the players in an often diverse logistics flow. Silent commerce takes the data-generation and -transmission activities out of human hands and puts it in a consistent electronic language that easily crosses political and geographic boundaries. The actual sensors used by different members of the logistics flow can even be of different types and from different manufacturers, as can the data-gathering/transmission equipment as well as the tanks in which the liquids are held. Unlike standard RFID applications that require standardization and integration of these elements along the entire length of the logistics flow, the point of connection among the different players within a Supply Chain for Liquids flow is electronic. Both the RFID for Liquids® and CPVR approaches rely on commonly formatted data rather than any kind of physical link among the players. This both eliminates the need for physical integration and vastly increases the speed with which the logistics flow in a diversified environment, such as cross-European, can be designed, implemented, and brought into operation.

Silent commerce is also the gateway to the next-generation use of the Internet, which European society is in some ways more ready for than the United States. Capturing data at its source and developing pervasive information about selected activities has been defined by some as the next focus of Internet utilization. Supply Chain for Liquids moves in this direction by providing a complete and universal picture regarding liquid products that are covered by the system. Because Supply Chain for Liquids utilizes process-based rather than product-based sensing devices, it can offer virtually universal information about product activity without any of the privacy concerns that are commonly voiced related to RFID systems for discrete products.

Alternative Approaches to Collaboration

Getting logistics-flow players with similar work styles and a common worldview to collaborate by extensive sharing of internal data is in many cases difficult, and even more so for players who speak different languages and do business in different ways. When that collaboration is redirected toward effective real-time handling of the logistics flow in a coordinated manner that does not require revealing company information but rather use of common logistics information, the collaboration receives a much higher level of acceptance and thus of effectiveness in achieving its goal. Supply Chain for Liquids' CPVR approach is particularly appropriate to a diverse environment such as Europe because each player acts in an independent yet coordinated manner with the other players, based on processing that resides within that player's own operation. This level of interactive independence is a very appropriate reflection of the relationships between entities within Europe, and thus has a much higher level of success than an approach that requires deeper interaction.

The "culture" of Supply Chain for Liquids is very much a mirror of the culture of business in Europe and other diverse, developed areas. The level of success in implementing a logistics system is directly related to the level of benefits that are derived from that system. Supply Chain for Liquids' approach, which directly addresses many European-centered logistics issues, enhances the likelihood of successful implementation and productive results.

Less-Developed Zones/Lack of Logistics Infrastructure

Another truly exciting scenario becomes clear when we think about Supply Chain for Liquids in terms of areas that have not yet reached the level of economic development normally associated with Western business practices. For developed countries, Supply Chain for Liquids represents a switch from one methodology to another, but for greenfield environments, the impact of Supply Chain for Liquids can be even more dramatic. In areas is which neither B2B (business to business) nor B2C (business to consumer) logistics flows have been developed — parts of Asia, Eastern Europe, and developing Africa, for example — the application of Supply Chain for Liquids opens tremendous opportunities for development in highly locale-appropriate directions.

Starting with the B2C segment, in some places such as parts of India, China, and Africa the logistics system consists of essentially manual collection and distribution of liquid products. There is very little infrastructure as we know it, including the lack of a developed retail or logistics system. In such an environment, the fundamental Supply Chain for Liquids approach offers an alternative, highly effective method for advancing local development. Rather than waiting for the entire retailing system to be developed and implemented, Supply Chain for Liquids offers the possibility of installing relatively simple tank-based outlets that focus on serving the population's liquid needs. The basic capability that Supply Chain for Liquids provides of bulk transport, storage, control, and dispense is of itself of high commercial value. Using even a simplified version of a tank-based kiosk, Supply Chain for Liquids offers the opportunity for low-cost distribution of basic consumer liquids. By placing such kiosks at multiple distribution points in a populated area, such a system could provide cleaning liquids, personal-care products, and beverages to the local population in a highly effective manner and with a minimum of overhead. In essence, Supply Chain for Liquids could replace a standard retail network for supplying liquid products. The beachhead of retail penetration could be achieved relatively simply based on liquid products, followed by further development of retail activity over time as the local culture adapts to such a methodology.

Similarly, Supply Chain for Liquids for B2B channels in undeveloped areas can serve a key role. With far less infrastructure and impact than required for traditional package-based operations, Supply Chain for Liquids can make both product and process liquids available to industry in a relatively inexpensive and convenient form. The fundamental bulk-based approach limits the cost of such a system, and full automation of the monitoring method could be adapted to partial automation to meet the operational and financial needs of each application. Supply Chain for Liquids could become the basic logistics methodology in locations in which only primitive, manually oriented logistics methods currently exist.

Many of the advantages listed above for developed, diverse areas apply even more so for less-developed regions. An example of this is the silent commerce aspect of Supply Chain for Liquids. In addition to the advantages of the use of technology for operational benefit and the way that it neutralizes cross-cultural differences, silent commerce offers strong advantages in less-developed environments because of the overhead/administrative tasks it eliminates in the different locations, as well as the training for those tasks among people of diverse backgrounds. A logistics system that depends on heavy manual intervention among employees who do not have the background and disciplines needed to execute these tasks properly is likely to fare poorly. The use of sensors and silent commerce to eliminate this weak point in the logistics flow provides the foundation for the overall Supply Chain for Liquids to operate effectively in these types of environments.

From this review of Supply Chain for Liquids' application in different environments, we can get a true feeling for the system's power. In its primary form for advanced Western economies, as applied to diversified and segmented economies, and applied to even relatively simple business environments, the Supply Chain for Liquids offers benefits and opportunities that are not available without it.

Additional Distributor Operational Issues

As the midflow agent along the Supply Chain for Liquids, the distributor connects the producer on one end with the customer on the other end. Working according to the methods described in this section, the distribution function supports the principles of Supply Chain for Liquids operation. There are several additional issues the distributor may need to address related to Supply Chain for Liquids activity.

Multiple Producers/Multiple Customers

The discussion thus far assumes the simplest situation, that of a distributor working with a single producer to distribute that producer's product to a set of customers. This is certainly the case for producers who run their own distribution operations, or who are the sole producer for a given distributor. However, distributors frequently handle the products of multiple producers, either competing products or noncompeting products, as part of their distribution activity. In fact, Supply Chain for Liquids encourages this situation through development of Complementary Supply Chains for Liquids[SM] (described in Chapter 10) as an additional efficiency to the distribution process. Let us take a look at what happens operationally in the more complex case, that of multiple producers and multiple customers, with the distributor in the middle of this network.

As we look at the Supply Chain for Liquids system, we see that there is no fundamental impact on the overall flow in a multiple-producer environment. The fact that the river has more tributaries and perhaps its delta is wider does not change its basic flow as a river. As we look at this scenario, we quickly discover that a multiple-producer situation is very similar to the case of a single producer with several production facilities. Instead of one producer pickup point, this situation may require pickup points at several producer locations. Several adjustments to the basic flow adapt it quite easily within this expanded framework. This can be handled in any of several ways:

- The producer locations can be viewed as extensions of the Supply Chain for Liquids, so the producer-to-distributor flow is simply an additional length of the Supply Chain for Liquids. In this case, Supply Chain for Liquids processing must take into account and coordinate the products, customers, and deliveries of the multiple producers. In any case, Supply Chain for Liquids considers multiple products from a single producer when planning deliveries and truck capacity, so multiple producers with their multiple products are an extension of, not a change to, this processing.
- Depending on geographic and other considerations, multiple pickup points can be handled in several ways. If products from different production facilities are delivered to a common set of customers, and if the production facilities are in reasonable proximity, the delivery trucks can circulate between the facilities to on-load the products prior to departing for the delivery run. In the case of distant production facilities or distinct sets of customers, delivery trucks can service one set of products/customers on one delivery run and a different set on a different delivery run, treating them as essentially separate activities. The combinations of these different conditions will lead to the most effective solution based on the factors involved.
- The producers might replenish product at the distributor location, so that from the distributor's perspective the Supply Chain for

Liquids starts at the distribution location. This scenario is more common in situations in which a producer has multiple production facilities and uses the distribution point as its stock-keeping location. Under this scenario, the producer-to-distributor replenishment process could be handled apart from, although driven by, the Supply Chain for Liquids distribution process that flows from the distributor to the customer. The Supply Chain for Liquids process from the distributor onward no longer "cares" which distributor any particular liquid comes from; the same algorithms regarding delivery planning, truck configuration, avoidance of cross-product contamination based on per-tank exclusions, etc. apply in multi-producer environments just as they do in a single-producer environment. Because each liquid product is identified by a unique product number and all of the information processing is handled based on product number, there is no danger that the products will become intermixed or that one producer's products will be delivered in place of another's. The delivery person performs the identical delivery as described in Chapter 10 of inputting the customer location, attaching the hose(s), and pumping the liquids without any impact that the liquids may be the products of different producers.

■ The distributor might relate to each producer's products independently, that is, it might carry one producer's products during one delivery run, and a different producer's products during a different delivery run. In this case, each delivery is for its own Supply Chain for Liquids, from a particular producer to that producer's customers, and so the entire distribution cycle works according to standard Supply Chain for Liquids principles.

In each of the above cases, some variations to the Supply Chain for Liquids flow may be introduced based on the particulars of the situation. The core processing and physical flow of Supply Chain for Liquids remain constant, as do Supply Chain for Liquids–related elements such as CPVR and the information flow of the system.

Distributing Liquid and Discrete Products

A key aspect of the Supply Chain for Liquids approach is treating liquids as liquids and avoiding the conversion of liquids to discrete products that occurs when liquids are placed in bottles, jugs, drums, or other containers. The benefits of this approach are clearly laid out in this book and are in clear contrast to the most common practice today, which is to treat all products as discrete products, including liquid products that have been placed in discrete containers.

For the distributor, the logistics of distributing a single type of product — either discrete or liquid — leads to a specific equipment configuration appropriate to that type of product. Discrete products are most generally distributed in box trucks, vans, or trailers, but liquid products are distributed in tank trucks or box trucks/trailers carrying tanks.

However, in the course of their business, many distributors handle both liquid and discrete items. For example, cleaning liquids are distributed together with cleaning equipment, beverages are distributed together with food and other discrete restaurant supply items, lubricants are distributed with automotive-maintenance equipment. Given this requirement to combine liquid and discrete products in the distribution process, there are a number of alternative approaches the distributor can use to address this situation:

- *Use of two sets of trucks*: On the face of it, duplicate trucks would seem to be cost-ineffective. However, the use of two sets of trucks — one for liquids and the other for discrete items — makes good economic sense in many cases. The savings resulting from the liquid-products trucks are clear, and the space freed up by eliminating liquids from discrete-based trucks provides larger effective capacity for discrete items and more effective delivery runs. Each situation has to be evaluated economically on its own merits, but the parallel-operation approach is effective in many circumstances. In any case, the only way to gain the full benefit of the Supply Chain for Liquids approach is to have a distribution capability dedicated to liquid products.

- *Use of a combination truck*: A combination truck is a box truck or trailer that holds fixed tanks for liquid products and, in addition, contains room for discrete products. Such a truck allows the delivery aspect of the Supply Chain for Liquids system to be carried out through attachment of hoses from the truck tanks to an external port on the site's wall and passing the liquid products to the on-site tanks. At the same time, the delivery person delivers discrete products to the site using the traditional delivery method. Although many of the benefits of Supply Chain for Liquids are reduced or eliminated under this approach (the ability to make off-hours deliveries, the noninteraction with site employees, etc.), in situations where most of the products delivered are liquids, supplemented by a small quantity of easy-to-move discrete products, this scenario becomes more attractive. This scenario also is effective if a lock-box arrangement allows off-hours delivery of discrete items as well as liquid products.

■ *Use of a variable-capacity combination truck:* This alternative is a variation on the previous option and allows the liquid-versus-discrete capacity of the truck to be varied for each delivery run. Instead of placing a fixed set of tanks on a truck, the tanks are off-loaded and on-loaded onto the box truck or trailer according to the needs of each delivery run. Tanks of various sizes are available that can be filled in advance and loaded on the truck in the number and size needed for the specific delivery run, thus providing the ability to balance the amount of space dedicated to discrete or liquid items on each delivery run. This approach preserves the delivery-flow aspect of the Supply Chain for Liquids system while allowing the truck to deliver discrete items at the same time and ensure maximum utilization of the space on the delivery truck during each run.

■ *Use of a multiple-use truck:* This arrangement combines aspects of each of the prior alternatives. A box truck is used that can be loaded with tanks for a liquid delivery run, or have the tanks removed for a discrete-item run. In some situations, this is a particularly attractive solution. Each delivery run is of one type or another; it is either for discrete items or liquid products, so the distributor gains maximum benefit from the Supply Chain for Liquids configuration. Because the tanks are off-loaded for a discrete-item run, they can be filled during that run and be ready to be loaded when the truck returns. Thus the delivery runs can be carried out at the most advantageous times, such as discrete products during the day and liquid products at night. This also certainly maximizes the utilization of the trucks within the distribution process.

Like almost all aspects of Supply Chain for Liquids, the combination of liquid and discrete products in the distribution system is flexible, with several alternative approaches available. The use of any of these approaches, or combinations/variations on these approaches, should be evaluated in terms of maintaining the integrity of a Supply Chain for Liquids system.

Facilities and Operational Adaptation

A distributor who enters into the Supply Chain for Liquids process comes with an existing operation in tow — most likely a warehouse, racks, forklifts, and a whole system for managing and moving product. As described previously, the distributor may be in the position of having to support multiple business methods simultaneously — discrete-based, liquids-based, a combination of these as required by products from different producers, and a transition period of moving between methods. This situation requires adaptations by the producer on a number of levels — organizationally, operationally, informationally, physically, and structurally, among others. The change-management issues that the distributor's organization faces in this situation are outside of the scope of this book, although these issues are significant and may well determine the success of the transition process. Our focus is on the physical and operational requirements that are placed on the distributor as part of the transition from a discrete-based to a Supply Chain for Liquids–oriented distribution system.

At the most obvious level are the physical changes that are required to run a liquids-based rather than a discrete-based operation. These changes include tanks of various sizes, characteristics, and capacities; piping to allow the flow of liquids to and from the required locations; control mechanisms for this equipment; etc. These are not simply physical changes carried out to continue the same method of operation, but rather significant improvements to achieve much higher efficiencies of operation. As described in Chapter 11, replacing racks with tanks provides for approximately doubling of the utilization of storage space, and to the degree to which previously unused space is used — higher levels or corner space, for example — the capacity of the storage facility is increased even more. Placement of piping to move liquid materials replaces the need for forklift movement of product within the distribution facility. In summary, the short-term costs of physical changes are more than outweighed by the long-term benefits of the changes, as is laid out in the Liquid Lens analysis (Chapter 3) that is performed as the first step of a Supply Chain for Liquids project.

More difficult than the physical change in a facility is the operational change that occurs among the personnel involved in the process. In some cases, the Supply Chain for Liquids process requires a different set of skills than are currently present in a facility, and more than this, it requires a different vision of how the distribution process will operate. Any process works best if those involved feel ownership of the process and responsibility for its success. Ownership can only occur after an employee achieves complete understanding of the process, including an understanding of the differences between the planned process and the current method of operation. One manner of approaching this situation is to run a pilot of the entire operation to let all personnel share an understanding of how product planning, control, and movement are handled under the Supply Chain for Liquids approach. An overview of the processes and procedures used in a Supply Chain for Liquids operation is provided in Chapter 10. This overview can easily be interpreted into the flow of work for each person associated with the distribution activity. This "day in the life" approach can be brought to life even more by using actual equipment or models of actual equipment at each point in the distribution flow, the actual computer screens and printouts that personnel will use during the process, and the actual step-by-step procedures that will occur during operation. This approach to training removes the mystery from the employees' perspective on the Supply Chain for Liquids system, and it provides an opportunity to achieve the kind of understanding that will support the proper operation and success of the system.

Any multicompany logistics project is certainly going to be more complex and more difficult than an internal logistics project, because different operating methods, management styles, and value systems are likely at work. In situations like this, although it is in some ways unpleasant, it is often most productive if there is an imbalance of power in the relationships between the companies involved. Trying to run an integration project as a democratic exercise is usually a longer, slower, less-complete project than one in which there is a clear decision maker who is in a position to listen to all sides and then make a decision and move things forward. At the end of the day, the objective is a successful, productive system for all involved, even at the price of flexibility in the roles of some of the parties during the planning and implementation process.

Chapter 8

Customer/User

The Supply Chain for Liquids® creates opportunities for the liquid products customer or consumer in two major worlds — the world that is and the world that is possible. "The world that is" refers to the operational improvements, cost savings, and revenue enhancements that Supply Chain for Liquids brings to current operations, including the current sales channels and points of customer interface. "The world that is possible" includes all the opportunities and methods for getting the product to the customer that have not been considered until now simply because the logistics methods in use could not support them. These include new distribution channels and locations, innovative presentation and dispense techniques, and even repositioning products in terms of their usage by consumers. In this chapter, we will take a close look at the Supply Chain for Liquids in terms of each of these worlds.

Business Perspective

Prior chapters have shown us how the flow of liquid products from the producer through the distribution system and up to the customer's facility is altered under the Supply Chain for Liquids approach. As we have done earlier, let us compare the Supply Chain approach with the Supply Chain for Liquids approach at a customer site to illustrate the differences between these approaches. We will use the example of beverages at a restaurant to demonstrate the approaches.

Supply Chain

Under Supply Chain, beverage syrups are delivered to the restaurant in bag-in-box (BIB) containers. The delivery person enters the facility with the BIB packages on a handcart, requiring that either the delivery must be scheduled during restaurant operating hours or someone must be available off-hours to accept the delivery. The delivery person takes the BIB packages to the back room or basement, rearranges the old stock and new stock to increase the likelihood of proper product rotation, and looks for someone to sign the delivery receipt. In some cases the delivery person may spend time chatting with restaurant personnel.

For ongoing restaurant operations, a restaurant worker periodically checks the level of liquid that is feeding a dispense unit, or notices that the BIB container is actually empty. This is a very inexact science. There is no specific indicator of the level of syrup in a BIB container, so a worker may slightly lift the BIB unit on the shelf to feel how heavy it is and thus guess how close it is to being empty. In many cases this is actually the "high tech" approach; the less sophisticated method is to know that syrup is low when a customer complains that the beverage coming out of the dispense unit appears weak or abnormally watery. The worker then goes to the basement or wherever the BIB units are stored, takes one from the shelf, works the valving to switch BIB units on the line, replaces the BIB container, and disposes of the prior container. Again, these steps are much more easily said than done. A typical five-gallon BIB unit weighs in the range of 50 pounds, and not all employees are strong enough to lift or move them. A BIB carton in the middle of a stack on the shelf means that the worker may have to remove several cartons to get the unit needed, and then put the other cartons back — a considerable physical effort. The storage area may be very crowded, making physical handling of the BIB units particularly difficult and even dangerous. In short, the handling of BIB containers is of itself a difficult process.

Restaurant employees also engage in a number of overhead activities related to beverage syrup. A restaurant worker periodically monitors the BIB containers and reorders product as needed. Expiration dates need to be checked from time to time to ensure that no out-of-date product is used. The lines from the BIB boxes to the dispense units, and the dispense units themselves, are supposed to be cleaned and rinsed based on an equipment cleaning schedule.

From the consumer's perspective, the beverages are dispensed directly from the dispensing unit into a cup, either by the restaurant server or by the consumer. In some cases such as drive-through at certain restaurants, this dispensing is done automatically, with a cup moved into position and filled based on the drive-through order, and then packed by the restaurant server and passed to the customer.

Adapted Supply Chain

Under Adapted Supply Chain, some movement toward exploiting the liquid nature of beverage syrups has already occurred. For selected beverages in certain restaurants, tanks have been installed that allow the syrup to be held in the restaurant in bulk form and pumped from the tank to the dispense lines. These systems remain relatively primitive. For example, they require that the delivery person pull a hose from the delivery truck into the restaurant and connect it to the tank, and go through an extensive manual process to execute the delivery. Restaurant employees monitor the quantity of liquid in the tanks and reorder product as necessary, although their product-handling activities are eliminated under this approach. Clearly this approach has been developed in a limited way using BIB-based thinking, and in certain ways the on-site tank is set up essentially as a big BIB container. The approach does not utilize the full Liquid Lens[SM] perspective, but does recognize the liquid nature of the product versus the discrete BIB units.

Interestingly, in many restaurants a more Adapted Supply Chain–type approach is in fact used for a nonliquid. In these restaurants, the carbon dioxide that carbonates the beverages is delivered through a port in the outside of the restaurant into tanks within the restaurant that are in turn connected to the dispense system.

Supply Chain for Liquids

Under Supply Chain for Liquids, the flow of liquids within the facility is oriented toward the liquid nature of the product. BIB containers are eliminated in favor of semi-bulk tanks within the restaurant. These containers require no human intervention for operation. They are filled from a delivery truck through a port outside of the building, and beverage levels in each tank are monitored using sensors. Inventory data from the sensors is fed to the central information system. The tanks are connected directly to the dispense lines so that the integrated flow is complete from the point of delivery through storage and to the dispense point. In more sophisticated environments, their valving is controlled by manifolds and coordinated with the cleaning-in-place (CIP) system to ensure proper hygienic conditions within the tanks. Because the tanks do not require human access, they are placed in an unused elevated space and thus free up storage space.

From the user's (restaurant employee's) perspective, all back-office activity related to beverages is forgotten history. Employees do not have to physically touch or move the product, reorder beverage syrup, worry about stock rotation, or perform any other activities related to beverages. Because the dispense bar is often put in the dining area and employees are not involved with the in-restaurant dispense, their only contact with beverages is periodic cleaning of the dispense equipment.

Optimal Supply Chain for Liquids

Optimal Supply Chain for Liquids means fulfilling the plan for implementing a Supply Chain for Liquids system, and then taking the operational advantages gained and using them to achieve additional business benefits. Internal business benefits are based on the operational efficiencies that are gained by implementing Supply Chain for Liquids, and external benefits relate to the additional service/dispense opportunities that are created by the system. Optimal Supply Chain for Liquids occurs when these elements are effectively planned and then brought to fruition during the implementation process.

This example indicates some of the many ways that Supply Chain for Liquids impacts the customer/user or consumer. As we explore these areas in detail, it is useful to distinguish among the players, as shown in Exhibit 8.1. In this example the customer is the restaurant/restaurant chain and the user is the person who physically works with the product, such as the restaurant employee. The consumer is the person who actually consumes the liquid, such as the restaurant patron. In other environments the customer/user/consumer roles would be different. For cleaning fluids in a factory, the customer/user/consumer would be the factory/maintenance person/cleaning person; for beverages at an amusement park, they would be the amusement park/refreshment-stand attendant/park-goer, etc.

Customer Level

For our purposes, the customer is defined as the business that is implementing/operating a Supply Chain for Liquids system, both corporate and the individual facilities. At the customer level the impact of Supply Chain for Liquids can be classified as business/efficiency. The investments in facility, people, and product are all reduced, and we can look at each of these separately.

In terms of the facility, the business can gain significant usage of what is in many cases the very limited resource of facility space. This is accomplished in several ways. The use of tanks that do not require

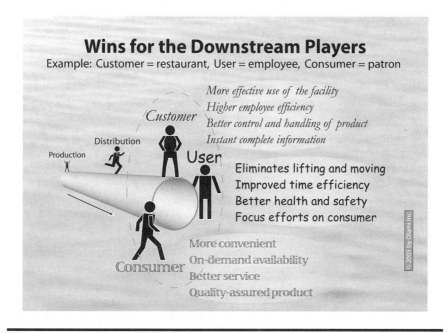

Wins for the Downstream Players

Example: Customer = restaurant, User = employee, Consumer = patron

More effective use of the facility
Higher employee efficiency
Better control and handling of product
Instant complete information

Eliminates lifting and moving
Improved time efficiency
Better health and safety
Focus efforts on consumer

More convenient
On-demand availability
Better service
Quality-assured product

Exhibit 8.1   Supply Chain for Liquids Provides Benefits for All Three Downstream Players

employee access means a large improvement in space utilization. Floor space in the storage area is freed up, as the tanks can be placed on the walls, overhead, or in above-ceiling spaces that are otherwise unused. Further, the storage tanks can actually be integrated into the public area or work area to take essentially zero space. They can be decorated and placed on the facility walls, built into counter space, or placed in other creative ways that take full advantage of the fact that they do not need to be either moved or accessed other than for maintenance. The use of Supply Chain for Liquids gives facility designers a whole new set of parameters to work with. If we extend the meaning of "facilities" to include product transport also, we have seen that a tank truck operating at night and delivering liquid product through an external port is a much more productive use of this resource than daytime delivery in which the truck spends more time both in traffic and idly during the movement of product into the facility.

The investment in people is both reduced and improved. A whole range of product-related personnel activities that are currently common in liquid-related operations are eliminated, as listed below. These are the reductions in personnel investment. The improvement in investment comes from a focus on what personnel *will* be doing rather than *will not* be doing: they will be spending their time on customer-facing activities, thus improving customer satisfaction levels and building the business. In addition to reducing employee operational activities, Supply Chain for Liquids relieves a whole flow of overhead related to monitoring and replenishing liquid product. The inventory-control functions that take place along the length of the supply stream are eliminated or reduced by central visibility into inventory information at all points along the stream, and the CPVR[SM] (Coordinated Procedures for Visibility Response[SM]) collaboration scheme directs the appropriate response to various inventory-related conditions that arise. Because Supply Chain for Liquids represents a single fundamental approach to liquid logistics, the operation of the system can leverage a very small number of dispatchers across a broad implementation of the system, even if specific parts of the implementation are adapted to the needs of particular liquids, customers, and conditions in local areas.

Investment in product must be measured systemwide, and the amount invested depends on product volumes, delivery strategy, geographic density of the sites, rate of product replacement, and many other factors. As a general Supply Chain for Liquids design concept, the quantity of product throughout the system is significantly reduced, although the quantity at each end-site may be increased slightly to allow maximum flexibility and efficiency in delivery planning. The amount of product at any given site, as well as the sizing of the tanks for the site, are determined using an algorithm including the factors listed above and other product-velocity information.

The close control of inventory levels based on virtually continuous reporting of on-hand balances along the logistics flow provides extraordinary flexibility in terms of product placement and replacement. In a period in which product specialization is growing and product life cycles are becoming shorter and shorter, tight control of product flow and the ability to quickly introduce, test, expand, or withdraw product according to highly targeted locations become particularly important and valuable.

Another customer-level impact of the Supply Chain for Liquids system relates to information. For an Internet-based information system, the customer has complete access to all product balance and movement information across all locations. This information can be summarized to provide "pulse" reporting, that is, top-level reporting that allows management to keep its fingers on the pulse of the business. In addition, the information can be analyzed with a high degree of granularity at the site/product/time level and compared across sites, products, or time increments. With proper security control, this information is available to the customer and whichever departments or personnel at the customer would be appropriate — logistics, finance, sales, etc.

The simplicity and efficiency of the Supply Chain for Liquids system may in fact cause a problem at the customer level for some customers.

In the case where the delivery is triggered, planned, and performed without site personnel even being involved in the process, there is a control element that may need to be introduced into the process. That is, the customer needs to know that the product and quantity for which an invoice has been generated was in fact delivered. There are a number of ways in which this situation can be handled without detracting from the efficiency of the process. Historical on-site balance information as described previously would allow the customer to view balance/fill information versus the invoices. A notification could be issued to the customer either at the point at which a delivery is planned or when a delivery has been completed, so that the customer can monitor the inventory change and confirm the delivery quantity. In any case, deliveries are performed against an overall blanket order, so the customer maintains control of the overall quantity and price for which deliveries are made.

We have seen the impact of the Supply Chain for Liquids approach at the customer level, that is, the company/facilities that are using the liquids. This impact is felt strongly in each of the areas described here — facility, people, and product.

User Level

The user is the person who works with a liquid, although that person may not be the final purchaser/consumer of the liquid. A user would be a server at a restaurant, car mechanic at a garage, machine maintenance person at a factory, custodian at a hospital, and anyone that handles and uses liquids at a facility utilizing the Supply Chain for Liquids approach. At the user level, Supply Chain for Liquids' impact relates to ease of use and time efficiency. Because all product movement from receipt through dispense is contained within the Supply Chain for Liquids equipment, many time-consuming but non-value-adding activities are eliminated from the work flow. The activities that become unnecessary at a user level under a Supply Chain for Liquids configuration include:

- Checking the on-hand quantity of liquid in the containers at a site
- Pulling liquid containers from storage and moving them to the point of usage
- Swapping empty/full liquid containers and disposing of the empty container
- Counting liquid containers for inventory purposes
- Cleaning up from container spills, fallen or damaged containers, etc.
- Performing all of the overhead functions required for product, such as inventory tracking, re-ordering, etc.

To the degree to which a good work environment and employee job satisfaction are important and productive, enhancing them through the elimination of drudge tasks such as these becomes more important. The employees' health and safety are also enhanced as the lifting, carrying, moving, opening, and disposing of containers containing liquids are no longer part of employee activity. Management at the user level also benefits as the distractions of mechanical overhead activities are reduced and more time and attention is paid to business-building activities.

Consumer Level

At the consumer level, Supply Chain for Liquids provides convenience and on-demand consumption opportunities, the net result of all the advantages and benefits at the customer level and the consumer level described in the preceding sections. As companies improve on current ways and develop new ways to serve the consumer as described at the customer level, and users are freed from diversions to better execute these methods as described at the user level, the consumer also benefits.

It is important to bring this discussion full-circle and to realize that the end is actually the beginning. The consumer-facing opportunities should be defined and developed, and should actually *drive* the design of the Supply Chain for Liquids. As described in Chapter 11, the ends of the Supply Chain for Liquids drive the middle, and the consumer end drives the production end if these are out of sync. The consumer experience should not "fall out" of the Supply Chain for Liquids system, but should be a key design element that shapes the system that feeds into that experience.

We have detailed here the impact of the Supply Chain for Liquids system from a business perspective and how it affects the activities of personnel at the customer, user, and consumer levels. The next step will be to look at these same processes from another angle, that of the technical perspective. Chapter 3 talks about the importance of keeping the business and technical aspects very close to each other. Each can drive the other forward, and this is one of the "energy engines" that the Liquid Lens directs us to use to develop as effective a system as possible. Not only must all of the business processes and benefits described above be supported by the technical side, but we expect that there will be business benefits that we can derive from technical capabilities that can be applied to the logistics flow. We do not expect to turn businesspeople into technicians or technicians into businesspeople, but we do very much expect to create an overlap between the two areas that will make each side more productive and work together to the benefit of the company.

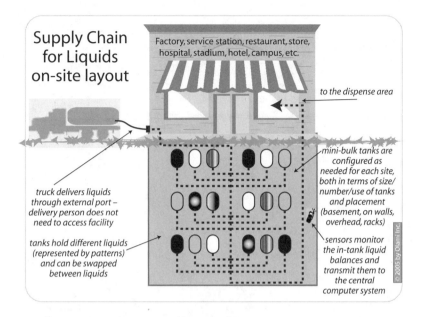

Exhibit 8.2   Supply Chain for Liquids Configuration at a Customer Site

Technical Perspective

With an understanding of how the Supply Chain for Liquids works for the customer from a business perspective, we can gain an understanding of how it works for the customer from a technical perspective. On-site Supply Chain for Liquids equipment includes the tanks, piping, monitors, and data-gathering and -transmission equipment needed to support Supply Chain for Liquids functionality.

Exhibit 8.2 provides an overview of how the Supply Chain for Liquids system looks at a downstream facility. A tank truck arrives and the delivery person connects lines from the truck to the secured external port at the facility, with one line for each different liquid. The liquids flow into the tanks in the facility, with one or multiple tanks dedicated to each liquid, as shown in the exhibit. The tanks can be placed essentially anywhere in the facility. From the tanks, the liquids flow to the dispense area for usage. Further details of each aspect of the product and information flows are given in the following subsections.

Tanks and Piping

The tanks and piping for any particular facility will be configured to the needs of that site in terms of materials, sizes, positioning, etc. However,

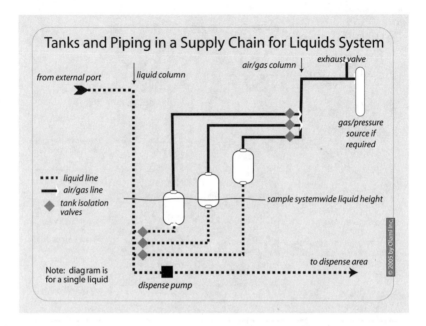

Exhibit 8.3   Flow of Liquid within a Customer Site under Supply Chain for Liquids

there is a basic structure to the way that the tanks are configured to meet the various operational demands of a Supply Chain for Liquids system. These demands include flexibility to change the tank configuration/liquid capacity at the site, elimination of user involvement in liquid holding and transfer, access from outside the facility through an external port, protection of the quality of the liquids in the system, and ongoing measurement of on-hand liquid balance, among others.

The fundamental characteristics of the tank/piping arrangement within Supply Chain for Liquids are shown in Exhibit 8.3. This diagram shows a sample setup for one liquid at a site. If there are, for example, eight liquids at the site, the configuration would be replicated (and adjusted in terms of number and size of tanks) for each of the liquids handled at the site. One liquid might have four midsize tanks, another two tanks, another three tanks, etc., but they would all follow the mechanical principles defined here.

One set of pipes is for the liquid and connects the external port with the tanks and the dispense line. These pipes, shown as dotted lines in Exhibit 8.3, are of material and sizing appropriate to the liquid and its usage, as described in the parameters defined below. The "backbone" liquid line leads from the external port to the dispense line, with a line to each tank coming off this central liquid column. This provides for the parallel tank arrangement that allows a great deal of flexibility in closing off and removing/cleaning any particular tank, versus a serial arrangement in which the tanks are essentially one long row, connected one after another. The big disadvantage of a serial arrangement among tanks, as with the serial arrangement among light bulbs in an electrical system, is that if any single tank needs to be taken off-line, the entire flow must be broken. The system must stop operating in order to clean or replace any single tank within the flow in a serial configuration. A serial arrangement amounts to a top-in bottom-out flow, with liquid flowing in the top of a tank and out the bottom of the tank.

As shown in the diagram, the liquid lines feed into the tanks from the bottom. As liquid is introduced into the system, it naturally flows to the lowest level and fills the lines and tanks from the bottom up. This arrangement allows gravity-driven flow of the liquid to the lowest point in the system, or at least gravity-assisted flow in the event that the liquids are propelled by a gas, as described below. This amounts to a bottom-in bottom-out liquid flow within the tanks, with liquids filling from the bottom of the tank and then flowing out of the bottom of the tank to the dispense line.

A different approach, that might be expected but would not work properly, would be a top-in top-out system. This is the approach often used with beer kegs, for example, using a stem or tube that extends to the bottom of the inside of the barrel and through which the liquid is forced out the tube at the top of the tank. This not only prevents the gravity-flow approach, but it requires higher system pressure to move the liquid and thus introduces additional mechanical requirements to create the pressure and to ensure that the system is leakproof at the higher pressure. Using the beer-barrel approach would also be a misapplication of the original reason for the top-out approach: beer kegs are often placed on the floor and must be easily tapped by the user, making top exit much simpler than bottom exit. Because both of these requirements are eliminated under Supply Chain for Liquids — an advantage of the system is that they can be placed almost anywhere and that the user does not need to access them — there is no reason to bring these characteristics to the Supply Chain for Liquids system.

The bottom-access points on the tanks are for liquids, and the top-access points are for air or gas. As the system is being filled with liquids, air or gas is pushed out of the top of the tank and vented, and as liquids are being used air/gas is introduced through the tank-top opening to prevent creation of a vacuum or as a propellant to move the liquid. A float valve can be placed at the top-access point, or further along the air/gas lines, to prevent liquid from moving beyond the tanks into the air/gas line or beyond the point at which the valve is placed. The air/gas lines that top-exit the tanks lead to a central air/gas column, as shown in the diagram, that corresponds to the central liquid column on the liquid side as described earlier. To exhaust the air/gas in the system during liquid fill, the air/gas lines lead to an external venting system to ensure that none of the vapors from the system are released within the facility.

If the system is to be pressurized, either to propel the liquids or for quality assurance purposes, these air/gas lines are attached to a gas source. This source provides the gas required for the system and maintains the pressure needed to accomplish the objective. For example, for liquids containing gases such as beer, this pressure is carefully set and maintained to avoid affecting the nature of the liquid itself. The pressure required for the propellant objective and the pressure required for the quality objective must be made to match. It should be noted that the propellant pressure need only be sufficient to move the liquid through the tanking and piping system and to augment the gravity-flow impact. Because pressure adds complexity to the system, it should be avoided if not required for the specific liquids involved.

Immediately after the final tank, at the beginning of the line to the dispense area, a pump is used to move the liquids from the tanking area to the dispense area. The tanks may be at a physically lower level than the dispense area, such as in the basement beneath the dispense area, so the pressure from this pump is what moves the liquid to the point of dispense.

The relationship between the gas and liquid sides of the system, together with the physical positioning of the tanks, are important design issues. A fixed pressure (or gravity) is applied to the liquids, rather than having the pressure in any particular tank being higher than the others and thus causing that tank to empty first. This use of pressure leads to a single liquid level systemwide for each particular liquid. That is, at any given moment, the height of the liquid will be the same throughout the system. In the diagram, several tanks have vertical overlap, that is, they are placed such that parts of different tanks are at the same vertical height. The line labeled "sample systemwide liquid height" shows the level of the liquid in a sample situation. At the point in time illustrated, the top tank of the three is empty, the middle tank is mostly empty, and the bottom tank is mostly full. In addition, the height of the liquid in the central liquid column exactly matches the height of the liquid at all points in the system. Using this effect, the total quantity of the liquid in the system can be measured using just one sensor, that which detects the height of the liquid in the central liquid column. With translation programming in the programmable logic controller (PLC) or central computer system that includes a map of the tanks — height of the bottom of each tank, height of the top of each tank, and diameter of each tank — as well as of the pipes, the single height reading can be translated into the quantity of the liquid in the system. As described below, this is one of several techniques available to continually monitor the quantity of liquid in the system.

Another effect of this approach to the tanks/liquids/air-gas arrangement is that it provides virtually complete flexibility in the placement of the tanks. They can be in proximity to each other, or they might be connected by pipes at some distance from each other. They can be at different heights, and of course they can be of different sizes. In many applications, storage space is at a premium — restaurants, health-care facilities, automotive maintenance facilities, etc. — so this flexibility is a real advantage to the Supply Chain for Liquids approach.

Because gravity is used to assist in the movement of the liquids, the dispense line — the line that goes from the tank area to the dispense area — must be physically lower than any of the on-site tanks. As noted above, the dispense points themselves can be higher than the tanks, with a pump on the dispense line then being used to propel the liquids from the tank area to the dispense area. Similarly, if the external port through which liquids are loaded from the truck is higher than the tanks, then it may be sufficient for gravity or a gas/air pump to propel the liquids from the truck through the external port and into the tanks. If any of the tanks are physically higher than the external port, then a pump must be placed adjacent to the external port to propel the incoming liquids from the external port and into the tanks.

The number and sizes of the tanks to be used at any particular site depend on many factors. These factors are combined during the planning process to define the entire logistics flow related to liquids: on-site tank configuration, truck-tank configuration, number of trucks, etc. The factors are evaluated both in terms of quantity of liquid and cost of each element — the costs of different-sized tanks, etc. The factors included in the algorithm to define the logistics configuration are described in the following subsections.

Liquid-Usage Quantities

The quantity of each liquid used at the site is measured in daily, weekly, or monthly increments, depending on the nature of the business and the planned replenishment cycle. This basic usage information will be adjusted by all of the subsequent factors to come up with the optimal system design. For a given usage quantity for a period of time, there are many trade-offs in how to design the system. For example, larger on-site inventory quantity leads to fewer deliveries, but it takes more space and requires more investment. There is no one right answer, but an evaluation based on the liquid-usage quantities adjusted for the additional factors listed here leads to the target design of the system.

Seasonality, Specials, Fluctuations

The liquid-usage quantities described above may have been defined in terms of the normal or regular flow of product. Each site, however, has to provide for exceptions to the regular flow. These exceptions may be periodic and over a certain period of time, such as seasonality. Beverage usage, for example, increases across the summer months. The exceptions may be based on planned events, such as special sales, e.g., a reduction in price of X percent leads to an expected increase in demand of Y percent. Unplanned fluctuations can also impact usage. A news report of a car that burned up because of lack of motor oil, for example, may lead to a temporary increase in lubricant usage as drivers respond by servicing their vehicles. In terms of the Supply Chain for Liquids process, another "planned uncertainty" to be taken into account is variations in the delivery cycle. If, as a result of this calculation process, it is determined that the liquids at a certain site are to be replenished every three weeks, we might determine that four weeks of inventory should be held at the site to take into account delays that may occur in the delivery cycle, such as holidays, weather conditions, etc.

Flexibility to Adjust for Trends and Changes in Liquid Usage

The tank's physical configuration must be able to fulfill changing needs in terms of increases or decreases in usage of different liquids. For example, if the seasonal decrease in one liquid's usage corresponds to the season's increase in usage of another liquid, the number and capacity of the tanks for each liquid could be set such that some of the tanks could be switched between the liquids based on seasonality. To account for a number of fluctuating liquids, the target configuration would be a relatively larger number of small tanks rather than fewer large tanks. This would allow tanks to be utilized for different liquids over the course of time, thus changing system capacity for specific liquids without the need for adding or removing tanks. This corresponds to the use of shelf space in the world of discrete products. Racking is planned for the correct amount of total storage space required for all products, but the use of the racking can be shifted between products across time according to changing needs. The multicapacity-tank approach under Supply Chain for Liquids accomplishes the exact same objective for liquid products.

Minimize Tank and Equipment Cost

As we are considering alternative scenarios for our equipment configuration, the cost of the equipment itself clearly plays a role in the calculation.

This touches on both the techniques used and the details of the equipment. In terms of techniques used, there may be regulatory requirements that must be met but that can be met in several different ways. For example, environmental regulations may dictate the use of double-walled tanks or, as an alternative, the installation of a catchment basin if the tanks are single-walled. Another example of the cost effect of different techniques is the liquid-level measuring equipment, as described later in this chapter. Based on a number of factors, we can choose from a variety of configurations, including liquid-level sensors in each tank, liquid-level sensors for each liquid column (that is, one sensor per liquid), flowmeters rather than liquid-level meters, etc. Evaluation of these alternatives should be done with cost minimization in mind and given the proper priority.

In terms of the equipment itself, different configurations will have different cost results. The material to be used for the tanks, the cost of different combination of tank capacity (such as multiple small tanks versus fewer larger tanks), the material to be used for the piping both in terms of cost and in terms of ease of installation/reliability over the course of time, the approach to be used for the tank trucks (described in Chapter 7) such as removable tanks versus fixed tanks — these are just some of the available equipment-related alternatives that will have a significant impact on the cost of the system. Unlike other costs, such as trucks, that are distributed across the entire system, on-site equipment directly impacts the profitability of the Supply Chain for Liquids approach for a particular site. Thus different equipment approaches may be used for low-volume sites as opposed to high-volume sites. As with all of the other factors listed here, the cheapest solution will not necessarily be the one selected. It is the optimal combination of factors that will define which alternative will be selected for each component of the system.

Minimize Inventory Investment

Inventory is like many investments: it consumes capital; as long as it exists, it is at risk of diminishing value; it leads to auxiliary costs such as storage and insurance, etc. In addressing the objective of minimizing inventory investment, there are several aspects that we need to properly take into account. Our view of minimized inventory must be systemwide rather than localized at any particular site along the logistics flow. In fact, some localized increase in inventory may lead to reduced systemwide inventory as well as greater systemwide efficiency. For example, higher on-site inventory balances decrease the frequency of deliveries required, obviate the need for interim positioning of inventory, and increase flexibility in the delivery process. In evaluating the need to minimize inventory investment, we must distinguish between the physical product itself and the financial arrangements related to the product. A higher inventory balance on the site does not necessarily mean that the customer's inventory investment has to increase. This might be considered as consignment inventory up to a certain point, for example, and because inventory usage is constantly monitored, the Supply Chain for Liquids system certainly supports this type of arrangement. The point is that the Liquid Lens approach — the systemwide view — applies to our objective of minimizing inventory investment, and that the overall objective can be achieved while fine-tuning the details to meet the overall needs of the system.

Maximize On-Site Space Utilization

Space is at a premium at many business sites. In high-cost urban areas, each square foot costs a significant amount of money, and even in less-expensive locations, the area within a facility, such as the back area or basement of a restaurant, is limited. Therefore, the degree to which the on-site equipment needed to operate the Supply Chain for Liquids system requires less space should be considered as a benefit in this analysis. Indeed, the analysis here should focus not on how little space the system will take up, but rather how much space the system will free up relative to space usage under the current operational method. "Space" does not refer here to absolute physical space, but rather to usable space. Generally anything within reach — within reach by a human in a person-based environment such as a storeroom or restaurant, or within reach by a forklift in a warehouse, etc. — is considered usable space, and space above that or below the floor is considered unusable. Thus in a storeroom, liquids that are held on shelves are taking up usable space, whereas liquids that are held in tanks between the tops of the shelving and the ceiling are actually freeing up space. These liquids are no longer stored on the shelves, so the space they used to occupy on the shelves is now available for other products. As described in Chapter 3, because the user no longer has to access the liquids at the point of storage — the liquids now being piped to a point of dispense — they can be stored in inaccessible areas. In addition to higher-level areas, places such as above the ceiling, in corners, under the floor, in the basement, or even protected outside areas become available for storage of liquid products. The evaluation should determine how much unused space is available at a site, how much currently used space can be freed up by using the Supply Chain for Liquids system, and how much (preferably all) of the currently used space can be freed up by moving the liquids currently stored there to unused space.

As described in Chapter 11, the comparison of currently used space to space required for liquids under the Supply Chain for Liquids approach is not a one-to-one correspondence. Liquids in packages take up more than twice the storage space that liquids in tanks require, so the tank that will hold the liquids will occupy less than half of the shelf space that was freed up. Moreover, the tank can be located in formerly unusable space. This should be taken into account in evaluating space utilization during the Supply Chain for Liquids planning stage.

Support Operational Needs Such as Tank Cleaning

In planning the system layout, operational requirements — maintaining ambient temperature, the type of tank cleaning required, batch control requirements, antiexplosive considerations, etc. — must be taken into account. Some of these require additional equipment besides the Supply Chain for Liquids tanks and pipes themselves, such as cooling/heating equipment, cleaning-in-place (CIP) equipment, etc. As described in Chapter 9, CIP requires its own set of equipment, including cleaning-fluid tanks, control mechanisms, piping and flushing systems, etc. Batch control within the Supply Chain for Liquids flow includes placement of manifolds to control liquid flow as well as the additional control capability within the on-site PLCs to manage batch separation and between-batch cleaning that may be required. Features such as antiexplosive capabilities may be more passive and relate to the planned electrical components and method used for the on-site equipment, without any impact on the logistics operations. In addition, the exact nature of the operational requirements depends on the liquids involved, the geographic location of the site and specific regulatory considerations at each location, different conditions in terms of site layout and liquid usage, and other factors. Any of these additional operational requirements for the on-site or on-truck configuration should be identified and taken into account during configuration definition.

Minimize Delivery Frequency

One of the small elements that makes a large difference in the overall effectiveness of the system is the delivery frequency, that is, how frequently a site requires a delivery to replenish on-site balances. Less frequent deliveries means lower investment in the means of delivery — the trucks, drivers, replenishment process, etc. — as well as more flexibility in the delivery process. However, as mentioned above in the description of on-site equipment cost, even the trucks, which may represent the single largest equipment cost in the system, become relatively inexpensive on a per-gallon basis as their cost is spread across all of the gallonage of all the customers for the useful lifespan of the equipment. The on-site equipment, in comparison, may have a much lower absolute cost, but their per-gallon cost is more expensive because it is spread only across the gallonage that moves through a particular location. Therefore, minimizing delivery frequency with the objective of decreasing truck investment should be examined carefully based on the specifics of the situation and not assumed to be an automatic, large savings. However, minimizing delivery frequency to gain overall operational efficiency and reduction in complexity represents significant savings and is a valuable goal to take into account in defining systemwide configuration.

Lowest Weight of Truck Tubes with Speediest Delivery Capability

The details of all of the processes related to the Supply Chain for Liquids distribution methodology must be taken into account in this analysis. For example, a very exacting engineering issue arises related to the tubing used to connect the truck to the external port as part of the site delivery process. Ideally, the tubes would be very large so that the liquid would move through them most quickly and minimize the amount of time the truck needs to spend at any single delivery stop. However, tubes filled with liquid quickly become very heavy as their diameter increases, to the point where they could not be pulled from the truck to the external port by the delivery person.

Another design issue is the bundling of multiple tubes for connection to the external port, again for the purpose of reducing the number of actions required by the delivery person and speeding up delivery time. Bundled tubes are less flexible and more difficult to handle than individual tubes; on the other hand, pulling/connecting/activating multiple tubes at the same time significantly speeds the delivery process. Other factors that come into play in evaluating truck tube configuration include the range of likely ambient temperatures during the delivery process that could impact the viscosity of the liquid during delivery, the maximum distance from the truck to the external port at different delivery sites, the "directness" from the truck to the external port (number and degree of turns in the tubes affects the liquid flow), the pipe material, the pressure under which liquids are propelled from the truck to the external port, the size of the tubes from the external port to the tanks inside the site, and of course the specifications and characteristics of the liquid itself. These factors do not come together in a "makes sense" approach; these are engineering issues that significantly impact the effectiveness of the delivery process and should be evaluated from an engineering perspective. The results of this analysis are then put together with the other factors listed here to come up with the overall equipment configuration.

Most Effective Truck-Tank Sizes and Configurations

A similar evaluation to that described above for the on-site tanks is performed for the truck tanks. In addition to the factors related to the actual tanks, a number of issues are taken into account in sizing the trucks themselves. The distance to be traveled by the trucks, the degree of highway versus urban activity, weight constraints for trucks in different types of travel or delivery areas, physical size (e.g., the need for narrow trucks for certain city environments), the use of different types of trucks for different delivery situations, and other factors are taken into account when determining the truck and truck-tank configurations. Regulatory constraints such as Department of Transportation rules may also come into play in determining the truck/tank layout and various equipment and features on the truck, depending on the types of liquids to be transported on the truck. There are many options related to the truck/tank configuration as described in Chapter 7 — tank trucks, box trucks, detachable trailers, removable tanks, etc. — with the cost, operational capabilities, and other advantages and constraints taken into account when designing the overall system.

Dispense Equipment

The Supply Chain for Liquids approach encompasses liquid dispense by the user at the point of usage or in preparation for usage. Liquid dispense takes on different forms in different environments. In a vehicle maintenance facility, it might involve dispense maintenance fluids directly into the vehicle through retractable tubes positioned near the service bay; for restaurants, it might be the beverage bar; in a factory, machine lubricants might be dispensed at selected points in the production area or liquids moved directly into the production process; in a hospital, cleaning materials might be dispensed in the area to be sanitized or into the cleaning equipment, and so on. In each case the Supply Chain for Liquids cycle is completed by dispensing the liquid directly at its point of need/usage rather than into an interim container for transport to the final point of usage. In any case, because ease of dispense/usage is an inherent benefit of a liquids-based system versus a discrete (container)-based system, the method of final usage of the liquid is taken into account in system design.

In fact, it is a fundamental principle of the Liquid Lens approach that it is the end point in the logistics flow, together with production at the beginning of the process, that drives the entire flow in-between, so that the logistics flow supports the dispense requirements at the end of the process. Given this, the layout of the dispense equipment, the quantity and nature of dispense points per site, the integration of the dispense equipment with the on-site Supply Chain for Liquids equipment, planning for the need to expand or change the dispense equipment either over the near term or related to ongoing development at the site, and other factors that affect the dispense process should be taken into account during this process. As the Liquid Lens approach directs, the dispense approach used in this analysis should not be the approach that is currently in place, but the approach that will become possible and will be used once the entire Supply Chain for Liquids program is in place. The opportunities available at the dispense point must be envisioned to avoid being constrained under the new system by the realities and understandings that are present in the current system. Again, the Liquid Lens approach tells us that this vision is not only from a technical perspective, but from a marketing, operational, financial, and strategic perspective, and all of these angles should be taken into account in envisioning the dispense system and laying out its exact configuration.

The process of laying out all of the factors and gathering the data required to perform the configuration analysis leads to additional clarification of the Supply Chain for Liquids vision. Within the overall Supply Chain for Liquids methodology, there is room for a great deal of variability of any particular aspect. Some sites may have many tanks of different sizes to accommodate their need for greater flexibility, but other sites with very stable liquid usage and no need for cleaning or other type of backup may use only one tank per liquid. Some sites may have more frequent deliveries than others; some trucks may be configured differently than others; some sites may have more complex, sophisticated, and frequent data reporting than others. These local variations, made to increase effectiveness both for each site and for the system as a whole, all fit within the overall framework of the Supply Chain for Liquids process and can be integrated into the system while still maintaining a high degree of efficiency and simplicity for the logistics flow as a whole.

In addition to the sizing and physical layout of the tanks, several other factors are taken into account related to the physical/technical characteristics of the tanks and pipes. The material that the tanks are made of, or at least the interior of the tank that comes in contact with the liquid, is selected based on several considerations. For quality purposes, the tank material allows us to control the environment that the liquid will be in for the entire length of the logistics flow, so materials are selected that will preserve product quality. In this light, we need to make sure there are no weak points related to materials throughout the liquid flow. For example, liquids that are sensitive to air or oxygen might be impacted if plastic tubing or pipes are used at any point in the flow, as this tubing may have a sufficient degree of permeability to impact the quality of the liquid. Even a short length of plastic piping may represent an unacceptable risk to product quality, and so must be avoided at any point in the logistics flow.

Another factor taken into account in selecting tank and pipe materials is the potential chemical or corrosive interaction between the liquid and the tank. Some chemicals, petroleum products, or even beverages may not have a significant effect on tank material, or the tank material on the liquid, for short-term storage periods. Even though the liquids are expected to flow through the tanks at a certain rate, one must assume that these liquids will occasionally reside in the tanks for an extended period. Thus planning for the long-term interaction between the liquid and the tank material is an important element in tank material planning. Periodic tank cleaning may mitigate the effects of this interaction, but even with cleaning there is likely to be long-term, virtually uninterrupted contact between the tank/pipe material and the liquid.

When considering the material to be used, especially for piping, installation issues should be included. Piping is used to connect the external port to the tanks and the tanks to the dispense line. For locations in which this piping will involve many turns or complexities of installation, the type of pipe material will have a large impact on the length and difficulty of pipe installation. For example, stainless steel piping may be preferable for a particular installation, but it also may be extraordinarily difficult to install, depending on the characteristics of the location and of the piping. Installation is, for the most part, a one-off activity at a specific site, but the problems involved in working with difficult materials in difficult conditions across multiple sites can be significant.

Regulatory issues may influence tank and pipe materials as well as other design issues. Legal requirements certainly come into play for liquids that are consumable, flammable, corrosive, explosive, or have any of a dozen or more mean and nasty characteristics. Beyond requirements as to the material itself, there are requirements related to structure — single-wall or double-wall construction, containment reservoir, automatic shutoff, and other design characteristics. If the system is to be pressurized, an additional layer of compliance rules must be taken into account. As if this were not enough, regulatory restrictions pop out from behind every rock — federal, state, county, city, health department, fire department, and so on and so on. These are not insurmountable, but the last thing you want to do is design your tanking/piping materials and configuration and then discover regulations that you did not take into account.

Last, but by no means least, the selection of materials depends on the cost of the alternative materials. Cost can be a complex concept. A more expensive material that will last for the expected lifetime of the system may end up costing less than a cheaper material that will need to be refurbished or replaced within a foreseeable period of time. Cost is put together with the other factors is selecting the tank/pipe material and the rest of the design elements.

Liquid-Level Monitors

Liquid-level monitors are available in several configurations and should be evaluated based on a number of characteristics of the environment in which they are to operate. As the overall Supply Chain for Liquids system is designed, the detailed demands on the monitors become evident. The following subsections address some of the basic issues involved in defining the application needs for monitors and selecting the appropriate monitors.

What Technique of Level Monitoring Is Most Appropriate?

Two common techniques are direct measurement and calculated balance. Direct measurement involves placing a device in the tank and measuring some aspect of the liquid: its height in the tank, its weight, etc. The measurement is then used with conversion data, such as the dimension of the container or the per-unit weight of the liquid, to calculate the quantity of the liquid in the container. Direct measurement is advantageous in that it is independent and thus not subject to the accuracy of other quantity information. A variation on the direct-measurement approach that can reduce the cost of the monitors is to have a liquid column for each liquid in the system, that is, one vertical tube that reflects the height of that liquid throughout the system, as shown in Exhibit 8.3. For example, there may be four tanks of a certain liquid, and they may be positioned at different levels vertically, with some of them horizontal to each other. In such a system, the height of the liquid will be the same throughout the system, including different tanks that are horizontal to each other as well as the liquid column. Therefore, from the height of the liquid in the liquid column and data about the physical positioning of the tanks, the total volume of the liquid can be calculated just by measuring the height of liquid in the liquid column. Under the liquid-column approach, only one sensor is needed per liquid to detect the height of the liquid column and then calculate the on-hand balance, rather than having a separate sensor for each tank holding each liquid.

The second technique, that of calculated balance, involves placing measuring devices at the points of inflow and outflow of liquids in the system, and calculating the on-hand quantity based on the formula: Previous Balance + Inflow − Outflow. The devices could be flowmeters placed specially for this purpose, or they could be other, existing devices. For example, the dispense equipment that is already in place may monitor the amount of liquid used, and this could serve as the outflow meter for Supply Chain for Liquids purposes. This approach is particularly applicable in situations in which the total-system quantity of each liquid, rather than the quantity of liquid in each tank, is to be measured. Several types of flowmeters and their functionality are described below. In cases in which the flow of liquids is not measured directly but is rather based upon input by the user, the accuracy of the data available to the Supply Chain for Liquids is subject to the accuracy of the manual reporting being performed.

What Size Are the Tanks in Which the Liquid Level Is to Be Measured?

Some measurement techniques, such as ultrasonic, require a minimum distance from the monitoring device at the top of the tank to the surface of the liquid, and cannot be used in small tanks. A float-based monitor, on the other hand, measures its position on a vertical axis and can be used in virtually any size tank. The size of the tank, in terms of its vertical height, is related to the placement of the tank within the facility, such as in an otherwise unusable space in which it can be laid horizontally rather than stood vertically. Thus the planned placement of the tanks in the site will affect the decision regarding the measurement method used. In addition, the shape of the container may impact the level-measurement process and the calculation of on-hand balance. For most standard-shaped tanks (round, cubical, cylindrical), the conversion from liquid height to liquid quantity is reasonably straightforward. For any off-shaped tanks, a measurement method should be used that will allow conversion to in-tank liquid quantity.

What Is the Degree of Accuracy Required for the Measurements?

The accuracy of the measurement (such as the height or weight of the liquid) impacts the accuracy of the liquid balance calculated based on the measurement. Further, an inaccuracy in the measurement will be amplified as it is converted into a quantity. The degree of accuracy required depends on a number of factors, including the size of the tank (for a large-circumference shallow tank, a small difference in the measurement of the liquid level can lead to a significant error in the calculation of the quantity of liquid in the tank), the planned replenishment cycle and the amount of margin of error built into the inventory and replenishment processes, etc. The cost of accuracy should also be taken into account. Some probes measure liquid temperature together with liquid height, and so provide the information needed to compensate for the impact of different temperatures on the height of the liquid. Such a probe is significantly more expensive than a height-only sensor, so that the ambient temperature in the area in which the tanks are to be placed, and the degree of variability in the ambient temperature and the impact of this variability on the liquid, should be determined as part of sensor-system selection. The issue of accuracy should be evaluated very carefully in light of the importance of the results of this issue. To go through the entire Supply Chain for Liquids planning and implementation process, only to discover that the level of accuracy provided by the on-site sensors is leading to erroneous readings and inappropriate actions, would be the height of being penny-wise and pound-foolish.

What Product-Related Factors Are Involved?

The nature of the liquid being measured may impact the functioning of the sensor used to measure it, or there may be specific requirements associated with different kinds of liquids. If the liquid is a food product, the sensor must meet the appropriate sanitary requirements, and if the liquid is flammable, the sensor must be protected and guaranteed spark-free. Other product-related factors to take into consideration include the presence of vapors within the container that could render certain types of sensors (such as ultrasonic/radar) inaccurate, the temperature or viscosity of the liquid that could impact sensor functionality, the method used to clean the tank (certain cleaning fluids might damage unprotected sensors), the caustic nature of the liquid that could affect the sensor or its functionality, the tendency of the liquid to gel or coagulate under certain conditions, etc.

What Are the Cost Considerations?

A company always wants to purchase the least expensive equipment that will meet its functional needs. Nevertheless, given that the major costs of Supply Chain for Liquids are the trucks and the on-site equipment — against which large savings are incurred throughout the process — there may be room to consider additional functionality or options that would enhance current or future operation of the Supply Chain for Liquids. Such functionality includes quality-related measurements in addition to quantity-related readings, or sensors with a higher degree of sensitivity. Quality-related measures such as temperature or pressure show when the liquid is being subjected to conditions that might impact the quality of the product, such as abnormal temperatures or pressures. Higher-sensitivity sensors would be those that measure levels continuously rather than incrementally and thus would detect even relatively small usages that may indicate theft or leakage of the product.

Standard Considerations Related to Equipment Purchases

Sensors often have target lifetimes, but they are sensitive pieces of equipment and subject to the problems related to normal usage. Given the geographic spread of the application for which the sensors are required, is ser-vice/replacement readily available? Does the vendor have other implementations of the sensors in a comparable environment? Sensors come in a wide variety of configurations, with models from the different manufacturers available to meet most standard needs, so it is most likely that sensors will be an off-the-shelf purchase rather than requiring any special functionality.

The first step is to know what we need, by asking the questions described above. Once the needs of the implementation in terms of the sensors have been defined, we can set about examining the types of sensors available and how each relates to the criteria defined above. Sensors can be divided into two general categories. "Continuous" sensors provide indication of the level of liquid in a tank, no matter what the level might be. "Point" sensors indicate whether there is liquid at the particular point at which the sensor is placed. Thus point sensors are noncontinuous; they show whether the liquid level is above or below each of the points at which point sensors are placed, but they do not indicate the exact level of the liquid at any given time. Some of the major types of liquid-level sensors are:

- *Electro-optic*: This point sensor uses an electrical beam and beam detector to identify whether there is or is not liquid at the particular level at which the sensor is set, and it issues the appropriate "yes" or "no" signal. The sensor is a self-contained unit that emits a beam of light and then detects the beam; if there is no interference with the beam, then the liquid is not present. If liquid is present at the level at which the sensor is set, then the beam is weakened or disrupted. The detector senses this disruption and reports that the liquid is at the level. Electro-optic sensors are used with general-purpose liquids that do not crystallize or condense, as these would disrupt the "read" and render the sensor useless. Electro-optic sensors are an economical solution for general-purpose point-sensing requirements.

■ *Ultrasonic*: This radar-type sensor is often placed at the top of a tank and measures the time required for an energy pulse to echo off the liquid surface to determine continuously the level of liquid in the tank. The time measurement is converted into a distance from the sensor to the surface of the liquid. Based on data regarding the dimensions (internal radius and height) of the tank, the amount of liquid remaining in the tank is calculated. Ultrasonic sensors are often used in the most difficult physical conditions, such as high acidity, pressure, or temperature of the liquid, although vapors emitted by certain liquids can affect the accuracy of the detection system.

■ *Float type*: This sensor consists of a float, conceptually similar to a ping-pong ball, that remains at the bottom of a housing as long as the liquid level is below the float, but rises as liquid reaches the level of the float. As the float rises, it touches or closes a contact, which provides an electrical indication that the liquid level is at or above the vertical level of the float. This is also a point sensor, which indicates the presence or absence of liquid at a specific point but does not give an indication of the continuous level of liquid in the container. Floats sensors are often used as switches or valves. As the float rises to the contact, the connection activates a switch to cause some other action, such as shutting down the pump that is filling the tank. Float sensors double as valves by closing off a pipe and preventing the escape of liquid, such as in a vent line in which gas is allowed to escape during tank filling but which the float closes to prevent liquid leakage from the vent opening. In a Supply Chain for Liquids system, float detectors/float valves can be placed at the top of each tank or as part of the exhaust valve, as illustrated in Exhibit 8.3.

A number of other types of sensors use different techniques to detect the level of a liquid. For example, capacitance or conductance liquid-level transmitters utilize the principle that an electrical circuit can be formed between a probe and a vessel wall. The circuit changes as the fluid level changes, which is then related proportionally to an analog signal. Similarly, a Hall-effect sensor utilizes electrical flow principles to measure liquid levels. Additional types of sensors include noninvasive radiometric sensors, hydrostatic sensors for less viscous liquids, and special sensors for both liquids and small-grained solids.

There are many variations of each of these types of sensors, and selection of sensors should be done based on the needs criteria described earlier.

Quality Sensors

In addition to placing sensors in the system to measure the quantity of liquid at any point in the supply stream, we can place sensors to measure quality-related characteristics of the liquid along the stream. These sensors can alert us to problems with the liquids themselves or conditions that could impair product quality, or alternatively, they can confirm that the product meets our requirements from a quality assurance perspective.

We should be careful to point out that the availability of quality sensors is the tail, not the dog, when it comes to overall thinking about quality. We can use the example of Frito-Lay potato chips to make the point. Frito-Lay had a great statistical quality control system in place that they relied on virtually exclusively for ensuring the quality of the product, including the required measurement techniques. The system measured characteristics of the product such as color, moisture, oil, and salt. There was only one measure that indicated a fault in the system: Frito-Lay potato chips were losing market share to its competitors. After a long series of examinations, Frito-Lay came up with a set of additional quality measures, these based on the consumer experience in addition to the specific characteristics of the potato chips. The types of potatoes used, the technique and thickness for slicing, the bag that was used, even the gas that was introduced into the bag to preserve freshness were taken into account in the quality process. The point of the story is that, in many cases, the quality measures that can be made by sensors are a necessary but insufficient way to measure overall product quality. The lesson here is to be careful in defining what gets measured and how. However, the subplot of the Frito-Lay story deserves a curtain call: they were measuring characteristics based on their internal perspective (how they produced the product) rather than from an external perspective (what the customer was looking for in the product). Do you imagine that there might be other companies that are still doing things the first way?

Once we have decided what quality parameters to measure and at what points to measure them, we can select the appropriate sensors. Sensors are available to measure a wide variety of liquid characteristics, including the following:

- *Temperature*: Both the temperature of the liquid and the ambient temperature surrounding the tanks holding the liquid at any point in the supply stream can be important to the quality of the product.

- *Pressure*: For pressure-controlled applications, pressure can be a critical factor to quality. Exceptional pressures, either low or high, can impact the gas content of a liquid or, alternatively, a change in pressure may be an indication of chemical activity within the liquid that is impacting product quality. Liquids that are held and transported under high pressure are also particularly sensitive to pressures beyond defined limits.
- *Chemical parameters and physical characteristics*:

    pH value

    Chlorine and chlorine dioxide contents

    Conductivity, including all ranges of conductivity or concentration in water, alkalies, or acids

    Oxygen, turbidity, and solids content

    Nitrate

    Photometer for the measurement of phosphate, ammonium, nitrate, nitrite, and other parameters

The flow of data from quality sensors can be the same as that for liquid-level measures, that is, the sensors can capture the quality-related data at intervals defined by the user and transmit the data to the central computer system at the required frequency. In some cases, quality-related data is more variable and thus more critical than quantity-related data, and so it may be captured and transmitted more frequently than quantity-related data.

Flowmeters

As described above, the sensor approach can be used to directly measure the quantity of liquid present, or the flowmeter approach can be used to measure the quantity of liquid that enters the system and the quantity of liquid that exits the system, with the on-hand quantity calculated based on these figures. If the flowmeter approach is to be used, the type of flowmeter needs to be evaluated. Although the turbine meter is commonly thought of as the major type of flowmeter, there are in fact many types with capabilities to service environments with different characteristics. A turbine flowmeter is one of several types of flowmeters classified as obstruction flowmeters because they place some sort of mechanism into the liquid flow. A turbine meter works based on fins that cause the turbine to rotate as the liquid moves across the unit, and a measuring unit that counts the rotations. The number of rotations translates into the movement of a certain amount of liquid through the unit. In contrast to obstruction flowmeters, restriction flowmeters place a reduction in the pipe and measure the pressure drop across the reduction to extract flow rate. Magnetic flowmeters use changes to a magnetic field as a conducting liquid flows through it to calculate flow rate. Each of these methodologies has different strengths and weaknesses, including accuracy, minimum flow rate required, cost, reliability, and complexity, and they need to be selected to meet the exact needs of each environment and point of measurement.

PLCs/RTUs

Another technical aspect of a Supply Chain for Liquids is the method used to gather the data at each site and transmit it to the central system. In general, this equipment consists of the following:

- *PLC*: A PLC (programmable logic controller), RTU (remote telemetry unit), or some other device accepts electronic signals from the actual measurement devices and performs some initial validation or processing of the data, such as location-stamping and time-stamping. A PLC is actually a small computer, although it does not look like a personal computer. It is enclosed in a casing that allows it to be placed in a harsh environment without affecting the circuitry, and it is programmed either remotely or by attaching another device such as a personal computer to it. In manufacturing environments, PLCs often perform a control function. For example, when the temperature of a piece of machinery gets too high (based on the reading the PLC receives from a sensor on the equipment), the PLC may increase the flow of cooling water to the machine (based on the PLC's connection to and ability to send a signal to a valve on a water line). For Supply Chain for Liquids purposes, PLCs are relatively simple and generally perform a monitoring and reporting function. An exception to this is the PLC on the delivery truck that both monitors and controls the flow of liquid. The PLC on the delivery truck monitors the quantity of liquid that is being delivered to a specific location based on a signal received from a flowmeter, and it sends a signal to close the valve for the liquid when the quantity of liquid reaches the target delivery amount.
- *Data logger*: A data logger holds data until it is passed to the central information system. A system may be configured to read data every 15 minutes, for example, but then transmit the data only every three hours. Such an arrangement provides the level of data detail required at the frequency required, but the data is held at the site between data transmissions. Similarly, there may be a disruption in the communications line that prevents a scheduled data transmission.

In either case, a data-logging capability is required at the site to hold data and make sure it does not get lost prior to being transmitted to the central computer system.

■ *Data communications equipment*: A communications device sends the data to the central computer system. The communications device not only transmits the data, but contains a verification function to confirm that all the data transmitted to the central computer system was properly received, and to resend any data that may have become corrupted during data transmission. As described in Chapter 10, the data transmission can be done through a telephone landline or through a mobile telephone, by radio, over the Internet, or through another data transmission method.

The PLC/data logger/data communications equipment described here is widely used for many types of applications, and it may be that a company already has some or all of this equipment in place or available for use by the Supply Chain for Liquids system. For example, if maintenance liquids are to be placed near production equipment within the Supply Chain for Liquids system, there may be PLCs and data-transmission units in place and already monitoring and controlling the production equipment itself. If such PLCs are available and have the capacity, they can be used both for the production-equipment monitoring/control function and the Supply Chain for Liquids function.

Dispense Control and Recording Devices

In some instances, it is necessary to either control a liquid being dispensed or record specific data to be associated with the liquid that is being dispensed. For example, an automotive maintenance facility might be set up such that a central inventory person must key a code into the computer controlling the dispense equipment in order for a mechanic to be able to dispense a certain quantity of motor oil. Another example would be for a machine maintenance person to be required to input a maintenance order number and machine number prior to dispense fluids for machine maintenance or repair. Dispense-control equipment is available that allows these types of safeguards. In addition, it can be set to meter the liquid based on a quantity input by the user; measure and dispense specific quantities of different liquids in the same dispense action; or control the temperature, rate of flow, or other characteristics of liquids as they are dispensed.

The input to dispense-control equipment is frequently done through the use of swipe cards or bar-code readers that allow input of data without the user actually having to key in information. For example, users may swipe their identity cards through a dispense machine to release the dispense, and the unit records the product dispensed, the quantity dispensed, the user number, the location or dispense unit used, and the time of day for control and reporting purposes. As described earlier, dispense-control equipment can also serve as part of the inventory-monitoring function, particularly in applications in which dispense is tightly controlled. Rather than having continuous-read sensors, the on-hand balance of a liquid can be continuously calculated by recording the amount of liquid fed into the on-site system during the delivery process (inventory addition) and using dispense data regarding liquid removed from the system (inventory reduction).

Looking at the Technical Issues through the Liquid Lens

In considering the technical aspects of Supply Chain for Liquids, such as the types of sensors or quantity-monitoring technique to be used, it is important to always go back and look at the situation through the Liquid Lens. For example, having considered the various types of liquid-level sensors that are available, we may discover that certain types of sensors provide capabilities that are more broadly useful in the Supply Chain for Liquids. Certain float-type sensors, for example, include temperature monitoring, so that the calculation of the quantity of liquid in the tank can be properly compensated for the temperature (expansion or contraction) of the liquid. In turn, the temperature-monitoring capability may add to the quality aspects of the Supply Chain for Liquids, and may even open new distribution channels for the liquid. Optimal Supply Chain for Liquids is all about putting the whole package together — equipment, techniques, technology, procedures, processes, information. As knowledge is gained related to any part of the Supply Chain for Liquids, its impact all up and down the Supply Chain for Liquids should be evaluated.

Another aspect of the Liquid Lens that should be taken into account when viewing technical issues is the concept of simplifying. It is important to distinguish simplification of the user process versus simplification of the technical process. For example, as described previously, PLCs are powerful pieces of equipment that have many capabilities that reach the processing level of a small computer. In addition, the PLC is the brain that receives signals from the sensors and can send signals to control units such as valves. Extending the utilization of an on-site PLC beyond simple monitoring and to an actual control function may require slightly more complexity within the PLC, but it can yield a great deal of simplification in the user's work flow. For example, in some quick-service restaurants, the beverage dispense unit in the drive-through area is connected to a PLC that receives beverage order information as it is keyed in by the drive-through attendant. The PLC moves a cup into place to be filled with ice and the ordered beverage, and then moves the filled cup to the drive-through attendant's position. This eliminates a number of steps required by the attendant and simplifies and speeds the drive-through function. In planning the technical flow related to Supply Chain for Liquids, the utilization of an existing PLC at a site, or reviewing the entire flow to best utilize a PLC that is to be introduced as part of Supply Chain for Liquids functionality, often yields an even more effective flow.

As we have gone through the technical aspects of Supply Chain for Liquids, we have seen that there are no black boxes — no secret technologies or hidden programming — required to make a Supply Chain for Liquids system work. Supply Chain for Liquids is a well-planned, well-executed combination of existing technologies, although each segment of that definition — well planned and well executed — is filled to the brim with demands on the company. Each of the parts of the system — sensors, PLCs, tanks, piping, information system — is readily available and needs to be applied properly to make up a Supply Chain for Liquids system. To coin an old phrase, all we need to do is reapply the wheel. Reinventing the wheel is easy, just like inventing the original wheel was easy. As folks dragged heavy things along the ground, they realized that when they put fallen trees under the heavy objects, the objects moved more easily. This inventing the wheel was not necessarily a great mental leap; indeed, the idea may have literally fallen on someone by accident as a tree fell across a path. Reapplying the wheel is a completely different story. I want the person on my team to be the one who reapplied the wheel, the one who said, "Instead of rolling this big thing over the logs and then running to take the logs from behind and put them in front, let's figure out a way to attach the logs onto it so the logs go along with it." Not only were there technological challenges involved ("Darn, one turn and it keeps falling off"), but there would have been the problem of inertial thinking ("How can we attach these logs to the bottom of this block?") and the usual organizational challenges ("But it's my job to move the logs to the front; you're a troublemaker who's trying to put me out of work"). Round was around long before wheels, but it was connecting round with heavy that was a really amazing thought. Reinventing the wheel is relatively easy: you put the obvious together. Reapplying the wheel is really hard: you connect two things that do not have an obvious relation between them.

A Supply Chain for Liquids World

The Liquid Lens directs us to envision what the overall flow of the Supply Chain for Liquids will be even before we begin any work to implement it, and to visualize the benefits that can be derived from the system even though it has not yet begun operating. One way to "jump forward" is to describe the results that will come from Supply Chain for Liquids operation. The story we tell in this section envisions the daily activities of an average person at the points at which she is touched by the Supply Chain for Liquids world, and in doing so we begin to break through the self-imposed barrier of "what is" and start the terrific process of imagining "what will be."

Lauren had to laugh as she walked across the factory floor. Even though they were odd, they added life to the place and certainly symbolized that things did not work the way they did before. First came the tanks for the Buildings and Grounds (B&G) Department. Acme Industrial Products Corp. had installed them first, in a non-mission-critical area, to see if the Supply Chain for Liquids concept (or AcmeFlow as it was named in the company) would work for the company as it appeared it would. Instead of buying building-care and grounds-care liquids in jugs and drums, Acme had installed a set of tanks to hold the liquids. There were about 20 tanks of different sizes altogether. Some held rotating products — lawn-care liquids in the summer, deicers in the winter — while others held products that were used year-round, such as floor waxes, disinfectants, and hand soaps. The tanks were hung on the wall, above the B&G storeroom and below the windows, and Lauren recollected the lively discussions that had accompanied the decision about the tanks. The B&G crew was proud to be the leader in the company to try out the new liquid holding and dispense method, but they were even more proud of their respective sports teams, and it showed. The biggest AcmeFlow tank was painted with the company's colors and logo out of deference to management. Bill, the B&G supervisor, was a big football fan, so the next biggest tank was painted like a football, with the local team's symbol emblazoned across the middle. The B&G crew had taken care of all the tanks; when they finished painting them as a baseball, a basketball, a soccer ball, a tennis ball, and a bowling ball, they started decorating them as other sports paraphernalia.

Lauren knew that for all of the good-old-boy camaraderie among the B&G personnel, it was their thoughtfulness that laid the groundwork for the future success of the Supply Chain for Liquids approach and its many benefits to the company. As part of the Liquid Lens process, for example, they had spotted the usefulness of making the external-port concept two-directional — the standard external port for receiving products from suppliers, and a separate external port to allow dispensing of grounds-care liquids outside the building. This saved the crew the trouble of coming into the building to get the fertilizers, waxes, and other materials they needed while working outside, and made it easier for them to do what they were so proud of doing, making Acme's property a beacon of quality and beauty for anyone who came near it.

It was only after the AcmeFlow system went into operation for B&G that another change took place, moving Big Jack. Big Jack had been sitting in his lean-back armchair running the B&G storeroom for as long as anyone could remember. Because he was an institution, all of the crew treated him with respect, but Lauren knew that at least some of the newer members of the crew resented Big Jack for endlessly shuffling paper all day while they were out in the heat and the cold. With the implementation of AcmeFlow, it was clear that a large chunk of administrative activity was removed from the storeroom, and with it the need for Big Jack to spend all his time there. With his usual finesse Bill, the B&G supervisor, saw an opportunity to introduce a bit of change to the usual pattern. He presented Big Jack with a list of the most prestigious activities that B&G performed — taking care of the flowerbed around the flagpole, making sure the main entrance to the facility was shipshape, painting the big sign on the lawn with the company's name on it, and the like — and let Big Jack select the ones he would do in addition to part-time work in the storeroom. Big Jack felt important, Bill got better use of Big Jack's time, and the administrative work that Big Jack had been doing was either eliminated or automated and actually got done better than when Big Jack was doing it.

As the pilot program for the Supply Chain for Liquids approach, the B&G department came through with flying colors. The financial savings were readily demonstrable, but it was the enthusiasm with which the department approached its role as implementation leader that really impressed management. The department continued to develop and exploit Supply Chain for Liquids capabilities well after the initial installation, and thought of the other departments that adopted the system later like kid brothers.

Lauren recollected the progression of AcmeFlow within the company after that. The next area of the company to work with suppliers to implement the Supply Chain for Liquids approach was the Engineering and Maintenance (E&M) group, which is responsible for product engineering, machines and machine maintenance, and all mechanical activity at the facility. In addition to product-related liquids, that is, the liquids used to make Acme's products, many process-related liquids were brought over to the AcmeFlow system. These included the oils and lubricants used on the machines and the cleaning fluids for tool and machine cleanup. E&M, being a more staid group than B&G, related to the Supply Chain for Liquids like traditional engineers. The main AcmeFlow tanks for process liquids fed not only to the maintenance shop but to the machine centers in the production area, and the ready availability of lubricants meant that preventive maintenance could be performed more frequently and yet with less effort. For reasons that E&M was unable to discern, the use of machine lubricants actually dropped significantly after the implementation of the Supply Chain for Liquids system, and the inventory shrink dropped from nearly 8 percent of consumption to close to zero. Because colors and dyes are part of many Acme products, E&M also extended the dispense capability of AcmeFlow to the production area for these liquids, thus simplifying their usage within the production process. As they used the system, E&M realized that it could be used for a chemical binder that was only used on products made during the summer months, but that did not justify installing extra tanks. In coordination with B&G, it was decided to install the tanks such that E&M would use them during the summer, and then they would be switched to B&G usage during the winter to provide extra capacity for chemical deicers. The difference between the two groups was accentuated on this point — E&M's uniform white tanks contrasted strongly with B&G's colorful sports collection, and after some discussion it was agreed that the shared tanks would be painted uniform green. E&M liked the single-color cleanness, and B&G said that all sports were played on turf that was represented by the shared tanks.

Following B&G, the food-service group came along quickly. When they found out that several local restaurants had adapted the Supply Chain for Liquids approach and that beverage syrup deliveries were being made routinely in the area, it was a relatively simple step for them to join the system. Their 12 tanks were placed on a wall in the main cafeteria, painted as beverage cans — including as beer and ale cans, although only soft-drink syrup passed through them. Some of the cafeteria employees were retirees, and they were happy when AcmeFlow was installed. They no longer had to lift the heavy bag-in-box containers that they used to have to connect to the beverage dispense lines. And for the cafeteria, which was always pressed for space as it tried to serve more diverse and healthy foods, the savings in space meant more room to hold the variety of foods that the cafeteria manager wanted to offer.

Grabbing a last cup of tea Lauren wrapped up for the day and started for home. On her way home from work she stopped by the Liqui-Quik kiosk to pick up a few items. The kiosk, located in a parking lot that was on her way home, sold the basic liquids she needed in whatever quantity she wanted. She usually purchased a gallon of each liquid, reusing the same bottles or replacing them with empty milk bottles. She liked buying in larger quantities instead of lugging many bottles home from the super-market, and she did not have to worry about running out of common household liquids. Handing the attendant the empty gallon jugs labeled "shampoo," "hand soap," and "dish detergent," she was happy to do something that was more convenient, environmentally useful, and less expensive than going to the store. Talk about easy — the attendant filled the jugs and put them right into her trunk; she did not even have to get out of the car. As a matter of fact, because the jugs were marked, the attendant knew just what she wanted, so she did not even have to stop the conversation she was having on her mobile phone during the entire purchase. Her son Alex had asked her whether it was not wasteful to sit in a car that was running while the attendant filled the bottles, and she was glad that he had that much environmental sensitivity. Because the whole transaction took about the same amount of time as buying a drive-through hamburger (or even quite a bit less, given the lines at mealtimes at the fast-food places), she said she thought the savings in packaging was very beneficial. Once Alex thought of it that way, he started to figure it out. For each gallon of liquid they purchased, they eliminated the need for about five bottles if purchased at the store, and if they purchased six liquids this way, on average about once every two months, and if a quarter of the families in town were to buy using the Liqui-Quik method, then the amount of landfill space that would be saved. Lauren saw that Alex's analytical mind would get him a job in the E&M department one day. During her most recent visit to Liqui-Quik, Alex was with her, and she explained to him how the system they used was very similar to the AcmeFlow system. This piqued Alex's interest; although the system was essentially invisible if you did not look for it, he liked the way it fit together and flowed for everyone's benefit.

As she stopped by the service station to fill up with gas, she noticed the tanks high on overhead racks at the back of the service bays. If it was not for AcmeFlow she would not have paid any attention, but she immediately knew that it was the same system. Walking over to where the mechanics were changing oil, she mentioned the tanks, just to see what sort of reaction she would get.

"It certainly opened up new opportunities for us. We used to have to stack five-gallon pails of motor oil there against the wall," said Emily, the head mechanic, gesturing toward the side of the service area where automobile accessories were stacked. "Now we've freed up space and can sell other products our customers need. It was always a hassle to get the pails, store them, move them, and pour the oil from them. And then we had to collect them up for recycling. All that is gone now. I like working on cars, and that's what I get to do." After listening to the mechanic, it seemed to Lauren that their experience with the Supply Chain for Liquids system was very similar to Acme's, even though they were working in different environments and with different liquids. She thought about suggesting that they paint the tanks, but decided to leave well enough alone.

Stopping by the university to pick up her husband, Lauren enjoyed a few minutes sitting under one of the huge oak trees on the campus. John came along and sat down next to her, and they exchanged their usual "What's new?"

"I finally broke down today and got one of the mugs," John offered. Lauren did not know what he was referring to, so he pulled it out of his briefcase. It looked like a regular beer mug, only plastic and with the University's logo on it.

"They've been offering them for a while now, but I was kind of skeptical. When I saw that so many of the students had them, I decided to try it out. Even sitting here — take a look." Lauren looked around and noticed something she had not seen before; many of the students had the mugs dangling from their backpacks. As she watched, she saw a couple of them stop at what she had thought was a water fountain, fill the mugs, and take a drink. Fill, drink, go.

"You buy the mug at the Student Center, and prepay for as many refills as you want. It comes with some sort of a chip embedded in it that keeps track of what you paid and how much money you have left. They have those drink fountains all over the campus. I like them. They're not obtrusive and very convenient. You just put your mug under the tap, push the button for the drink you want, and out it comes. I thought it would be a rip-off, but a little display on the fountain tells me how much money I have left, so I know that I'm not getting cheated. They have a machine at the student center where you can pay in more money. You just put the mug on the machine and insert the money, and the whiz-bang chip adds it right on."

It sounded interesting to Lauren. As she watched, she saw how easy it was to get a drink and be on the way, with no garbage or waste at all. John did not know much about the drink fountain, with no attendant and no apparent way of keeping track of how much beverage was left inside. John said he had never seen a truck driving around refilling them, and they certainly had not laid pipes to each one. Lauren suspected that a Supply Chain for Liquids system was lurking here, and that if John would come by on certain nights he would see some sort of small tank truck circulating on the grounds, quickly hooking up to each fountain, and shortly after that moving on to the next one. She did not want to encourage him to investigate, but she made a mental note to think about how AcmeFlow could be expanded by using this additional functionality. Come to think of it, there are many places where this smart-mug form of Supply Chain for Liquids could be used. Lauren thought perhaps she would throw it into the air with Alex and see what happened.

When they got home, John put the gallon jugs under the sink, and the family decided to go out to eat. They debated quick-serve versus quick-casual and decided on the closest restaurant, because it was getting a little late and they were all pretty hungry.

Lauren was not surprised by the evidence of a Supply Chain for Liquids system that she saw at the restaurant, such as the external access box she noticed on the side of the restaurant. She was not even surprised by the beverage bar out front of the restaurant for customers who wanted to stop by for something to drink without going into the restaurant. What did surprise her was the JavaMover truck that drove past while they were eating. It was a small box truck, actually narrower and taller than trucks Lauren was familiar with. While she watched out the restaurant window, the truck stopped at six different stores along the boulevard: one coffee bar, two newspaper stands/convenience stores that Lauren knew sold coffee, two restaurants, and one other business that Lauren could not see what it was. At each stop the driver jumped out, pulled a hose from the right side of the truck to a connector, waited a few moments, reeled the hose back into the truck, and was on his way to the next stop. Lauren was not familiar with coffee concentrates, and in fact had watched an employee at a convenience store near the factory move from coffee pot to coffee pot, brewing the different flavors. It had struck Lauren even then as an enormously time-consuming process that kept the attendant so busy that it sometimes caused customers to have to wait to pay for other products. It just had not occurred to her that coffee could be handled through the Supply Chain for Liquids system. As she watched the JavaMover truck, though, she saw how efficiently liquid could flow. Almost as soon as she noticed it, it had finished its deliveries and was gone.

The family skipped dessert and made its way home. Lauren turned in, thinking about the things she had seen during the day and wondering how she could make use of them.

Supply Chain for Liquids as an Internet-Purchasing Enabler

The usage of Supply Chain for Liquids as a complete system provides tremendous benefits. As emphasized in Chapter 3, which focused on the Liquid Lens approach, it is the wholeness of all of the parts integrated into a single system that gives Supply Chain for Liquids so much value. Even so, the system is adaptable to many different types of needs related to different liquids, different supply chains, different companies, and different environments. Further, the system can be adjusted to accommodate various types of needs. Even relatively minor adaptations of different aspects of the system can make it even more appropriate for specific applications. One of these applications is the trend toward Internet-based purchasing.

Internet-based purchasing serves both B2B (business to business) and B2C (business to consumer) relationships. In both cases, a store's Internet site defines the shopping experience by presenting the products available and allowing the user to enter orders for those products. Depending on the situation, the Internet purchasing interaction can present the entire range of products available or limit the products to those in which the customer has an interest.

As Internet purchasing has become more commonplace, one of the main difficulties that has emerged is not with the Internet aspect of the purchase, but rather with its logistical and delivery aspects. The Internet aspect is quite well developed, with virtual shopping carts, product selections, and check-out lines being streamlined and convenient. For the supplier, though, getting the goods to the customer after the purchase has been the real challenge of achieving success with Internet-based purchasing. This is demonstrated most dramatically in the B2C world, with some of the more-spectacular crashes during the Internet bubble involving Internet-based grocery shopping. The current Internet marketplace is showing a bit more sanity, and companies have been far more careful in building Internet-purchasing capabilities combined with various delivery methods that support the convenience offered while controlling delivery costs and maintaining profitability.

From a Supply Chain for Liquids perspective, Internet purchasing dovetails quite completely with the Supply Chain for Liquids system. Supply Chain for Liquids is built to make the logistics flow of liquids as convenient and cost-effective as possible, and to minimize the need for customer involvement in the delivery process. This complements completely the Internet's proffered convenience, with the actual ordering process requiring minimal effort from the customer. The adaptation of Supply Chain for Liquids to Internet purchasing involves a number of steps that actually enhance the Internet purchasing experience:

- The sensor system can notify the user of a replenishment requirement, allowing the user to confirm/adjust the replenishment order or to create a replenishment order for a separate set of products. As part of this Internet interaction, the user can be presented with product-usage history, prior-order information, and other factors that the user may want to take into account in placing the replenishment order. Alternatively, if the user prefers to monitor the balance of liquids and place the replenishment order directly, the sensors can be eliminated from the system, and the user's Internet purchasing transaction serves as the trigger for the replenishment activity in the Supply Chain for Liquids system.
- Similar to an Internet package-tracking system, the sensor can notify the user of the status of a replenishment order at each step of the replenishment process. From the point of triggering the replenishment using the previously described methods, the replenishment

order is scheduled by the system, the truck is dispatched, and the actual delivery is made. The data for this transaction are transferred through the Internet, and can be made available to the user either passively (as updates on an inquiry screen) or actively (as messages that are sent to the user). In either case this capability improves the user experience by providing a feedback loop regarding the status and execution of the replenishment process.

These adaptations are available for both B2B and B2C environments, and so Supply Chain for Liquids applies to and enhances each of these forms. In a sense, the ongoing development of Internet-based purchasing is a partial and preliminary effort at achieving a Supply Chain for Liquids system. It is based on using innovative technology-based methodologies to radically change the purchasing activity, and to cut out many of the steps, costs, and complexities from the act of ordering product. Supply Chain for Liquids is based on the same principle — using innovative technology-based methodologies to cut costs and complexities — and extends the application of the principle from the purchasing act alone to the entire supply cycle for liquid products.

Chapter 9

Special Operational Considerations of Supply Chain for Liquids

Supply Chain for Liquids® as a general approach follows the methodologies described in the preceding chapters. However, in addition to the basic flow, many liquid products and applications have special characteristics or requirements that must be taken into account in designing and operating the Supply Chain for Liquids system. Some of these considerations and their special handling are illustrated in Exhibit 9.1 and described in this chapter.

Batch Control

Many liquids can flow through the system without identifying specific batches or lots of product. During the replenishment process, new liquid is added to the liquid that is already in the system to increase the balance of on-hand product. For some liquids, there is no need to segregate the batches or lots. In such cases, the lot number of the major portion of the liquid in the system at any given time might be known, but the specific lot number of any particular portion of the liquid is not useful information. In addition, because the tanks are periodically cleaned, it is possible to know the lot numbers that passed through the tanks since the last cleaning, although not specifically of each quantity of liquid still in the tanks.

Special requirements adjust the shape of
Supply Chain for Liquids but it remains
complete as a system

batch control – for liquids that require batch or lot number tracking throughout the supply stream, the isolation valves are automated and controlled by the PLC

pressurization and gas blankets – the gas source provides positive pressure and the gas vent is set to maintain system pressure

reverse flow / reverse logistics – trucks are dispatched with specific tanks empty, to be filled with the returning liquids during the run

Supply Chain for Liquids

cleaning methods and systems – cleaning equipment is added onto the Supply Chain for Liquids equipment, and activated either manually or automatically under the control of the PLC

liquid seeding – marker materials are introduced into liquid products to provide identification and traceability of each liquid

© 2005 by Olemi Inc.

Exhibit 9.1 Supply Chain for Liquids Adapts to Special Logistics Requirements While Maintaining Its Major Elements

For other liquids or other applications, however, the identifiability and traceability of individual batches must be maintained. This could be for regulatory purposes, for quality purposes in the event of product defect or recall, or based on customer specification. Some types of pharmaceutical liquids and fluids, for example, are more likely to require batch control than nonconsumables.

Batch-identification capability does not affect the Supply Chain for Liquids concept. The need for batch control of liquids should be considered more of a tactical consideration than a strategic consideration in Supply Chain for Liquids design. All of the principles of Supply Chain for Liquids still apply to the system as a whole. A layer of complexity is added to the system in segregating different batches, tracking the movement of batches, and performing whatever between-batch processes are required. Let us examine more closely where this complexity comes into the process and how it can be handled.

For a batch-controlled liquid, the producer is already identifying and segregating batches during production and in producer storage, so there is no change required at that stage. Moving downstream, liquids are transferred to tanks in bulk trucks or to bulk tanks at the distribution center. A series of steps are required as part of these transfers to maintain lot traceability. These steps are handled automatically in that they are controlled by the equipment and by the information system, and do not require manual activity or user intervention:

■ *Tank isolation*: The tank receiving the liquids must be empty to avoid mixing a prior batch with the current batch. The degree of separation required between batches dictates whether some residue between batches is acceptable, or whether the separation must be absolute. It may be enough simply to empty out the tank even if a residue remains, or it may be necessary to perform some sort of cleaning process between the batches using one of the cleaning methods described below. In either case, the piping arrangement found in a standard Supply Chain for Liquids configuration is not sufficient for batch-control purposes. Rather, this piping must include electronically controlled valves that can close off and isolate any particular tank. The valves have the capability of physically closing the pipes to and from a specific tank, as well as the intelligence to receive a signal from the PLC (programmable logic controller) to move to the open or closed position. Note that the valving system referred to here relates to the valves that isolate a single tank from the remainder of the system, not to the valves that allow a specific tank to be swapped from one liquid to another.

■ *Replenishment*: During the replenishment process, all tanks connected to the piping for the same liquid must be individually isolated, that is, the valves to and from these tanks must be closed while new liquid is being loaded into the system. This will prevent cross-contamination of batch numbers between batches of existing liquids in the tanks with the batch of liquid being replenished. Just as the required degree of segregation of liquids in the tank must be determined, so too the degree of segregation of liquids in the pipes must be defined. If the residual quantity in the pipe is not meaningful, there may not be a need to clean the pipes between batches. If complete segregation is required, several alternative approaches are available. Interbatch mixing in the pipes can be completely avoided by cleaning the pipes between batches, or by having separate pipes/tanks identified by batch rather than just by product. In this case, multiple sets of tanks at a site contain the same liquid, albeit from different batches. As product is physically passed in a batch-controlled fashion, the information about the product is passed from the source information unit (such as the truck) to the target information unit (such as the on-site PLC). This information includes not only quantity information, but the batch number as well.

■ *Usage*: As product is used (for example, passed from the on-site tanks to the dispense system), the valves are opened on one tank at a time to allow liquid to flow out of a specific tank at a specific time. The batch number of the product in that tank is passed to the receiving system (in this example, the dispense system) in a manner similar to that described above. The information systems control the opening/closing of each tank to ensure that batch integrity is maintained in each tank throughout the system. This information is archived to allow future traceability of batches in the event of a problem with the product.

■ *Batch completion*: The process of batch control is completed at the time at which a tank is identified by the sensor system as being empty. In addition to closing off the empty tank and opening the valves on another tank to continue the flow of liquids, the system can trigger a cleaning process for the empty tank. A cleaning-in-place (CIP) system can act as a subsystem to clean and sterilize any tank that has been isolated from the remainder of the system. The information system would not mark a tank as being available to receive a new batch until it had received a signal from the CIP system that the cleaning process had been successfully completed.

Based on this description, it is clear that batch control adds a level of complexity to the system, as would be expected. As mentioned above, the purpose and finiteness of the need for batch control dictate the physical requirements and complexity of the batch-control system within Supply Chain for Liquids. These requirements are incremental rather than fundamental. The information system and PLCs are already required for the standard Supply Chain for Liquids system, and these are simply enhanced for inclusion of batch-control functionality. Similarly, isolation valving is included in standard Supply Chain for Liquids design; it is the ability to open or close them based on a signal from the PLC that differentiates them in a batch-control environment.

Pressurization and Gas Blankets

In addition to batch control, special processing may be required for a number of other types of Supply Chain for Liquids applications. Although some liquids will tolerate exposure to air and can use gravity flow to move to the dispense line, others require pressurization or the presence of a gas blanket to preserve product quality. Liquids that contain gases, such as beer, require careful pressurization to maintain the gas content of the liquid as well as to serve a foam-control function, and high-viscosity liquids such as juice concentrates require pressurization to move product through the system.

Pressurization/gas blanket is accomplished by placing a gas source at the head of the gas/air line as shown in Exhibit 8.3. Because the system has a single liquid level across all of the tanks and pipes, and all liquids are flowing in a downward direction, the pressure from this gas source will be equal at all points of contact between the liquid and the gas. The liquid will be propelled uniformly from the highest level of the system to the lowest level of the system, and behave in a highly predictable manner. The mechanics of pressurization are described in more detail in Chapter 8.

If the gas is to be used to protect rather than propel the liquids, the gas source can provide a reliable blanket over the liquid to prevent exposure of the liquid to air. A nitrogen blanket, for example, will ensure that air does not enter the system and will not come into contact with the liquid until the point of dispense. In this situation, the pressure of the gas within the system is significantly lower, and will thus place correspondingly smaller demands on the system for strength of tank and pipe material, propulsion requirements, etc.

Reverse Flow/Reverse Logistics

Another situation that commonly arises for companies dealing with liquid products is the need for reverse flow, that is, returning the liquid product from the customer to the producer or some other location. Collection of used motor oil is an example of this type of situation. The Supply Chain for Liquids model handles reverse flow within the framework of the model, with some adaptations. For example, the flow of liquid from the truck to the tanks in a site is usually one-directional. In the event of reverse flow, the on-site tanking and piping system, including pressurization to move the liquid from the tank to the truck if needed, must be appropriately designed. With reverse flow, the planning system for the truck tanks includes empty tanks that are filled during the truck run, as opposed to the usual practice of full tanks being emptied during the run. That is, the system tracks how much returning fluid is to be picked up at each site, and provides for enough empty capacity in truck tanks to collect this quantity. An additional factor is that separate piping should be in place in the on-site system for the returned liquid to prevent contamination of fresh liquids by that being returned. Again, separate piping for each product is already an inherent part of the Supply Chain for Liquids basic design, so this does not fall outside of the overall structure of the system.

During the Supply Chain for Liquids planning process, the quantity of reverse-flow liquids should be projected carefully. Reverse-flow liquids often represent a relatively high percentage of original liquid volume, including 60 percent recycling of used industrial and lubricating oils nationwide. An analysis of a particular Supply Chain for Liquids application may indicate that reverse-flow liquids will clog up the logistics flow by requiring too much space in the delivery/reverse-delivery trucks. If this is so, separate reverse-flow runs would be appropriate to maintain the efficiency and utilization of the delivery trucks while still providing for the reverse-flow capability.

Another version of reverse logistics is not truly "reverse" as described above, but does relate to post-usage liquids and is an important representation of liquid logistics. Wastewater and other outputs of business or residential facilities may be channeled to specialized treatment facilities or may be treated as sewage. Although wastewater is usually piped to the location of treatment, wastewater treatment is actually a production process of its own that involves chemicals added to processes in different quantities to achieve the required result, usually a specified level of purity for the water or other liquid. The liquid flow of the waste liquid as well as of the chemicals used to treat the waste can be monitored and controlled using the techniques described here.

Liquid Seeding

Some companies that produce or distribute liquids need to seed their liquids, that is, put some sort of identifying marker in their liquids. Liquid seeding may be required for security purposes, such as to identify the source of explosive chemicals and thus be able to trace their usage, or to allow detection of certain materials that would otherwise be much more difficult to detect. Liquids are also seeded to prevent counterfeiting or piracy of the product, with the seeds used as a tool to identify the genuine product. Liquids that are later applied or utilized in other applications, such as printing inks, are seeded to allow identification of the application item, such as a specific document. A common method of seeding is the use of taggants, extremely small pellets that look like powder, with unique characteristics that provide the unique identification required in liquid seeding. Taggants can be introduced into the liquid at the point of production or at a later point in the liquid-logistics process. Their use is described in more detail in Chapter 6.

Handling of the special characteristics listed above — batch control, pressurization and gas blankets, reverse flow/reverse logistics, and liquid seeding — can be engineered into the system and do not deflect from basic Supply Chain for Liquids processes. Part of the power of the overall Supply Chain for Liquids framework is the common methodology that allows the system to function across a broad scope of operations while offering wide flexibility in the details of any particular installation. This is reflected in the system's ability to handle the special characteristics of each application of the process.

Cleaning Methods and Systems

For some liquids and environments, the tanks and pipes may need to be cleaned periodically, either for hygienic purposes or for switch-over of a tank from one product to a different product. Because we do not want to move the tank to clean it, we install a cleaning-in-place (CIP) system to perform the cleaning function without having to remove the tank.

CIP systems are available at many levels of complexity. In cases in which a tank will be cleaned very rarely, such as once every several months or more, the CIP method can be virtually entirely manual. The maintenance person may disconnect the fittings, drain or vacuum out the residue, introduce some sort of degradable cleaning solution to clean the inner surface, and rinse the tank and reconnect the fittings. Although manually intensive, this approach is most appropriate for infrequent or difficult cleaning environments.

The next level of CIP system is manually initiated but internally self-operating. The user places a bottle of the cleaning solution in a special compartment near the tank and attaches it to a line connected to the tank. After ensuring that the tank is isolated from the rest of the system, the user presses a button to initiate the cleaning cycle. The CIP control unit sprays the cleaning solution into the unit, and then sprays a rinsing solution or water into the unit to remove the cleaner. The CIP system is designed so that a nozzle within the tank sprays the solutions along the interior walls of the tank, combining mechanical and chemical cleaning actions. The user then ensures that the cleaner and rinse have drained from the tank, shuts off the fittings, and reactivates the tank for use. This approach is appropriate for periodic tank cleaning and in many cases represents a good balance between cost and functionality.

Completely automatic CIP systems perform the cleaning function fully automatically and without any user intervention. These are common in applications in which a highly hygienic environment is required and the liquid lends itself to the growth of bacteria, such as the holding and processing of milk or other dairy products. In these situations, the CIP system is integrated into and controlled by the PLC as described in Chapter 8. The PLC detects that a tank has become empty, isolates the tank by closing the tank valving, initiates and completes the CIP process, and reactivates the tank. The cleaning solution is fed into the CIP system continuously so that the CIP cycle can take place as needed upon the emptying of the tank and then return the clean tank to service as quickly as possible.

Another aspect of the CIP process is cleaning the piping to the tanks, between the tanks, and from the tanks to the dispense point. Cleaning the pipes is more complex than cleaning the tanks for several reasons. First, it is relatively easy to put ingress and egress points in a tank and to isolate the tank and CIP system as a closed system. Pipes are inherently a one-way system, and the draining/cleaning/rinsing process often requires manual steps (such as putting a container at the dispense point to catch the cleaning and rinse solutions) as well as wasting a certain amount of product as it is washed out of the pipes during the cleaning process.

Several solutions are available for pipe CIP capability. The design of the piping and its associated valving define the method by which the pipes can be cleaned. For example, the tank/pipe flow might be integrated in such a way that the CIP action automatically extends to the pipes as well as the tanks. CIP systems that propel remaining liquid out of the pipes with gas, and then clean and rinse the lines prior to allowing refilling of the lines with the product, reduce the amount of product wasted during the CIP process. In some cases, however, cleaning of the pipes is segregated from the cleaning of the tanks, and pipe cleaning is a more labor-intensive activity.

We have looked at several exceptional requirements that might be placed on a Supply Chain for Liquids system, and we have seen that the basic system can be adapted to each of them. Batch control, pressurization and gas blankets, the needs of reverse flow and reverse logistics to move liquids from downstream back upstream, liquid seeding, and system cleaning do not impact the applicability of the Supply Chain for Liquids concept to a particular application. What is important to keep in mind for these and the many other exceptional considerations that might arise is to apply Liquid Lens[SM] thinking to the exception as well as to the general flow, in order to maintain the Supply Chain for Liquids character of the system.

Chapter 10

Managing the Supply Chain for Liquids

This chapter looks at Supply Chain for Liquids® from the perspective of managing the process of introducing and executing a Supply Chain for Liquids process. There are three phases to managing the Supply Chain for Liquids: planning, implementation/transition, and maintenance. As described in Chapter 11, the Supply Chain for Liquids approach starts from the ends and moves toward the middle, adapting the middle of the flow (transportation, distribution, and storage) to the needs and methods of the beginning (production) and the end (consumption) of the flow. Proper execution of these steps leads to attaining Optimal Supply Chain for Liquids status. For many reasons, however, the producer may not be able to jump from its current operational method to the Optimal Supply Chain for Liquids method, but rather must move through one or a series of interim steps on the path to Optimal Supply Chain for Liquids configuration. During this transformation, the methods used increasingly emphasize the product and deemphasize the packaging as the logistics focus. A sample sequence showing this evolution is as follows, using distribution of motor oils to a garage/quick-lube facility as the example:

- *Supply Chain*: The motor oil is placed in one-quart containers by the producer. The quart containers are placed in cartons, the cartons are arranged on pallets, and the pallets are moved through the Supply Chain, including producer warehouse, distributor warehouse, retailer warehouse, and storeroom at the garage. At the garage the mechanic opens a carton, removes several one-gallon containers, and pours the oil into the vehicle. The containers are then dispensed into the garbage and taken to a landfill. When the stock of oil looks low, the garage supervisor calls the distributor to deliver more. The distributor maintains a level of stock and, when the inventory level goes down, calls the producer to deliver more. The producer keeps stock of the oil and sends out shipments based on orders from the distributor.

■ *Adapted Supply Chain*: Supply Chain members realize that the user is not an individual car owner who wants to keep a spare quart in the trunk, but a higher-volume user (a garage) for whom one-quart containers are inefficient. In recognition of this usage pattern, somewhat larger motor oil containers are used, such as five-gallon pails, fifty-five–gallon drums, or even three hundred–gallon inter-mediate bulk containers (IBCs). In addition, some dispense equipment is put in place, such as spouts, to more closely match the dispense and consumption needs of the user. The remainder of the logistics steps remain in place as previously. The Supply Chain is to some degree adapting itself to liquids, but it is clearly still thinking like a Supply Chain for discrete products.

■ *Supply Chain for Liquids*: The members of the Supply Chain for Liquids supply stream have looked at the entire flow through a Liquid Lens^{SM} and identified the most effective flow of product and information between producer and consumer based on the liquid nature of the product. They have developed a plan for transitioning from the current configuration through several interim configura-tions to Optimal Supply Chain for Liquids. Motor oil is being delivered in bulk trucks to tanks at the garage, and dispense lines run from the tanks to each of the bays. The information flow back to the distributor and producer is based on sensors in the tanks, although for an interim period the replenishment order is approved by the garage supervisor prior to being acted on by the central computer system. Rather than relying on historical data for analysis of seasonality and trends, the garage owner prefers to manually guide the replenishment process by adjusting the orders based on current conditions. When the central computer system generates a planned replenishment order, it is presented to the garage owner on the computer at the garage, and the owner approves or adjusts it before it is acted on by the Supply Chain for Liquids system. Again, the entire flow is liquid-oriented, and the remaining pieces are to be implemented according to a clearly defined plan.

■ *Optimal Supply Chain for Liquids*: The entire flow of product and information is truly liquid-oriented, and it is the most effective flow that the participants are able to define. The product flows only in bulk, from the producer through the bulk trucks and on-site bulk tanks to the points of dispense at the bays in the facility. The information flow is as hands-free as possible. Liquid-level sensors transmit data to a central information system that provides graphs and reports defined by management as well as triggering the replenishment cycle. The members of the Optimal Supply Chain for Liquids are constantly on the lookout for techniques and technologies that will allow them to further improve their processes, reduce costs, and improve their competitive position, but to this point they have implemented the system as well as they are able to define it.

This evolution will look different in every situation, depending on the nature of the liquid, the players, the process, operational requirements, and other factors. What this example demonstrates is the process of moving from Supply Chain to Optimal Supply Chain for Liquids, a process that involves thought, planning, coordination, and action to achieve the massive benefits of a Supply Chain for Liquids environment.

Although this approach is logical, there are many considerations to take into account in each of the steps of the Supply Chain for Liquids process. Issues of managing the Supply Chain for Liquids in each of its steps — planning, implementation, and maintenance — are described in the following sections.

Designing the Supply Chain for Liquids

John A. Roebling had a big advantage over us when he designed the Brooklyn Bridge — the fact that it was not there. He could stand on one side of the East River and imagine the future structure to be whatever he wanted it to be. In fact, it was probably only because he started with literally a clean sheet of paper that he was able to design what would later be called "the most completely satisfying structure of any kind."

We can build a very satisfying Supply Chain for Liquids structure, but we first need to get rid of lots of mental baggage to be able to start out with a clean sheet. It is natural to be limited in our thinking by accepted wisdom and by ingrained habits. At best, we sometimes have insights that allow us to tweak a current system to enhance it or make it more efficient. For the most part, though, these lead to evolutionary changes that improve the system, not revolutionary changes that jump the company ahead.

In order to enter the process of planning the Supply Chain for Liquids, we need to make sure that we have created an environment that will free us up to accomplish what we can accomplish. There are many aspects to such an environment — mental, political, physical, financial, and personal. Because this is a book about liquid logistics and not about change management, we will not explore this area in detail, but clearly many change-management issues come into play when approaching Supply Chain for Liquids.

■ The entire Supply Chain for Liquids planning process should be viewed through the Liquid Lens, as described in Chapter 3. We start at the ends of the process — production at the beginning and consumption at the end — and profile the liquids and their usages. In many cases the production end will be relatively simple and the consumption end more complex. Different users utilize the liquids in different ways, and by profiling these different usages, we begin to draw a picture of our logistics flow. Using a petroleum products producer as an example, this profiling for a particular company might be as follows. The profile would show that the producer produces all of the products in the same manner, with production runs followed by packaging operations in which the liquids are placed in various types and sizes of containers. The usages of the products are as follows:

  – *Application 1: Motor oil used in do-it-yourself form at home to top off the oil level or perform do-it-yourself oil changes by the vehicle owner*: The user purchases five to six quarts of motor oil at a retail outlet or service station and stores it at home or in the vehicle. Periodically, the user checks the level of oil in the vehicle and adds oil as required, most likely in small quantities. It is important for the user to be able to hold the oil in very small, mobile containers, as the oil needs to be readily available. Product is currently distributed by shipping pallets to the retailer's distribution center. Retail sales of motor oil in this channel account for 8 percent of the company's sales volume.

  – *Application 2: Motor oil used at do-it-for-me (DIFM) centers (quick-lube shops, automobile dealers, service stations, fleet maintenance facilities, etc.)*: A DIFM center uses an average of X gallons of motor oil per month. It is kept at the facility in bottles or barrels and dispensed by the mechanics into vehicles in four- to six-quart quantities. The producer currently uses a distributor to move pallets or cartons to these types of facilities. This channel accounts for 76 percent of the company's volume.

  – *Application 3: Industrial users in a manufacturing environment*: A factory uses petroleum products in several ways. Petrochemicals are used to make components of many products, milling fluids are part of the production process, and machine lubricants are used continuously in the maintenance function. The producer uses trucking services to ship product to these locations. Some of these products are stored in cans or jugs, and others in 55-gallon drums. This channel accounts for 16 percent of the company's sales.

This profile shows several sample products and usages for a company as an illustration for this exercise. When done for the purpose of designing a Supply Chain for Liquids process, the full scope of the liquids' current and projected usages would be included in the list. The list lays out the ways a company's products are being used and what weight each of these usage methods has in terms of the company's overall business. This profile is initially focused purely on the logistics of liquid products. It does not yet take into account other considerations, such as the marketing or finance aspects of product distribution. To come up with the optimal solution, we must maintain our razor-sharp focus on what we want to accomplish. Other factors will be used later to either adjust the optimal solution, or the factors will be adjusted so that we can achieve the logistically optimal solution.

When depicted graphically as shown in Exhibit 10.1, it becomes easier to sense the blank space in the middle that exists in its current configuration but remains to be filled in for the Supply Chain for Liquids vision. As a matter of fact, if we look at the diagram and keep the existing systems out of mind, the diagram essentially calls out to us with the opportunities that are waiting for us. We can think of this diagram as a form of business meditation, using the quick-and-dirty method of leaving a blank white space on a piece of paper instead of the intensive and much longer-duration mind-clearing methods used in regular meditation techniques. Practitioners of meditation know that the first step in the process is to release all of the noise from our heads and our hearts and make room for something else. Our corresponding technique is to clear out a space in the middle of the page in order make room for a logistical "something else." It is important to note that although we included the current distribution channel in the original profile, we did not bring this information over to Exhibit 10.1. This information will be used later, but for now it is excluded, as it would work against our objectives were we to include it in the diagram. We need to clear out everything but the essentials from Exhibit 10.1. At this stage, the question is not, "What is missing from this picture?" but "What *should* be missing from this picture?"

Our first response to the blank space should be to "go with the flow," so to speak, and examine our gut reaction to the blank space based on the information on each side of it. This is the most hypothetical response,

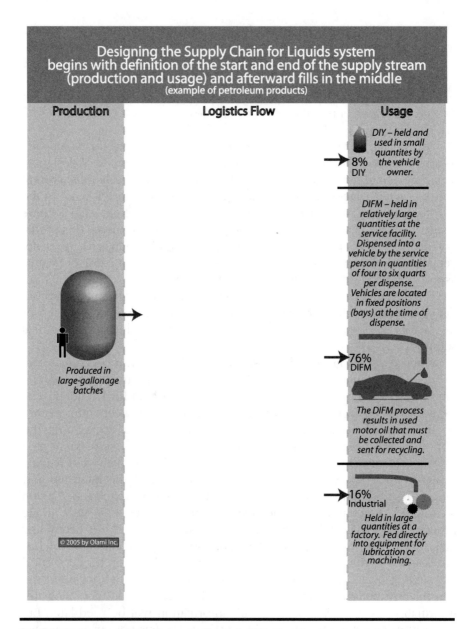

Designing the Supply Chain for Liquids system begins with definition of the start and end of the supply stream (production and usage) and afterward fills in the middle
(example of petroleum products)

Production   **Logistics Flow**   **Usage**

DIY – held and used in small quantites by the vehicle owner.

8% DIY

DIFM – held in relatively large quantities at the service facility. Dispensed into a vehicle by the service person in quantities of four to six quarts per dispense. Vehicles are located in fixed positions (bays) at the time of dispense.

76% DIFM

Produced in large-gallonage batches

The DIFM process results in used motor oil that must be collected and sent for recycling.

16% Industrial

Held in large quantities at a factory. Fed directly into equipment for lubrication or machining.

© 2005 by Olami Inc.

Exhibit 10.1   The Blank Space Is the Key; It Is the Starting Point for Planning a Supply Chain for Liquids System

coming from the heart rather than the head. How much of this response will survive to the end configuration is irrelevant; it is important to feel and to capture this "ideal" approach initially. In fact, this is the most productive moment to go as far outside the box as you can, to think of the ways that the left side of the page can be connected to the right side of the page. There will be plenty of time for analytics during the process, so let us take advantage of the emptiness of the page as much as possible to conceive different ways to fill it in.

The next step in working with the blank space — that is, in designing our Optimal Supply Chain for Liquids — is to lay in the absolute must-have characteristics of the supply stream. In general "must-haves" relate to either quality or legal issues; many other "must-haves" are really "want-to-haves" or "already-haves" in disguise. For example, if wine must always be protected from exposure to oxygen or it will spoil, this is a "must-have." Similarly, if we are legally mandated to track a chemical by batch or lot number to allow traceability, this would qualify as a "must-have." Notice that even the "must-haves" must be carefully phrased. Although a nitrogen blanket is most commonly used to protect wine from exposure to oxygen, the nitrogen blanket is not the "must-have," but rather the protection from oxygen. For any given "must-have" that we define, we will likely find a number of ways either in the product or in the process to address it. We do not want the definition of the "must-have" to limit our ability to come up with the best combination of product and process.

To help us break out of standard analytical thinking and more effectively explore alternatives, as the next step let us start with extreme solutions and then work our way back to "standard." Extreme solutions include ideas such as: What if we were to produce at each user location? What if we were to lay a pipe from the production facility to each user? Extreme solutions are almost never viable as is, but they do serve two very valuable purposes. First, they help us break our thinking out of the box and create innovation upon which forward-leaping success is based. Second, there is often some element of an extreme solution that can become part of a very practical solution. In the samples described above, each extreme solution has a potentially viable element. What if we were to produce at each user location? Perhaps we cannot do all of the production at a user location, but there are products for which production is done even at the point of dispense. Beverage syrups are carbonated and combined with water, and some soap concentrates are diluted with water very close to the point of usage. Are there any production steps for this product that could be performed close to the user that might impact the logistics flow? Similarly, with the extreme solution of a pipe from the production facility to the user, what form of logistics would be most similar to laying a pipe? Are there parts of the logistics flow in which pipes could be used? These are the kinds of questions that can be very effective in envisioning an alternative, and possibly much more effective, logistics flow for liquid products. If we start with "what is" in terms of logistics flows and try to imagine "what could be," we are limiting ourselves from the start. If we start with "what would we want to do logistically with our liquid products if we could" and then filter for reality, we have a much better chance of creating a much better solution.

As we lay out the logistical possibilities for our liquid products, we do not initially filter or evaluate them. As mentioned above, an idea that is on the whole not feasible may contain elements that are very beneficial, so for the time being we record and explore the ideas without putting a block on any ideas or parts of ideas. A description of the formats and forums that could be used for this exercise would take up several chapters and again fall under the rubric of change management. Depending on the environment and motivation, this design process could be handled in a number of different styles and scales. It could take place informally within the operations group of a company, or it could be a formal multi-disciplinary project crossing several departments or multiple companies.

Following the development of ideas and alternatives, these are then evaluated, recombined, juggled, adapted, and concretized through what-ever process is appropriate to the specifics of the situation. This process is undertaken within the framework of the business-evaluation and project-development process that is already in place at the company. The goal of this process is to come up with one or a set of solutions that are realistic, even if far-reaching, and an overall program for moving from the current logistics methods to those envisioned as a result of this effort. It is important that the final objective be clearly defined and illustrated; only by doing so will everyone involved be able to keep their "eyes on the prize." As described earlier, "know your goal" is a critical if often overlooked element of any effort, and having a clearly defined goal helps guide all activities along the way.

Having reached this stage, we have done a significant part of the groundwork of envisioning the Supply Chain for Liquids. We know broadly where we are and where we want to go, and thus can lay out a plan for moving along the Supply Chain for Liquids process — transitioning from Supply Chain to Adapted Supply Chain, jumping to Supply Chain for Liquids, and then achieving Optimal Supply Chain for Liquids status. As we develop this program in more detail, we can define what will be involved from a personnel, organizational, financial, and equipment per-spective, and how we plan to proceed in each of these and other areas. Finally, we can project the impact of this effort in terms of internal effectiveness and external competitiveness, and take into account all of the other areas of the company that will serve to shape our final design.

Having sketched out the Supply Chain for Liquids planning process, it must be emphasized that the flow described here is simplified to avoid getting lost either in the detail of the effort or in the breadth of the issues involved. Many factors are brought into play in this process, from business intelligence to technical capability, from partner politics to product life-cycle position. But knowing the track we are on will help us get there, and the Supply Chain for Liquids planning track will help us get the business results we need.

Implementing/Transitioning to Supply Chain for Liquids

The implementation approach to Supply Chain for Liquids includes incremental steps that allow a company to proceed and benefit without requiring an Evel Knievel-type leap across a huge abyss. Like a low-carb diet, some benefit is gained by some adherence, and greater benefit is gained by greater adherence. One of the joys of Supply Chain for Liquids, like a joy of a low-carb diet, is that it recognizes that we are human. Implementing the Supply Chain for Liquids from a greenfield situation, or transitioning to the Supply Chain for Liquids from an existing logistics environment, involves constant evaluation and adjustment while keeping true to the principle of "know your goal."

The implementation of Supply Chain for Liquids through its phases — Supply Chain, Adapted Supply Chain, and Supply Chain for Liquids to Optimal Supply Chain for Liquids — includes three aspects: the organizational aspect, the equipment/mechanical aspect, and the information-system aspect. The design integrates all three aspects into a single unit, and the implementation of the three aspects is done in parallel and in synchronization with each other. Although any particular implementation will have its own set of issues, we can lay out the major considerations of each of these aspects.

Organizational Aspect

The process of change often leads to entrenching of positions. The first instinct when an earthquake occurs is to grab on and hold on, and the first instinct when change is in the air is to view it as a threat. This is perception, and in fact real change and real progress often have winners and losers. Some makers of slide rules never recovered from the invention of the pocket calculator, but it is not certain how many people actually long for the "good old days" of the slide rule.

In moving to a Supply Chain for Liquids, there are likely to be winners and losers, both externally and internally. Some of a company's partners may not want to participate in the process for reasons of their own, and some internal personnel may see that their position will be adjusted, reduced, or eliminated under this scheme. Who can express it better than Niccolo Machiavelli:

> It must be considered that there is nothing more difficult to
> carry out nor more doubtful of success nor more dangerous to
> handle than to initiate a new order of things; for the reformer
> has enemies in all those who profit by the old order, and only
> lukewarm defenders in all those who would profit by the new
> order; this lukewarmness arising partly from the incredulity of
> mankind who does not truly believe in anything new until they
> actually have experience of it.

This sentiment is included not to scare anyone from pursuing Supply
Chain for Liquids, but rather to help them pursue it with the best chance
of success possible.

Supply Chain for Liquids commonly has a complexity, though, that
requires special attention. Getting as close as possible to the "ideal"
solution may involve some trade-offs and repositioning in parts of the
operation. For instance, the Supply Chain for Liquids approach might
ideally offer an opportunity to cut out part of the logistics process for
liquid products that the company may need for its nonliquid products or
for other purposes. An example of this is that a Supply Chain for Liquids
configuration can cut out the middleman; the distributor with all its
warehouses, transport trucks, and overhead might be shown to be extraneous given the efficiencies that are available from the producer delivering
directly to the customers. As happy as the producer might be to do this,
the producer may be dependent on the distributor in many other ways.
The distributor may handle products that can be moved through the
Supply Chain for Liquids but also products that are sold in small packages
or low quantities. The distributor may provide services to the end customer
that the producer cannot or is not interested in providing. In other words,
the producer may want to cut the distributor out of some parts of the
logistics process while leaving other distributor activities in place.

Each industry and many subindustries have their own balance of power
between the producer, the distributor, and the customer. The resolution
of the issue of adjusting the logistics flow will be guided to a great degree
by the politics of this relationship. What is useful, though, is to approach
the issue of partner relationships with the same open frame of reference
that was used in designing the Supply Chain for Liquids to begin with.
There is benefit to be had from Supply Chain for Liquids, and often great
benefit. Benefit properly defined and presented is an incentive for change
that can break down resistance, even if it is well-entrenched and long-
established. Most companies are not in a position to either make or receive
"an offer they can't refuse"; instead, changing the rules of the game
provides opportunities to redefine the roles and benefits of each partner.
An example of a logistics situation that was very tough at first but ended

up being inclusive of all involved comes from the early days of Pennsylvania oil. Edwin Drake had drilled the first successful oil well in Titusville in 1859, although he was unsuccessful at getting anyone to buy the smelly, mucky gunk and ended up dying broke. On the other hand, in 1865 Sam Van Syckel built a five-mile-long, two-inch pipeline to move the liquid from the oilfields to the railroad yards, and had to bring in armed guards to protect the line from the teamsters and railroad thugs who saw him taking away their hauling business. Everybody thought they were fighting over a very small pie and so they fought over each piece. Andrew Carnegie even dug a big hole in the ground to store 100,000 gallons of oil in anticipation of the supply of oil running out and prices going up. But as we know, the development of the product and the system ended up providing plenty of logistics work for everyone. More pipelines were built, railroads move petroleum and petroleum products, trucks move petroleum in their own segment of the supply stream, and all contribute to the success of the petroleum distribution system.

An additional perspective beyond the balance of power between the players in a given relationship is the balance between this relationship and its competitors. The common goal of players is or should be to build competitive advantage and demolish the competition. The niceties of the relationship between partners may pale in comparison to this objective. Fighting over one pie leads to winners and losers, but working to make the pie bigger can make winners out of everyone in the relationship.

The issue of winners and losers is fluid. Philo T. Farnsworth was the formal "winner" in the sense that it was established in a court of law that he invented television. On the other hand, David "The General" Sarnoff made himself the de facto winner by running with television and making the most out of it he could. It is sometimes a useful question to ask yourself: Do you want to end up like Philo T. Farnsworth or like David "The General" Sarnoff?

Case Study: Acuity Specialty Products

The simplicity or complexity of a company's Supply Chain depends on a number of factors: the number of products and the configurations of those products that it offers, the number and types of industries and customers it serves, its sales and distribution channels, and its geographic spread, among others. An excellent example of a company that deals with liquid products in a highly diversified environment is Acuity Specialty Products, with headquarters in Atlanta, GA. Acuity's businesses include Zep Manufacturing, Enforcer Products, and Selig Industries which service the institutional, industrial, and retail markets in North America and Western

Europe. Zep Manufacturing alone supplies over 11,000 products to 300,000 customers, focusing mainly on maintenance and sanitation fluids.

Ed Walczak, vice president of operations at Acuity Specialty Products, laid out the issues involved in Supply Chain for Liquids for his company. Interestingly, the commonality of logistics issues across liquids-based operations in multiple industries was readily apparent. Walczak's 22 years of experience in operations and Supply Chain management includes extensive background in both Consumer Packaged Goods (CPG) consumable liquids and industrial cleaning and maintenance fluids, and he drew the parallels between the logistics aspects of the different types of liquids in the different industries.

For the most part, the production aspects of Acuity's operations service a make-to-stock operation, while Selig Industries's business is more oriented toward make-to-order products. The blending and packaging operations result in a variety of liquid containers from one-quart bottles through 275-gallon totes. The major factor that influences the size of the containers is the usage by the customer; volume and method define the size and shape of the container. To match the diversity of its product offering and its customer base, Acuity has designed its logistics strategies along several different lines. These are described in the following subsections.

High Number of Small Sales Orders

With a customer base as large as that serviced by Acuity Specialty Products, many of the customers place frequent orders of relatively low quantities each. To address this segment of the business cost effectively, Acuity utilizes third-party delivery services such as United Parcel Service and Federal Express. This approach is most effective in cases in which a salesperson's visit to the customer is not justified for each delivery. Acuity is pursuing the partnership with delivery-service companies even further by consolidating all shipments to be made through such carriers into distribution centers near the carriers' hubs, rather than having the individual distribution centers work separately with the carriers based on proximity of the distribution center to the customer. This approach promises several levels of efficiency for Acuity for this sector, both in the interaction with the customer and the interaction with the carrier.

Accounts Serviced by Sales Representatives

The next segment of Acuity Specialty Products's customer base is serviced by the sales representatives. In many cases the sales representatives serve multiple customer-facing functions: delivery, order taking, monitoring inventory quantity, stock rotation, and product merchandising, among others. Acuity considers this customer contact a critical element of its sales effort, from both a logistics perspective and from a sales perspective, so the company is continuing to work to enhance this function. A separate position is being created for a person who will circulate among customers to perform the logistics-oriented tasks, such as inventory review and order generation, thus freeing the sales representative to focus on sales-related functions. Technological capabilities, such as handheld order-taking devices, are used to make this function as effective as possible.

Shipments to larger retail customers are also done through warehouses, and Acuity has found ways to achieve efficiency on this path also. The per-store staging approach led to high levels of manual activity, with any given product being picked a number of times as it was staged for different stores. By coordinating with the customer's cross-dock practices, Acuity now picks products for an entire shipment of as many as ten to fifteen stores, with breakdown performed at the transfer point. Any given product will be picked one time, in sufficient quantity to supply the entire shipment, but product is still separated by order at Acuity's dock. This allows significant improvement in picking efficiency, but additional opportunities remain to maximize the density of products on the trailer. Additional collaborative studies are under way to allow the customer to save money through higher freight efficiency and lower freight cost while Acuity streamlines its logistics function.

Industrial Accounts

The third branch of Acuity's logistics strategy relates to industrial customers. Based on the needs of these customers in terms of volume of product and method of usage, the fluids might be delivered in 55-gallon drums or in the larger totes described previously. Recognizing that disposal of the empty container can be a significant problem for the customer, Acuity provides trip-lease arrangements for industrial customers to facilitate the return of the container. The company has found that it is most cost effective to outsource the container-return function, and so provides contact information to the customer to call directly for container pickup.

Bulk Industrial Customers

Some of Acuity's customers use fluids in larger bulk form, and the company provides this logistics methodology as well. For example, some food-processing customers have extensive centralized cleaning systems that utilize large quantities of cleaning fluids that are stored in tanks at the customer site. For these customers Acuity utilizes a tanker truck or split tanker load and delivers product directly to the tanks. Although these customers constitute a small portion of the total customer base, they represent a high-growth opportunity, and Acuity has developed this Supply Chain capability to serve its needs. On the other hand, bulk deliveries are an important channel for deliveries that the company receives from its suppliers, in addition to IBCs and 55-gallon drums. For production purposes Acuity's liquid supply system is fully automated with a central control center channeling the flow of major ingredients into the blending kettles, and then, after production, to the bottling facility.

To support these logistics methodologies Acuity Specialty Products utilizes a network of 28 distribution centers in addition to production facilities. Walczak's vision for increasing utilization of these resources focuses on several areas:

- Although CPFR (collaborative planning, forecasting, and replenishment) is not currently a priority, CRM (customer relationship management) is a major focus for Acuity Specialty Products. Analysis of customer order patterns and suggesting additional order products are among the key objectives of the CRM system.
- Data mining is the next step beyond data availability. Walczak sees a lot of value in the information that Acuity generates internally and receives from external sources such as customers, and the company is looking to exploit that information for Supply Chain improvements.
- Among the large number of warehouses, a certain amount of buffer has slipped into inventory balances to guard against uncertainties of inventory demand. A goal of the company is to identify the exact levels and locations of this buffer and to reduce them as much as possible.

Each of these areas is made more complex by the range of customers and products that Acuity's logistics systems need to support. In this sense, Acuity is very representative of the challenges facing companies in a highly complex, high-volume liquid-products environment.

The Acuity Specialty Products case study, as well as the discussion above regarding adjustments to the "ideal" (such as the role of the distributor), focuses on external elements of the organizational aspect of Supply Chain for Liquids implementation. The many internal organizational aspects of such an effort fall under the heading of change management, but we will focus on one of these concepts because it is an excellent general principle, and because it is based on liquid-related imagery.

In any aspect of company operation, but particularly during a period of transition and even more so during times of significant transition, many employee behaviors and decisions will need to be made for which there is no set rule. Situations arise for which there is no precedent that impact to a greater or lesser degree either the company itself or one of its customers, and for which action must be taken reasonably quickly. Even though the rules or precedents may not be in place, there are guidelines that can steer the employee's behavior in such situations and direct the outcome to a productive direction for the employee, the company, and any others involved. These guidelines can be presented in the form of a "waterline" image.

The waterline refers to the point on a ship that makes the difference between little damage and very serious damage. The waterline is the level of the water on the outside of the ship. If a hole is made in the side of the ship above the waterline, then the damage does not represent a threat to the ability of the ship to proceed with its activities. The damage needs to be repaired, but the order of magnitude of the damage is limited. On the other hand, a hole in the ship below the waterline represents a real and immediate threat to the ship and its passengers and contents. The issue is not just the repair of the hole; it is the water that is rushing in that if, left unaddressed, will sink the ship.

This imagery from the high seas can be translated into guidelines for employee behavior, as shown in Exhibit 10.2. We divide the image into

Exhibit 10.2 Employees "On the Bridge" Guide the Ship; Those "On Deck" Move the Ship Forward; but Those "Below the Waterline" Threaten the Voyage

three zones. The gold zone is high on the bridge, viewing the way toward clear sailing. The green zone is on the decks, keeping things shipshape. The red zone is below the waterline — territory that can sink the ship. To round out the maritime metaphor, it is important to define clearly the port toward which the ship has plotted its course — in this case, the successful implementation and operation of the Supply Chain for Liquids system.

Exhibit 10.2 shows how the waterline approach clearly lays out the kinds of activities that are considered to be part of each zone of behavior. For each zone, the "theme" of the zone is shown with examples of behaviors for that zone and the expected result of working in that zone. The behaviors can be adapted and defined according the specific situation at any given company. An example of each of the zones is as follows:

- *Gold zone*: The gold zone encompasses outstanding activities that show positive initiative by an employee. Gold activities go beyond the routine tasks and everyday responsibilities and allow employees to demonstrate enterprise, display strong understanding of the company's values and goals, and participate actively in building the company. These kinds of activities are normally considered management-level tasks, but it is important that gold-zone behavior be available at all levels of the company. For example, the gold-zone tasks shown in Exhibit 10.2 are, for the most part, personal characteristics that are beneficial to the company. For example, company employees can influence others positively, take initiative, develop their communications skills, and display other character-istics listed for gold-zone behavior. It is up to management to follow through on the result of these types of behavior — to pay attention and see when it is happening, to recognize the behavior of high-performing employees, and to express this recognition in a manner that encourages the ongoing growth of the employee. It is particularly important that gold-zone behavior be strongly and visibly reinforced to prevent management from focusing solely on the red zone and turning the waterline concept into a carrotless stick used mainly for disciplinary or negative purposes.

- *Green zone*: The green zone represents good, solid activity by an employee in line with job requirements and normal expectations of behavior. Most employees operate in the green zone most of the time. Rather than describing exceptional behavior, the green zone serves to define company standards and values in terms of employee behavior. Some companies emphasize teamwork, while others reward individual work; some focus on professional devel-opment, while others emphasize error-free performance of current tasks, etc. The green zone provides an opportunity to express the kinds of behavior the company wants and expects to receive from its employees. The result of green-line behavior is also solid if unspectacular, such as the employee's continued growth and development within the company.

■ *Red zone*: The opposite extreme from the gold zone is the red zone. These are the activities that employees should avoid and that put their position with the company at risk. It is usually easier for management to define red-zone activity than gold-zone activity, and the entire waterline approach should be handled in a positive way to avoid turning it into a not-very-well-disguised threat to employees. Having said this, it is useful in situations in which employees have greater degrees of freedom of action to clearly identify what behavior is considered out of bounds. The waterline/red zone does not take the place of formal disciplinary/removal procedures that may be defined in company policy or mandated by legislative or work-agreement rules, and that often require a formal written warning and other very specific steps. However, it does provide a clear and readily recognizable method of communicating company expectations to employees.

The waterline approach is useful during Supply Chain for Liquids implementation and operation for a number of reasons. The Supply Chain for Liquids approach focuses on brains rather than brawn. Instead of throwing lots of resources at the logistics flow, the system minimizes the resources used and makes the most of them. Each person involved in the flow can significantly impact the effectiveness of the flow and can carry a significant share of the responsibility for the success of the flow.

The availability of guidelines to direct behavior in undefined circumstances is particularly useful in this environment. The waterline image — and the associated gold, green, and red zones — is easily communicated and highly effective. The images of waterlines and sinking ships are readily familiar and easily grasped. These images (and their associated behavior zones) serve as an effective code for employee behavior. "That's a gold-zone idea" effectively communicates to an employee that an idea is a good one and is recognized as benefiting the company, and "Let's be careful about getting close to the red zone" is a clear warning of the possibility of unacceptable actions.

Both the internal and external elements of the organizational aspect of Supply Chain for Liquids implementation will determine the success of the project. The topics we will discuss below — the equipment and mechanical aspects and the information system aspect — are technical in nature, and these clearly must be in place for the system to work. It is a tremendous mistake to overlook the organizational aspect during planning and execution of a project such as Supply Chain for Liquids. If you do not grab the alligator by the tail, it may come around to give you a heck of a bite.

Equipment and Mechanical Aspect

The plan for acquiring and installing the physical side of Supply Chain for Liquids has already been defined during the design phase. This plan includes the equipment to be utilized within the framework of Supply Chain for Liquids, the sequence of purchasing and installing the equipment across the Supply Chain for Liquids phases, and the resources required to install and operate the equipment.

The detailed plan for the specifications of the equipment to be installed at each site and at the central location for the operation of the Supply Chain for Liquids system, which also defines the information flow and processes/procedures related to the system, is based on the parameters and conditions within which the system will operate. These parameters cover all aspects of the logistics flow. The following shows a sample of the data that should be gathered to engage in the detailed specification process, broken down by information related to customer sites, related to products, and related to suppliers.

Analysis of Customer Sites

- *Number of sites*: The total number of sites to be serviced by this application
- *Site dispersion*: The total miles and travel time from the central site to the most distant site
- *Site density*: The average miles and travel time between adjacent sites
- *Dispense configuration*: The average number of dispense points per site, per "site category" listed below
- *Dispense dispersion*: The average distance from the location of the central tanks on the site to the dispense points
- *Site categories*: Types of sites based on volume (If all sites are relatively consistent, there would be only one category, or there may be "large" and "small" categories, or more categories. The percentage distribution of category types across the total number of sites should be defined.)
- *Fill distance*: The average and minimum/maximum distances in feet from the truck parking position to the external port, and from the external port to the on-site tank location

- *Fill accessibility*: Accessibility/limitations to accessibility of the truck to the external port that would limit the ability of the truck to deliver with complete flexibility
- *Site ambience*: Conditions that influence temperature of on-site tanks, that is, are tanks held in a space that is maintained at room temperature, or in a space that changes with outside temperature
- *Special considerations*: Special considerations at the customer sites or at particular customer sites

Analysis of Products

- *Total products in the application*: The total number of unique products handled through Supply Chain for Liquids
- *Total product categories*: The total number of product categories; list the categories and the specific products that are included in each category
- *Total products per site*: The total number of unique products maintained at any specific site at a given time
- *Product usage per site*: Profile of product volume usage; laid out by product by month by site category as defined above
- *Current product inventory per site*: A general idea of the inventory levels of products (number of days of inventory) that are currently being held at each site to measure how the operational projection will compare with this number
- *Product volume seasonality*: The degree to which usage volume changes across a year
- *Product mix seasonality*: The degree to which the relative usages between products change across a year, which would indicate the degree to which tanks can be switched from one product to another during the course of a year
- *Frequency of spiking*: The presence of product-usage peculiarities that we need to take into account in planning the system, such as spikes in usage that will disrupt the regular distribution cycle
- *Shelf life*: Shelf life or other storage issues related to any product
- *Batch traceability*: The need to be able to trace any products by batch or lot number
- *Product environment constraints*: Constraints related to product environment such as min/max temperature, spark-free requirement such as for the sensors in the tanks with the product, etc.
- *Product propellant constraints*: Limitations or issues related to propelling product from the truck to the on-site tanks and from the on-site tanks to dispense — description of physical layout related to gravity feed, gas, pumps, etc.

- *Tank multiproduct constraints*: Limitations on flexibility of tank usage across liquids (for example, once one specific category of liquid has been put into a tank, another specific category may not be put into that tank)
- *Cleaning requirements*: Requirements as to both the frequency and method of cleaning on-site tanks
- *Product specs*: Relevant data related to each product such as MSDS, product behavior such as viscosity, impact of product characteristics on tank specification such as corrosiveness, etc.
- *Nonprogram products*: Description of the need for distribution/delivery of products outside of the Supply Chain for Liquids program

Analysis of Suppliers

- *Number of suppliers*: The total number of suppliers that will supply product used in this application
- *Supplier density*: The average miles and travel time between suppliers
- *Fill time*: The average amount of time a truck will need to spend at a supplier location for filling, including both wait time and actual fill time
- *Suppliers per run*: The average number of suppliers at which a truck will need to be filled with different products for each delivery run
- *Products per supplier per run*: The average number of products that will be filled from each supplier for each delivery run
- *Supply constraints*: Constraints in planning delivery from suppliers to customers (for example, are all products available from all locations of a single supplier, or are there limitations in the supply algorithm?)

These data together with other relevant information provide the foundation for numerical projection and operational planning for the flow of product and the flow of information through the system.

The major elements of the Supply Chain for Liquids system are detailed in Chapter 8 and can be summarized as follows. The configuration for any particular installation will be specific to that site, but some of the common equipment and mechanical elements are described in the following subsections.

On-Site Tanks

At the user site, these is a set of mini-tanks to hold the on-site liquid inventory. There is one set of tanks for each liquid, and the tanks/pipes for separate liquids constitute separate and independent systems. For quality purposes, the tanks can be made out of the liquid's native material, that is, the same material as used for tanks and equipment in the production process. This will prevent any degradation of quality while the liquid is held in the tanks at the user site.

The on-site tanks are sized based on the usage volume of each liquid. For higher-usage liquids, a set of larger tanks is used; for lower-usage liquids, smaller tanks are used. For maximum flexibility, total capacity is divided among a number of tanks so that tanks (and thus capacity) can be switched between different liquids as required. For example, two liquids with countercyclical usage and 600 gallons per month combined total usage could be held in four 150-gallon tanks rather than two 300-gallon tanks. In this way, the on-site capacity of one liquid would be 450 gallons during its heavy season, and capacity for the second liquid would be 150 gallons. When the seasons change, two of the tanks can be switched from the first liquid to the second liquid, so that at that point on-site capacity for the first liquid would be 150 gallons and for the second liquid 450 gallons. The sizes of the tanks and plan for switching tanks between liquids based on seasonality or other factors are derived from data regarding liquid usage that is collected and evaluated during system design.

Piping

Like the tanks, the piping connecting the tanks and feeding to the dispense line can utilize materials that are native for the liquid and thus enhance product quality. This is balanced against ease of use and impact on quality. For example, for certain liquids the tanks may be made of stainless steel. Due to the high degree of difficulty of running stainless steel pipes in complex environments (with many bends and turns), it may be determined that specialty plastic or rubber pipe will be used instead. In addition to pipe placement, factors taken into account in determining the piping material to be used are cost, impact on quality, cleaning considerations, technical specifications such as the internal pressure in the system, and related factors.

Valving

Valving, like piping, must meet the quality requirements contained in the system. A number of other factors are taken into account related to the valves in the Supply Chain for Liquids system. Valves are used to isolate specific tanks for the purpose of cleaning or swapping a tank between different liquids. In cases in which the cleaning process is automated so that a tank is cleaned automatically as soon as it becomes empty, the valves/manifolds will be connected to the control system so that the isolation of the tank, running of the cleaning process, rinsing, and reopening of the valves will be executed automatically within the system. For this to occur, the valves must be motorized for automated opening and closing rather than purely manual operation.

Sensors

The sensors inside of each tank are the physical equipment that provides visibility into inventory levels at all points along the Supply Chain for Liquids. A sensor reads the liquid level in the tank using one of the methods described in Chapter 8 and passes the data to the control equipment described in the next section. Different types of liquids under different conditions will require specific types of sensors, as is also described in Chapter 8.

A standard Supply Chain for Liquids configuration envisions one sensor, of whatever type, inside of each tank. As described in Chapter 11, however, the on-site layout, including the sensors, is the most cost-sensitive piece of the entire Supply Chain for Liquids system. As related to sensors, if there is one sensor per tank and four tanks for a given liquid, then there will be four sensors for that liquid alone. The cost of those sensors must be spread across the volume of that particular liquid in that particular location. An alternative approach to the one-sensor–one-tank approach is the liquid-column approach. A principle of liquids is that the level of a liquid will be the same at any point within a single system, whether there are multiple branches, tanks, pipes, etc. Within Supply Chain for Liquids, this is a liquid column, a single vented vertical pipe that is part of the system for this liquid. Measuring the height of the liquid in the liquid column will show the systemwide level of the liquid, and this is achieved using a single sensor for the liquid. The flip side of this cost saving is the complexity that this approach adds to the information-processing aspect of the system. For any particular height of the liquid, the system needs to know what tanks are at that height together with the vertical configuration of the tanks, that is, how a single vertical height translates into a total volume of liquid in the system. Although a set of algorithms can perform this calculation, care must be taken that when a tank is switched from one liquid to another, the calculations for both liquids involved are adjusted to properly reflect the on-hand quantity of each liquid based on the column height of each liquid.

Control Equipment

The control equipment such as a PLC (programmable logic controller) or RTU (remote telemetry unit) is the device that gathers data from all of the sensors at a site and transmits it to the central computer system. One such unit is needed at each site and can be sized to handle all of the sensors and whatever quantity of data is to be generated by the site. The unit is programmed to accept the readings sent by the sensors and perform some initial validation and processing of the data. The unit can also perform such standard tasks as stamping each piece of data that is received from a sensor with date/time/location/product information, so that this information is included when the data is forwarded to and processed by the central computer system.

Data Transmission

The transmission of data from the site to the central computer system can take place by any of several methods, depending on the characteristics of the site and the central computer system. If both the site and the central computer system are connected to the Internet, this is often the lowest-cost and simplest data-communications method. Many locations, however, are not connected to the Internet, and a standard telephone line can be used for dial-up connection and transmission of data. The dial-up transmission can be set for off-peak telephone usage times such as lunch hour or overnight to avoid disrupting telephone usage. For more remote locations or locations in which a separate telephone line is required in any case, a cellular telephone could be integrated into the PLC/RTU unit and the data transmission performed through a cellular connection. Such units often have a logging capability to hold data for the period between transmissions to the central computer system, and also to allow the system to continue to operate even if the data-transmission capability is temporarily lost. Technical details, such as whether the central computer system polls the sites to request the data transmission or the sites transmit the data according to a time sequence, are worked out according to the specific communications configuration. In any case, both data security (that data is not being stolen during transmission or, if it is at risk, that it be encoded during transmission) and data integrity (that all data is transmitted fully and accurately) are key considerations in designing or selecting the methodology to be used for data communications.

The frequencies of data collection (from the sensors) and transmission (to the central computer system) are determined by the level of visibility that is required to fulfill the business and operational objectives of the Supply Chain for Liquids system. A company might want to see hourly information regarding product inventory and usage, even though it only reviews and acts on the data twice each day. In a situation such as this, the PLC collects data from the sensors each hour according to a clock in the PLC, and then validates, logs, and stores the data. Twice each day the PLC transmits the data to the central computer system and, having verified that the data has been received fully and correctly, clears out the log file. Any combination of data collection/data transmission can be used to meet the application need, for example, collecting data from the sensors every 15 minutes and transmitting it to the central computer system each hour, etc.

Trucks and Tanks

The physical arrangement of the tanks on the trucks is comparable with that of the on-site tanks. The truck tanks are multicompartmented to provide flexibility for the mix of liquids to be carried on each run. That is, the mix of liquids to be delivered will be different on different runs. On one run, the combined quantity required across the delivery sites for liquid A might be 450 gallons and the combined quantity for liquid B might be 150 gallons. On the next run for the truck, the requirement for liquid A might be about 300 gallons and for liquid B about 300 gallons. Based on analysis of usage of the different liquids, the truck would contain tanks that would provide flexibility to meet this situation. In this example, four 150-gallon tanks would fill the need for this capability, and valving between them would allow three tanks to be filled with liquid A and one tank with liquid B on the first run, and two tanks each on the second run. This is clearly a simplified example, but it demonstrates the design and usage of the truck tanking system that is available under Supply Chain for Liquids.

Another feature of the truck tanking is the pressurization required to propel the liquid from the truck to the on-site tanks. This pressurization can come from any of several sources. For example, the truck might carry either pumps or a gas supply, or each site might be equipped with a pressure outlet that is hooked to the truck as part of the delivery process to serve to propel the liquid. The amount of pressure required, the use of gas or air, and other factors must be taken into account in determining which approach to take.

The design of the truck itself can also be adapted to the needs of the application. Among the alternatives are a standard tank truck, a box truck containing tanks, a detachable trailer, or a tanking system that can be removed from the bed of the truck. Each of these configurations contains the tank system described above, and each of the alternatives satisfies the conditions and requirements of a different operating environment. A standard tank truck is already built to contain and handle liquids, but a box truck is more protective of the tanks from extreme outside temperatures. Detachable trailers provide flexibility in the filling process, as an empty trailer can be left at the fill site to be filled while another, full trailer is used on the delivery route. Detachable trailers also allow for double-pulling of two trailers for an extended distance before being joined to separate cabs for delivery, a scenario that is described in more detail in Chapter 7. A tank system that can be removed from the bed of the truck, like a detachable trailer, allows quick turnaround of the truck by simply replacing the empty tank system for a full one, thus getting the most delivery usage out of the vehicle.

Truck Control Equipment

Like the on-site system, the truck contains a PLC/RTU unit to monitor, control, and report liquid activity on the truck. This control equipment accepts data from the central computer system during truck fill, monitors and records activity during the delivery run, and passes data back to the central computer system at the end of the run.

A major feature of the truck control system is the measuring and shutoff of each liquid as it is transferred to the site. As described later in this chapter, the central computer system tells the truck how much of each liquid to transfer at each customer site. The delivery person enters the customer number of the site at which the next delivery is to be made into the PLC/RTU on the truck and then connects the hoses to the external port at the customer site. Upon activating the liquid delivery flow, the PLC/RTU monitors the quantity delivered of each liquid and then closes the shutoff valve for each liquid when the quantity delivered matches the scheduled amount of liquid to be delivered to that customer. A backpressure sensor also trips the shutoff valve in the event that, for whatever reason, the on-site tank system for that liquid has filled before the end of the delivery cycle.

The actual quantity of each liquid delivered to each customer is recorded by the truck control equipment and passed to the central computer system at the end of the delivery run. This information is used for several purposes. First, it is the basis for reporting the delivery of product to the customer and any invoicing or other transactions required. Second, discrepancies between the planned delivery quantity and the actual delivery quantity indicate a problem with the system, and these are investigated to identify and resolve the source of the problem.

The specific details of the equipment and mechanical aspects of implementing or transitioning to Supply Chain for Liquids must be defined for each installation. Technical factors such as flow rates, hose diameters, pump pressures, and others impact the operational results in terms of delivery speed, number of customers served per run, and truck utilization. All of these factors must be put together using the one-system concept of the Liquid Lens.

Information System Aspect

The information system elements can be as simple or as complex as required to support Supply Chain for Liquids activity. Depending on the company's existing central computer system and the information flow it will require from Supply Chain for Liquids, there are several alternative approaches to developing the Supply Chain for Liquids information-processing system.

One direction is to fully integrate the processing into the programming in the central computer system. Under this approach, Supply Chain for Liquids processing is treated the same as any other information processing needed to support the operation of the company, and appears on the users' computer screens as part of the same programs that the users utilize in their daily work. From a user perspective, this simplifies the work flow in that the Supply Chain for Liquids process is a seamless part of the information flow. Fully integrating Supply Chain for Liquids processing from a technical perspective, however, is a relatively complex task, as is any significant change to existing computer processing. It involves analysis of the current program flow to identify the exact points of integration with the Supply Chain for Liquids processing, and then changing a flow that already works, thus putting the existing operations at some risk. At least for initial efforts related to Supply Chain for Liquids, this approach may be overkill in supporting Supply Chain for Liquids processing.

Another alternative is to create Supply Chain for Liquids processing as a front-end or independent module that interfaces to the processing in the central computer system. This alternative uses an approach similar to other software systems such as a route-planning module that accepts data from the central computer system and then passes data back to the central computer system, but performs actual processing independent of the programming in the central computer system. Certain elements of Supply Chain for Liquids — such as CPVR^{SM} (Coordinated Procedures for Visibility Response^{SM}) as described later in this chapter and tank-sizing and -configuration algorithms as described earlier in this chapter — lend themselves to the modular approach. As a whole, Supply Chain for Liquids can be set up as a front-end system as described below, although there are specific points at which it must interface with the central computer system. For example, the Supply Chain for Liquids module receives product and customer information from the central computer system to validate the codes being used in the Supply Chain for Liquids module, and passes data on actual deliveries to the accounting system for invoicing purposes. As much as possible, master data should be held by the central computer system, with the Supply Chain for Liquids module serving as a slave that interfaces with data and processing in the central system.

In any case, the planning and creation of the programming is made relatively simple by considering that the Supply Chain for Liquids, from an information perspective, is a transaction-based system with a specific trigger for each transaction. Planning and developing the programming therefore becomes an exercise in laying out the transactions that will take place in the system, defining what physical-world event will trigger each computerized transaction, and describing the informational effect or result of each transaction. This is done in two stages. First, the scope of the Supply Chain for Liquids module is laid out to provide the framework for planning and coding Supply Chain for Liquids–related programs. Second, a list of the specific events and transactions with their processing implications is laid out. Each of these is described in more detail below.

The first definition is exactly what processing is to be included in the Supply Chain for Liquids module. At its highest level, this definition can be done in table or bullet-point format, as this is the global framework to ensure that we have included all of the required processing areas. The definition includes an identifying series number that will subsequently be broken down into more-detailed processing steps. An example of such a definition in bullet-point format is as follows:

- Master Data (1000 series)

  Master data — 1100: Defines the master data that will be required to run the Supply Chain for Liquids module, and whether each piece of master data resides in the central computer system or within the Supply Chain for Liquids module. Master data refers to customers, products, trucks, sites, tank types, etc.

- Routine Activity Processing (2000 series)

  Delivery analysis — 2100: Relates to the analysis performed by the computer system prior to truck loading. This includes replenishment requirements planning, such as identifying all of the tanks that require replenishment and their quantities, filtering replenishment requirements against truck capacity, on-site and truck-tank reconfiguration requirements, etc.

  Delivery preparation — 2200: Based on the 2100-series programs above; controls and monitors the flow of products into trucks and the downloading of required data to the trucks

  Delivery execution — 2300: Controls truck activity during the delivery run, including site identification, valve control, actual quantity delivered, and unused product returned to warehouse

  On-site activity — 2400: Monitors, controls, and reports on-site activity, including both operational and quality-related data that are monitored at each site

- Special Activity Processing (3000 series)

  On-site tank reconfiguration — 3100: Process additions or changes to on-site tank configurations, such as addition of tanks, switching tanks between liquids, etc.

  CPVR processing — 3200: Processing related to the CPVR system as described earlier in this chapter

  Customer interface — 3300: Presents site and product information to customers with security access and controls the access that customers have to data regarding their sites

This layout shows us the activities that are to be included in our Supply Chain for Liquids system and provides a framework for further detail and development. It is the overall roadmap to further develop the conceptual and technical aspects of the Supply Chain for Liquids module such as the sample section described below.

Exhibit 10.3 provides a sample of the kind of specification that can be easily written to support one part of the Supply Chain for Liquids flow. This example shows several of the transactions related to the 2200-level activity, delivery preparation.

In this case the specification is laid out in a tabular format. The columns shown in this specification are:

- *Txn Num*: The transaction number associated with this transaction. This is the next-level breakdown from the series number in the overall transaction structure described above.
- *Event description*: An operational description of what this transaction does and how/why it occurs.
- *Event trigger*: The act that triggers the execution of this transaction. This is described operationally, but from a programming perspective this will be used to prepare the computer processing associated with this event.
- *Data from*: Where the data in this transaction is coming from. Codes such as TRK RTU (the RTU/PLC on the truck), SCLM (Supply Chain for Liquids module), and ERP (enterprise resource planning or the central computer system) are used to specify the data-from and data-to entities.
- *Data to*: Where the data in this transaction is transferred to.
- *Data layout*: The actual data contained in this transaction. In this example the data layout is shown as transaction identifier code and transaction variables. The transaction identifier code is entered at the beginning of the transaction and distinguishes each type of transaction so that the computer system can process it properly. Transaction identifier codes TRKFILL (TRucK FILLing transaction)

Sample specification for Supply Chain for Liquids processing flow
Sample related to deliver preparation activity

Txn Num	Event Description	Event Trigger	Data From	Data To	Data Layout	Result
	Delivery Preparation					
2200						
2210	The truck tanks are filled with the appropriate liquids – The Warehouse Operator fills the truck tanks in preparation for the next delivery run. The product and quantity for each line on the truck have already been calculated by the Supply Chain for Liquids Module	The Warehouse Operator enters a "Truck Fill" transaction, including the truck number and line number on the truck. The shutoff valve closes when the fill quantity has been reached	SCLM	ERP	TRKFILL, ttt, nn, aaaa, cccc • ttt is the truck number entered by the Operator • nn is the line number entered by the Operator • aaaa is the actual quantity at aaa.a gallons detected by the flow sensor • cccc is the calculated quantity at ccc.c gallons for this line	Liquid inventory balance on truck is increased and in warehouse is decreased. If there is a mismatch between the quantity-to-load calculated by the SCL Module and the quantity actually loaded, an error message is issued
2220	Request to download next day's deliveries – The Warehouse Operator requests that the system download the next day's delivery information to the truck	The Warehouse Operator enters this transaction on the truck RTU	TRK RTU	SCLM	DELREQ, ttt • ttt is the truck number entered by the Operator or sent by the RTU	The SCL Module prepares to transmit the next day's delivery data to the specified truck
2230	The next day's deliveries are downloaded to the truck – The next day's delivery plan (account, line, quantity) is downloaded to the truck. During the delivery, the Truck Operator will then need only to enter the account number, and the load quantity will be set automatically	SCLM performs this transaction based on receiving transaction DELDNLDREQ	SCLM	TRK RTU	DELDNLD, nn, aaaa, qqqq [multiple records] • nn is the line number • aaaa is the account number • qqqq is the quantity at qqq-q gallons	The truck RTU knows what quantity of each line to deliver to each account
2240	Truck ready – The Operator reports that the truck is fully loaded.	Warehouse Operator enters "Truck Ready" transaction	TRK RTU	SCLM	TRKRDY, ttt • ttt is the truck number entered by the Operator or sent by the RTU	The truck is ready for the next delivery run

Exhibit 10.3 The Transaction-Based Orientation of the System Guides the Information Flow

and DELREQ (DELivery REQuest transaction) are among those shown in Exhibit 10.3. Transaction variables identify for the computer programmers the data elements that will follow the transaction identifier code in comma-separated format.

■ *Result*: The condition that results from the execution of this transaction.

Completing the specifications in a format such as this has many advantages. Operational personnel can read through the "event description," "event trigger," and "result" columns and get a plain-English understanding of the flow of the system and how users will interact with it. Computer programmers can use the "event trigger," "data from," "data to," and "data layout" columns as the basis for coding specifications. Multiple sets of computer programmers are generally involved with projects such as this, including central computer system programmers, PLC/RTU programmers, etc., and this document provides a common set of parameters for them to work from. Most importantly, a single specification document that can be read and understood by everyone means that everyone is singing from the same hymn sheet — always an important step to ensure that the song comes out right.

Maintaining a Supply Chain for Liquids System

Maintaining a system after it has been implemented can be tough to do, as George Washington found out just three years after the American Revolution ended in 1783. "No Morn ever dawned more favourable than ours did — and no day was ever more clouded than the present!" the president-to-be wrote to James Madison regarding Shays Rebellion, the armed uprising that resulted from the inequities that were already occurring in the young American economic system. Although Daniel Shays's rebellion did not bring down the system, it did have a big impact on restructuring the system. The extent of the rebellion shook up the powers that be, and the causes of the rebellion were an important part of the discussions that surrounded the replacement of the Articles of Confederation with the Constitution.

A standard approach to any system or process is first to implement it and then to maintain it. These are two different phases that require two different sets of skills. Implementation requires skills and activities such as planning, engineering, creation, installation, training, change management, coordination of players, and a "spike" of effort in various directions. Maintaining a system for the most part means running it, managing it, providing ongoing training on its usage, and dealing with the "bumps" and tweaking for the deviations from norm that occur in the course of daily operation.

A company that follows this path will not gain maximum benefit from Supply Chain for Liquids. The concept of "maintaining" the Supply Chain for Liquids should be replaced by the concept of "leveraging" the Supply Chain for Liquids. Like most systems, Supply Chain for Liquids consists of a base investment that a company will want to exploit as much as possible by finding as many uses for it as possible. Unlike many systems, Supply Chain for Liquids creates new opportunities for the company that did not exist before it was put into place, so maintaining Supply Chain for Liquids "as is" from the point of operation misses out on these potential usages of the system. Supply Chain for Liquids should include a bit of a Shays' Rebellion to periodically adjust itself to changing conditions.

Let us use another type of system as an example to clarify this point. When a company puts in a time-and-attendance system to track employee work time, it expects the result to be a more efficient time-and-attendance process, with the resulting controls, reports and analyses, and cost savings. Once a time-and-attendance system is implemented, it is expected to run and yield its benefits, but in most cases there is no expectation that it will lead to some other result or benefit for the company, and no effort is made to explore other results or benefits.

To this we contrast our thinking about a Supply Chain for Liquids system. An operating Supply Chain for Liquids system links us with our partners all along the supply stream, from the raw-material suppliers through the end customers. It supports the ongoing flow of product in one direction and information in the other direction to make the logistics stream as effective as possible. It can be expanded as much as possible to achieve economies of scale and maximize the financial return on investment. This is the "maintenance mode" for Supply Chain for Liquids that, to use the language of logic, is necessary but not sufficient to gain maximum benefit from Supply Chain for Liquids. A "leverage mode" lets us benefit from the rich potentialities that Supply Chain for Liquids has to offer. Among the characteristics of leverage mode are:

■ New marketing, sales, and distribution channels, as described in Chapter 11. Because the movement and configuration of the physical product is different under Supply Chain for Liquids than it is in its ordinary packaged configuration, the product can be distributed, offered, and dispensed in ways that are not possible in the ordinary configuration.

■ Complementary Supply Chains for Liquids^{SM}, as described later in this chapter. After one stream of Supply Chain for Liquids relationships has been established, it can be expanded not just vertically

— end-to-end — but also horizontally, with liquid-related companies that are operating in parallel to the Supply Chain for Liquids.

■ Competitive battle, as described in Chapter 3. Your ability to offer
Supply Chain for Liquids may well "change the rules of the game"
and allow you to choose not only the battlefield, but also the
weapons that will be used in your competitive struggle. You can
leverage the Supply Chain for Liquids system not only internally
and among your partners, but in the way that you relate to your
competition as well.

■ The techniques offered by Supply Chain for Liquids allow a company to establish industry standards and assume industry leadership
in a number of areas: services provided to customers, quality
assurance, and pricing, among others. Industry leadership in these
areas can be translated into broader positioning of the company
so that Supply Chain for Liquids serves the highest levels of
business strategy.

The method and degree to which Supply Chain for Liquids can be
leveraged by any particular company depends on many factors. The key
is to make sure that "leverage mode" operates beside "maintenance mode"
once Supply Chain for Liquids has become operational.

A Day in the Life of a Supply Chain for Liquids Company

One way that we can pull together our description of Supply Chain for
Liquids is to run through how it "feels" — what the world looks like from
within the Supply Chain for Liquids process. Who does what, what flows
where, how does a person know what to do? By walking through the
Supply Chain for Liquids processes, we can round out the picture of what
it is all about. We will run through a one-day cycle of Supply Chain for
Liquids, referring to events that happen before or after our focus period.

This example is, of course, generalized for illustrative purposes, and
each organization performs the activities, and assigns responsibilities, that
are appropriate for that organization. However, this example covers the
major activities — delivery preparation, including both information and
truck preparation; delivery; on-site operation; operational activities; management activities; and customer/supplier activities. For simplicity, it does
not include details such as various housekeeping activities like information
setup and maintenance. This overall flow is appropriate whether there is
one delivery run daily per truck or more, or whether the deliveries are
made at night, during the day, or a combination. The overall flow can
accommodate these and other tactical decisions within the overall Supply
Chain for Liquids process.

The description that follows is for Optimal Supply Chain for Liquids including a full and fully integrated information flow. As discussed earlier, a system such as this can be implemented in stages, with partial manual processing leading up to optimal automation. Examples of points at which manual processing can be used are included in this description.

Delivery Preparation — Information

The following flow relates to planning for truck deliveries under the Supply Chain for Liquids system. These can be deliveries to customer sites, deliveries from a producer to distribution sites, or other distribution/delivery planning. This process precedes the physical preparation of the truck and truck loading, as described in the next section.

Dispatcher

The dispatcher receives a delivery-preparation report generated by the central computer system. This report is "user ready" for finalizing the delivery run for each truck, and all the processing and information described below are included in it.

Delivery-Preparation Report

The delivery-preparation report has taken into account all of the factors related to planning a delivery run, including the following:

1. The delivery-preparation report is based on the signals received from the on-site systems as to the inventory balance and usage pattern for each liquid at each site. Based on the input or calculated replenishment point for each liquid, the central computer system has identified sites at which a liquid balance is at a low threshold and should be replenished within a specific time horizon. To maximize delivery efficiency, if a truck is to make a delivery at a site, it will replenish all the liquids at that site, even if only one or two specifically need replenishment while the remainder need only be topped off.

2. The delivery-preparation report takes into account any CPVR indicators required, as described below. Although there may appear to be a shortage of product at a certain point in the supply stream, overstock at a subsequent point must be taken into account in determining the proper replenishment action. CPVR addresses adjustments of this type.

3. The delivery-preparation report takes into account route planning and standard delivery runs or schedules that may be in place. Route planning can be part of the central computer system's processing, or the central system might be supplemented by a software package dedicated to this purpose. Because of the speed with which deliveries occur under the Supply Chain for Liquids system, it is possible that a truck will be used for two delivery runs per day, such as day and night. If so, route planning should be smart enough to know whether a route is being run during a high-traffic period, with slower truck movement and fewer deliveries across the same period of time, or during a low-traffic period that will speed truck movement, increase delivery capability, and shorten delivery time. Under Supply Chain for Liquids, the time-of-day limitations that are common for delivery planning in standard/ Supply Chain environments are irrelevant, as product is delivered externally and without site entry or personnel interaction, so it is assumed that this is not part of delivery planning here.

4. The delivery-preparation report takes into account the configuration for each truck for which a run is being prepared: capacity, including the number and sizes of on-truck tanks; limitations to on-truck tank usage (some tanks may be dedicated to consumable products and others to nonconsumable products, for example); allowed weight; size limitations for specific delivery areas; etc.

5. The planning for the route takes into account the sources of the liquids to be delivered during the run. If all liquids being delivered during a run are coming from the same producer, then the truck-fill process is simplified, whether the run is actually being performed by the producer, a distributor, the customer's truck, etc. By the same token, if for example the delivery is being performed by a distributor, the same result could be achieved by having liquids from the different suppliers held in bulk tanks at the distributor site. However, if liquids for a particular delivery run need to be loaded from multiple supplier sites, this must be taken into account during delivery-preparation planning.

6. Finally, the delivery-preparation report can also provide signals regarding other activities that need to be performed and that will impact the delivery configuration but are not directly part of the delivery process. An example of this is the need to change the on-site tank configuration for a particular customer site due to shifting patterns of usage among the liquids at the site. Although this is not directly a part of the delivery process, it affects delivery in several ways. The dispatcher who plans the delivery runs might be the same person who plans the maintenance runs, and so would

want visibility into this information during delivery planning. If on-site tank reconfiguration involves minimizing the quantity of certain products at the site to permit or simplify the reconfiguration process, the dispatcher should be aware of the pending reconfiguration to fine-tune the on-hand quantity at the site to best balance the reconfiguration activity and avoid the possibility of stock-out of any liquid.

The delivery-preparation report contains other information required in any particular environment, and it is formatted in the most effective manner for each environment.

Dispatcher

Having received the delivery-preparation report as described above, the dispatcher finalizes routing the trucks for the delivery runs. The process of truck routing under Supply Chain for Liquids is similar to any standard routing operation in which orders and products are assigned to trucks, trucks are assigned to routes and customers, and quantities are checked against delivery requirements. The dispatcher ensures that certain "finesse" issues are addressed, as described in the delivery-preparation report section above, and inputs into the central computer system or dispatching system any adjustments required to the delivery plan. This information is then passed to the appropriate areas through the reports or displays that are available to them.

As noted above, there is an entire group of setup activities that go into the preparation of the computer system for use, such as data related to customers, sites and site tanks, trucks, products, suppliers and supplier tanks, orders, etc. Because these are not part of the work flow described here, these have been excluded from this description.

Delivery Preparation — Truck

This section relates to the physical activities involved in truck preparation, based on the planning and information preparation described in the prior section. For the most part, these physical activities take place at the location at which liquids are loaded onto the truck.

Warehouse Operator

The warehouse operator is the person responsible for the loading of the trucks. Although, as we shall see here, their methods of working are vastly different, the warehouse operator's function is parallel to that of the forklift driver in a standard truck-loading environment, and this analogy can be used to understand the warehouse operator's function in this process.

The warehouse operator first ensures that the truck has been processed since its prior delivery run, that is, the tanks have been emptied and cleaned if required, the inventory balances shown for the truck have been reset, etc. The warehouse operator then uses the truck-loading report to configure the truck and load the liquids.

Truck-Loading Report

The truck-loading report may be a physical document, or depending on the degree of automation that has been installed as part of the Supply Chain for Liquids process, it may be signals that the central computer system sends to PLCs and manifolds that automatically control the truck-configuration and -loading process. The latter approach encompasses full automation of the truck-loading process. A mixed system could be used, for example, computer control of product quantities and manual setting of the valving between tanks on the truck. The truck-loading report defines the activities to be performed by the warehouse operator.

1. First, the physical configuration of the truck tanks is defined, that is, which tanks on the truck will be linked together for the next delivery run. The number and sizes of the tanks on the truck that are dedicated to a particular liquid on a particular delivery run determine the capacity in the truck that is available for that liquid. Switching the tanks between different liquids for different delivery runs provides a great deal of flexibility in the quantities of different liquids that are delivered on different runs. Because the delivery plan is based on the most-recent readings regarding the remaining inventory balances in the site tanks, truck planning and loading can be done with a high degree of efficiency in terms of loading exactly the products and quantities that will be delivered during the next delivery run. If the tank configuration has not changed from the previous delivery run for this truck, this is noted on the report; if there are changes from the previous tank configuration, these are highlighted on the report on an exception basis.
2. The liquid to be loaded into each tank grouping is shown, together with the quantity of each liquid. Again, if this activity is performed manually, it will be printed on the report; or these may be settings that are transferred to the flowmeters that control the flow of liquids to the tanks in the truck.

Warehouse Operator

Based on the information shown in the truck-loading report, the warehouse operator makes the physical changes to the truck and loads the truck. First, the warehouse operator changes the valve settings so that the proper tanks are interconnected as shown on the report. The design of the valving system should be such that setting and checking the valve settings/tank interconnections is as simple and error-free as possible. Next, the warehouse operator connects hoses from the supply tanks to the truck tank lines to load the liquids onto the truck. Just as care is taken during standard delivery planning as to the order on which products are loaded onto the truck, so that the earliest deliveries are for the first accessible products on the truck, in parallel under Supply Chain for Liquids, care is taken to ensure that proper quantities of specific products are loaded into the proper tanks on the trucks. Even in the "worst case" that this is purely a manual function, however, Supply Chain for Liquids makes these processes as error-proof as possible through the use of matching fittings on the connectors between a supply tank and its corresponding truck tanks so that only the desired liquid can be loaded into the tanks, sight-glasses that allow reconfirmation of the quantities of liquids loaded, etc.

In a more automated environment, the flow of liquids through predefined connectors and flowmeters that cut off the flow of liquids when the required quantity has been loaded make the system even more fail-safe. In such an environment, the recording of the truck loading, with its corresponding decrease in the supply tank balance and increase in the truck tank balance, would also result automatically from the loading process. Similarly the next step, that of the details of the actual delivery plan, is handled differently depending on whether the system is automated or manual.

Delivery Report

The delivery report shows each customer to be reached during the delivery run together with the specific products and quantity of each product that is to be delivered to each customer. In addition, the delivery report shows the information included in a standard routing report, such as the sequence of customers for the delivery run, special instructions or conditions, etc. Again, the delivery report may be entirely or partially printed, or it may be in the form of data that is downloaded to the PLC on the truck if a truck-based control and reporting system has been installed.

Warehouse Operator

If the delivery system is computer-based, the warehouse operator enters an instruction into the computer system to download the delivery report information from the central computer system to the PLC on the truck. The PLC on the truck will control the flow of each liquid at each site and ensure that the proper quantities have been delivered at each point on the delivery route. Following this download, the warehouse operator enters a "load complete" transaction to show that this truck has been loaded from both physical/product and information perspectives and is ready for the delivery run.

Although the warehouse operator's function was earlier compared with that of the forklift driver in a standard environment in terms of getting the truck ready for a delivery run, as can be seen from this description, the nature of the work is far different. The forklift driver has a great deal of physical activity to do — retrieving product, staging it, loading it onto the truck — with a relatively low level of sophistication required. The warehouse operator in a Supply Chain for Liquids environment has a physically less demanding job — connecting tubes, switching valves, monitoring liquid flow — but in a manually oriented scenario, the operator has to pay much more attention because all the settings must be correct for the process to work right. In a more automated environment, this requirement is not quite as critical, and the warehouse operator's job is less demanding.

The Delivery Process

This section describes the activity that occurs during the actual delivery run as the driver performs a delivery at each customer site.

Driver

The driver brings the truck adjacent to the external port on an outside wall of the site. After unlocking the box, the driver attaches the hoses from the truck to the coupling units inside the external port. The shape of the coupling units, a pin system that is different for each external port, or some other simple method is used to ensure that the proper hose from the truck is attached to the proper line from the external port to the mini-tanks inside the facility.

After the physical connection is made, the driver keys the customer's site number into the PLC in the truck. An even more advanced version of the system transmits a signal from the external port to the PLC in the truck, thus eliminating any possibility of driver error.

Truck PLC

The PLC matches the current site number to the liquids/quantities information for the site that was downloaded from the central computer system during the "delivery preparation — truck" process. In this way, the PLC knows the type and quantity of each liquid that is to be delivered to this particular customer. The PLC displays the customer or site name, and upon confirmation by the driver the PLC opens the valves for the liquids required and begins to deliver the liquids.

As the flowmeter on each liquid line reaches the required delivery quantity for that liquid at this site, the PLC shuts the line and stops the liquid flow. After the delivery quantity of all liquids has been delivered, the PLC displays a "Delivery Complete?" message, and upon confirmation from the driver, the PLC updates the truck inventory balance and the information to be passed to the central computer system regarding site inventory receipt. Any discrepancy between the planned delivery quantity and the actual delivery quantity, such as if a line was shut off during delivery for any reason, is flagged for investigation by the dispatcher. In addition, the reading from the flowmeter inside the site is also compared with this quantity to confirm that the delivered quantity was received by the customer site.

Driver

Following the completion of the flow of product to the site, the driver disengages the lines from the external port, locks it, and drives to the next site. As can be seen from this description, the nature of the driver's work is different from that in a normal store delivery scenario. In many instances under a standard delivery methodology, the major part of the driver's function is physically hauling the product, be it in cases, barrels, etc., from the truck to the storage area inside the site. In addition, the driver frequently enters the facility, takes the order, enters it into a handheld device, and prints and returns the receipt. All of these activities are replaced by the act of hooking and unhooking the hoses, and activating the process through the truck PLC. The duration of each delivery stop is also much shorter, as the unloading/hauling/rotating/moving process is replaced by the flow of liquids through the hoses, at whatever rate has been designed into the system.

On-Site Operation

This section describes the Supply Chain for Liquids–related activities of personnel at a user site.

On-Site Personnel

There are no ongoing activities required of on-site personnel related to the Supply Chain for Liquids system. Depending on how the system is designed and implemented, there may be periodic tasks required related to the system, such as activating or checking the tank/pipe cleaning system, changing valve settings to reconfigure liquid capacities in the tank system, etc. One of the major advantages of the Supply Chain for Liquids system is that it relieves on-site personnel of the many physical and administrative tasks that are ordinarily associated with handling and using liquid products, as described in detail in Chapter 8. As such, in addition to the extensive cost savings and streamlining that accrue to the producer and the distributor under Supply Chain for Liquids, there are also considerable benefits for the customer/user.

On-Site Management

As a management tool, Supply Chain for Liquids provides benefits both to company/corporate management, as described below, and to site management. With the appropriate security, the manager of a store, restaurant, garage, factory, or other facility has instant Internet access to product inventory and usage information down to the level of detail defined for the system. For example, if the sensors in the tanks take readings every 15 minutes, the site manager can get detailed information about product usage traffic as well as immediately spot exceptions that may be causing inventory loss. Corresponding information can be compared across different sites supporting district, regional, or companywide analyses and corrective action.

Operational Activities

This section describes the operational activities, beyond the actual delivery cycle, that are connected to Supply Chain for Liquids.

Production Planning and Inventory Control

While production feeds product into the Supply Chain for Liquids system, Supply Chain for Liquids feeds information back that can be a powerful tool in making production and inventory/distribution decisions. Using the Supply Chain for Liquids methodology, the production-planning function can see in both directions. For its own products, it can see the balances and movements of inventory for the length of the Supply Chain for Liquids, and thus can make the most appropriate production decisions to minimize systemwide inventory while maintaining required service levels. For ingredients and products it receives from suppliers, production planning can know exactly how much is available and where it is located. For on-site inventory, Supply Chain for Liquids offers real-time inventory balances with complete accuracy.

In addition to excellent visibility, the CPVR approach described later in this chapter offers coordinated guidance to production and inventory responses to changing conditions. CPVR (Coordinated Procedures for Visibility Response) means that the production-control group will be directed to take actions that are coordinated with the actions taken by all of the partners for the length of the Supply Chain for Liquids. As a result, the production-control department is able to make the decisions that will ensure that product gets into Supply Chain for Liquids as needed — a complete circular flow of information and product.

Management Activities

This section describes the management interfaces with the Supply Chain for Liquids system.

Marketing

Supply Chain for Liquids offers marketing a level of interaction with the customer that is only available otherwise through point-of-sale data. Data is available by customer or by product, down to the time-of-day level, based on the granularity with which the data is being captured. With easy comparison between different combinations of data — product, location, time, channel, etc. — marketing can detect trends that would have otherwise remained hidden in lumpy data.

Finance

Inventory investment can be brought down two ways: by lowering the cost of the product or by lowering the amount of product in the system. Supply Chain for Liquids supports both of these objectives. The simplified operation that eliminates packaging and handling at many points along the logistics flow takes costs out of the process and makes margin available to the players. At the same time, the streamlined flow with a high level of visibility allows less product to support a higher level of service. Even more, the amount of product in the system is closely definable; there are no "black holes" where the quantity of product is unknown or disappears. The many ancillary benefits of Supply Chain for Liquids — lower insurance costs, reduced space requirements, lower manpower needs, and better utilization of resources such as delivery trucks — only serve to sweeten the deal. Finance's relationship with Supply Chain for Liquids is a happy one indeed, and the finance perspective can be an important contributor to making sure the Liquid Lens is in sharp focus.

Human Resources

Although human resources does not work with the Supply Chain for Liquids system directly, the system has a large impact on operational personnel. There is a large safety benefit to Supply Chain for Liquids versus standard systems. In the warehouse area, for example, all products are in enclosed tanks and flow without having to be moved by operating personnel, versus the forklifts, racks, broken packaging and products, and other hazards that characterize standard operational environments. Delivery personnel do not have to lug cartons, tanks, or other heavy containers of products into the customer site and frequently down stairs or into backrooms. Instead, they simply attach the delivery pipe to a connector near the delivery truck. On-site there is much less risk of spillage, falling goods, slipping, or other hazards associated with containers that have to be stored, moved, opened, and poured. In these indirect ways, Supply Chain for Liquids simplifies the human-resources function and makes for a better working environment for the employees.

Environmental Compliance

From an environmental perspective, Supply Chain for Liquids is a vast improvement over standard logistics methodologies for liquids. The advantages of each step of Supply Chain for Liquids for the environment are detailed in Chapter 11. Reduced environment-related activity multiplies its own benefits. Not only is the logistics system itself "cleaner" in an environmental sense, but the reduction in paperwork, tracking, reporting, cleanup, and other environmentally related activities amplifies this benefit.

Customer/Supplier Activities

This section describes customers' and suppliers' activities related to Supply Chain for Liquids.

Customers and Suppliers

As a fully Internet-based system, Supply Chain for Liquids supports full and instantaneous availability of information. Supply Chain for Liquids supplies that information directly from the source — from sensors located in the tanks holding the liquid products. This information in its raw form or processed to add or protect information can then be made available to customers and suppliers, each to view its own data and position. The CPVR program described later in this chapter provides an additional linkage in unifying the Supply Chain for Liquids flow from supplier through producer and distributor to customer and consumer.

A day in the life of Supply Chain for Liquids shows many players working together in a well-coordinated flow of product and information, with many benefits derived from the fact that it is a fully liquids-based effort.

RFID for Liquids

RFID is growing in importance as major retailers and government agencies drive implementation of the technology — like it or not — by their suppliers. RFID (radio frequency identification) in its standard usage consists of tags that are applied to products, cartons, pallets, or containers that can be read by RFID readers at various points throughout the Supply Chain. RFID provides the ability to track virtually 100 percent of inventory at every point at which an RFID reader has been installed. This lofty goal is seemingly ideal from a Supply Chain management perspective, but the reality of RFID is somewhat more mixed. There are some very valid reasons why RFID's penetration of the marketplace is meeting resistance. There are plenty of opinions on and information about RFID in general available in the marketplace, and because understanding RFID itself is not our objective, we will not explore that topic here.

A close look at the major benefits and the major drawbacks of RFID, however, reveals something astonishing: Supply Chain for Liquids provides almost all the major benefits and avoids almost all the major drawbacks of RFID for discrete products! The method and monitoring of liquid flow in Supply Chain for Liquids amounts to RFID for Liquids®, and companies that produce, handle, distribute, or sell liquid products actually have an enormous advantage over those that handle discrete products in terms of the issues related to RFID. You might say it was not planned that way, but it sure works out that way. Sometimes the bear gets you, but sometimes you do get the bear.

Let us look more closely at Supply Chain for Liquids as an RFID application, and we will see that liquid products are in fact way ahead of the curve in this area. In standard RFID, a tag travels with the product and is read by readers along the Supply Chain, thus providing data on product movement and balances. In Supply Chain for Liquids/RFID for

Liquids, the "tags" are the product itself within the producer tanks, distributor tanks, on-site tanks, etc. The sensors along the supply stream, rather than just reading the presence of the product, read also the quantity of the product present. There is no need for the physical tags such as in standard RFID, as in a properly constructed RFID for Liquids system the sensors directly provide the data on product movement and balances. With discrete products, you must use tags because you cannot know the products' precise physical position to determine, for example, their quantity based on their volume. In Supply Chain for Liquids/RFID for Liquids, we use the fact that liquids always gravitate to the bottom of a tank and sit with a level surface to determine their quantity based on their volume, thus exploiting this huge physical difference between discrete and liquid products for business benefit. RFID and RFID for Liquids are in one sense identical, in that they both use sensors to track product through the logistics process with a high degree of accuracy. But for the most part, that is where the similarity ends.

To fully understand Supply Chain for Liquids/RFID for Liquids's relationship to RFID, let us lay out the major benefits and the major drawbacks of RFID as they are commonly presented. First we will simply list them, and then we will review each one in detail and examine it in light of Supply Chain for Liquids capabilities to understand that RFID for Liquids is in fact a radically more attractive process than standard RFID.

Some of the major benefits usually cited for RFID are:

■ Compliance with customer requirements
■ Real-time information about inventory movement and balance
■ Labor savings through automatic data capture without human intervention
■ Improved sales performance through reduced stock-outs

Facing these benefits are some of the predominant drawbacks of acquiring, implementing, and operating an RFID system:

■ Per unit cost
■ Technical coordination of tag and reader technologies
■ Infringement of privacy
■ Balance of benefit

Now let us look at each of these benefits and drawbacks and show how Supply Chain for Liquids changes the paradigm for the better in all cases. A comparison of the flow aspects of RFID and RFID for Liquids is illustrated in Exhibit 10.4.

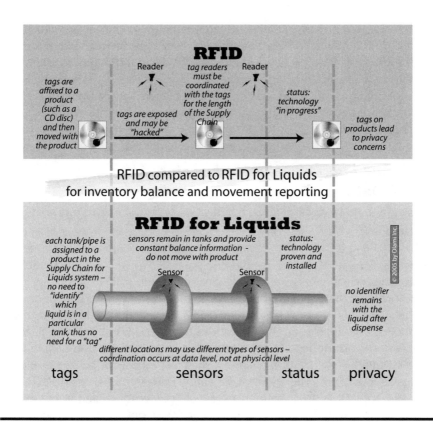

Exhibit 10.4 RFID for Liquids Provides Virtually All the Benefits of RFID for Discrete Products without the Drawbacks

Compliance with Customer Requirements

Early efforts at broad implementation of RFID have been led by the downstream end of the Supply Chain, including major retailers and government agencies. Inasmuch as the general consensus is that the advantages of RFID accrue mainly to the retailer/user, with advantages to the producer being marginal at best, downstream initiatives and leadership are to be expected.

This paradigm is completely changed in the RFID for Liquids approach, because the RFID element in Supply Chain for Liquids is not an add-on cost for the producer as it is in standard RFID (see Per-Unit Cost below), but rather it is an integral part of a cost-reducing, margin-generating system. The entire Supply Chain for Liquids package reduces costs, as described in Chapter 11, and the savings that result from RFID for Liquids are distributed all along the Supply Chain for Liquids — producer, distributor, and customer.

Therefore, rather than creating an adversarial relationship in which the producer is "required to be in compliance" with customer requirements, the RFID for Liquids functionality within a Supply Chain for Liquids system offers benefits to all the players. The success of many efforts is commensurate with the incentive to participate, and any of the players in a supply stream may initiate movement toward and derive large benefit from the Supply Chain for Liquids approach.

Real-Time Information about Inventory Movement and Balance

As mentioned above, this benefit is essentially identical in RFID and RFID for Liquids. Both use sensors to detect the presence of product at specific points along the logistics process, and both transmit this data to a central information system for use by the companies involved. Although the two approaches may be "essentially" identical, there are still several large differences between them that are very much to the advantage of RFID for Liquids. The relatively inexpensive passive RFID tags are very limited in the maximum distance allowed between the tags and the reader, and in the rate at which multiple tags can be read. They are, for the most part, used in well-defined processes with a set rate of movement, such as products or packages moving on a conveyor belt. The distance limitation means that passive RFID tags are less applicable to situations in which the reader cannot be moved relatively close to the tag, such as during an inventory count in a warehouse. Therefore, passive RFID is applicable to tracking inventory *movement* but less so for inventory *balance*. In cases in which the actual distance exceeds the readable distance, the balance is calculated when the movements of the tags are detected by passive RFID, but it is not directly measured.

Within Supply Chain for Liquids, the sensor in the tank is monitoring the *balance* of product at any given time, and so is providing a much more reliable measure of on-hand inventory. Detecting inventory movement using RFID often requires the much more expense active RFID capability, with RFID tags that are many times more expensive than passive RFID tags. Supply Chain for Liquids provides options for both capabilities. A sensor in a tank monitors the on-hand balance of the liquid product in the tank at any time, and a flowmeter in a supply or dispense line can measure product movement through that point.

Labor Savings through Automatic Data Capture without Human Intervention

Neither RFID nor RFID for Liquids requires human intervention for actual data gathering, although the capabilities in terms of what data can be gathered are different between the two approaches, as described above. Even assuming full automation of the RFID process — printing the RFID tag, attaching it to the product, reading it remotely — there are likely to arise steps that do require human intervention. Given that RFID systems are based on a multiplicity of tags, one per unit being monitored, a certain percentage of tags will not provide data accurately. This can result from any of several causes, such as a physically faulty tag, the tag being separated from the unit, malfunction in the reader, periodic distortion of the signal between the tag and the reader, etc. In the event that any of these or other causes leads to a discrepancy in inventory information, such a discrepancy must be manually investigated and resolved. Because RFID for Liquids does not rely on an amount of equipment corresponding to the quantity of product, but rather on a single fixed measuring unit at each point of measurement, the likelihood of malfunction and the corresponding need for corrective intervention is reduced. There is simply much less equipment involved in the whole system.

Improved Sales Performance through Reduced Stock-Outs

Within the provisions of the comments above regarding benefits and the following comments regarding drawbacks, the two approaches, RFID and RFID for Liquids, provide the same support to sales performance through reduced stock-outs. RFID for Liquids also matches standard RFID in creating new sales and marketing opportunities for companies. RFID paves the way for monitoring consumer purchase patterns in real time and suggesting add-on purchases based on the customer's existing basket, as well as providing flexibilities in the check-out process that are not available without RFID. As described in Chapter 11, Supply Chain for Liquids creates sales and marketing opportunities as well as distribution-channel opportunities that are not available in manually supplied product environments.

Some of the common drawbacks of RFID, together with the comparative functionality of RFID for Liquids, are discussed in the following subsections.

Per-Unit Cost

RFID can be expensive, and this expense is compounded by several factors. First, as described above, the costs of RFID may not be evenly distributed among the players in the Supply Chain. In an environment in which the producer bears the greater part of the cost while the customer enjoys the greater part of the benefit, there is a true imbalance of incentive to participate in the effort. The issue of cost related to RFID is also amplified by the fact that RFID is inherently a recurring cost that increases with usage of the system: the more products/cartons/pallets/packages that are tagged in an RFID system, the higher the cost due to the per-tag cost. This is part of the reasoning for the per-pallet or per-carton approach rather than a per-unit approach in current mandates for RFID for discrete items. RFID has not yet reached the point where it can track individual units of lower-cost items cost effectively.

In contrast to the cost structure of standard RFID, RFID for Liquids is a *per-process* cost, not a *per-product* cost. That is, there is no RFID for Liquids cost incurred per unit of product as there is with the tags in standard RFID. Further, the costs associated with RFID for Liquids as well as the savings are spread throughout the Supply Chain for Liquids. As described in Chapter 11, some of the major costs are the tanking systems at the producer, distributor, and customer; the trucks; and the monitoring and feedback equipment. The major benefits are the savings in material by the producer and labor/handling at the distributor and customer. All the players have an investment to make, and all the players stand to gain from a Supply Chain for Liquids system, making it a much more attractive proposition for the system as a whole.

Technical Issues

There are a number of technical issues that stand in the way of massive implementation of RFID systems. The limited range of the tag-reader connection in a simple RFID configuration is a significant drawback in certain RFID applications. Depending on the type of RFID system to be implemented, the radio frequency used by the system in a location becomes an issue. The coordination among multiple RFID systems will clearly be increasingly problematic as RFID technology is adopted. If a retailer receives products from two different suppliers that use two different types of RFID tags, the retailer will need to install and integrate multiple types of RFID readers to support the technology. In general, extensive effort must be invested, and compliance with Supply Chain–wide methodologies for the physical aspects of RFID is required in order for RFID to work properly among multiple players.

These issues do not exist in RFID for Liquids simply because the RFID portion is fixed at specific points in the Supply Chain for Liquids and does not travel along the Supply Chain, as do RFID tags. In fact, RFID for Liquids adapts itself to the most appropriate technology at each particular point in the Supply Chain for Liquids. For example, the sensors in the producers' tanks may be point-monitors, in the trucks they may be flowmeters, at the distributor they might be float sensors, and the customer might use electrooptic sensors, each being the most appropriate type of sensor for that particular piece of the Supply Chain for Liquids. The units likely are from different manufacturers that work with different protocols and techniques related to sensing inventory balances. The point at which these pieces interrelate is not at the physical level but at the data level. After the sensors transmit data to a PLC, the format of the data that the PLCs transmit to the central computer system must be consistent and standardized. As described earlier in this chapter, it is relatively simple to standardize the data aspects of an RFID for Liquids system, certainly much simpler than standardizing the physical aspects of an RFID system for discrete goods in which there is a physical connection (the tag and the way it is read) between the players.

Privacy Infringement

A drawback to RFID that has been more visibly and vocally expressed is the concern that an RFID tag serves to invade the privacy of a person who purchases an item affixed with an RFID tag. An RFID-ed world could bring even deeper knowledge of consumer behavior, even well after the point of purchase. There is no lack of horror stories of the possibility of Big Brother (or Big Thief) driving down the street and knowing exactly who has what goods and appliances in which house. The desire to avoid this point of resistance may again have played into decisions to approach initial RFID implementations only at the pallet or carton level rather than at the individual-product level.

These concerns, of course, do not apply to RFID for Liquids. The RFID aspect of Supply Chain for Liquids is purely within the logistics process from the producer to the customer, and it is not physically associated with the product in any way. Thus the privacy issue is also a nonissue when it comes to RFID for Liquids.

Balance of Benefits

The fact that there are so many Web seminars dedicated to the topic of "making the business case for RFID" is an indication that it is not always easy to do. As described previously, in early implementations of RFID the benefits are weighted toward the user, while the costs are weighted toward the manufacturer.

RFID for Liquids within the context of Supply Chain for Liquids cancels this imbalance, because it is not a scheme thrown on top of an existing logistics flow, but rather a completely modified logistics flow. Costs and complexities are removed from every step of the process, starting with the producer. There are operational benefits all the way around; how the players in the logistics flow decide to divide up the freed-up margin and additional revenue opportunity will be decided in each case separately.

In essence, you put in Supply Chain for Liquids and you get RFID for Liquids for free, including so many of the benefits of RFID as described above without the drawbacks. Out of the two alternative paths, for discrete products or for liquid products, RFID for Liquids is a much simpler, proven capability. More comprehensive information about RFID for Liquids characteristics and capabilities can be found at www.RFIDforLiquids.com, the Internet site of RFID for Liquids.

CPVR

The information side of the Supply Chain for Liquids must be completely integrated with the product side of Supply Chain for Liquids, as described above. However, there are many configurations that the information side of Supply Chain for Liquids can take. The description above uses a VMI (vendor-managed inventory)-type approach; another approach to the relationship among the players along the Supply Chain for Liquids is a collaborative effort.

Supply Chain for Liquids offers an alternative approach to the collaboration models that are commonly available. The approach offered by Supply Chain for Liquids — CPVR (Coordinated Procedures for Visibility Response) — applies the Liquid Lens principle of "snatching simplicity from the jaws of complexity" to create a light, easy-to-operate approach for companies along the Supply Chain for Liquids to interact with each other. This may be an interim step as the partners in the Supply Chain for Liquids move toward the VMI-like capability that Supply Chain for Liquids offers, or it might be defined as the ultimate objective of the information flow within the partners' Supply Chain for Liquids definition.

Existing collaboration models are "heavy" in the sense that they add complexity to a company's planning and execution by overlaying comanaged processes on top of the company's own processes. This includes sharing information about the company's plans and strategies with its Supply Chain partners so that all can understand the vision and direction in which each of the partnering companies plans to move. Although this approach may work in selected circumstances, the drawbacks are obvious. Basically, you have to agree to get married before you have your first date. Many companies are reluctant to commit to sharing their most intimate plans, in addition to investing in the bureaucratic overhead required to undertake such extensive collaborative activity, even if it is in the name of Supply Chain efficiency. Perhaps the most telling fact about currently popular collaboration models is that it is estimated that only 3 to 8 percent of companies are actually working according to these models — not a large penetration rate for a method that gets quite a lot of noise and notice.

The Liquid Lens leads to a different paradigm for interaction among the players along the Supply Chain for Liquids. Instead of the massive effort required for collaboration as traditionally defined, CPVR utilizes a "cellular automata" approach. It takes a page from another complex situation that was converted into a relatively simple procedure for resolution. Let us take a look at an example of where the cellular-automata approach has been used, and then we can see how we will apply the principle to Supply Chain for Liquids collaboration.

"Cellular automata" says that instead of doing things in a massively large way, do them in a very small but very smart way. A well-known example of the approach is the paint shop at the General Motors assembly plant in Fort Wayne, IN. In the early 1990s, the shop was running 60 vehicles an hour through a set of paint booths. Selecting which booth to run any particular truck through was a complex task, as wait times, color changeovers, and production line efficiency had to be taken into account in making the decision. The computer software required to control this process was extensive and complex, and it was not clear that the results were the best available.

In 1992 a manager at GM, Ernest Vahala, agreed to use the cellular-automata approach proposed by Dick Morley to control the assignment of trucks to paint booths. Under Morley's approach, the massive software-based decision-making process previously used to channel trucks to the booths was replaced by very small, nimble logic at each booth. The logic at each booth was simply a coordinated procedure for responding to the situation at any given moment. That is, each booth had a set of rules that amounted to an internal decision-making process to evaluate how much that booth "wanted" any of the trucks waiting in the common queue, based on the booth's current situation — the color of paint it was currently running, the number of trucks currently in the booth's own queue, its production rate, etc. For any given truck that arrived at the paint work center, the paint booths were polled by a simple central computer program, and whichever booth "wanted" the truck the most got it. This cellular approach to decision making — in which each alternative (booth) evaluated the situation and these evaluations were compared rather than using a centralized command-and-control approach — radically simplified the process. It is estimated that the programming and implementation of the cellular approach required one one-hundredth of the effort needed for the centralized approach, with the corresponding savings in cost. And it saved GM $1 million in paint, to boot.

With this background on cellular automata, let us think about the common approach to collaboration along a Supply Chain. We try to get everybody together and work out a massive centralized plan for everyone to follow. We then have to build equally massive (or even more massive) procedures for changing the plan, including proposing changes and reviewing, approving, and disseminating them. This is a very centralized approach that gets heavier as it grows.

Supply Chain for Liquids offers a key element to completely change this paradigm, that of visibility. Like the paint booths, each player along the Supply Chain for Liquids can have all the information it needs to respond to changing circumstances and make decisions for itself. Again, like the paint booths, the key to having this approach function properly is to ensure that the individual responses are ultimately coordinated. We need to develop Coordinated Procedures for Visibility Response (CPVR). That is, the players along the Supply Chain for Liquids do not need to sit down and work out the whole massive plan, but they do need to develop the very smart decision making that each player will use in response to the data that has now become visible to the players. That is, it is not the data that will be common between them, but the rules for responding to that data.

Let us work through a simple example. In a Supply Chain for Liquids that consists of three players — the producer, the distributor, and the customer — there will be rises and falls of inventory levels at each site as well as in transit between the sites. Without visibility into the inventory position throughout the entire Supply Chain for Liquids and coordinated procedures for developing a response by each player, the usual reactions would set in. A slight rise in demand at the customer level would lead to shipment from the distributor and a proportionally higher replenishment order from the distributor to the producer to cover what may be an increased level of demand. The producer sees that the distributor is taking more product and so increases production to cover the anticipated increase in demand. These responses take place even within the context of the massive approach to collaboration, because the all-inclusive collaboration mechanism is not responsive enough to handle these short-term or inter-mediate-term shifts in activity.

The CPVR approach looks at this entire situation differently. Each player is aware of product balance and activity throughout the Supply Chain for Liquids because of the fully integrated approach to processes and information that is a cornerstone of the Supply Chain for Liquids approach. The players have worked together to set up a set of coordinated procedures for responding to the information that comes back from this visibility — CPVR. Thus, when demand at the customer rises slightly, each player will run this new set of facts through its own coordinated procedures and come up with the most appropriate result. The producer, for example, will process information about product balances and movement at the customer as well as at the distributor to reach a decision on what action to take. Because the algorithms used by each of the players have been coordinated (they are coordinated procedures) and they are working from the same data (resulting from the visibility that Supply Chain for Liquids provides), the result will be a synchronized response to whatever events or shifts occur. In addition, each player can build into its procedures additional algorithms related to internal data. For example the producer might take into account production resource availability, planned future supply and demand of a product, etc. in determining its course of action. If a new production order is entered as a result of this process, this will become part of the data that will be taken into account during the next run of the coordinated procedures.

The real-world nature of the CPVR approach is shown in its adaptability. The cliché that change is the only constant happens to be true in the case of Supply Chains. Players are added to or removed from a Supply Chain, or adjust their roles within the Supply Chain. A Supply Chain grows more complex through the expansion of manufacturers, products, or customers; changes in the competitive environment lead to proactive or reactive behavior by the Supply Chain, and so on. In an environment as dynamic as this, keeping one collaboration mega-system going is very difficult — difficult to keep up to date, difficult to adapt to the changing environment, and difficult to manage. By dividing the relationships between the players into manageable segments, the adaptability offered by CPVR matches the adaptability required by the marketplace. CPVR is the "float like a butterfly, sting like a bee" approach to multientity interaction. With a predefined set of rules applied across a Supply Chain, CPVR applies those rules no matter what dynamics are occurring within the Supply Chain. If adjustments are required to address specific situations that arise or changing circumstances, those adjustments are pinpointed right into the specific places where they are required, without affecting the entire organism.

The relative simplicity of the CPVR system as illustrated in Exhibit 10.5 is reflected in the steps involved in creating CPVR. The first step is to identify the players to be involved in the CPVR relationship and the situations to be addressed through CPVR. In the second step, the actual coordinated procedures are prepared and implemented. Finally, CPVR is brought into operation, and the coordinated procedures are tuned or expanded to encompass additional aspects of the relationship among the players. Let us go through each of these steps in more detail.

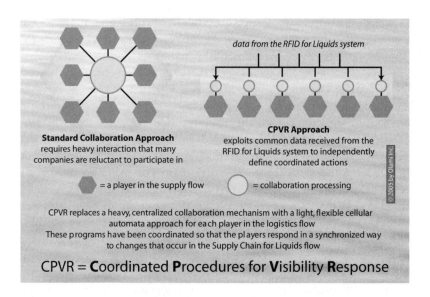

data from the RFID for Liquids system

Standard Collaboration Approach
requires heavy interaction that many
companies are reluctant to participate in

CPVR Approach
exploits common data received from the
RFID for Liquids system to independently
define coordinated actions

= a player in the supply flow   = collaboration processing

CPVR replaces a heavy, centralized collaboration mechanism with a light, flexible cellular
automata approach for each player in the logistics flow
These programs have been coordinated so that the players respond in a synchronized way
to changes that occur in the Supply Chain for Liquids flow

CPVR = Coordinated Procedures for Visibility Response

**Exhibit 10.5   CPVR Is a Completely Different Approach to Collaboration between
Companies along a Logistics Flow**

Establishing the CPVR Relationship

The first step is to establish the CPVR relationship among the companies
along a Supply Chain for Liquids. CPVR services an operational focus for
groups of companies that want to optimize specific activities, such as
levels of inventory along the length of the Supply Chain for Liquids, but
for any of a number of reasons do not want to engage in an extensive,
expensive, and complex process of sharing their business strategies,
forecasts, and internal information. The CPVR framework allows such
companies to operate independently but in coordination, serving the best
interests of all but protecting each from undesired and unnecessary
exposure to the waves in the supply stream.

Because any given company can be involved in multiple Supply Chains
for Liquids, it might establish a CPVR relationship within each group of
companies with which it works. This does not involve replication of a
heavy set of activities within each Supply Chain for Liquids. Rather, to
the degree to which the company replicates its coordinated procedures
across multiple Supply Chains for Liquids, they may be activated with
relatively little incremental effort. For identical procedures, it would involve
virtually no effort.

According to the Liquid Lens approach, the ultimate configuration of
the Supply Chain for Liquids will be planned before any work is done to

move toward the Supply Chain for Liquids. Included within overall Supply Chain for Liquids planning is the approach to be used for CPVR — exactly what data the Supply Chain for Liquids will need to provide to the CPVR function, and how CPVR will operate within the Supply Chain for Liquids. Alternatively, with the availability of data to provide the required visibility, CPVR could be overlaid into an existing relationship. CPVR is a rules-based approach rather than a data-based approach in the sense that it creates rules for the behavior of each of the players in the light of the continually shifting data that is processed through CPVR. This is different from the players sitting together and trying to work out the actual numbers by which they will operate.

Once a group of partners have determined that they want to engage in a CPVR relationship, they define the parameters on which they will focus. Because a major benefit of the Supply Chain for Liquids approach is visibility — visibility into inventory levels of liquid products all along the Supply Chain for Liquids, and the derivative visibility into inventory movements — a primary parameter for CPVR focus is the appropriate response by each member of the Supply Chain for Liquids flow to shifts in inventory levels at any particular point along the Supply Chain for Liquids. Specifically, the coordinated procedures will evaluate all of the parameters that are relevant to each player's response and drive all of the players' responses toward a single synchronized result.

Preparing and Implementing Coordinated Procedures

After the players have organized themselves and determined the spheres on which they will focus, they move to the second step, which is to prepare the coordinated procedures that each will use to operate the system. Recollecting the paint booths in the example given earlier, in which each individual booth evaluated its condition independently using a coordinated set of rules to achieve the best result for the whole system, the partners prepare together the coordinated procedures that will be used by each player.

In determining the nature of the response, the partners seek to determine the parameters needed to define the response. In the example of a highly simplified producer-distributor-customer Supply Chain for Liquids flow, if the partners want to know whether activity at the customer should trigger the producer to ship product to the distributor, they might determine that the following parameters are needed:

- *Current balance at the customer:* The quantity of the product that is currently on-hand at the customer site

- *Rolling-week activity at the customer:* The quantity by which the on-hand balance at the customer site has decreased over the past seven days
- *Current balance at the distributor:* The quantity of the product that is currently on-hand at the distributor site

Current balance data at each point in the Supply Chain for Liquids is readily available from the transmissions of the sensors at these points, and from the current inventory balance at each point in the Supply Chain for Liquids, periodic product activity can be readily extrapolated. That is, as each player is receiving the source data from the sensors, each can include in its coordinated procedures system a formula to calculate usage over a predefined period, such as the prior week.

Based on this set of data, the coordinated procedures at the producer can perform the calculation defined by the partners. The partners can build the coordinated procedures in such a way as to protect from overreaction by the distributor and the producer to events at the customer. For example, while the on-hand balance at the customer may have fallen below the reorder point, the coordinated procedures might identify that activity over the past week was within a normal range and that there was sufficient product at the distributor to cover the normal flow. A parallel set of coordinated procedures at the distributor would reach the same conclusion, thus triggering a replenishment shipment to the customer but not an unusual order from the producer. Thus, CPVR/Supply Chain for Liquids serves to "massage" the level of inventory along the Supply Chain for Liquids and ensure optimal levels of inventory at all points rather than having each player react to conditions presented by its immediate customer.

The example above is of course simplified for illustrative purposes. Additional complexities only mean that additional variables need to be added into the coordinated procedures, not that the CPVR system itself needs to be any more complex. In addition to taking into account the on-hand balance and periodic usage information, the coordinated procedures may need other data such as expected seasonality, trends, or promotions so that each player will recognize these rather than viewing them as a rise in base demand. Each player puts into the "pool" of rules those variables required for the coordinated procedures to function for each player. These variables represent visibility into the future to complement the visibility provided into past and current conditions as provided directly from the Supply Chain for Liquids. It is important to note that these variables are denominated as percentage changes the company anticipates over the specific period such as a week, and do not require that the company disclose further details beyond those needed for CPVR functioning.

As another example, the raw data showing the inventory level at each location might show a total quantity, rather than that portion that is allocated or available to this Supply Chain for Liquids. The player responsible for that point, such as the distributor, might need to throw an additional variable into the "pool" available for the coordinated procedures, that of the percentage of the inventory that should be taken into account in determining the on-hand balance for the purpose of this Supply Chain for Liquids. The coordinated procedures at the player and the other players will then take this percentage into account when processing the coordinated procedures to come up with the appropriate result.

Again, let us be clear on the two main points that differentiate this approach from other common approaches to the same situation. First, the visibility offered by Supply Chain for Liquids and exploited in CPVR prevents overreactions or underreactions to inventory situations. Without these mechanisms, a blip in demand at the customer could lead to a perceived bulge in demand by the distributor and a flood of demand at the producer, with each party overcompensating for the set of facts available to it. Second, this coordinated response takes place with minimum overhead in terms of sharing data/plans/forecasts, acquisition or development of synchronization programs, etc. The highly targeted, independent but coordinated set of procedures is a streamlined approach to dealing with the complexities of inventory, just as the base approach dealt with the complexities of paint-booth scheduling as described in the example above.

Operating/Expanding CPVR

After the preparations of the prior steps, the third step involves operating the CPVR system and expanding its usage. Because CPVR is a front-end system rather than an integral part of a company's legacy or ERP system, there is a lot of flexibility as to how it is brought into operation and subsequently tuned and expanded. The results of each CPVR run might be presented to the orders department to evaluate the appropriate response versus that suggested by the ERP system or other source of order information. Once the CPVR system is tuned and has been proved to be operating properly, it can be bridged directly into the ERP system to trigger the appropriate actions as have been defined in the coordinated procedures.

A key to the successful implementation, operation, and expansion of a CPVR system is the coordination among the partners in developing the coordinated procedures, the rules by which each partner behaves based on a series of predefined parameters. This one-off coordination process for development or for each enhancement replaces extensive ongoing coordination, which is handled automatically by the CPVR system once it has been properly implemented. The system can be compared to the automatic pilot of an aircraft, whose captain is using a system that has proved reliable and who has ensured that the data that has been fed into the system is accurate (that the coordinates for Jamaica have been entered, for example, and not Johannesburg). The captain will not leave the cockpit or abandon the controls, but he or she can rely on the system to do the bulk of the work and allow the captain, or orders/inventory person, to monitor the system to ensure proper functioning and focus on any nonroutine events that may occur.

From a technical perspective, the implementation and operation of the CPVR system is relatively simple. Because different partners are sharing data but not code, each can continue to operate in its own native computer processing environment using the definitions in the coordinated procedures as their "programming specs." There is no need for the players to move to the same computer language or operating system, and the shared aspect of the system is data rather than programs. The base data for the system, that being transmitted by the sensors at each location along the Supply Chain for Liquids, is readily available to all partners, particularly if the transmissions are Internet-based. This technology also simplifies the sharing of parameters in the "pool" that the partners create and maintain for auxiliary information not supplied by the sensors. Again, in deference to the IT (information technology) people, CPVR is a *relatively* simple system versus a much more massive and complex planning and collaboration scheme, but it is not a one-day development job. The investment in thought and development up-front pays itself back in the effectiveness of ongoing operations, especially in a system that must be built to handle continually shifting conditions. Further information about the structure and usage of CPVR can be found at www.SupplyChainForLiquids.com, the Internet site of Supply Chain for Liquids.

Complementary Supply Chains/Complementary Supply Chains for Liquids

Because of the flexibility that Supply Chain for Liquids offers, it creates an additional opportunity for adding value to producers, distributors, and customers — that of Complementary Supply Chains for Liquids. Complementary Supply Chains^SM or Complementary Supply Chains for Liquids operate in the same "universe" of distribution/customer base but are noncompetitive and so can add mutual value in several ways. For example, automotive repair facilities use several different categories of liquids. They use lubricants and maintenance fluids in performing the actual work, and they use cleaning liquids such as hand cleaners and floor cleaners as part of the peripheral or support activities in the facility. In this example, the Supply Chain for Liquids for lubricants is complementary to the Supply Chain for Liquids for cleaning products. These are noncompetitive products in that a producer of lubricants is not likely to also produce floor-cleaning materials, and yet both types of products enter the same distribution area and reach the same customers.

What are the advantages of Complementary Supply Chains for Liquids? There are several benefits to multiple Supply Chains for Liquids working in concert. First, the combined use of logistics resources reduces the per-unit investment in distribution activities. One truck visits a set of customers and supplies a broader range of liquid products. The infrastructure needed to support the logistics effort for each type of liquid is created once rather than twice, saving money for all the players.

From an operational perspective, a Complementary Supply Chains for Liquids becomes feasible when two or more producers share a common set of customers for noncompetitive products. The logistics aspects are simplified to the degree to which there is geographic proximity between the production or distribution points of the two producers, so that trucks can be filled at each and then proceed on a delivery run. The nature of the products themselves is actually a relatively minor issue in a Complementary Supply Chains for Liquids scenario; the tanks in the trucks and at the customer facility can be completely segregated by type of liquid, so that at no point will one of the liquid types contaminate the tanks or pipes of the other.

Perhaps even more important than the operational advantage of Complementary Supply Chains for Liquids is the business advantage. Producers of different types of products that come together to create a Complementary Supply Chains for Liquids are in fact providing more of a "full service" offering to their customers. Like automobile manufacturers who are trending toward purchasing complete subsystems from suppliers rather than individual components that they then would have to assemble in-house, customers benefit from broad-scope supplier relationships that are able to service a broader spectrum of the customer's needs.

As described in Chapter 5, the power balance in any given Supply Chain/Supply Chain for Liquids relationship will guide the initiator and the character of the Supply Chain for Liquids. Even so, there are competitive aspects of Complementary Supply Chains for Liquids that can influence the power relationship. In a situation dominated by a single major supplier for each of several different types of liquids, offering a Complementary Supply Chains for Liquids approach could be a method for the number two or three player for each type of liquid to strengthen its position. In the above example, if the number three player in the lubricants area was to join with the number two player in the cleaners area, both might be able to benefit in strengthening their market positions. The ability to create and participate in such a buxom Supply Chain for Liquids goes beyond the advantages of Supply Chain for Liquids itself and becomes a strategic business tool.

To further illustrate the Complementary Supply Chains for Liquids concept, we can distinguish between an all-purpose distributor and Complementary Supply Chains for Liquids. An all-purpose distributor carries all of the materials required by several types of customers. For example, a janitorial-supply house might carry all of the materials, equipment, and supplies that a customer might need related to cleaning. Such an all-purpose distributor could service several different types of customers such as factories, hospitals, etc. From the perspective of each of the customers, the all-purpose distributor fulfills all of the customer's needs in the specific area of cleaning materials.

This can be contrasted to the relationship defined in Complementary Supply Chains for Liquids. In such a relationship, multiple types of liquids are combined in the Complementary Supply Chains for Liquids — for example, cleaning fluids and automotive lubricants. The customer has the availability of liquids for both of these purposes from the Complementary Supply Chains for Liquids. On the other hand, such Complementary Supply Chains for Liquids generally focus on only one type of customer. For the relationship in this example, the type of customer would be automotive-related — automobile dealerships, service stations, quick-lube operations, fleet-repair or municipal garages, etc.

Complementary Supply Chains for Liquids are the logical next step beyond Supply Chains and Supply Chain for Liquids. Supply Chains and Supply Chain for Liquids offer many advantages over a company operating independently; as described above, and Complementary Supply Chains for Liquids offer additional opportunities to the producer, the distributor, and the customer. After a company successfully builds its Supply Chain for Liquids relationships, it can further enhance its position by then arranging them into Complementary Supply Chains for Liquids.

Points of Integration — Supply Chain for Liquids and ERP Systems

Because the Supply Chain for Liquids system is designed as a complete and integrated system in itself, it must also be integrated into the flow of information and operations for the remainder of the company. The specific points of integration vary from system to system, and are defined during the planning process as described in the Liquid Lens methodology. The transactions internal to the Supply Chain for Liquids system are described in greater detail earlier in this chapter. Here, we are reviewing the transactions that move between the Supply Chain for Liquids information system and other information systems such as the central computer system. An overview of the points of integration that may be required for the Supply Chain for Liquids system as related to passing information to or receiving information from other company systems includes the following areas:

- *Accounting/accounts payable*: For the company receiving the products, the delivery event triggers a receiving transaction that is matched against a purchase order (in general, a blanket purchase order is used with the Supply Chain for Liquids system to avoid having to issue a purchase order for each delivery). The details of the exact quantity of each product delivered are passed as part of the transaction. Pricing is extracted from the purchase order, leading to the creation of an accounts payable entry for the delivery. Special conditions, such as a consignment arrangement as described in Chapter 7, would be treated as appropriate.

- *Accounting/accounts receivable*: For the company supplying the products, or for the company providing the Supply Chain for Liquids delivery service, the delivery event triggers an accounts receivable transaction. For the supplier, this would be for the quantity delivered at the price defined in the purchase order issued by the customer. For the distributor/delivery company, this would be based on the agreed-upon terms. The distributor may charge based on quantity delivery, number of products delivered, fixed fee, or some combination of these or other types of charges.

- *Inventory/supplier*: During the truck-filling operation, the total quantity of each liquid transferred to the truck is reported by the flowmeters that control the liquid fill. This reduces the on-hand quantity of each liquid at the supplier as of that point in time. The product is considered in transit, or in the truck inventory location, until it is delivered to each customer.

- *Inventory/customer*: The actual quantity of each product moved from the delivery truck to the customer site is transmitted to the customer's inventory system. Although the Supply Chain for Liquids system monitors inventory balances for operational purposes, the customer may need to have the information available to record on-hand inventory balance for accounting purposes, monitor system accuracy, etc.

- *Route planning*: Once the Supply Chain for Liquids system determines the deliveries to be made during a particular delivery run,

338 ■ Supply Chain for Liquids

the specific sequence and mapping of the delivery route may be done by an external software package. The route-planning software does not necessarily need to be provided with information about the products to be delivered at each site, but it can create the most efficient delivery plan for each truck.

- *Warehouse*: Loading the trucks may require preparation by the warehouse in terms of truck movement and product flow/positioning, as well as preparing the trucks such as cleaning or setting the intertank valving. Warehouse personnel should be alerted as to the loading plan for the next delivery run so that loading can be performed as efficiently as possible.

- *HR/personnel*: Because delivery becomes a 24-hour process, shift work for drivers, warehouse personnel, and others involved in the delivery process may be necessary. Personnel planning, as well as legal requirements such as work-hour limitations, need to be based on up-to-date information and plans for near-future delivery activity. The Supply Chain for Liquids system can supply the data required to support this planning and monitoring, although it is not able to handle these issues itself.

- *Maintenance*: The equipment used in the Supply Chain for Liquids system requires periodic maintenance, including the on-site tanks and piping, the truck tanks and piping, and even the communications equipment. In addition, it may be a maintenance function to change the configuration of on-site tanks, such as adding tanks or switching tanks between liquids. The maintenance department should keep track of equipment activity and perform ongoing maintenance at predetermined time-based or quantity-based intervals.

- *Management reporting/marketing*: The Supply Chain for Liquids system, including the RFID for Liquids and CPVR processes, contains a large amount of information about a company's internal operations as well as the behavior of its suppliers and customers. It is certainly in a company's interest to pass this data to an executive information system, marketing system, or other analysis mechanism. This is data to be mined and its value extracted to the benefit of the company, its strategy, and its marketing effort.

In some cases there will be other system interfaces, and in other cases the Supply Chain for Liquids system will be relatively self-contained. The extent, complexity, nature, and timing of the intersystem interfaces are defined during the system planning process, and they are activated with the activation of the Supply Chain for Liquids system.

Outsourcing Supply Chain for Liquids Functionality

Under the assumption that somebody else can do certain things cheaper and better, companies are turning to outsourcing as a way of handling some of the tasks that otherwise would be handled in-house. Because outsourcing is a viable option for certain aspects of Supply Chain for Liquids functionality, it is worth looking at outsourcing and understanding the points at which outsourcing can play a role in Supply Chain for Liquids operation.

Outsourcing means having another company perform some of the functions that your company would normally perform, either as if the outsource provider is a part of your company or by providing the functions as a service to your company. For the most part, companies consider outsourcing to be noncore processes, that is, processes that are relatively standard but, although important, not part of the unique, core strength of the company.

An early target for outsourcing was the computer department, or at least parts of the computer department. Information system communication is a good example of a readily outsourceable function. Setting up large-scale data communications networks is a highly specialized activity that requires a very specific level of expertise, can be cleanly identified as a "piece" to be handled by somebody else, and requires fairly constant attention for maintenance, troubleshooting, and upgrading. Outsourcing goes beyond purchasing the network from a vendor; it means the supplier is responsible for all aspects of operation and maintenance of the network. This applies in general to other outsourcing situations, although the exact definition of responsibilities is always an important part of establishing an outsourcing relationship.

Outsourcing is done for a wide variety of functions, but there are several areas in which it is most common. These include human resources, facilities operations and management, training, and procurement. In addition to these, the most widespread outsourcing functions are finance and accounting, customer care, logistics, engineering/research and development, and sales and marketing. As a company exploring the most effective ways to establish a Supply Chain for Liquids system, several of these functions are of particular interest.

The first aspect of Supply Chain for Liquids that we can examine for outsourcing is that of product handling. Outsourced logistics is often labeled "3PL" for "third-party logistics," in which another party besides the manufacturer or the customer provides the logistical activities. The concept of 3PL covers a lot of ground, both literally and in terms of the specific logistics capabilities that are covered. In terms of product handling,

3PL companies provide basic truck- and fleet-management services, warehousing and fulfillment services, shipment consolidation, international and intermodal transportation, as well as some processing and services such as product setup or installation during delivery. The 3PL suppliers go well beyond the physical handling of goods and offer such information-based services as freight payment, transportation/freight planning and optimization, import/export documentation, and order processing. This survey of 3PL service offerings shows that, unlike the situation even ten years ago, 3PL is a well-developed source of comprehensive logistics services. In terms of the services offered, 3PL covers not only the routine delivery activities of the standard Supply Chain for Liquids configuration, but also many variations that we expect to occur in extended-distance or extended-complexity Supply Chain for Liquids situations.

For our purposes, the availability of these services is promising but not enough. Many of the services offered by 3PL companies apply to both liquid and discrete products, so we can view these companies as a potential resource for at least some logistics needs. Going beyond this, we need to ensure the availability of 3PL services that support liquid-specific needs, starting with the tank trucks and extending to tank-based warehousing and the expertise to handle liquid products. The field narrows considerably based on these criteria, as many 3PL companies specifically do not have liquid-oriented capability and actually avoid involvement with some types of liquids such as dangerous chemicals or other materials subject to hazmat (hazardous materials) regulations. The 3PL companies that do provide services for liquid products in some cases have a focus on a particular type of liquid, limiting the choice of liquid-oriented 3PL providers even further for any given producer and product type. In planning our Supply Chain for Liquids system, we can look for 3PL providers as an alternative to controlling the logistics internally, although our success in finding one will depend on the specific type of liquid products involved and the specific logistical services we are seeking.

Whether we decide to outsource the logistics side of the Supply Chain for Liquids system or run it using internal resources, the second major area that we might want to consider outsourcing is the information-flow side of the system. The information flow of Supply Chain for Liquids consists of a number of elements, including the physical equipment (sensors/PLCs/data transmission as well as the computers involved), the software and information flow, and the information handling and actioning, such as the dispatching function. In considering outsourcing, we first need to clearly define for ourselves which elements we would like to outsource and which elements should be handled in-house. We might define, for example, that the moving of information should be outsourced and the use of information should remain an internal activity. Under this definition, all of the data-collection and -processing activities — equipment at the site and on the trucks, the PLCs and data-communications devices with their programming, the computer and software that process the information and support the flow — are candidates for outsourcing, while the dispatching, truck loading, and management activities remain in-house. This kind of information technology outsourcing is relatively common, and outsource suppliers are available who can provide the complete scope of services including both hardware and software. This area also lends itself to outsourcing because the exact scope of the outsourcing can be defined with a high degree of precision, so that one of the foundations of a successful outsourcing relationship — clear definition of the roles, responsibilities, and expectations of each of the parties — can be met relatively easily.

Once we have identified those aspects of the Supply Chain for Liquids system that we plan to outsource, we proceed through the process of identifying, selecting, and working with outsourcing suppliers. This process has its own set of "do's and don'ts" for which there is plenty of information available and which is outside the scope of this book, but several of these issues should be mentioned in light of Supply Chain for Liquids requirements.

Outsourcing projects are sometimes undertaken with the understanding that the outsourcing supplier will take over the current operation and run it for a period before undertaking changes to improve efficiency or reduce cost. This allows both parties to fully understand each other and develop their working relationship under relatively stable conditions, and then enter into the change process with a stable foundation in place. For a company that is moving to a Supply Chain for Liquids system, outsourcing part of the system represents both a tremendous opportunity and a tremendous risk. The good side of change is not only the expected accomplishments and benefits, but also the opportunity to introduce additional adjustments that individually would be much more difficult. For example, moving from in-house responsibility for certain functions to outsourcing those functions, if handled as a stand-alone act, could easily turn into a political battle with a great deal of negative disruption. Introducing outsourcing as one piece of a larger change process, that of Supply Chain for Liquids, gives it a context that puts less focus on it as a separate act and provides the business proposition for going in that direction. Even more important, change on a significant scale provides an opportunity for a company to examine its strengths and weaknesses, and to focus on its strengths while mitigating its weaknesses. Properly handled, outsourcing serves as an excellent means for a company to minimize the negative effects of whatever weaknesses it has. The instability inherent in change offers key elements of the phrase "the power of flexibility, the evil of certainty" to come to full fruition.

The risk side of introducing an outsourcing element during the transition to Supply Chain for Liquids is the complexity involved in change on top of change. As both the outsourcing activity and the changed logistics system come on-line, it is unlikely that things will work exactly as envisioned. From the outsourcing perspective, this raises the possibility of conflict between the company and the outsourcing provider in terms of roles and costs, a conflict that will likely not serve either party well. If both parties go into the arrangement with a good understanding of the potential problems and with excellent communications, these types of problems can be avoided for the most part or at least resolved quickly and effectively once they arise.

Another common issue related to outsourcing that particularly needs to be addressed as related to Supply Chain for Liquids is performance measurement. Outsourcing relationships are set up based on activity-measured results in the sense of sharing risk and sharing reward ($X per site serviced, with the outsourcing provider being paid more for greater success and less if fewer customers are involved), based on fixed payment for services performed within a predefined range ($Y as long as the system runs with zero site stock-outs and a maximum systemwide inventory of Z gallons, with penalties for exceptions), or some other payment scheme. These performance measurements, like measurements used for incentive-based pay for employees, must be set up very carefully to avoid driving the outsourcing supplier in a direction that is actually counterproductive to the goals of the company. Like incentive-pay measurements, they may well require tweaking after they are put into place to handle unforeseen conditions or results. Under conditions in which outsourcing is brought into operation together with the Supply Chain for Liquids system, this tweaking must be taken into account when establishing the relationship between the customer and the outsourcing provider. This will be much easier if both sides have a very clear idea of the other's goals and priorities, so that detailed changes to the performance measurement/payment structure can be made within the framework of mutually understood positions.

Outsourcing provides an alternative approach to addressing various aspects of the Supply Chain for Liquids system. Awareness of the ups and downs of outsourcing, in particular as it is related to Supply Chain for Liquids, can make the effort more successful and avoid unnecessary bumps along the way.

Obstructions to Supply Chain for Liquids Implementation

The process of planning, implementing, and operating a system of the nature of Supply Chain for Liquids does not stay "under the radar," but rather is more likely to become a high-profile activity among the departments and companies that are involved in the effort. As with any such effort, there will be advocates who invest energy and effort into it as well as sharpshooters sitting on the side with their rifles in the crooks of their arms, ready for the slightest stumble so that they can start shooting. This for-or-against picture is reasonably common in any project, but those who set their objective as the success of the effort are in the best position to recognize, and hopefully even understand, the concerns of those who are less receptive to the effort. The following subsections describe some common obstacles that a Supply Chain for Liquids project may face.

Channel Conflict

The creation of a new channel in the supply stream means that some of the other channels will either adapt or dry up. Like the stagecoach driver watching the railroad being built, a group threatened by the fight-it-or-join-it question will respond in different ways. The adaptive ones will learn to work with the Supply Chain for Liquids system and excel at it, like the stagecoach driver learning to be a train engineer. Others will fight the development in whatever way possible. The analogy of Supply Chain for Liquids to stagecoaches and railroads is not at all complete; once the railroad was built, nobody needed the stagecoach any more. Both a producer and a customer may well need to keep working with a distributor for products that fall outside of the Supply Chain for Liquids, as detailed earlier in this chapter. In some situations such as this, there may be much more at risk in terms of antagonizing the distributor than is to be gained from implementing the Supply Chain for Liquids system. For this reason, the inclusive approach — which ends up not only keeping the distributor in place, but providing the distributor with more powerful capabilities, albeit much different from a standard Supply Chain — should be considered when mapping out the approach to Supply Chain for Liquids.

Recognition/Distribution of Benefit

Some of the benefits of Supply Chain for Liquids are clearly definable, as laid out in Chapter 11, and these benefits lead to a quantifiable increase in the margin pool available from operating a Supply Chain for Liquids system. Other benefits clearly occur, but these are more difficult to define, such as overhead savings and increased revenue opportunities. This situation leads to potential obstacles to acceptance of Supply Chain for Liquids in two ways.

The first cost-related obstacle has to do with defining the benefit for each player. Even with a carefully defined projection of the financial benefits of implementation of the system, each player will view the costs and benefits from a different perspective. What one player might perceive as a clear benefit might appear to be a marginal or even doubtful result to another player. Without a clear vision by each participant of the likely benefits of the system, it is doubtful that all will come aboard.

The multiplayer situation also creates room for disagreement over dividing the net benefit, even if all agree as to what the total benefit is likely to be. It is in the nature of the Supply Chain for Liquids system that all of the players work as one integrated flow, resulting in cross-benefit by each from each. What is the proper formula for dividing the freed-up margin? Given the large quantities of product (and money) that are involved in some logistics flows, this issue can be an impediment to proceeding with the implementation of the system.

Target Customer Base

The Supply Chain for Liquids system has an "ideal" customer configuration in terms of size, volume, number of liquids, geographic density, and other factors. As the customer base falls away from this target profile, the margins become marginal, and the relative benefits decrease. The 80-20 rule is likely to apply with some variation on that percentage. The larger customers in a potential Supply Chain for Liquids arrangement are more capable of supporting the system and gaining more from it, while smaller companies may be undercapitalized, slower to embrace change, or may not see as much relative benefit. The system needs a certain threshold to operate productively, although the cost/complexity of the system is to some degree adaptable to more limited circumstances. Identifying the required customer base, and making sure it meets the threshold of a successful system, should be an early task in the project.

These barriers are not insurmountable, and they do not even apply in every case. However, they are common issues that may come up, sooner or later, during planning for a Supply Chain for Liquids system.

Chapter 11

Business Benefits of Supply Chain for Liquids

In addition to the many advantages of Supply Chain for Liquids® in the logistics and operational areas, the approach offers many business-level benefits. The impact of Supply Chain for Liquids on such areas as marketing/strategy, finance, and environment means that it should be considered an important business tool in addition to being a dynamic technical capability. Let us take a look at each of these areas in detail.

Marketing/Strategy

When you can do the kinds of things that Supply Chain for Liquids lets you do, and your competitors cannot, then you are in a powerful strategic position. As described earlier, Supply Chain for Liquids lets you move product faster and cheaper, and into places you otherwise cannot. Let us take a look at some of the marketing implications of Supply Chain for Liquids. These are shown in Exhibit 11.1 and include:

- *New sales and distribution channels*: New outlets for your company's products
- *Innovative product/product usage configurations*: Different ways for customers to use your company's products
- *Higher on-premise penetration to lead off-premise sales*: Marketing focus on the "hearts and minds" battleground

new sales and distribution channels
higher on-premise penetration
better quality product
EXPANDED SERVICES OFFERING - NON-PRODUCT ATTRIBUTES
Marketing Benefits
of Supply Chain for Liquids
MORE NIMBLE PRODUCT PLACEMENT
innovate product configurations
CUSTOMER AND CONSUMER WIN

Exhibit 11.1   Marketing Hype Is Backed Up by Real Value under Supply Chain for Liquids

- *Expanded services offering*: Nonproduct attributes that make the product more attractive
- *Improved information on user/customer behavior*: Closer profile of the usage/purchase transaction
- *More-nimble product placement*: Logistics support for marketing prowess
- *Enhanced quality assurance*: Tighter control and monitoring of quality-affecting conditions
- *Numerous customer benefits*: Easily definable "wins" for the customer

Each of these marketing benefits is described in more detail in the following subsections.

New Sales and Distribution Channels

The marketing mind is always seeking new ways to look at a product. Within this thought process, though, marketing is constrained by the realities that it is aware of related to the product. If the product is only sold in three package sizes — half-gallon, one-gallon, and two-gallon jugs, for example — then the marketing mind is likely to think about how to go about marketing the product within these packages.

If you completely remove the package and its handling from the equation, on the other hand, you are able to break through this constraint and thus be on the road to thinking of new ways to market, distribute, merchandise, sell, and provide your product. You can take your thinking to the other extreme and work back from there: if I could have my product — the product itself, not the package — "appear" anywhere and in any way, where and how would I want it to appear? At first blush this may seem extreme, but this is in fact what the traditional "four P's of marketing" (product, price, place [distribution], and promotion) are really all about. It has just been that the constraints of traditional logistics systems have kept the marketing effort farther away from the "ideal" situation than does the Supply Chain for Liquids approach. Supply Chain for Liquids not only opens up new avenues, but even encourages the use of methods and media that have not existed in a practical way previously.

Let us take a couple of specific examples to work through this process. Purveyors of beverages, personal-care products, home-cleaning fluids, and other home-consumer liquids usually think along the traditional lines of discount chains, department stores, grocery stores, quick-serve stores, and the like as sales channels. However, the message coming back from the marketplace related to such liquid products may indicate that these channels are not serving customers' true desires. The popularity of larger-quantity or higher-convenience sales channels means that customers want to be able to choose for themselves the balance between price and convenience, and want different options in doing so. Examples of these sales channels are warehouse stores that sell larger-than-standard unit sizes of many types of products, Internet or fax buying options that allow a customer to place an order and have it delivered to the home or office, and do-it-yourself stores at which a customer wants a better price in return for willingness to add a labor component to the finished product.

Putting together these two factors — our liquid products being constrained by the packaging in which it is offered, and the customers' desire for flexibility in size, place, and effort related to the product — a marketing person might make the leap to a new way to offer the product. The marketing mind would lay out some of the key factors as follows. A person going to a do-it-yourself store is already into the mind-set of investing some extra effort to save some amount of money. Convenience means bringing the product close enough to the customer that there is a recognized value to an alternative sales channel. Using the Supply Chain for Liquids approach, the liquids provider is able to offer the product in bulk form into whatever size or type of container suits the customer. Putting this together, the marketing mind might say, let us create a kiosklike liquid dispense channel at or adjacent to wholesale club-type facilities and let the customer dispense the product either into containers provided by the customer or several larger-sized containers offered at the kiosk. The customer drives up to the kiosk, be it physically adjacent to the building or in the parking lot, and either self-dispenses or attendant-dispenses selected liquids into whatever size containers the customer provides and places the containers directly into the vehicle. The Supply Chain for Liquids allows effective design of the kiosk facility, including number and quantity of liquids to be stored and appropriate liquid-replenishment capability to ensure that stock-outs do not occur. The marketing mind knows that it has to work through the details and that the end channel may be in some ways different from the initial vision, but the Supply Chain for Liquids has provided the freedom and flexibility to think in such nontraditional ways.

Having thrown off the limitations of logistics-bound marketing capabilities, the marketing mind might also think down another channel. Internet-, fax-, or phone-based buying means that the customer places an order for products and has them delivered to the home or office. Much of this process is constrained by the fact that these products are usually discrete items, that is, they must be delivered and physically received in some way by the customer. Just as Supply Chain for Liquids provides a radically changed construct for delivery of liquid products to businesses without requiring the customer's presence, so too could this approach be applied to residential or office-park deliveries. With an appropriate version of Supply Chain for Liquids's on-site mini-tank arrangement installed in the home, common home-use liquids are delivered directly and independent of whether the customer is at home or not. From the customer's perspective, some of the heaviest products usually purchased at the store — bottles of soaps, shampoo, cleaners, beverages, and so on — are off the shopping list forever, and these products are available at home, with no effort, and for all intents and purposes never running out. A parallel capability serves offices at office parks, college dormitories, and other similar consumer product-consuming locations.

Supply Chain for Liquids opens up a new perspective on "the art of the possible" in terms of sales and distribution channels related to liquid products. In the absence of the constraints of discrete items, these channels look completely different.

Innovative Product/Product Usage Configurations

Under the Supply Chain for Liquids approach, you are able to leave your liquid product in its native (liquid) form as far down the supply stream as you would like, even to the point of dispense. This means that you can now think of exactly how the customer wants to use your product, and bring the product configuration or product usage configuration even closer to that desire. In doing so, you make your product more attractive to the customer and create sales opportunities for yourself.

Let us use as an example of this point the consumption of beverages in out-of-doors environments. The kinds of venues included in this example are amusement parks, sports stadiums, university campuses, and other locations at which consumers become thirsty and would like to purchase beverages in varying amounts, quickly and at their own convenience. Although dispensing machines serve this function inside of buildings, they are less common in external environments.

In these venues, a common approach is a beverage stand, with an attendant selling the beverage or filling a cup with beverage, and collecting money from the consumer. The attendant also performs the back-office functions of monitoring the amount of stock at the stand and replenishing the beverages as required. Anyone who has been to these places knows that the longest lines may well be at the refreshment stands ("Yes kids, I know you're thirsty, but can't you see there's a line here?"). Supply Chain for Liquids allows us to think of a different paradigm for this transaction, one that is much more flexible in terms of the physical processes related to the product. Assuming that the attendant is the constraining factor, can we get by without an attendant? With Supply Chain for Liquids, this becomes a realistic alternative. Addressing the other constraining factors may lead to a scenario such as this: the consumer purchases a mug for a price that includes deposit against the purchase of a certain amount of beverage. The mug contains a computer chip that keeps track of the available deposit amount. The consumer goes to a beverage dispense center and dispenses beverage directly into the mug, which automatically reduces the available deposit amount. The consumer has complete flexibility; the mug can be refilled at any dispense point as often as needed to slake the thirst, and the entire transaction takes the amount of time it takes to fill the mug. When the deposit amount reaches zero, the consumer has the option to replenish the deposit at points designated for this purpose, and in any case keeps the mug. The monitoring and replenishment of the stand's beverage supply is done through Supply Chain for Liquids, so that the need for an attendant for this purpose is eliminated.

What has Supply Chain for Liquids allowed us to do here? It has created a new product-usage methodology that serves everybody's interest. By making our beverages available more conveniently, we encourage consumption by the consumer, or more accurately, make it easier for the consumer to use our product. We reduce the cost of the transaction by eliminating the attendant in addition to other benefits of the location, such as reduced trash. We provide a positive experience with our product for all involved, that is a powerful tool.

Once you have gone through this process, you can then do the "double reverse" that the Liquid Lens[SM] values so much. You got rid of the packaging to create new opportunities. Now, with those new opportunities, are there new types of "packaging" that can help expand the opportunity even further? Of course we are not talking about traditional packaging of the kind we got rid of to begin with, but rather nontraditional packaging of whatever configuration it might be — self-forming holders, expandable tubes, or whatever works based on the usage of the product by the consumer combined with the flexibility of product form and placement that Supply Chain for Liquids offers. As Supply Chain for Liquids opened up new opportunities by getting rid of packaging, it is not afraid to create even more opportunities by providing for new forms of "packaging" and product usage.

Higher On-Premise Penetration to Lead Off-Premise Sales

A marketing issue that is particularly appropriate to beverages is the interplay between on-premise and off-premise sales. "On-premise" refers to channels in which the beverages are consumed at the location at which they are purchased, such as restaurants or bars, and "off-premise" refers to channels in which the beverages are purchased at one location, such as a grocery store, and consumed at another location. In many cases the on-premise arena is seen to be a "battleground" that influences behavior in off-premise purchasing. There is something of chaos theory in this approach, like the butterfly flapping its wings in China leading to rainstorms in Omaha, with a small change in on-premise activity leading to a relatively larger change in off-premise activity.

To the degree to which a beverage producer places importance in on-premise activity, Supply Chain for Liquids becomes a much more important tool. Supply Chain for Liquids addresses many of the key beverage-related logistics issues and results in a more effective logistics flow than the traditional Supply Chain. The on-premise/off-premise issue simply serves to magnify the benefits of Supply Chain for Liquids in the beverage world. Getting your product through the Supply Chain for Liquids into on-premise accounts will result in a corresponding expansion of your off-premise sales.

Supply Chain for Liquids provides another interesting slant as related to the on-premise/off-premise issue. For beverages that are distributed and dispensed through the Supply Chain for Liquids system, there is no consumer packaging. The beverage is dispensed directly into whatever cup or container the consumer drinks it from, so there is no bottle or can. This makes the on-premise path much more suitable as a product-testing and -exposure channel than a path that requires additional investment in packaging. All of the branding in the on-premise route comes from the signage, banners, graphics, advertising, and other forms of collateral that surround the product. For product testing, market research, and other forms of "temporary" distribution, the low-cost, highly targeted capabilities that Supply Chain for Liquids offers provide a lot more flexibility at much lower cost than conventional logistics approaches. Beverages in this mode can be easily incorporated into the supply stream without disrupting the standard logistics flow.

Expanded Services Offering

Many producers or distributors offer a variety of services along with their products to increase the total value of the relationship to the customer. These services may relate to expertise and advice on the use of the product, such as is offered by some chemical and lubricant manufacturers. It may relate to supplying equipment to use with the liquid products, such as is offered by some cleaner manufacturers. Many companies offer such adjunct services that, in addition to the product itself, are needed to differentiate that company and that product from its competitors, and lead the customer to purchase the product.

Supply Chain for Liquids represents a highly valuable service that a producer or distributor can offer to the customer. By working with the customer using the Supply Chain for Liquids methodology, the producer or distributor is in effect offering many significant benefits to the customer such as:

- *No product handling by employees*: The employees never have to handle, move, lift, place, or check product, or dispose of the packaging. This eliminates not only the physical effort involved in handling, but also the time employees have to spend on handling product. Adjunct benefits include reductions in insurance claims because of the decreased risk of accident or injury, and increased job satisfaction as one of the most difficult tasks in the workplace — physically lifting, moving, and placing packages and product — is eliminated.
- *More effective use of facility space than bottles or other containers*: As described later in this chapter, liquids in tanks take up less than half the space of the equivalent quantity of liquids in packages. Furthermore, there is a great deal more flexibility in the physical placement of liquids under the Supply Chain for Liquids system than with a packaged-products system. Because the tanks holding the liquids do not have to be readily accessible by employees, they can be put overhead, on walls, or in other unused space. This is in contrast to packages of liquids that usually sit on the

floor or on shelves, taking up valuable, usable space within the facility. Facility owners thus get much better space utilization with Supply Chain for Liquids, saving money and creating space for additional revenue-generating products or activities.

■ *"Never check/never out" inventory management*: From the customer's point of view, there is never a need to check liquid inventory levels and no concern about running out of inventory. The customer (a restaurant, quick-lube facility, hospital, factory, printer, etc.) actually does not have to think about liquid inventory at all under the Supply Chain for Liquids system. Liquid products are always available with literally no effort on the customer's part.

■ *No disruption at the site during product delivery*: There are various levels of disruption that often occur during the delivery process. Informally, the delivery person may spend time chatting with company personnel and distracting them from their work. More significant is an extended interaction between the delivery person and company personnel in terms of clarifying the types and quantities of products to be delivered. In some cases the delivery process physically disrupts a company's operations because of material movement from the truck to the storage location and rearranging product in the storage area. All of these levels of disruption are eliminated in the Supply Chain for Liquids scenario. Delivery is done from outside the facility, and so there is no physical relationship between the delivery process and ongoing activity at the site, and there is no interaction between the delivery person and customer personnel. The Supply Chain for Liquids system is physically designed so that the user's dispense process can continue even while the producer's/distributor's replenishment process is taking place. In terms of the employees' work, personnel do not even know that a delivery is being made. The work flow at the customer site maintains its efficiency even while deliveries are being performed.

■ *Eliminate inventory shrink caused by theft, spillage, residual product, etc.*: Every contact between an employee and a product is an opportunity for inventory shrink. Whether intentional or accidental, every time a person touches, moves, or even gets near a product, there is a possibility of affecting the product, and the law of likelihood says that damage will happen a certain percentage of the time. Under the Supply Chain for Liquids approach, the only direct contact between a person and the product is the point at which the product is dispensed. Up to that point, the product is contained within the tank/piping system and is not accessible by employees. In fact, the Supply Chain for Liquids system is particularly vigorous in its prophylactic approach to inventory shrink. By continuously monitoring inventory levels, the Supply Chain for Liquids detects unusual usage activity that might indicate leakage or theft. This is in contrast to discrete-based systems, in which shortages are only detected based on a physical inventory count that may occur weeks or even months following the act that led to the shrinkage. Under the Supply Chain for Liquids system, the customer gains better control of inventory and reduces loss of inventory to shrinkage.

■ *Safer work environment and more environmentally friendly work method based on the elimination of the physical product-handling tasks*: Moving, placing, and handling bag-in-box containers, 120-pound pails, 55-gallon drums, and other forms of liquid-product containers can be hazardous. The periodic injuries and damage that occur with packaged products — such as dropped containers, spilled liquids, product falling from the shelf, and the like — do not occur under the Supply Chain for Liquids system. The customer also benefits from the elimination of packaging waste and the need to dispose of or recycle the packaging material.

■ *Includes a range of liquid products, even at the same facility*: The customer can use the same system to cover product liquids, process liquids, cleaning fluids, beverages, chemicals, and any other types of liquids used in the customer facility. This provides the customer with a broad opportunity for cost savings, operational efficiency, and revenue enhancement.

■ *Employees focus on serving consumers/users rather than on over-head activities*: More of the company's resources are dedicated to consumer-facing service activities rather than backroom-facing overhead activities.

Offering customers the Supply Chain for Liquids methodology is a highly attractive "carrot" that can have an important impact on the final decision to purchase a company's product.

Improved Information on User/Customer Behavior

As described in Chapter 10, Supply Chain for Liquids does not lead to consumer privacy issues, as have been raised with RFID (radio frequency identification) technology for discrete items. However, from within the final dispense location — such as the restaurant, vehicle maintenance facility, hotel or hospital, etc. — Supply Chain for Liquids is able to track highly detailed usage data. In contrast to sales-tracking systems whose only visibility into usage behavior is the periodic reorder of the product,

Supply Chain for Liquids allows detailed information about the time, location, and quantity of product usage. When supplemented with dispense-control devices as described in Chapter 8, this can be extended to the level of the individual using the product, the purpose of its use, or the detailed task to which it is being dispensed.

Information on product usage is always valuable in understanding how the marketplace relates to the product, and Supply Chain for Liquids serves to increase that understanding. From a marketing perspective, Supply Chain for Liquids provides not only usage information, but also early-warning signals regarding shifts in product usage or customer behavior. Changes in the quantity used, time of day at which the product is used, geographic distribution of usage, spikes or valleys of usage, and other data that is available from a full Supply Chain for Liquids system provide important insights that will impact or even guide marketing actions.

More-Nimble Product Placement

With the marketing mind breaking the world down into highly focused customer segments or clusters, targeting product to the specific cluster becomes ever more important. An extension of this need is the ability to move product in and out of the marketplace at market speed based on seasons, trends, major events, and other factors. And it goes without saying that product stock-outs do not fit well in the marketing mind.

Starting with the last point first, one estimate has it that U.S. retailers are losing nearly 4 percent of sales per year as a result of out-of-stock inventory. Marketing and sales go to all this effort to get the customer to buy our product, and four times out of one hundred, we say to the customer, "Sorry, we cannot really sell it to you." One important contributor to this situation is that we do not even know the product is out of stock because what is actually available to the customer is invisible to us. This is one of the important contributions of the Supply Chain for Liquids approach — visibility into what is available all the way along the supply stream, including product in the on-site tanks waiting to be dispensed to the user or consumer.

Product movements in and out of the marketplace are common. They may happen over a relatively short horizon or over a longer time period, or the duration of the product life cycle may not be estimable in advance. An example is synthetic motor oils, which are in the process of penetrating the marketplace, although at various speeds through different channels. To properly monitor and respond to changes in the lubricant market, the logistics system has to be sensitive to the various trends that are taking place related to lubricants and be able to report product activity all along the logistics flow. Trends relating synthetic lubricants impact both these products and conventional lubricants, thus making it doubly important for producers to keep close watch on product activity.

Finally, the logistics system must be able to place and track product at specific locations, zones, or regions to address different customer segments. Within the geographic region covered by one distribution center, there may be many segment-related zones, so tracking product to the level of the distribution center does not satisfy this marketing need. Not only does the appropriate product need to get to the right locations, but its performance there must be tracked and reported to allow constant tuning of market segmentation. Supply Chain for Liquids provides this capability to the level of detail required to ensure that logistics and marketing are working in sync out in the field.

Enhanced Quality Assurance

The logistics system can either enhance or detract from product quality. Most obviously, the longer a time-sensitive product sits in our distribution system, the smaller is the window that is available for it to sit in the retail or sales system. The conditions of the distribution system can also impact the quality of the product. The types of containers the product is in, the ambient temperature, opportunities for product contamination, the methods used to physically handle and move products and their containers, all of these impact the condition that the product will be in when it reaches the consumer. From the consumer's perspective, the quality of the package may be associated with the quality of the product, so that not only product deterioration, but also damage to the package detracts from perceived product quality. Damage to bottles, packages, or cartons is eliminated, as these are not used in a Supply Chain for Liquids system. A more detailed examination of product-quality issues is found in Chapter 8.

Supply Chain for Liquids addresses and resolves many of the product-quality issues. By reducing or eliminating the number of interim steps in the supply stream, the Supply Chain for Liquids system moves product from producer to consumer faster, thus providing fresher, higher-quality product for the consumer. Better visibility into inventory levels all along the supply stream allows close control over product velocity within the logistics system as well as the duration of its stay within the system.

The Supply Chain for Liquids system allows the product to remain in its native environment throughout the logistics process. Assuming that the materials used to hold the liquids at the producer are optimal in terms of product quality, the same materials can be used not only at the producer site, but throughout the logistics flow. Beverages that maintain their quality better in stainless steel containers, for example, can be transported in stainless steel truck tanks and placed in stainless steel on-site mini-tanks, thus protecting their quality right up to the point of dispense.

Environmental sensors for conditions that affect product quality can be included in the Supply Chain for Liquids system, such as monitors of either the liquid temperature or the ambient temperature surrounding the tanks. These sensors continuously or periodically report environmental conditions and allow Supply Chain for Liquids players to either correct any exception conditions or isolate product that has been exposed to damaging conditions. Monitors that directly measure quality characteristics of the liquid, such as clarity or gas content, can also be included in the system.

From a marketing perspective, these Supply Chain for Liquids capabilities provide a level of assurance that product is reaching the customers at the level of quality that we have specified for its use in the marketplace. Although Supply Chain for Liquids may be viewed primarily as a logistics tool, its marketing impact is broad and deep. The factors listed here are significant or critical to many companies, and they should be evaluated in reviewing the company's logistics approach.

Financial/Cost Savings

Our discussion on marketing/strategy laid out the revenue-enhancing aspects of Supply Chain for Liquids, and in this section we will look at the reverse side of the coin — cost reduction. Although the specific financial impact of Supply Chain for Liquids will vary by market and company, we can compare a typical Supply Chain for Liquids scenario with a typical Supply Chain scenario to get an idea of the major areas of cost savings available from Supply Chain for Liquids.

We can break down the total cost savings to a company from Supply Chain for Liquids into two categories. The first category is the reduced cost of the product itself, that is, the "unproductive" costs that are eliminated from the process in the Supply Chain for Liquids approach and thus can be deducted from the total cost of the product. Whether these reduced costs are passed along in terms of a price reduction for the product or are absorbed as additional margin is a completely different question.

The second category of savings is the reduction of the amount of product that needs to be in the logistics flow to support the same level of sales, that is, the reduction in inventory investment. To the degree to which less inventory is needed in the logistics pipeline, the holding costs for the inventory — both directly in terms of the product itself and indirectly in terms of the facilities and activities required to hold it — are reduced. We will examine the two categories separately, and then combine them to show the total savings available from the Supply Chain for Liquids approach.

Product Costs

For this examination of reduced product costs, we will use the Supply Chain for Liquids diagram we developed in Chapter 5 that overlays the Supply Chain for Liquids flow on top of the traditional Supply Chain flow. We will identify in Exhibit 11.2 the points at which there is a financial

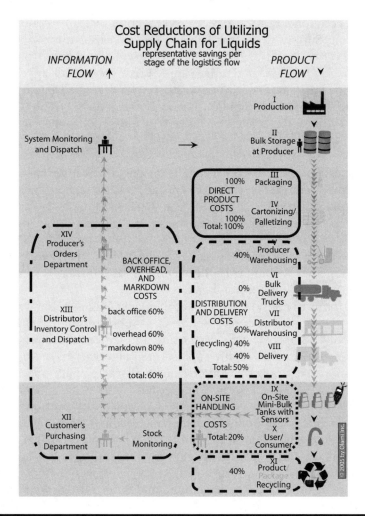

Exhibit 11.2   The Reduction in Complexities under Supply Chain for Liquids Brings Reduction in Costs All along the Flow

impact between the two approaches, and at each point provide an estimate of the impact based on standard assumptions. This is meant to provide a framework for a company to evaluate the financial impact of the Supply Chain for Liquids system; the exact numbers will of course be different in each situation. To the degree to which any particular cost element is higher or lower for a company than the figures defined here, the total financial impact of Supply Chain for Liquids will change accordingly.

Direct Product Costs

The first cost component is the direct product costs that are reduced or eliminated using Supply Chain for Liquids. To be conservative, we will assume that the savings in direct product costs will result only from the reduction in packaging used under the Supply Chain for Liquids approach, although this may not necessarily be accurate. As described earlier, the additional marketing and distribution channels created by Supply Chain for Liquids lead, in some cases, to changes in the product that actually reduce the cost of the product or increase the revenue/margin opportunities with the same product.

Packaging can range from an insignificant part of product cost to a substantial component of the total cost of the product. According to an analysis by Food & Drug Packaging in June 2002, packaging costs range from 4 percent of product cost for cosmetics to 24 percent for soaps and detergents, and can reach 50 percent or more for some types of products. Packaging encompasses the direct package material for the liquid, such as the bottle, together with a carton in which one or more bottles can be placed and a pallet holding a number of cartons.

Of course, for us to consider the cost of the packaging material without taking into account the resources required to perform the packaging operations would be an oversight. Packaging and cartonizing operations range from purely manual to highly sophisticated automated systems. For manual operations, a group of workers might fill each bottle, place the bottles in cartons, load the cartons onto pallets, and walk around the pallet with the shrink-wrap material in hand. Automated systems perform all of these tasks, including optimizing the pallet configuration for dimensions based on shipping origin or location, customer-specified pallet type, and other factors. In either case, packaging execution is a cost above the packaging material itself. The overhead costs associated with the operation including space, maintenance, management, and other factors are further loaded onto the packaging cost.

A relatively hidden cost related to products and their packaging relates to space usage. The space requirement for bottled liquids in cartons on pallets is quite high. The liquid content of a standard configuration (six one-gallon bottles to a carton, seven cartons to a layer, five layers to a pallet) is 210 gallons. But the amount of space required by the loaded pallet, assuming packed dimension of 42.5 inches by 37.0 inches by 61.5 inches and excluding the pallet itself, is enough capacity for just over 418 gallons. So we are taking 418 gallons worth of space to hold 210 gallons of liquid — almost exactly double the actual liquid content. You can thus imagine a pallet full of cartons to be essentially a big half-full tank of liquid. Again, there is clearly a cost aspect to this condition that we could assign to the product/packaging, but for the purpose of our conservative approach to this financial evaluation, we will take it into account in only a minimal way.

Another aspect of product cost, that of increased product in the pipeline, is also incurred in the packaging process. In operations in which packaging is a separate work center rather than a continuation of the production work center, the packaging work center faces the normal issues of work-center scheduling such as capacity limitations, queues, changeovers, etc. Packaging equipment can be expensive relative to the mixing tanks used in the actual production process. In such cases, companies may choose to use as few packaging machines as possible to service as many production lines as possible. Proliferation in numbers, sizes, and configurations of packages has only made the work of the packaging line more complex. Taken together, these factors lengthen the overall pipeline by adding an additional stage — packaging — to the pipeline.

The package-based approach to selling product inherently impacts the quantity of product in the logistics pipeline in another way. The same liquid product — the liquid itself — that is offered in different sizes or types of packages essentially becomes different products for logistics purposes as well as to the users. Thus a store shelf with three gallons of cola in 250-ml cans, three gallons of cola in 375-ml bottles, and three gallons of cola in two-liter bottles is not the pipeline equivalent of nine gallons of cola. The consumer selects the package as well as the product, and these are not interchangeable. Rather, the customer may forgo buying the product if there are only the small can and bottle on the shelf and not the larger bottle, thus bloating the level of inventory in the pipeline, because each product/package combination has to have its own level of safety stock at each point in the logistics process, including the point of purchase. Product will remain in the pipeline if it is not in a desired package, even though the liquid itself is the same liquid product. Product demand is not completely elastic in terms of packaging, leading to higher levels of inventory in the pipeline and a corresponding increase in inventory investment. Conversely, to the degree to which packaging can be removed from the logistics/usage equation, pipeline inventory and the investment in it are reduced.

For products that pass through a Supply Chain for Liquids system, the costs of packaging, cartonizing, and palletizing, and the related costs described above are reduced to zero, that is, the cost reduction amounts to 100 percent for these cost items. From a financial perspective, several other questions arise immediately to complete the analysis. What percentage of total product cost is represented by packaging cost, that is, what part of product cost does the 100 percent savings apply to? If packaging costs and related items as described above amount to 15 percent of total product cost, then by this evaluation we have increased margin by 15 percent of total product cost.

Another question is whether the elimination of the material, labor, and process costs described above will actually lead to 100 percent cost savings, or whether some of the costs will remain in place. For example, a company is unlikely to buy a somewhat smaller packaging machine to service packaged goods just because it has moved some of its product to the Supply Chain for Liquids system. More likely is that it will either find other uses for the equipment, or it will remain with some excess capacity. From a product-costing perspective, though, that cost should be redistributed across the products that are using the equipment, and not applied to products that do not run through those machines. If the company is relatively "loose" about throwing overhead across all its products, rather than tuning its product-costing scheme to the specifics of each product or product type, then the savings may appear to be less than 100 percent.

Distribution and Delivery Costs

The next set of costs we can examine that are associated with the traditional Supply Chain approach are distribution and delivery costs. As shown in Exhibit 11.2, these costs are incurred in the following steps:

- Supplier warehousing, including all internal activities such as receiving, picking, counting, moving, etc.
- Trucking from the supplier warehouse to the distribution center
- Distribution center, including the same types of activities that take place in the supplier warehouse
- Delivery from the distribution center to the customer site
- Package removal/disposal/recycling

The costs of package recycling are included in this set of costs under the view that both delivering the packaged product and removing the waste that results from the product package are considered to be parts of the distribution process.

In Chapter 7 we described the activities that typically occur in the supplier warehouse and in the distribution center, and our interest here is in the costs of those activities and in the quantity of liquid they add to the pipeline. Further, the leap in efficiency and visibility under a Supply Chain for Liquids system may actually allow elimination of one or both of these centers. If the virtually complete transparency offered by Supply Chain for Liquids allows production to match distribution needs, then the "buffer stock" use of warehousing and inventory to prevent stock-outs is significantly reduced. Even without such a radical alteration of the distribution structure, the Supply Chain for Liquids approach offers extensive cost-reduction opportunities.

Under Supply Chain for Liquids, the discrete-unit approach to product — racks, forklift trucks and drivers, manual movement, picking and staging, truck loading — is replaced by a much simpler approach. As described earlier, product is piped from the production process into holding tanks, and then piped to the trucks for transport and delivery. As anyone who has worked with warehouse systems knows, racking is not cheap, and we can take the cost of an extensive racking system to more or less correspond to the cost of a tank system for the same quantity of product. It should be remembered that a tank system holds several times more product than a racking system for the same amount of warehouse space. As we saw earlier, even within a single pallet of bottled liquid, only about half the space is actually used for the liquid product. Add the empty space between shelves of a rack system together with the aisle space needed for forklift access to the rack and the overhead space between the top of the rack and the ceiling of the warehouse (as rack heights are limited by forklift reach as well as by warehouse design), and it is a simple calculation to show that a tank system holds four to ten times more liquid product than a traditional rack system in the same amount of space. It is this differential in actual space utilization that leads to the equivalence of the per-unit cost of racks to the cost of tanks and their associated plumbing and controls.

Given this "wash," the remaining costs that are reduced or eliminated under Supply Chain for Liquids versus supply chain represent pure savings. If we can considerably reduce reliance on the distribution center as an inventory buffer (owing to the factors described above) and thus its scope, scale, and size, we have achieved a quantum change in the cost equation. Even without doing so, however, the cost implications of Supply Chain for Liquids are clear. Savings include the following areas.

Forklifts, Including Equipment, Drivers, and Maintenance

Most warehouses are forklift-intensive, including receiving and put-away, stock movement and rotation, picking, staging, and truck loading. Both the direct and indirect costs (such as product and property damage caused by forklifts) and pipeline time associated with these activities are eliminated. If there is an alternative or adjunct to forklifts in place in any particular facility to move packaged product, such as conveyors or an automated warehouse system, these are also eliminated by the tank/pipe-based product flow in Supply Chain for Liquids.

Inventory Shrink

Theft, damage, mislabeling and mislocation, erroneous counts, and all such "pure loss" costs are essentially eliminated under the Supply Chain for Liquids approach, as described in more detail below. Even the costs associated with identifying the shrink and verifying inventory — the periodic physical inventory including counting, tabulating, reconciling, and updating the results, together with the effort required to investigate the causes of differences — are radically reduced.

Management and Overhead

The reduction in warehouse personnel and significant simplification of the product-tracking and -movement process allows reduction in the manpower, supervision, and overhead required to run a warehouse. Movement of liquids takes place by opening or switching valves rather than physically moving product packages, and depending on the degree of sophistication and availability of HMI (human-machine interface) software, this might be accomplished by one operator in a control room rather than numerous warehouse personnel. Other overhead items such as insurance, maintenance, equipment, administrative activities, and personnel support functions are correspondingly reduced.

Trucking and Transportation

Cost savings result from the extraordinary efficiency of truck runs under the Supply Chain for Liquids scenario. Truck utilization is improved through the effective loading that results from the high degree of product visibility that Supply Chain for Liquids offers. The external-delivery approach and resulting off-hours trucking runs enable scheduling of deliveries during low-traffic periods, allowing trucks to cover many more stops than under a standard configuration. The costs of the trucks are distributed across an even broader set of customers and delivery activity than trucks delivering discrete products, thus making the per-quantity cost of trucks and trucking very small. All of these factors come together to reduce the cost of trucking in both the transport and delivery functions.

An issue that arises in adopting the Supply Chain for Liquids approach is that of duplicate truck visits to the same customer. That is, in many situations the fact that a Supply Chain for Liquids truck delivers bulk liquids to a specific customer does not eliminate the need for a truck carrying nonbulk liquids or other discrete items to visit the same customer. On the surface, this might seem to be an added cost, but in many cases it proves to be an added savings. Removal of these liquids from the discrete-items truck allows loading of more discrete items on the truck and thus makes that transport or delivery run more effective. This is especially true when the capacity of the truck is the constraint to the number of customer deliveries that can be made in a given delivery run, which is usually the case.

Further, the replenishment pattern for liquid products is often different from that for discrete products, so that delinking the replenishment runs for the two types of products is actually more suitable for both of them. In a janitorial-supply distribution operation, for example, "durable" discrete items such as mops and towels need replenishment less frequently than "consumable" liquid items such as soaps and floor cleaners, so there is an inherent sense in disconnecting cycles for the two types of products.

Package Disposal

The cost of package disposal or recycling is eliminated under Supply Chain for Liquids, because the packaging is itself eliminated. These costs often take the form of haulage of the waste material — in the form of garbage, cardboard carton, plastic jugs, steel drums, etc. — from the user site to the recycling center or garbage dump. Another cost incurred as part of this process is the preparation required for the disposal process. This includes breaking down and bundling the cartons, cutting up the drums, crushing the plastic jugs, etc. In any case, these are costs incurred within the Supply Chain system that are eliminated under the Supply Chain for Liquids approach.

Just as earlier we saw that the producer enjoys significant cost savings from the Supply Chain for Liquids system, in this section we have seen wall-to-wall savings (literally and figuratively) from the model for the distributor. Based on these savings factors and standard distribution and delivery figures, we can conservatively set the figures for savings in distribution and delivery costs derived from the factors listed above as 40 percent for producer warehousing; 0 percent for trucking from the producer to the distribution point, as this physical movement of the product is required in both cases; 60 percent for distribution warehousing; 40 percent for delivery because of the efficiencies from off-hours delivery and the external-delivery method; and 40 percent for the elimination of package recycling (as product recycling may remain), for a combined savings on distribution and delivery costs of 50 percent. As described below, these figures are intended to provide a structure within which a particular company can project the financial impact of the Supply Chain for Liquids system, and the results will be different for every company. The steps required for tuning these numbers, as well as for translating them into a percentage of total product cost and then combining them into total pipeline investment, are given below.

The next section discusses the financial impact/cost savings for the downstream end of the supply stream.

On-Site Handling Costs

The next set of costs eliminated from the system under a Supply Chain for Liquids configuration are those associated with on-site handling of the product. "On-site" may refer to a restaurant, an automotive repair facility, a factory, or other facility that represents the user end of the Supply Chain for Liquids flow. An extensive description of the types of users and applications for the Supply Chain for Liquids system is found in Chapter 4, and this analysis is applicable to each of the industries listed there.

It is important to distinguish between the cost savings that are available from the Supply Chain for Liquids system and the decision as to how those savings will be used. Our objective here is to identify costs that are removed from any point in the entire system; how the savings/benefit will be distributed among the players along the Supply Chain for Liquids is a separate question that is not addressed here.

The on-site efficiencies gained through Supply Chain for Liquids handling result from the many steps that are eliminated from the on-site process. Activities that are eliminated include:

- Acceptance of incoming goods, including counting received product; put-away, including replacement of existing product to ensure proper product rotation; and receipt signing and other interactions with the delivery person.
- Retrieving product from storage and preparing it for use. In a restaurant, this involves moving a bag-in-box (BIB) unit to the BIB rack and switching dispense-line attachments, or taking bags of ice cream mix or jugs of cooking oil to the appropriate equipment and filling the equipment. In an automotive-service environment, it involves swapping 55-gallon drums, retrieving jugs of lubricant from the storeroom, or whatever method is used to bring maintenance fluids to the point of usage. In a hotel or hospital, it may

be to get a jug of soap concentrate, mix it with water, and put it in a bucket for use. For a maintenance engineer in a factory, it could involve carting several bottles of machine lubricants and fluids to a work center in which preventive or repair maintenance is to be performed. In any case, this activity involves on-site personnel performing some act of moving the liquid to make it ready for usage. It is natural that product will stock-out during periods of heavy usage during the day, which are exactly the times when employees should be focused on serving customers and users. Thus the cost of this on-site inventory-handling activity encompasses both employee time required to perform this activity and the reduced level of customer service that results from the employee handling product rather than performing customer-facing functions.

■ Dispense and actual usage of the product. The "zero-line" of liquid usage is that the right liquid be readily available at the point of need in a form that requires as close to zero effort as possible. Anything short of the zero-line measure means increased employee activity during the act of dispensing and usage.

There are many examples of usage effectiveness as well as usage ineffectiveness. A mechanic fixing a car in a repair bay might have a retractable hose of motor oil within arm's reach, or might have to fetch the oil as described above. A restaurant employee might have a beverage-dispense unit nearby, but physical proximity alone may not be good enough. If the employee has to hold the cup and the valve handle while the beverage is poured into the cup, this comes at the cost of employee/customer facing time. A dispense unit in which the employee hits a button and the proper amount of liquid flows into the cup, while the employee is free to do something else, reduces the employee cost of that act, although this must of course be measured against the cost of putting the more sophisticated dispense unit in place.

From a Supply Chain for Liquids perspective, the dispense issue is a primary focus. Indeed, as described in Chapter 2, it is a driver of the design of the entire system. Assuming that the point of customer/user contact is "what it's all about," making that point as effective as possible should be an important consideration in the design of the entire flow. As described in Chapter 10, focusing on the customer/user interface is a key part of the Supply Chain for Liquids planning process and should include as many of the logistics-flow players as possible.

These efficiencies can be translated into cost savings in several ways. Dispense systems are generally cost-justified as an opportunity to increase employee efficiency and thus expand operational activity without adding personnel. Alternatively, these efficiencies can be viewed as creating the possibility for reducing employee headcount while supporting the same amount of business activity, which also amounts to a reduction in the per-volume cost of the business. The Supply Chain for Liquids aspect additionally creates the direct connection between the liquid-holding tanks and the dispense unit. The user's ability to dispense the liquids without having had to take any action to feed liquid into the dispense unit is a large savings, as described above. Additional associated cost savings, as described below, include reductions in insurance premiums because the Supply Chain for Liquids system reduces worker exposure to injury-causing activities.

Given the above factors, an estimate of on-site cost savings based on a standard operation for the backroom activities such as inventory put-away, movement, and replenishment; for on-site space made available under the Supply Chain for Liquids system; and for retrieval, pouring, and actual usage of the liquid is a combined 20 percent reduction in on-site costs.

Back-Office, Overhead, and Markdown Costs

Less obvious but equally as real are the back-office and overhead costs that are loaded onto Supply Chain activity, together with an even more hidden and normally less controllable set of costs that we can group together as "markdown costs." The back-office and overhead costs are more closely associated with the information flow from the customer site back to the distribution and production points, rather than with the flow of product itself.

The flow of information under the Supply Chain for Liquids scenario is automated from the source of the information through to the person who is in a position to act on the information as required. The source of the information is the point at which the product itself is held: monitors in the tanks at the user site, on the trucks, and in any interim inventory holding location such as a distribution center or producer's warehouse. The base information that is available is current on-hand balance at each location at any given point in time, with additional information such as recent usage history generated as needed for a particular application.

Although the source information can be distributed to any member of the Supply Chain for Liquids, these do not represent costs incurred as part of the Supply Chain for Liquids. This is in contrast to a normal Supply Chain sequence as defined in Chapter 5, in which the same data is handled several times along the Supply Chain and is in fact manipulated in a way that is counterproductive to the efficient and effective operation of the Supply Chain as a whole. Each point at which the data is handled in the Supply Chain — the count person and reorder person at the downstream site, the inventory person and purchasing person at the distribution center, and the orders person at the producer — represents a cost that is eliminated under the approach that allows direct access to source data. Under a scenario in which the Supply Chain for Liquids information system processes the source data and presents it to the dispatch person at the producer ready to initiate replenishment action, all of the costs that are normally incurred in handling the data along the Supply Chain are eliminated. This includes not only the individuals who handle the data directly, but the systems and infrastructure that each creates to perform this task.

In cases in which interim steps in the supply stream, such as distribution centers, are reduced or made more efficient rather than eliminated, the Supply Chain for Liquids still serves to reduce the amount and thus the cost of data handling. With the inclusion of CPVR^{SM} (Coordinated Procedures for Visibility Response^{SM}) processing (described in Chapter 10), source data is preprocessed based on rules set up in advance, and the information system presents the user with the suggested course of action in terms of inventory ordering or movement. This directed action, which is based on coordination with the other players in the logistics flow, reduces the burden on inventory control personnel to evaluate inventory conditions prior to taking action. The result is less effort/cost invested in planning and controlling inventory while achieving lower systemwide levels and thus lower cost of inventory.

The final set of costs that can be radically reduced or eliminated are the "markdown costs." These are often taken for granted as being part of the normal cost of doing business. Not so under the Supply Chain for Liquids approach.

Examples of some markdown costs are:

- *Product damaged during handling*: For liquid products in packages, it is almost never the product itself that is damaged during handling, but rather the packaging. Because of the dependence on packaging in a normal Supply Chain environment, damaged packaging is in fact equivalent to damaged product. This dependence is broken in Supply Chain for Liquids, and there is very little opportunity for damage along the Supply Chain for Liquids stream.

- *Theft*: Anyone who has worked with inventory knows that theft knows virtually no bounds. The case of the garage sale in which a whole table full of carbide inserts were beautifully arranged and ready to be sold at an excellent price — carbide inserts stolen from a nearby factory, and useless to anyone who does not have high-precision material-forming equipment — shows that virtually anything can and will be stolen. Supply Chain for Liquids has several advantages over Supply Chain in reducing theft. First, normal Supply Chain puts the product in an easily stealable form, such as a quart bottle that fits neatly inside a lunch box. To steal from a bulk tank, you have to bring your own bottle and fill it from the tank yourself, and in a Supply Chain for Liquids environment, there is not necessarily even ready access to a tank. Second, in Supply Chain, theft is only revealed weeks or months after it occurs during the physical count of inventory. With continuous monitoring, any unusual inventory dispensing — unusual quantities or unusual times of dispense — can be spotted and investigated immediately. As a generalization of this last point, the psychology that often seems to be at work is that if nobody is watching, then it is alright to steal; whereas if the company is keeping a close eye on inventory, then thieves should look elsewhere for things to steal. Supply Chain for Liquids puts that eagle eye on all liquid products.

■ *Inventory shrinkage*: This granddaddy of all cost categories covers the "we really don't know what happened to that product" category that occurs more often than companies are willing to admit. For example, it is estimated that nearly $6 billion worth of inventory is lost each year by retailers in the United States due to administrative errors alone. Supply Chain for Liquids by its nature combats inventory shrinkage. It keeps the product in tanks and pipes from the point of production to the point of dispense, a much more secure environment than bottles, cans, jugs, and jars that can so easily grow legs. It is constantly monitored throughout the pipeline, and any discrepancies between the balance that should be in any location and what is actually in that location can be identified and pursued immediately. Finally, it keeps the whole product pipeline "skinny." The same inventory buildup points that are created to protect the Supply Chain from stock-outs due to lack of visibility into demand also serve as the invitation points for inventory shrinkage in whatever form it may take.

■ *Product obsolescence/replacement*: Supply Chain for Liquids is extraordinarily useful for situations in which liquid products have relatively short life cycles, high seasonality, or other characteristics that demand highly responsive inventory levels and a flexible inventory-holding system. The complete visibility into inventory position over the whole length of the Supply Chain for Liquids allows the players to "close the spigot" at the producer end and closely monitor the quantity of product in the Supply Chain for Liquids versus demand at the consumer end. The on-site tanking system allows tremendous flexibility in the quantities of different liquids held on-site and in the interchanging of holding capacity between liquids. From a cost-control perspective, these capabilities minimize product disposal due to obsolescence, allow fine-tuning of transition to replacement products, and allow full control over the timing of new-product introductions to completely use existing product.

■ *Warehouse misplacement, mislabeling, etc.*: Physical systems, even RFID systems, are subject to the costs of mislabeling, misplacing, and otherwise "losing" inventory. This can occur in any number of ways. The identifying tag can get ripped from the product packaging; an error or discrepancy on the production/packaging line can lead to mislabeling of some packages; the put-away location of some product can be misreported as another location; unrecorded or erroneously recorded product movements can take place, and so on. Each of these instances represents product costs. When finished product is "misplaced," it has already incurred all the costs of reaching that status (production, quality control, packaging, handling, etc.) but will not generate the associated revenue. Moreover, the employee effort required to identify a "lost" or "found" product, trace its source, and take corrective action can often be significant. Customer orders that are lost due to product unavailability, or additional production runs generated to create product that in fact already exists, are other costs related to this problem. Because Supply Chain for Liquids moves product within closed systems and does not utilize individual units or labeling of units, the chances of such events occurring (with their associated costs to the company) are significantly reduced. Because inventory levels are reported automatically by the sensors, the points of possible error in a Supply Chain for Liquids occur following one-off acts, such as switching a tank from one liquid to another and not properly reporting it to the system, rather than during the normal course of ongoing activity.

■ *Quality impairment during process*: Product that goes bad in the view of the customer or consumer represents a cost to the company. The cost may be in replacement product, customer-service efforts to resolve the perceived problem, or lost customers. Even more insidious, quality-impacted product can damage the company's reputation and create unhappy customers whose impact on sales goes beyond isolated cases. The costs of these events can range from minor to extensive. Supply Chain for Liquids enhances product quality in a number of ways, such as preserving product in its native environment and allowing continuous monitoring of quality-related parameters. These quality-related capabilities are described in more detail in Chapter 10. Their cost implications can be evaluated based on the current costs a company incurs for quality-related issues.

The scope and distribution of back-office, overhead, and markdown costs vary from company to company, as will the savings in these areas from moving to the Supply Chain for Liquids approach. We can project these savings for activities related to products moving through Supply Chain for Liquids as 60 percent for back office, 60 percent for overhead, and 80 percent for markdown costs, with a combined cost savings of 60 percent.

Having identified the savings in each of the areas described above — direct product costs; distribution and delivery costs; on-site handling costs; and back-office, overhead, and markdown costs — each company needs to take two steps to complete the financial picture for itself. First, it needs to fine-tune the percentage estimates shown above based on its own operations to come up with the relative savings for each of these areas for that specific company. Second, the company needs to lay these relative savings against the breakdown of product costs for the company to come up with a weighted savings projection appropriate for the company. For example, a company can (1) review its product costs in terms of a standard breakdown of categories such as material, labor, overhead, distribution, and GS&A (general, sales, and administrative) and (2) identify the percentage of total product cost for each. It can then apply the percentage of savings to the appropriate category to identify the total savings in product cost. For example, if the material category represents 20 percent of the product's total cost, and if we have identified that packaging and related savings will reduce material costs by 30 percent, then the savings in total product cost that derives from packaging savings is 6 percent. By repeating this exercise for each of the other cost categories, a company can come up with a projected overall savings in product cost that will result from use of the Supply Chain for Liquids system.

For purposes of illustration, we can apply the product-cost savings figures to a sample set of product-cost categories to see how this process works. The relative weight of each category that makes up total product cost — material, labor, overhead, distribution, and GS&A — is different for every company. To simplify this illustration, we will say that the cost of the product is divided evenly among these five categories. Thus each category represents 20 percent of the total cost of the product in this example.

In developing the product-cost savings figures, we did not break down the costs according to these product-cost categories, but rather according to where the savings occur in the Supply Chain for Liquids flow. There is therefore not a clean one-to-one correspondence between the two sets of figures. When creating these figures for a specific company, we structure them such that the application of product-cost savings to product-cost categories will be clear. In any case, we can apply the cost-savings numbers we developed earlier to the product-cost categories as follows:

- *Material*: The material category corresponds to the packaging shown in the "direct product costs" savings item. Using 30 percent as the packaging component of material, the 100 percent cost reduction shown in Exhibit 11.2, and the material-costs assumption of 20 percent of total product cost, we arrive at a total product-cost savings of 6 percent that can be attributed to the elimination of packaging under Supply Chain for Liquids.
- *Labor*: The labor category is normally associated with the actual production operation. Although there are many labor-saving points throughout Supply Chain for Liquids, we will not include them in the labor category for the purpose of this example. Rather, we will include them in the distribution and back-office categories, so the cost savings here is defined as 0 percent.
- *Overhead*: The 60 percent savings shown for "back-office, overhead, and markdown costs" applied to the 20 percent of product-cost category defined for overhead yields a 12 percent savings in total product cost as a result of overhead reductions in the Supply Chain for Liquids system.
- *Distribution*: With a combined "distribution and delivery costs" savings of 50 percent applied to the distribution product-cost category of 20 percent of total product cost, the result is a 10 percent savings in total product cost derived from the efficiencies in distribution that Supply Chain for Liquids offers.
- *GS&A*: In our example, we have not clearly defined the cost savings that apply to this product-cost category, so we set the savings in this category at 0 percent.

Summarizing the results of this simple example shows the savings from the Supply Chain for Liquids system as follows:

Material costs	6%
Labor costs	0%
Overhead costs	12%
Distribution	10%
GS&A	0%
Total	28%

That is, with the generalized assumptions and conservative estimates that we used in this example, Supply Chain for Liquids has the financial impact of reducing the cost of product by 28 percent. Again, it should be noted that we are referring here to product cost and not product price. What a company does with the knowledge of the cost of its product is a completely separate issue.

Quantity of Product in the Pipeline

Up to now, our view of the financial impact of Supply Chain for Liquids has focused on reducing the cost of the product by eliminating unnecessary steps and complexities that add to the direct cost of the product. The other side of this coin is the savings derived by reducing inventory in the supply stream. Investment in inventory ties up capital; by reducing inventory levels, we can either reduce the amount of capital required to support inventory or lower the cost of financing the inventory.

Additional cost items are commonly included in inventory carrying costs, such as the costs of holding and handling inventory, costs for the space that the inventory occupies, and the risk costs associated with inventory damage/obsolescence/etc. For the purposes of this analysis we have included those items as product costs above and will avoid double-counting them here. Our objective here is to estimate the amount of inventory that Supply Chain for Liquids will allow us to remove from the supply stream that, together with the reduced cost of product defined earlier, will give us our total inventory savings based on moving from Supply Chain to the Supply Chain for Liquids system.

Supply Chain for Liquids reduces inventory in the logistics flow in a number of ways. The visibility that the approach provides allows much tighter control over pipeline inventory quantities, faster identification of low stock levels, and reduction of buffer stocks that are often used to protect against the problems caused by a lack of visibility. We can use the experience of companies that have moved to RFID systems for discrete items, which corresponds to the RFID for Liquids® functionality that is part of Supply Chain for Liquids, to provide direction on the order of magnitude of inventory reduction that results from such a move. Figures vary based on industry, company, and type of product from 5 to 40 percent, but a figure of 20 percent inventory reduction appears to be a fair estimate for our purposes.

Supply Chain for Liquids also reduces inflow inventory through the velocity at which it is able to move product. The delivery process, which exploits low-traffic off-hours conditions and pumping the product through an external port rather than requiring the delivery person to enter the site, is built to move product faster than one that does not offer these functionalities. The speed and responsiveness of the delivery process allow less product to do more in terms of servicing the supply stream. We will assign a 4 percent reduction in systemwide inventory level to this agility within the Supply Chain for Liquids system, totaling a 24 percent reduction in systemwide inventory under the system.

Combined Financial Impact of the Supply Chain for Liquids System

We have reviewed the cost impact of Supply Chain for Liquids throughout the various stages of the product pipeline. As mentioned at the beginning of this section, the cost impact involves two aspects. First, the reduction in steps and costs represents a direct savings to the system. Second, the reduction in the amount of product in the system represents a reduction in the inventory investment required to operate the system.

The true financial power of the Supply Chain for Liquids approach is revealed in putting these two factors together, as shown in Exhibit 11.3. The first graph relates to the reduced per-quantity cost of the product, and the second to the decreased quantity of product throughout the pipeline. It is the third graph, which combines these two into the reduced dollar investment in the pipeline, that is the overall measure of the value of the Supply Chain for Liquids approach to all the players together. This represents the total margin that is freed up in the system, to be utilized to cover the costs of implementing the system, distributed to the participants, reduce the end cost of the product to the customer, or battle the competition in some other way. In any case, this represents the "win" from implementing the Supply Chain for Liquids approach.

Cost of Implementing and Operating a Supply Chain for Liquids System

Financially, the Supply Chain for Liquids system represents a dramatic reduction in costs and creation of a margin pool for the players involved. Like any effort, the net cost of the effort must be evaluated together with its benefits and limitations in the specific marketplace in which it is being considered. In evaluating Supply Chain for Liquids, it is important to identify two different types of costs. The first type is the set of one-off setup costs. These would relate to the up-front capital investment that would be paid off over the life of the project, such as the tank systems and the tank trucks. The second type relates to activity costs, the variable costs incurred by the volume of deliveries that take place at any given location.

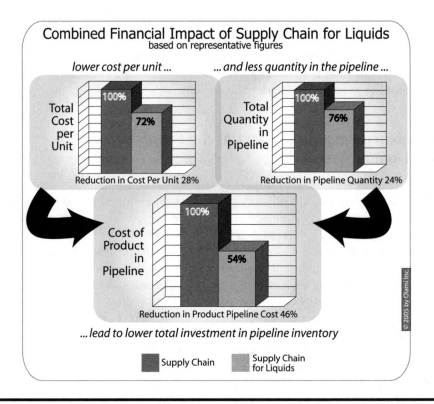

Combined Financial Impact of Supply Chain for Liquids
based on representative figures

lower cost per unit ... ...*and less quantity in the pipeline ...*

Total Cost per Unit — 100% / 72%
Reduction in Cost Per Unit 28%

Total Quantity in Pipeline — 100% / 76%
Reduction in Pipeline Quantity 24%

Cost of Product in Pipeline — 100% / 54%
Reduction in Product Pipeline Cost 46%

... lead to lower total investment in pipeline inventory

■ Supply Chain   ■ Supply Chain for Liquids

© 2005 by Olami Inc.

Exhibit 11.3   Reduction in Per-Unit Cost Together with Reduction in Pipeline Quantity Lead to Lowered Investment in Pipeline Inventory

Although they represent the larger financial outlays, the centralized costs such as trucks, information system support, warehouse tanks, and the like — when distributed across enough delivery points — become very small per unit of liquid. Because of the simplicity of the Supply Chain for Liquids system, there are no points of high complexity and no "black boxes" that require particular investment, so the system can be designed and acquired knowing all the costs in advance.

The critical point in the cost of the Supply Chain for Liquids system is the per-site cost, particularly the tank system and information-gathering and information-transmitting equipment. The cost of the equipment at each particular location is distributed only across the activity at that location, rather than over systemwide activity. Clearly, the installation of highly sophisticated high-cost equipment in a low-volume environment will raise the per-quantity cost of the product to an unacceptable level. This is the reason that the range of equipment described in Chapter 8 is so important. If the low volume of a particular liquid at a particular location dictates lower-cost equipment with reduced functionality, there are in fact alternatives available that reduce the cost in return for a lower level of functionality. For example, instead of a level monitor that continuously measures the level of liquid in the tank, allowing the system to read the quantity in the tank at any time, a less-expensive alternative is a point sensor. A point sensor is placed at a specific point in the tank and identifies whether the liquid level is above or below that point. Other than the yes/no signal regarding that particular point, such a sensor does not measure how much liquid is in the tank. It is possible to put multiple point sensors in a given tank, and thus for example get a signal when the tank is down to 25 percent of its capacity and again when it is at 10 percent of its capacity. However, this approach leaves the system blind as to liquid usage during the entire period from when the tank is full until it goes down to 25 percent, again between 25 and 10 percent, and then again less than 10 percent. For low-volume liquids, however, this might be a completely acceptable level of data flow, in that the cost of these monitors would not add significantly to the per-quantity cost of the product. In fact, the delivery to any particular location is likely to be driven by the higher-volume liquids for which there will be continuous level sensors, with lower-volume liquids replenished during each delivery run to that location. The tanks for the low-quantity liquids can be sufficiently large to virtually ensure that there will not be a stock-out of the liquid. With this in mind, the minimum sensor requirement for a low-volume liquid is a "hot-shot" signal at quite a low level, such as 10 percent, that will notify the system that a replenishment order is required in the very near term. An alternative approach that also helps reduce the cost of the monitoring system is the liquid-column approach as described in Chapter 7.

Other pieces of the Supply Chain for Liquids system can be put together according to the needs of the specific application. The information system may be as robust as described in Chapter 10, or it could be a much simpler configuration that flows the data into a standard min/max inventory system, with more intense intervention by the dispatcher. The compartmentalization of the tanks on the truck and the configuration of the on-site tanks can be highly flexible through a valving system, or it could be relatively fixed using a simpler equipment configuration. In each case, there are trade-offs between the cost of the system and the capabilities that it provides.

Case Study: JohnsonDiversey

The logistics dynamics of liquid products are pointedly different from the dynamics of discrete products. Indeed, the very nature of liquid products is defined differently from that of discrete products. These dynamics are demonstrated by the logistics processes in place at JohnsonDiversey, a company that provides cleaning and hygiene solutions to the institutional and industrial marketplace, serving customers in the hospitality, food service, retail, food and beverage, and health-care sectors as well as building-service contractors. The scope of JohnsonDiversey's operations is demonstrated by its global reach, with sales in over 60 countries.

A case in point is the Supply Chain operations that JohnsonDiversey set up in China. Andrew Bielby — who in his position as Supply Chain director guided the development, growth, and operation of production in and export from China — is deeply familiar with the dynamics of liquid logistics. Combining an extensive background in operations and strong sensitivity to economics, Bielby provides a broad overview of the key issues in logistics for liquid products.

In describing the types of liquids included in the production and distribution process, Bielby points out that many are produced using relatively simple technologies that do not require extensive plant or capital investment. Because these products are of low dollar value, the logistics costs — for example freight — quickly become high relative to the produced cost of the product. Historically, this has led to the establishment of many small factories located close to the target market. This has been the tried and true model of many companies.

Like many companies, however, JohnsonDiversey determined that it is effective to have production facilities in China, even though such factories export up to 80 percent of their output to Japan, Europe, and the United States. The factory was initially set up to meet Chinese regulatory requirements, but the company soon realized its export potential. This decision also took into account the insource/outsource issue to determine exactly which products to produce at the China facilities. Bielby describes some of the major factors included in the insource/outsource evaluation as:

- *Volume*: Given the volume of product to be produced, a company must determine whether its value to the company justifies tying up internal resources.
- *Technology*: If the product involves a specific technique or technology, a company must decide whether that technology should be kept in-house, assuming that outsourced processes will find their way into the marketplace and to the competition one way or another.
- *Value/geography*: For some products, the lack of value added during the manufacturing process together with the relatively high cost of freight force a company to produce close to the customer.
- *Product lifecycle*: A company is less likely to insource a product with an uncertain future, particularly a product with a low volume or one that is nearing the end of its lifecycle.

- *Availability of outsourcing*: A company must evaluate how closely the resources available for outsourcing match the company's needs, and determine whether outsourcing is a viable option based on the cost of outsourcing and its value to the process.

Analysis of a matrix showing these and other relevant factors led to specialized solutions for various products. For example, many products are produced in a super-concentrated form and diluted with water by up to 95 percent at the customer site prior to use. In addition, the dosing bottles are an integral part of the product as received by the customer. A good illustration of a situation in which the cost of freight is not always the driver is Bielby's calculation that it was cheaper to ship large volumes of low-value empty plastic dosing bottles to the United Kingdom than to produce them there. The conversion-cost/supplier-margin requirements in China are so dramatically lower that they more than offset the cost of shipping "air" halfway around the world.

As Bielby points out, this solution is to some degree counterintuitive. Shipping bottles filled with air would seem cost-ineffective, but at the end of the day it is the numbers and not intuition that direct the results.

This solution provides insight into the special nature of liquid logistics in a number of ways:

- The product and the packaging are considered separately as part of logistics planning and execution, whereas for discrete products, the packaging is most often considered part and parcel of the production process and of the product itself.
- The bottle serves several functions. It is used as the dilution bottle (essentially part of the application process) and the final dispensing bottle (as a control mechanism, it is the dispenser that will not allow competitors' products to be used in the company's placements). The bottle includes a special fitting so that only the company's bottles can be inserted into the correct dispense units the company has installed in the field. Another bottle design, appropriate for a different field configuration, is a bottle that contains concentrate but includes a dosing and dilution mechanism. This type of bottle is attached to a water hose and is then ready for dispense by the user.
- In both the bottle configurations described above, the dispense process is incorporated into the design of the bottle. In fact, the dispense equipment in the first configuration represents one of the largest capital costs associated with the product. As can be seen here, the packaging of the liquid takes on a high level of importance related to the product as a whole. In fact, Bielby points out,

a company is in some ways at its weakest in supplying bulk liquids in bulk containers, as there is the highest degree of interchange-ability at that point. In JohnsonDiversey's case, considerations of the packaging together with service, training, and quality come together as the "total package" that the customer is buying.

Having said this, there are cases in which nothing but bulk deliveries make economic sense. Based on Bielby's analysis, some liquids are delivered to some customers by tanker truck. In-flight catering kitchens, for example, use dishwashing detergent virtually continuously, and they do not want to have the disruption of having to change drums or perform other logistics tasks. In any case, the detergent is a low-price item that does not justify investment in packaging and the return cycle of empty drums or intermediate bulk containers (IBCs). Other customers such as large food-producing companies or breweries use liquids in similar ways, and the full-bulk approach is most applicable to many of them.

JohnsonDiversey has designed other logistics channels to meet the specifics of on-the-ground conditions and customer requirements. In a large commercial laundry, for example, JohnsonDiversey cleaning products are held in tanks and are pumped into the washing machines under the control of an advanced system of automated pumps. The controller manages both chemical dispensing and records the quantities dispensed, as well as other data regarding the wash process. However, the equipment has no continuous external connectivity, so the data from the controller is reviewed by on-site personnel or technicians, and the chemical replenishment process performed manually.

Bielby sees a number of additional trends related to cleaning products and their packaging. On the one hand, bag-in-box offers advantages to customers and is increasing in Western countries. At the same time, Bielby has witnessed a large movement toward recyclable plastic drums in Japan due to environmental concerns, with up to 80 percent of the drums returned after use. A third is movement to higher concentrations. The product configuration, packaging, and logistics method of each region is matched to the conditions in that region.

The final major logistics trend that Bielby commented on was that of "portfolio rationalization," the reduction in the number of SKUs (stock-keeping units) as well as the number of suppliers, warehouses, and inventory quantity with which the company works. Rather than impairing product availability, this initiative both improved customer service and resulted in significant cost savings. As it turned out, the proliferation in the number of products did not lead to the customer feeling that greater selection was available, but rather confused the customer as well as company employees and was determined to be a hindrance rather than a contributor to marketplace success.

Environment

We normally think of the environmental impact of liquids in association with the manufacturing processes related to these products: the consumption of resources, pollution generated, land usage, etc. When viewed through a Liquid Lens, production is literally only the beginning of the environmental impact of liquids. How are the liquids transported — how far, how frequently — and what are the environmental consequences of the transportation method? What packaging is used to hold the liquids, how much environmental damage is done in creating the packaging, and what happens to the packaging after the liquid has been used? At what points in the flow are spillage and leakage likely to take place, and how do such events affect the environment? Is the supply stream built in such a way that there are multiple storage points along the way, each with its own land-use and traffic issues, or are such operational inefficiencies eliminated and the environmental impact of the logistics flow decreased?

The environmental impact of the supply stream goes far beyond the production of the liquid product itself. In this chapter we will go through the Supply Chain for Liquids as we developed it in previous chapters and evaluate the steps of the system from an environmental perspective. The scale of liquid usage is so large that even modest use of Supply Chain for Liquids principles yields huge environmental benefits. Chapter 4 lays out the volumes of some key liquids in different industries and gives an idea of how large the river of liquids flowing through the American economy really is.

Environmental compliance has gone through a long evolution since the "dirty old days" of air you could not see through and rivers that caught fire. But the legislation that has brought us a cleaner world has not always been easy for industry to swallow. Environmental achievements have not slowed the demand for new regulation; rather, environmental awareness has sparked ever-increasing attention to factors affecting environmental quality. An example of this is the European Union's current approach to the chemical industry. Against a background of an enormous increase in the production of chemicals, the need for a new EU chemical strategy has been broadly recognized. The REACH laws (Registration, Evaluation and Authorization of Chemicals) shift the burden to producers and manufacturers regarding information and handling of chemicals. This legislation is being considered based on the estimate that 30 percent of the total burden of disease in industrialized countries can be attributed to environmental factors, and focuses on the "cycle of pollutants, how they mix and move in the environment." This legislation relates to some of the exact issues that the Supply Chain for Liquids addresses and resolves.

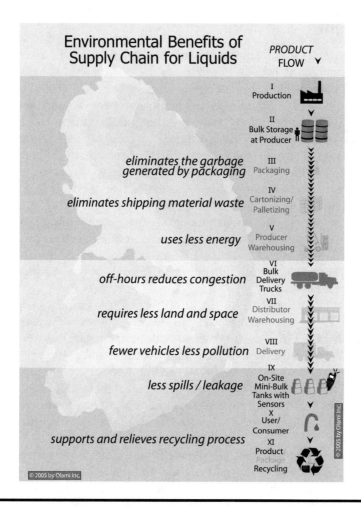

Exhibit 11.4   The Environment Is Another Big Winner from Supply Chain for Liquids

With the above background on the nature of environmental issues related to Supply Chain for Liquids, let us revisit our analysis of Supply Chain/Supply Chain for Liquids as we developed it in Chapter 5. In addition to the operational efficiencies described in the earlier chapters, we can examine each step in the Supply Chain/Supply Chain for Liquids flow as shown in Exhibit 11.4 from an environmental perspective.

Step 1: Production, and Step 2: Bulk Storage at Producer

From an environmental perspective, there is no difference between the production process as it relates to Supply Chain versus Supply Chain for

Liquids. However, to the degree to which the Supply Chain for Liquids is extended upstream from the producer to its suppliers, the environmental benefits described here accrue to the production process. This does not refer only to the liquid ingredients used to produce liquid products, but to all liquids purchased and used in the production facility — cleaning materials, lubricants and other machine maintenance products, and building maintenance materials such as waxes and coatings. These materials in particular are often purchased in plastic jugs and bottles, and moving their handling to the Supply Chain for Liquids system yields the environmental benefits related to packaging described below. The experience of one producer may also be telling in terms of the impact of the Supply Chain for Liquids method. When considering implementation of Supply Chain for Liquids practices, the company contacted one of its major customers to review the impact of the change on their relationship. It turned out that the customer had a problem with the local environmental protection authorities that they had not been able to figure out how to solve, in terms of a local warehouse that was under threat of penalty or closure. In reviewing the customer's needs and the producer's suggested approach, they both realized that the proposed Supply Chain for Liquids method resolved the problem beautifully.

Step 3: Packaging, and Step 11: Product/Package Recycling

The amount of packaging used for liquid products, and the environmental benefit of the Supply Chain for Liquids, is quite literally mountainous. The number of disposable containers of all types — plastic, tin, BIB packaging — used in B2B (business to business) sales in the United States exceeded 25 billion in 2002 alone, or a litter of 80 bottles for each person in the country.

Even at an estimated recycling rate of 25 percent for these containers, the environmental benefit of eliminating packaging is enormous. The best way to recycle is to eliminate the need for recycling. The elimination of the entire recycling process for these containers — on-site storage at the customer site, transporting the containers to the recycling facility, operation of the recycling facility — frees up the land and energy resources used in this process. Even greater are the environmental benefits associated with the elimination of the remaining 75 percent of packaging that is disposed through garbage collection, incineration, landfills, etc. Given the volume of containers, some 2000 garbage trucks are operating throughout the United States each day just to remove disposable liquid-packaging waste.

The protection against chemical and other liquid residues is another benefit of Supply Chain for Liquids. When containers that have been used for liquids are thrown away or placed for recycling, a certain amount of the contents of the containers will have remained inside the containers. That last little pool of liquid at the bottom of the container does not disappear; it will either leak out or be washed out into the sanitation system. Given the number of containers described above, and the nasty nature of some B2B liquids, the environmental benefit of eliminating this "last drop" is significant.

Looking at "how nature does it," we note that liquids have an interesting and environmentally efficient way of dealing with their own packaging. The surface tension of a droplet or bubble of liquid creates a "skin" from the liquid molecules themselves, which serves as the "packaging" for the droplet. Less environmentally friendly is the fact that water has a very strong cohesive force and thus a high surface tension, so we add soap to water to reduce the surface tension, allowing greater penetration of cloth so that we can clean our clothes better — at the cost of polluting the water that comes out of this process.

Step 4: Cartonizing/Palletizing

Many types of packaging such as jugs and bottles are placed in cartons, and the cartons are placed on pallets at the end of the packaging process. These cartons and pallets, in addition to the direct packaging materials described above, come at an environmental price, and their elimination under a Supply Chain for Liquids approach radically reduces that price. Although many cartons and pallets are built for repeat use, they eventually end up in the garbage dump or recycling process, just like the packaging materials described above. Cartons and pallets are wood- and wood-derivative products, and about six million tons of pallets and ten million tons of cardboard boxes are landfilled each year in the United States. The use of plastic and metal pallets has increased to the point that they have captured about 11 percent of the pallet market, with the resulting environmental deterioration resulting from the use of these materials.

Step 5: Producer Warehousing, and
Step 7: Distributor Warehousing

Huge 500,000-square-foot warehouses are commonplace in the liquids Supply Chain to hold the volumes of liquids commonly held in the warehousing and distribution process. The size and resources needed for warehouses are inflated by the fact that, due to packaging practice, only 62 percent of the volume of a carton actually holds liquid product. That is, a one-gallon bottle placed in a carton takes up enough space for 1.6 gallons of liquid. Including the empty space surrounding product held on a rack in a warehouse — between the product and the rack above, aisle space for the forklift, etc. — well less than half of the total space is actually used by the liquid. Supply Chain for Liquids also lends itself to vertical space usage and is not limited by the reach of forklifts, rack strength, or other factors. Translating this to a physical warehouse facility, it is clear that 500,000 square feet of warehousing sitting on a footprint of twelve acres, for example, is equivalent to a liquid-oriented warehouse sitting on under nine acres that would still enjoy a modest increase in product capacity. The environmental impact of actually running the warehouse or distribution center — energy consumption, generation of waste, etc. — would be lowered by a corresponding amount. The savings in energy of even a small reduction in warehouse space would be considerable in light of U.S. Department of Energy figures showing that large warehouse buildings consume a total of 285 trillion BTU of fuel for their operations.

Step 6: Trucking, and Step 8: Delivery

Not only does standard Supply Chain practice add packaging material on top of the product, as well as requiring storage space for the product together with its packaging, but then when the product is finally moved, along goes the packaging together with the product. It is like adding insult to injury. Given the space usage of packaging described above, it requires 160 trucks to move the same amount of product under traditional Supply Chain thinking as 100 trucks using a Supply Chain for Liquids method. Those other 60 trucks are using fuel, creating pollution, and impacting the environment in all of the worst ways for material transportation. But the reduced number of trucks under the Supply Chain for Liquids approach is only one aspect of the environmental advantages of this system. As described in Chapter 5, the limitations of the Supply Chain approach mean that product must be delivered during receiving hours, usually during the day. Supply Chain for Liquids is much more flexible, and so delivery can take place based on routing efficiency, such as at night. The operational efficiencies described in Chapter 5 translate directly into environmental benefits. A truck that can cover 18 stops under Supply Chain for Liquids in the same time that a truck makes 12 stops using standard Supply Chain practice has a much higher product-to-pollution ratio, making it a win-win-win situation for the distributor, the customer, and the environment.

Step 9: On-Site Handling and Storage

The operational efficiencies of a Supply Chain for Liquids on-site storage system are described in Chapter 5, and the reduction in packaging-waste disposal are described above. Because jugs and containers are not being handled by the user, spillage is minimized and the risk of environmental contamination is reduced.

The general trend toward convenience outlets in a number of industries — convenience stores for beverages, do-it-for-me oil changes at quick-lube shops, etc. — means that a higher number of smaller sites are being created that handle liquids of different types in different ways. The total number of convenience stores in the United States, for example, has grown to over 132,000 or an average of more than 2600 per state. This spreads the environmental issues related to liquid handling at convenient stores over a very wide area. Of greater concern environmentally are the 15,000+ quick-lube sites spread across the United States, of which 87 percent are independently owned. Providing the methodologies that minimize spills and leakage from each of these sites — and that simplify and encourage the recycling of used motor oil and other automotive maintenance fluids — is critical to their operation in an environmentally sound manner. Supply Chain for Liquids meets exactly these criteria.

Step 10: User/Consumer

As described in Chapter 8, the user may have a vastly different consumption experience when using liquids that have come through a Supply Chain for Liquids rather than a Supply Chain. However, assuming that the dispense/usage of the liquids is identical in both cases, there are no environmental implications to the use of either method.

In terms of environmental friendliness, in summary you could say that the connection between the Supply Chain for Liquids and the environment is "in the stars." Aquarius, the water bearer (or "Supply Chain for Liquids person"), is a blazing part of nature for all to see. In a cosmic extension of Supply Chain for Liquids, it is said that Zeus poured all the waters from the heavens out onto the Earth to wash away and destroy the wicked and evil people. This brought forth a fresh start for Deucalion and his wife, Pyrrha, who threw stones over their shoulders to create a new race of men and women. Perhaps it may be said that implementing a Supply Chain for Liquids system is the business equivalent of entering the Age of Aquarius.

Achieving OSCFL Status

"Until the wind and the rain alone shall wear them away." John Gutzon de la Mothe Borglum took the long view in describing the durability of his most ambitious work, Mt. Rushmore. It would be great to create something that would simply stand there and draw awed crowds, but that is not what Supply Chain for Liquids is all about. Supply Chain for Liquids is more akin to the corner bakery; the cookies have to be good every day in order for customers to keep coming back. It is not just that the *product* has to be good, but the *process* must also be good if the result is to be a consistently good product. Similarly, Supply Chain for Liquids must always perform at a market-competitive level. Built into the logistics system must be the mechanisms to constantly upgrade the flow based on changing customer requirements and evolving technological capabilities. This capability is part of optimal Supply Chain for Liquids status.

Optimal Supply Chain for Liquids is product-independent in that the nature of the product is not the focus of Optimal Supply Chain for Liquids. Like the ISO quality standards, where quality is defined by repeatability and measurement of processes rather than by characteristics of the products themselves, Optimal Supply Chain for Liquids focuses on the Supply Chain for Liquids process that a company has undertaken.

Because Supply Chain for Liquids is such a large and flexible opportunity that can be handled in so many different ways, Optimal Supply Chain for Liquids is made up of three aspects of the Supply Chain for Liquids process: envisioning, execution, and evolution. Achieving Optimal Supply Chain for Liquids status means that all of these elements have been successfully addressed, and addressed as a continuous cycle. Major elements of Optimal Supply Chain for Liquids are described in more detail below.

Envisioning

A successful process starts with a vision, and envisioning encompasses all aspects of a Supply Chain for Liquids project up to the point of execution. In addition to the formal planning process and other elements included in the Liquid Lens approach as described in Chapter 3, envisioning includes the method used to communicate the vision, the level of management involvement in the front-end processes, and the establishment of a formal methodology for approaching the Supply Chain for Liquids project. The reason for this emphasis in optimal Supply Chain for Liquids is that preparation is nine-tenths of success, and an Optimal Supply Chain for Liquids approach sets a company up to succeed rather than laying the groundwork for failure. The importance of this approach cannot be overemphasized. Sun Tzu put "Laying Plans" as his leading chapter in *The Art of War*, and concludes it by saying:

> The general who wins a battle makes many calculations in his temple before the battle is fought ... the general who loses a battle makes but few calculations beforehand. Thus do many

calculations lead to victory, and few calculations to defeat: how much more no calculation at all! It is by attention to this point that I can foresee who is likely to win or lose.

A Supply Chain for Liquids project, like many business activities, should be planned as if a battle were about to take place. Those who do so are working according to Optimal Supply Chain for Liquids principles, and those who do not can still accomplish Supply Chain for Liquids operation, but it is unlikely that this will be at the same level as that achieved from full preparation. How can Supply Chain for Liquids operation be achieved "by accident"? Many systems evolve over time and are actually patchworks of different technologies implemented at different times and for different objectives. The result of such a process may include sensors and a reporting system that bears some resemblance to a Supply Chain for Liquids system, but the lack of systemwide planning means that the flow is not fully integrated or does not take full advantage of the liquid nature of the product. But like those "free prize" offers of a "blender" if you will just listen to a sales pitch — where the prize turns out to be a crappy plastic hand-turned mixer instead of a real blender — a haphazardly evolved system is just not going to get the job done as well as the real thing.

The envisioning stage of an optimal Supply Chain for Liquids project is characterized by a certain amount of vagueness embedded in a great deal of clarity. The vagueness relates to the specifics of the planned system — what the Supply Chain for Liquids system will look like, how partners such as suppliers and customers will relate to it, and all of the other issues that are addressed during the envisioning/planning process. The clarity relates to how the company approaches the project, communicates the goals of the project, and lays the groundwork for the execution phase. That is, the method to be used to conduct the project must be completely defined even while the specific contents and anticipated results of the project are not yet known. Optimal Supply Chain for Liquids does not allow the uncertainty (the contents) to cloud the clear (the method).

The envisioning process for Supply Chain for Liquids incorporates the Liquid Lens methodology described in Chapter 3. The true value of Supply Chain for Liquids is in its foundation as a logistics-oriented system, rather than merely being an adaptation of a discrete-based system for liquid purposes. The Liquid Lens serves to focus on and clarify the liquid-specific aspects of the logistics system, and thus convert a standard Supply Chain approach into a Supply Chain for Liquids approach. Full adherence to all aspects of the Liquid Lens approach lays the groundwork for achieving Optimal Supply Chain for Liquids status, that is, the most effective liquids-based logistics system that the company is able to plan and execute. Let us look at several Liquid Lens techniques that lead to optimizing the Supply Chain for Liquids process.

Logistics Characteristics of Liquid Products

As a liquids-based system, it is natural that Supply Chain for Liquids will take advantage of the fundamental characteristics of liquids. The basic characteristics are that they flow, leading to the use of tanks/pipes, and that they have a constant level, leading to the use of sensors to measure the level and thus the volume of liquid at specified points along the supply stream. With these two characteristics in mind, we can create a Supply Chain for Liquids system that works according to the principles that we have defined in this book. An optimal approach goes farther than this. Did we look at all of the characteristics of our products, including those listed in Chapter 3, and examine the logistics implications of each? Did we follow the entire flow of the liquids from the point of production to the point of dispense to identify the conditions they would be in for the whole path, with any characteristics that might be influenced by those conditions? These types of activities mean going beyond obvious techniques and taking full advantage of the liquid nature of the products we are working with.

The liquid nature of the product may also lead to optimization in a different direction. As discussed in Chapter 3, "production" steps of some products may be moved well downstream, as far as the point of dispense. Such a move may involve producing the product to "age" along the logistics process, introducing chemical or other reactions downstream, or keeping ingredients separate further down the supply stream and combining them at the customer or point of dispense. An Optimal Supply Chain for Liquids approach includes an examination of this possibility and including it in the Supply Chain for Liquids design to the degree that it is appropriate.

All Parts of the System Work Together

The Liquid Lens tells us that all the parts of the system should be one integrated flow, each part playing off the strengths and limitations of the other parts. One way of measuring whether we have optimized this factor is to ask what capabilities each piece has that is *not* being utilized by the other parts of the system. That is, where are the points of nonintegration between the parts of the system, and where are there capabilities that are not being used to logistics advantage? Another way of measuring whether we have optimized the interaction between the different parts of the system is to identify where "buffers" are required, usually manual interventions in a process. Manual activities often fill in disconnects between parts of a system and show inefficiency in the system. An optimized system does not mean that manual steps have been eliminated; manual activities should be provided for at the appropriate control points throughout the flow. Full automation of every buffer may not be possible or cost-effective, so that manual interventions would stay in place. Identifying the buffers during the envisioning stage, and determining that each of them is in fact required or justified, is a step toward ensuring the implementation of an Optimal Supply Chain for Liquids system.

Finding New Opportunities through the Liquid Lens

Supply Chain for Liquids is not just doing better what we are already doing, but rather it is intended to create opportunities that do not currently exist. Optimization of new opportunities is not a quantifiable activity, but the process undertaken to seek and develop new opportunities testifies to the level of effectiveness of the effort in this area. We can ask certain questions that will point to the nature of the process. During the Supply Chain for Liquids planning process, who was involved in the effort to identify new opportunities — operations, sales, marketing, finance, product development, strategy/top management, R&D? How well did each area grasp the potential of the system and develop plans for taking advantages of the opportunities that a Supply Chain for Liquids system offers? How much contact was made with suppliers, customers, and potential customers, and how early in the process, so that they could interact on the potential benefits to be gained from Supply Chain for Liquids? Out of the plans that were developed based on both the internal and external forums, how specific were they? The results of such a forward-looking process are more optimized if they include specific action steps, responsibilities, and a timetable for carrying out the defined plans. The effort becomes Optimal Supply Chain for Liquids when a review of the activities shows that planning related to new opportunities was broad-based, specific, and then during the execution/evolution phases led to results that would not have been available without implementation of the Supply Chain for Liquids system.

Wider Impact of Supply Chain for Liquids

Any venture of the type and magnitude of Supply Chain for Liquids will create surprises, that is, it will produce results, issues, or problems that were not foreseen during the planning process. A measure of how well the envisioning process is optimized is how much "firefighting" occurs during execution and evolution — how much of the implementation is proactive and deals with activities that were planned for, versus unexpected activities that move the effort into reactive mode to deal with unanticipated situations. The occurrence of many unexpected or unplanned situations may indicate problems with the planning process that would prevent the Supply Chain for Liquids system from being considered optimal. Defective planning includes failing to be sufficiently inclusive in having all affected groups involved in the planning and preparation for the system, failure to understand and follow through on the impact of the changes included in moving to a Supply Chain for Liquids system, and failure to communicate the overall vision for the system as well as the detailed plan and operation of the system among all the parties involved. Such situations inhibit a company from realizing the full value of a Supply Chain for Liquids system and from achieving Optimal Supply Chain for Liquids status.

Simplify

A fundamental principle of Supply Chain for Liquids is to eliminate complexities and costs rather than build additional systems and procedures on top of the liquid-logistics flow. A measure of the effectiveness of the envisioning process is how well the Supply Chain for Liquids "diet" worked. That is, to what degree is the logistics flow fundamentally simpler under Supply Chain for Liquids design than under the prior operating method? To what degree is the fact that we are working with liquid products reflected in the streamlining of the projected supply stream? Like a diet, there is no clear border between "it worked" and "it worked optimally," but the degree of simplification relative to the prior system, and the degree of simplification in absolute terms such as in the total number of touchpoints as described later in this chapter, are measures of how much the plan for the Supply Chain for Liquids system has been optimized.

These measures of how well a company adhered to the Liquid Lens approach during the envisioning process point to whether the company has achieved optimal Supply Chain for Liquids status.

Execution

Machu Picchu is extraordinary in many ways. Starting with pretty tough conditions — the top of a peak in the Peruvian Andes that is generally covered with clouds — the founders of Machu Picchu put together a settlement that fused amazingly to the physical and spiritual environment in which it was placed. The layout of the place conformed to and took advantage of each aspect of the terrain for different purposes. The rock outcroppings were incorporated as part of the walls of houses and other structures, the (relatively) flat parts were extended by terraces for agriculture, and the water flow took advantage of the natural terrain. The harmony of the basic environment with the structures that have been put on top of it is striking. Beyond this integration with the setting, the builders constructed structures of great precision, with large multifaced stones fitting together without any gap and also without any mortar. Spiritually, the Incas put the whole thing together as well, from the caves from which life sprang to the column on the mountain to which the sun was hitched. The place is almost breathtaking in the extraordinariness of its execution.

What makes extraordinary — or in our case, optimal — execution? An Optimal Supply Chain for Liquids system is more than just a logistics system that works. First, it reflects an optimal planning or envisioning process, and it is true to that process in its execution. The "system" nature of the process is evident. Just as visibility into product throughout the supply stream has become clear, so the visibility of each player into the operation of the whole system and his or her position within the overall system have become clear. Like a building that proclaims the skills of its architect, an Optimal Supply Chain for Liquids system makes clear the integrated and innovative thought that stands behind it.

Second, optimal execution is measured by the results it leads to. The fulfillment of Supply Chain for Liquids metrics, as described later in the chapter, is an indication that the process is working optimally. The achievement of operational, financial, marketing, and strategic/business goals strengthen the optimal nature of the implementation. To use an image described earlier, if the pile of results in one corner of the room is very high, and the pile of excuses in another corner is difficult to find, then the company is headed in the direction of running an Optimal Supply Chain for Liquids system.

All of this does not mean that the execution or result of Supply Chain for Liquids has to be flashy or highly visible to be optimal. Like Machu Picchu, which escaped the conquistadores' attention by being essentially invisible to them despite all of its internal glories, an Optimal Supply Chain for Liquids system blends into operations without fanfare. In many ways, optimal execution is in fact measured by the degree of invisibility. If the users at a site never see a delivery person, never are involved with product logistics, and yet never run out of product, then the system is doing all it can do for them and is running optimally from their perspective.

Evolution

An Optimal Supply Chain for Liquids system plants the seeds for its own growth. If a company has created an environment in which the Liquid Lens and the Supply Chain for Liquids approaches feed on themselves and are constantly streamlining and expanding themselves, then it has achieved Optimal Supply Chain for Liquids status. This condition expresses itself in several ways.

Optimal Supply Chain for Liquids status results from a system that incorporates not only one-off reductions in costs and complexities, but also ongoing savings and efficiencies for the company and the supply stream. We expect, for example, that moving to handling of liquids in tanks at a warehouse or distribution center rather than in containers/pallets will lead to a cost reduction in the operation of the warehouse facility, but we would like to go beyond this. Are the resources that were freed up by moving to the Supply Chain for Liquids system being utilized for other purposes, or have they been removed from the company? Are the successes of implementing a Supply Chain for Liquids system being continued to expand the benefits of the system, or have they stagnated into a steady state? These are the issues that distinguish an Optimal Supply Chain for Liquids system in evolutionary mode.

Another measure of the achievement of Optimal Supply Chain for Liquids status is the organizational result of having undertaken the process. Successfully undertaking a major business initiative leaves an organization in a different state than it was before it was started. This can be compared to undertaking a major quality project. If you have been involved in a TQM (total quality management) project, you may have made an astonishing discovery — that as soon as you get where you originally decided to go, you realize that the opportunities to go further are even larger than the opportunities that have been created thus far. This revelation fits well with the requirement for evolution, the continual adaptation of an organism both to changes within the organism and to changes in the organism's surroundings. If you undertake all of the mechanical aspects of a project and reach each of the particular objectives defined in the original plan, then you have been successful at Supply Chain for Liquids. But if you blow past those objectives with a whole array of new opportunities and new initiatives based on where Supply Chain for Liquids has brought you, then you are in Optimal Supply Chain for Liquids territory. Optimal Supply Chain for Liquids is characterized by endless horizons.

Achieving Optimal Supply Chain for Liquids status means having fulfilled all aspects of the process — envisioning, execution, and evolution. When the envisioning process is complete and comprehensive, when execution follows the plan with positive adjustments during the implementation process, and when evolution ensures ongoing adaptation of the system, then a company has achieved Optimal Supply Chain for Liquids status. Further information about formal recognition for having achieved Optimal Supply Chain for Liquids status can be found at www.Supply-ChainForLiquids.com, the Internet site for Supply Chain for Liquids.

Supply Chain for Liquids Metrics

When we design or implement a Supply Chain for Liquids system, we want to know how well it is doing and how well we are doing. As part of the Supply Chain for Liquids process, we create a set of measures that will draw a picture of the proposed system's performance and our current performance.

Metrics — General Considerations

Before reviewing some specific metrics that might be useful in evaluating the Supply Chain for Liquids, we will address some of the basic concepts of metrics.

Metrics Can Be Very Powerful, but in Their Power They Can Be Very Dangerous

We can use incentive compensation as an example of the use of metrics that can lead to the wrong result. It is not uncommon that after an incentive plan is put in place, some aspects of a business start to suffer. If a plan incentivizes the quantity of production without addressing the quality of production, the quantity of good pieces is likely to go up, but the quantity of bad pieces may go up just as much or even more. If an incentive plan addresses both quantity and quality, workers may be in conflict over what work to perform. For some products, quantity/quality improvements might be easier than for other products, and suddenly the first shift might be doing all the production for the "easy" products, leaving the second shift to dog it with the tough ones. Such a situation can lead to problems not only internally, with conflict between employees or groups of employees, but also externally, such as with missed shipments and a decrease in the level of customer service.

It is clear that the right metrics must be defined, but in addition, the right combination of metrics must be defined. The balance of metrics, and the proper weighting of each, is a critical but sometimes overlooked aspect of metrics development.

The Common Phrase Related to Metrics Is That "What Gets Measured Gets Attention," but the Importance of Metrics Goes beyond the Pure Numbers

The metrics concept easily rolls into the concept of nurturing: anything that is nurtured, that is paid attention to, that is watered, and that is given air and sunshine will flourish, while anything that is not nurtured will not flourish. To the degree that metrics get people to pay attention to a certain area, that area will thrive. The story is told of the manager who would hire a summer intern to perform a certain study each year. Each year an intern was hired, the same study was performed and results reported, and the intern left and the report was forgotten. Each year, the same thing happened. When the manager was asked why she had the same study done every year and never implemented the findings, she replied that this process was well worth the effort. Each year there was a noticeable improvement in the area being studied while the study was under way, and the improvement lasted four to six months after the completion of the study. The benefit to the company was far more than the cost of the intern, so the manager was happy to do it each year. As long as someone was paying attention, the work was done more effectively. This story demonstrates the power of nurture, which could be considered to be a side effect of metrics: if you pay attention to it, it will grow.

There Are Different Ways to Design and Deploy Metrics, and They Have Different Meanings and Different Objectives

There is an important distinction between what we could call performance metrics and management metrics. The difference essentially is that one tells you how well you are doing, and the other tells you what is wrong. This difference is very important. Normal metrics are designed and thought of as positive measures, with the goal of maintaining or improving a product or process that already exists. The fundamental assumption is that you measure something that "is," a condition or process that already exists. A different kind of measure is specifically designed to tell you what you do not want to know. You think of the worst things you could find out about your company or the area of operations you are responsible for, and you put in metrics for exactly those items. In creating this type of metric, you do not start out with what "is" and how to measure it; you start out with the measurement and figure out what the "is" is that could provide the data. These metrics are meant to let you know as early as possible what you are likely to find out later in any case, and hopefully to find out before real damage is done. Perhaps we can understand this by contrasting it to Mary Poppins's tape measure. When she pulls it out to measure the children, the result is not in inches or centimeters but rather a very blunt "measure" of the children's personalities. In truest management style, however, when Mary Poppins measures herself, the result is without equivocation — "Practically perfect in every way" reads the measurement.

What is the worst thing you could find out — what is your worst fear — about the logistics operation, for example? Perhaps it is that your competitors are beating you to the punch, that they are moving their product into the market faster than you are getting your product to the market, with all the implications of that speed. If that is true, you may not be as good as you think you are, and you definitely want to find that out as quickly as possible. In this case, you would define the method that could most effectively provide data to support this metric. The simplest method would be to discover if some other function in the company is already gathering this data or is in a position to gather it easily. For example, a field-service group could sample competitors' packages and record the production date on the label. A second level of data source would be to actually gather intelligence regarding competitors' operations. Sun Tzu said that spies are a critical element in the art of war, and industrial espionage is certainly a commonplace practice for just this type of information. Another route would be to buy the information. Industrial data services offer a huge amount of data and are often able to put together the right pieces to come up with the desired result. In any case, the starting point of this kind of measure is not "What can we measure?" but rather "What result are we afraid of seeing?"

Even the Most Precisely Defined Metrics Can Go Astray unless Everyone Understands Exactly What Is Being Measured

Even the simplest measure, such as "gallons produced per day," is subject to multiple interpretations that lead to different understandings and actions. Is it total gallons, or gallons of good production? Is it actual production of liquid, or the quantity that came off the packaging line? Is it production runs that were started, or production runs that were completed? During many years as a consultant, I learned how much people assume things that are different from what other people assume, and I learned the importance of asking different people in a company where certain key figures come from and what they mean. Far more often than you would think, there is not just one answer, but a series of different answers based on the understandings that different people have. We can use an out-of-this-world liquid example to illustrate the point.

When Percival Lowell discovered the canals on Mars, he was able to make conjectures about the canals and about Mars in general from some of the measures he took and observations he made, including the intelligence of the Martians that built the canals. The canals were a reddish color and moved slightly as he observed them. The problem with this metric is that what he thought he was seeing was not what he was actually seeing at all. Because of the reflective nature of the telescope he was using, he was not observing the canals of Mars, but rather the inflamed veins inside his own eyes. Talk about not understanding the metrics! And to carry the parallel further, Lowell's fame and expertise led others to follow his findings and lay out charts based on them. One misinterpretation of the metrics proliferated throughout the whole field either because of "fear of the boss," a "desire to believe" what was so exciting to believe, a "groupthink" mentality that did not want to question the findings, or any of the other reasons why scientists of yesteryear and businesspeople of today get caught in metrics traps.

The nature of metrics in Supply Chain for Liquids is different from metrics in measuring a single company's performance or a specific aspect of company performance such as production or sales. Supply Chain for Liquids runs the length of the logistics flow from the raw-material supplier to the point of dispense by the user, and as described in Chapter 3, Supply Chain for Liquids is created as a single integrated flow. Therefore it would be misleading to measure only one part of the Supply Chain for Liquids, because it would not reflect the integrated-flow nature of the process. Thus the metrics should be created systemwide whenever possible, or put in combination to reflect systemwide conditions, rather than reflecting only a single aspect of the system.

The basic metrics for the many aspects of standard Supply Chain are described in numerous articles and resources and need not be repeated here, as they apply to Supply Chain for Liquids as well. Our focus in this book is on the differences between Supply Chain and Supply Chain for Liquids, so we will describe the metrics that apply to Supply Chain for Liquids over and above those that apply to Supply Chain. In general, these fall into two categories. The first metrics we want to review are those related to the business-level objectives that led us to implement Supply Chain for Liquids, and the second are those that measure the results of Supply Chain for Liquids as against the earlier Supply Chain configuration.

Business-Level Metrics

The first set of metrics we want to define are those that measure the results of Supply Chain for Liquids in the broadest business sense. If we ask ourselves the question, "Why are we going through the Supply Chain for Liquids process?" then the first set of metrics measures the answers to this question. For example, if the answer to the question is "to beat the competition and be more profitable," then market share and profitability should be the top metrics. The metric is the "answer," and before setting it, we should make sure that we have defined the "question." Business-level metrics measure the answers to business-level questions. They do not care about the detailed logistical or operating aspects of Supply Chain for Liquids. They measure the things we wanted to change by putting the Supply Chain for Liquids approach into play.

Let us focus on the "first cause" motivation for undertaking Supply Chain for Liquids. Suppose we had been operating under some form of Supply Chain, saw what Supply Chain for Liquids could do for the company, and decided to upgrade to Supply Chain for Liquids. Within "what Supply Chain for Liquids could do for the company," we will find the objectives of implementing the approach together with the business-level metrics to measure the achievement of those objectives. At this level, we focus on (that is, we measure) *what* the result is, not *how* it is achieved. It could be stated in a number of different ways, and it should be stated in the terms the company used in approaching this project:

- *We see Supply Chain for Liquids as a weapon in our company's battle against our competition*: There are many detailed aspects of this objective, such as services provided to the customer as a differentiator under Supply Chain for Liquids or customer "lock-in" once Supply Chain for Liquids is implemented. As a business-level metric, though, this is not appropriate because we do not want to get lost in that level of detail. The measurement we should establish and track related to this business-level objective is the amount of business we have won from competitors and the amount of business we have lost to competitors in those markets in which we are implementing Supply Chain for Liquids. The metric of overall market share is less appropriate in this case, as it also includes overall expansion or contraction of the market. We could have a net gain in business from competitors but still lose market share if the market is growing faster than are our gains. We can battle the competition in many ways, but if at the end of the day we have not taken business away from our competition, then we have not achieved the business objective that we set for ourselves in undertaking the effort.
- *Our focus is on improving profitability by using the Supply Chain for Liquids approach*: A company might decide that profitability is the driving motivation for a Supply Chain for Liquids project, with the benefits of increased profitability and the use of the funds generated to be decided separately. Supply Chain for Liquids provides for savings in certain logistics areas, such as packaging, while incurring expenses in other areas, such as the on-site tanking system, although those expenses are comparable with the cost of racking for the same quantity of liquids. A company that is focused on profitability from this effort will pull together cost information under the prior methodology as well as under the Supply Chain for Liquids methodology, together with changes in the revenue flow, to be able to identify and track margin improvements from

the system. Cost reductions include both direct costs such as packaging and savings in indirect costs such as insurance and space. As a business-level metric, this will be at a consolidated level; the details of the component cost and revenue streams will be shown in the function-level metrics.

■ *We want to exploit the opportunities that Supply Chain for Liquids provides in new channel development, both for our existing products and for new product introductions:* This business objective relates to revenue enhancement as opposed to cost reduction, as emphasized in the previous objective. A company with this objective is not necessarily considering using Supply Chain for Liquids in its current operations but rather to increase sales through the addition of sales and distribution channels. As a business-level metric, the new channels that utilize the Supply Chain for Liquids approach should be identified and their volume and profitability tracked.

■ *Supply Chain for Liquids fits our corporate strategy of continued innovation and market leadership:* Some companies set innovation as a value within their corporate culture, and innovative approaches are valued because of the intrinsic benefits of the approaches and also to reinforce the marketplace's perception of the company as an innovative leader. Other companies specifically follow a copycat approach, waiting for the innovator to break through an innovative barrier and then duplicating the effort while incorporating lessons learned from the original innovator. In this case, the business-level metrics related to Supply Chain for Liquids might be more subjective than objective — results of the effort as reflected in the press or in the marketplace, the degree to which the Supply Chain for Liquids approach is incorporated into the company's selling and marketing effort, and similar indicators of the Supply Chain for Liquids effort as innovation. Again, although such subjective metrics are legitimate in some cases, the actual analysis on whether to implement Supply Chain for Liquids and to track its function-level results would be completely objective.

Business-level metrics are stated in terms of, and measure, business-level issues that represent the company's highest objectives to be achieved with Supply Chain for Liquids.

Function-Level Metrics

Although business-level metrics are critical to making sure we keep our eye on the "big picture," top-level action takes place based on operating-level activity. Function-level metrics are used to identify, monitor, maintain, and enhance the activity in different functional areas of the company, all of which come together to lead to the business-level results.

As stated above, typical Supply Chain metrics, including basic function-level metrics, are widely discussed and well described in the literature, and thus will not be restated in detail here. One of the major differentiating aspects of Supply Chain for Liquids is the ability to reduce complexity in the logistics flow, and a metric we can use related to complexity is that of touchpoints. A touchpoint refers to each time an act is performed on a product. At the most general level, the more touchpoints there are, the more activity/complexity there is, and the greater are the costs incurred along the process. The next level of information beyond the quantity of touchpoints is the content of touchpoints — the actual costs or energies occurred at each touchpoint. A reduction in the number and content of touchpoints — touchdowns — is generally good; correspondingly, an increase in the number and quantity of touchpoints — touchups — is generally bad.

Touchpoints do not relate just to when a person touches a product, but to any act that is performed on a product — moving, put-away, picking, packaging, and the whole list of operations that a product undergoes. Of course many touchpoints are necessary in any particular supply stream, and many are very effective in adding value to the product. Thus each touchpoint is normally evaluated separately for its effectiveness. What the Supply Chain for Liquids approach does, however, is create an integrated scheme that inherently allows for the elimination of many touchpoints as part of a single process. Examples of touchpoints for steps along a Supply Chain are shown below. The groupings of the touchpoints, the individual touchpoints that can be evaluated or eliminated, and the details and cost/benefit of each touchpoint must be identified for any particular implementation:

- Production (no logistics-based touchpoints)
- Bulk storage at producer (no logistics-based touchpoints)
- Packaging (note that touchpoints of the packaging are considered touchpoints of the product, because under the Supply Chain configuration, the package is considered part of the product)
  - Planning packaging line activity
  - Planning packaging materials
  - Purchasing/producing packaging materials
  - Receiving/inventorying/issuing packaging materials
  - Running the packaging line
  - Maintaining the packaging line
- Cartonizing/palletizing (also considered touchpoints of the product)
  - Planning cartonizing line activity
  - Planning carton materials
  - Purchasing/producing carton materials

- Receiving/inventorying/issuing carton materials
- Running the cartonizing line
- Maintaining the cartonizing line
- Purchasing/producing/repairing pallets
- Running the palletizer
- Maintaining the palletizer
■ Producer warehousing
- Putting the product into inventory at the producer warehouse, including both physical put-away and recording the product location
- Inventory activity at the producer warehouse: periodically counting the product, checking product quality, etc.
- Producer inventory planning and control: monitoring the inventory balance and requirements for the product, and entering production orders as required
- Picking and staging product: preparing the product for transport from the producer warehouse to the distributor or customer, including physical movement of the product and the planning/ recording of the picking/staging activity
■ Trucking
- Moving the product from the producer's warehouse to the distributor or distribution center
■ Distributor warehousing
- The physical and clerical activities associated with receiving product at the warehouse and placing it in inventory
- Inventory activity at the distributor warehouse: moving, counting, or checking the product held at the distributor warehouse
- Distributor inventory planning and control: evaluating product supply with product demand and taking the replenishment actions required
- Preparing for product delivery: delivery planning, picking and staging the product, and loading the delivery trucks, including both physical product movement and the associated clerical activities
■ Delivery
- Delivering the product to the customer site and putting the product in the required location at the customer
■ On-site handling
- Rotating product for quality purposes
- Taking product from on-site inventory for usage
- Handling product at the point of usage
- On-site inventory planning and control: comparing on-hand product balance with planned needs and ordering additional product as necessary

- User/consumer
  - Opening the package and pouring out the required quantity
  - Returning the unused portion of liquid
- Product/package recycling
  - Placing the container for refuse or recycling, or preparing the container for return and reuse

Each touchpoint can be broken down to more-detailed activities if appropriate, and the costs and benefits of the touchpoint defined. Any logistics operation should be evaluated for unnecessary or wasteful activities. The general rule of thumb is that activities that do not add value to a product should be targeted first for elimination. The Supply Chain for Liquids approach provides a framework that is more likely to lead to reduction in touchpoints and simplifies their identification and analysis.

As we have been developing the concept of Supply Chain for Liquids in this book, we have pointed out the many benefits that Supply Chain for Liquids offers relative to Supply Chain, and so these relative benefits are the metrics that we want to focus on here. Let us extract these metrics from the preceding chapters and lay them out here, so that each company can then put them together into the set of function-level metrics that are important to that company.

- Financial
  - *Per-unit cost of product*: The total of direct and indirect costs of the product. As we have seen in Chapter 11, costs are reduced in virtually every segment of the supply stream under the Supply Chain for Liquids system, but a per-entity (producer, distributor, customer, etc.) analysis of product cost is not sufficient. The per-unit cost of the product as accumulated throughout the entire logistics flow, that is, the total of all costs of the product incurred throughout the flow, is the most effective metric related to per-unit cost.
  - *Amount of product in the logistics flow*: The total quantity of product that is on hand at all of the points in the logistics flow plus the quantity that is in-transit within the logistics flow. A streamlined logistics-planning and -execution system will reduce the total amount of inventory in the system, starting with the producer's warehouse and going through the customer's warehouse, although inventory may actually rise at particular points in the system to accommodate the most efficient logistics flow.
  - *Total investment of product in the logistics flow*: The per-unit cost of product at each point in the flow multiplied by the quantity on hand at that point yields the total inventory investment at that

point, and summing these across all points in the logistics flow gives the total financial investment in inventory along the entire supply stream. The total cost of inventory to support a specific level of sales is an effective metric, whether the objective goes in either direction: either increasing the level of sales supported by the same inventory investment, or decreasing the inventory required to support a specific level of sales. It is also useful to compare these figures across different slices beside different flows for a single product. For example, comparing the investment for two products that pass through similar flows, or the same product that passes through different flows (such as a bulk channel and a packaged channel) can provide important information regarding the logistics effort required to support sales for each product/channel.

■ Marketing/strategy

  – *On-premise and off-premise penetration*: The financial metrics shown above address the expectation that costs will be reduced under a Supply Chain for Liquids system, and that total investment in inventory will also come down. Another result of this effort is revenue enhancement, the ability to increase sales in a number of ways. The first metric relates to increased sales through existing on-premise and off-premise channels. Supply Chain for Liquids works directly in the on-premise arena — restaurants, vehicle-service centers, factories, hotels, etc. — and so we expect to increase sales as the benefits of Supply Chain for Liquids take effect against the competition. In addition, on-premise sales are often a leader for off-premise sales, as customers who use a brand on-premise select it for off-premise consumption also. Thus we expect to see a rise in off-premise penetration that reflects that of on-premise sales.

  – *Sales in new sales and distribution channels*: Beyond increased sales in existing channels, our objectives for the Supply Chain for Liquids system may include the creation of new sales formats and distribution channels. As described in Chapter 8, the user experience may be significantly enhanced as the result of the implementation of a Supply Chain for Liquids system, both through improvements in existing methods and in the creation of new customer-interface points. The entire cycle of new placement opportunities, similar to that of new product introduction, is accompanied by metrics that allow evaluation of both the introduction process and the channel itself.

  – *Quality assurance*: Quality is often part of a marketing effort, as a product's purity, freshness, and other characteristics are emphasized and included in the product's image. The availability of quality-related metrics based on sensors along the supply stream allows a company to claim and live up to the highest levels of quality for the product right through to the point at which it is dispensed to the user/consumer.

■ Environmental

  – *Reduction in waste generation*: The most direct environmental metric related to the Supply Chain for Liquids system is the reduction in material used in the logistics process, specifically, the elimination of containers, cartons, and pallets. This is not a metric in the usual sense of trying to improve performance or reduce waste, because the elimination in packaging for products that flow through the Supply Chain for Liquids system is 100 percent. A company can define the quantity of packaging and other waste reduction that results from implementation of Supply Chain for Liquids in the on-premise portion of its business, as well as the percentage of waste eliminated across its total distribution operation, both on-premise and off-premise.

  – *Reduction in air pollution*: The reduction in pollution that results from the efficiencies inherent in Supply Chain for Liquids can be measured in a normalized manner, such as the number of gallons of truck fuel required per gallon of product delivered. Because between-customer transit time is reduced due to off-hours operation, and at-site delivery time/truck-idle time is reduced because of the much quicker product delivery process, truck usage is made much more efficient, and truck-generated pollution is correspondingly reduced. The metric of fuel per gallon of product is derived from total gallons of fuel used and total gallons of product delivered; the absolute quantity of gasoline savings is also an indicator of reduction in air pollution.

  – *Warehouse-related reductions in air, land, and water pollution*: The environmental metrics associated with changes in warehouse operation under Supply Chain for Liquids fall into several categories. Each of the changes relates to the reduction in a specific type of environmental impact. Tank-based warehousing takes up a smaller footprint for the same amount of liquid product, thus reducing land pollution by taking less land for a warehouse or freeing up space in an existing warehouse so that additional warehouse space does not have to be built. Eliminating the need for forklifts and other mechanical transport devices within a warehouse decreases the air pollution that they generate or the use of resources required to run them. Damage to packaging that results in product spills and the resulting water pollution is eliminated. Each of these savings can be measured relative to the corresponding metrics for packaged-based operations to show the differential under the Supply Chain for Liquids system.

These are not all of the metrics that can be used in a logistics system, and many types of metrics are described in the standard Supply Chain literature. The metrics mentioned here are among those that differentiate a Supply Chain for Liquids system from a standard Supply Chain system, and quantify the differences between them.

Supply Chain for Liquids Society

It is common for people in a certain business to identify themselves according to the industry that the business is in and to participate in activities of that particular industry. For example, people in the health-care industry read health-care newsletters, go to health-care conventions, and belong to health-care associations. Retailing is the same way, hospitality is the same way, and every other industry is the same way. Like natural selection and the gene pool, though, there is atrophy in commonality and power in diversity. The health-care industry and the retail industry each have something to offer the other when it comes to Supply Chain for Liquids: within the context of those points in which the operations of each are similar, each can demonstrate tools and techniques that could be adapted for use in the other. A productive method for handling floor wax in the health-care industry might be adaptable to the handling of grape drink in the retail industry.

For this reason the Supply Chain for Liquids Society serves to cross-fertilize the industries in which liquid products are produced, handled, or used. The Society provides informational and educational forums in the spirit of the Liquid Lens, assuming that a person responsible for distributing automotive lubricants is open to learn, adapt, and utilize an idea or technique used by a person responsible for distributing beverages in a prison. One of the most powerful characteristics of Supply Chain for Liquids is its flexibility. The exact same principles hold true for virtually any type of liquid, in any quantities or configurations, and in almost any application. This gives the Supply Chain for Liquids Society its value to liquid-logistics practitioners.

By its very nature, the Supply Chain for Liquids Society defines liquids as an industry in the sense that it is the liquid nature of the product, and not the particular usage or characteristics of the product, that is the primary focus. The various issues raised in this book — the cross-industry nature of liquid usage, the physical characteristics of liquids, common techniques related to liquid logistics, the nature and operation of the supply stream — all deal with liquids generically rather than any specific liquid or type of liquid in particular. As in any industry, each company and each product will have its own specific characteristics, and the Supply Chain for Liquids approach is tuned to each application inside each vertical industry. This does not diminish the importance of liquids as a separate industry. More information about the Supply Chain for Liquids Society can be found at the Web site www.SupplyChainForLiquids.com, along with other Supply Chain for Liquids–related features.

Chapter 12

Supply Chain for Liquids for Discrete Products

This book is about supply streams for liquid products, and the discussion has focused on a trademarked approach — Supply Chain for Liquids®. As we have seen, Supply Chain for Liquids can provide huge leaps forward for the Supply Chain for liquid products — logistically, financially, operationally, and in many other ways. Supply Chain for Liquids is a powerhouse concept.

In this book we have focused only on liquid products, or those products that to some degree behave like liquids, as described in Chapter 1. As one last step in this process, we can look into the possibility of making the Great Leap Backward. If Supply Chain for Liquids is seen as the next step forward beyond Supply Chain, can we take Supply Chain for Liquids principles and apply them back to the discrete products that make up the bulk of Supply Chain activity?

We do not have to work very hard to see the value of this exercise. While many companies use a lot of liquids in either their products or their processes, they also use discrete products throughout their operations, again related to both products and processes. If even some of the benefits of Supply Chain for Liquids could be brought to bear on their discrete products, the advantage would be significant, even if not to the full degree of Supply Chain for Liquids for liquid products.

An additional reason to ask this question is that even companies whose core products are all liquids — lubricants, liquid soaps, beverages, chemicals, oils, etc. — may need to handle some of them as liquids using the

405

Supply Chain for Liquids method while handling others as discrete products, such as liquids packaged in bottles, jugs, or drums. As we described in Chapter 3, part of the planning for Supply Chain for Liquids includes identifying which parts of the business utilize each type of distribution channel — those that can utilize a Supply Chain for Liquids system and those that cannot. Motor oil is an example of a product that follows both of these flows. Motor oil sold to quick-lube shops or automobile dealerships, for example, fits the profile of products that benefit from the Supply Chain for Liquids, while motor oil sold at retail for home use, in very small quantities per purchase and in very small containers, is more appropriate for a discrete (container) approach. Because these channels are generally completely separate from each other, using Supply Chain for Liquids for some products/channels and standard discrete-based Supply Chain for other products/channels does not inherently represent any type of a problem. Each type of customer is handled in the appropriate way. But these companies, having gained the benefit of Supply Chain for Liquids for one set of customers, could further enhance their operations by bringing at least some of the Supply Chain for Liquids approach to their discrete-product channels.

On the face of it, the relationship between the liquid and discrete approaches may seem "black and white" and mutually exclusive, but there are already cases in which crossover exists between the two. An example of this is the "ice cream" you buy at some fast-food restaurants. While it behaves as a discrete item when dispensed to the customer — ice cream sitting on top of a cone or in a cup — it is actually a liquid from the point of production through the entire distribution process until it is poured into the ice cream dispense machine. Only within the dispense unit is it partially frozen to take on its solid form. In other words, this is a solid that could benefit 100 percent from the Supply Chain for Liquids approach. Because it is a liquid during its entire lifetime up to the point of dispense, it could flow through the Supply Chain for Liquids system just like any other liquid. In addition to food products, other products used in manufacturing and construction environments, such as epoxies, adhesives, and polyurethanes, behave in a similar way and could also utilize the Supply Chain for Liquids approach.

A broader application of Supply Chain for Liquids principles to discrete products focuses on the *processes* rather than on the *products* themselves. So now let us look at the processes that characterize Supply Chain for Liquids versus Supply Chain and see how discrete products can be put through similar processes, or at least processes that offer some of the benefits of the corresponding Supply Chain for Liquids process.

One of the key elements that differentiates liquid logistics from discrete logistics is the ability to move product as a flow rather than as individual units. Liquids move continuously along the path or channel that has been defined for them, while discrete items are moved, usually manually, from place to place. Liquids use a mechanism that is in place — a pipe or tank — to control their movements, while discrete items are normally moved by equipment that moves with the product — a forklift, hand truck, by hand, etc. If we think about situations in which discrete products move according to a Supply Chain for Liquids-type flow, we quickly arrive at what is considered to be one of the greatest breakthroughs in industrial history — the mass-production assembly line.

The classic image of such a production line, that of a long line of car doors suspended from a conveyor line in an automobile assembly plant, well illustrates the parallel between Supply Chain for Liquids and this approach for discrete items. With Supply Chain for Liquids, the product flows along the path of the pipe and within the pipe; with mass production assembly, the product flows along the path of the conveyor line, generally either on or under the line. What does this mean? It could be showing us that handling discrete products as closely as possible to the way that liquids are handled represents the most effective approach to logistics for discrete products. A mass production line mimics the flow of liquid products in a pipeline as closely as it possibly can for discrete products. Could it be that this model, discrete products mimicking liquid products, can advance the logistics related to discrete products — a sort of "Adapted Supply Chain for Discrete"? Could it be that much of the development of the discrete world — from the printing press in place of handwritten works to the assembly line in place of handmade units — represents an attempt at convergence of the discrete and liquid methods? Let us look at these questions more closely and find out if what goes around does indeed come around.

After only a first-pass look at moving products, we saw that in some cases movement of discrete products is considered to be at its most effective when handled in a way similar to that in which liquid products are moved. Handling discrete products in a flow, such as on a production line, closely resembles a liquid flow. Now let us look at another stage of the logistics process for discrete items and see whether there is a comparison to liquid logistics. If so, we may be able to validate this comparison and want to explore it in more detail.

The comparison of the production line to the delivery truck focused on a point-to-point flow, the most simple movement of discrete products (and, correspondingly, liquid products) from one point to another. A more complex comparison is the many-to-one flow that characterizes a different step in the liquid-logistics flow — moving product from several different tanks at the production or distribution facility to the truck for transport or delivery. As we have described, a liquid product can be placed in any number of tanks that are connected through piping. As the "picking" process occurs, these liquids flow from the tanks through the pipes and to the truck. We can compare this with a standard discrete process in which a picker or forklift driver goes to a location in the warehouse where the material is kept, picks it, carries or moves the material to a staging location, and from there loads it on the truck. In this scenario, the picker is moving together with the material. If we apply the liquid-logistics approach to discrete products, it would look something like this. Discrete products are located in any number of bins throughout the warehouse facility. These locations are not necessarily physically connected, but they are logically connected so that all the locations in which a specific product is found can be readily identified. As the picking process occurs, these discrete products "flow" from the locations to the staging area near the truck. As described above, this "flow" corresponds to the piping in which liquid products move, and it can take any of a number of formats.

If we take a look at the discrete flow we have just described, we see that it is nothing more or less than the pinnacle of warehouse logistics for discrete items — an automated warehouse system! An automated warehouse, such as with conveyors that take product from its rack position and move it to a staging area, is similar in flow to a corresponding system for liquids. We can take this comparison further and say that the advantages of automated warehouses are in some cases the same as those for the Supply Chain for Liquids system: reduced space usage for the same amount of product, less manual involvement in the logistics process, etc. This is not to say that an automated or semiautomated warehouse is for everyone. Relative to a system for liquids, they are expensive and complex to implement. What we do learn from this is that we can validate the comparison between liquid and discrete logistics and go to the next step to see what we can learn from liquid logistics for application to discrete logistics.

One of the characteristics of the Supply Chain for Liquids approach is that it is very difficult to measure quantities of liquids directly, so we do not even try. This book focuses quite closely on always having visibility into the quantity of liquid in any particular location, and yet out of all the methods that we have described, we did not suggest at any point that the quantity be measured directly. For example, in a 300-gallon tank, we do not measure how many gallons are in the tank. We can indirectly measure the quantity in the tank in a number of different ways. We can measure the height of the liquid in the tank, and based on the physical dimensions of the tank we calculate the volume of the liquid. Similarly, by measuring the weight of the liquid in the tank, or the pressure on a sensor in the bottom of the tank, and knowing the weight per unit, we calculate the quantity of liquid in the tank. We accomplish the same thing by measuring the flow of liquid to and from a tank using flowmeters. We know how much liquid was inside the tank to begin with, and based on the flow of liquid into the tank and out of the tank, we calculate how much liquid remains in the tank. Again, however, we have determined that an indirect measurement method (taking another measurement and converting it to quantity) is a much more effective approach than direct measurement of how much liquid is in a tank.

Let us see how this principle applies to discrete products. We are so used to counting things that it might not occur to us that a different method could be more effective than direct counting. Or to put it differently, because of the methods and equipment that are generally in place, one-to-one counting is the most common and most effective approach under current conditions. We would not think of other methods of counting within the framework of current conditions. As with Supply Chain for Liquids, the only way we will be able to create a more productive logistics approach for discrete products is to design a complete, integrated system of equipment, technology, and procedures that takes into account the exact nature of the discrete product. We must remember the Liquid Lens^SM principle that says we do not solve problems in isolation. Instead, we create entire systems that work together to support the processes we want to operate.

The exercise of looking at Supply Chain for Liquids principles applicable to discrete products follows the same process as that for liquid products, as described in Chapter 3. The initial drivers are the form of the product at the point of production and at the point of usage. From this we derive the best configuration of the product, including its packaging, for the logistics flow from the point of manufacture to the point of usage.

Because the production and consumption forms of any discrete product are based on the product itself, this analysis must be done for each product. For our purposes, we can take a look at some of the general principles that apply to many discrete products. For starters, we lay out all the ways in which quantities can possibly be measured, and then the kinds of systems that would be required for each measurement method. Beyond that, we go through the remainder of the Liquid Lens process and evaluate our envisioned scenario against the constraints in which we operate.

Discrete products are usually measured one-to-one, that is, we count individual units, and the total of the units is the count of the product. In some instances we might take into account the packaging method and use it to our advantage to slightly simplify the counting process. For example, if there are four bottles to a carton and 72 cartons to a pallet, then we can physically count the cartons or pallets and then perform the appropriate multiplication to come up with the total number of bottles. In many ways, RFID (radio frequency identification) tags simply take this same process to the next step. We count the tags on the products/cartons/pallets and sum the count to come up with our inventory. In this sense, RFID is the next technological step in an existing process, not an innovative process of itself.

Applying the Liquid Lens approach to discrete products, we can quickly come up with other ways to determine the quantity of product in any particular location without the need to count — or have somebody count — the individual units. The first approach would be gravimetrically, which is based on weight. Given a uniform weight of the product including its packaging, or similar enough weight that we could calculate the number of units in a group based on the weight of the group, measuring the weight of the group leads to a calculation that yields the number of units in the group. Similarly, for products that have specific dimensions such as height, measuring the height of a group of the product can lead to a calculation of the number of units in a group. A different approach from these is visual identification. For example, by using currently available imaging techniques, a camera pointed at a warehouse rack can identify the quantity of product on the rack. Additional approaches to measuring the quantity of product in an area would relate to specific characteristics of the product, such as magnetic or chemical emissions from the product.

Let us take a step back and be clear on what we are doing here. We are looking at the *process* rather than the *product* as the focus of our attention. Rather than using a standard approach that views logistics per each individual item, we are viewing logistics as a process through which many items move. By considering the possibility of having inventory counting and tracking as part of the process — for example, a pressure sensor on each rack that tells us the total amount of product on the rack — we are building the tracking system into the process rather than attaching it to each individual product, such as with an RFID tag. This corresponds to the Supply Chain for Liquids approach of having a sensor in each tank of liquid. Similarly, it focuses on the measuring and segregates the identification aspect. In Supply Chain for Liquids, a tank is assigned to a product, so that it does not have to be continually reidentified. Similarly, under this approach for discrete items, an area is identified as containing a specific product at a specific time, and so does not require reidentification with each measurement. Like the tanks, the flexibility of having product stored in different locations is taken into account in creating the system, but this flexibility is not so dynamic as to be a constantly changing variable.

After developing a list of the alternative approaches to inventorying discrete products and sorting through their implications, we can identify the most appropriate approach for each channel to be addressed. This may, and probably will, require adaptations in our thinking. For example, the common pallet in all its variations of size, material, and construction is a workhorse of discrete-product manufacturing and distribution. It is virtually always simply the base upon which cartons or products are placed for movement. Converting the pallet from a simple carrying unit to an inventory-control and -monitoring mechanism is beyond common practice, but it is one of the approaches that would fit into a scheme to apply the Liquid Lens approach to discrete products.

So far, we have briefly reviewed two aspects of Supply Chain for Liquids — material flow and quantity capture — and seen how they relate to logistics for discrete products. In each case, we saw that the methods used for liquid products can potentially be adapted for use with discrete products. This same possibility applies to the other characteristics of liquid products as described in Chapter 3. The methods cannot be applied in the same ways as they are to liquid products, but there is certainly enough similarity that a company looking at Supply Chain for Liquids for its liquid products would be well served to apply the same thought processes to its discrete products.

Chapter 13

Conclusion

If you guessed that this book is really a love song to liquids disguised as a business book, you are exactly right. Liquids are a joy to work with and full of possibilities that have not nearly been exploited in the world of logistics. The first thing we need to do is stop looking at them as the poor cousins of discrete items and begin to notice the terrific opportunities they offer. The ugly duckling can truly become a beautiful swan. This exercise is full of fun, but of course its objective is completely serious; whatever business we are in, we are here to trounce the competition. Smart logistics for liquid products — Supply Chain for Liquids® — is a great way to do this. Additional resources and tools for undertaking this initiative can be found at www.SupplyChainForLiquids.com, the Internet site for Supply Chain for Liquids.

To use a phrase that has a completely different meaning in the liquid world than it does in the discrete world, in this book we have "just touched the surface" of liquid logistics. In the discrete world, to "just touch the surface" means that we have been introduced to the topic but have not gone very far in investigating all of its richness and possibilities. There has been contact, but there has not been real impact. In the liquid world to "just touch the surface" has a completely different effect. Even putting just one finger on the surface of a pond of water causes rippling in all directions, and when those ripples are reflected back, they very quickly lead to cross-rippling that feeds on itself. In the normal course of events, these waves will move back and forth, and only after a period of time will the pond return to its smoothness as long as we do not "touch the surface" again. We would like to think that we have just touched the surface of liquid logistics in the liquid sense. Yes, we have only just begun to explore the topic, but even this introduction will lead to ripples and cross waves that will only become yet more intense and more exciting as we touch the surface some more.

As we discussed in this book, the culmination of a project such as the implementation of Supply Chain for Liquids is not the end of anything; it is only a point at which it becomes clear that it is just a beginning. We can say the same thing about having gone through this book on Supply Chain for Liquids. Finishing this book only serves to give us a moment to reflect on how enormous are the horizons that are open in front of us in many directions with liquids and liquid logistics. Properly planned and performed, this adventure through territory that is, for many companies, unexplored should be as exciting as it is rewarding.

Internet Resources

3D Movies, BadFads Museum; http://www.badfads.com/.

A Silver Lining? *Living on Earth*, Mar. 5, 1999; http://www.loe.org/.

Agency for Toxic Substances and Disease, Public Health Statement for Hydraulic Fluid, Agency for Toxic Substances and Disease Registry, Sept. 1997; http://www.atsdr.cdc.gov/.

American Park Network, History of the Statue of Liberty; http://www.americanparknetwork.com/.

Anon., History of the Bridgewater Canal, Penine Waterways; http://www.penninewaterways.co.uk/.

Anon., Where to Recycle in the Flathead Valley, Flathead Valley Community College, Kalispell, MT; http://mail.fvcc.edu/.

Archer Daniels Midland, Transportation Services Summary; http://www.admworld.com/.

Are Fast Food Restaurants Responsible for America's Weight Problem? CNN Transcripts, July 27, 2003; http://www.cnn.com/.

Aviation Turbine Engines, *Chevron Aviation Fuels Tech. Rev.*, 2000; http://www.chevron.com/.

Avis, Quotable Facts; http://www.avis.com/.

Barrels and Barriques, Santa Margherita, Dictionary; http://www.santamargherita.com/.

Bear Stearns Equity Research, Tracking to the Future: The Impending RFID-Based Inventory Revolution, June 2003; http://crimsonsoftware.com/.

Beetle, P.L., Silos: An Agricultural Success Story, Cooperative Extension, University of Wisconsin; http://cecommerce.uwex.edu/.

Bettin, W.J. and Baker, H.E., Breaking the "Liquid Logistics" Paradigm, Staff of the Quartermaster Professional Bulletin, U.S. Army Quartermaster Center and School, Fort Lee, VA, Spring 2002; http://www.quartermaster.army.mil/.

Bhatia, P. and Gilbert, G., Now's the Time for RFID, *Line 56 e-Business Executive Daily*, Apr. 22, 2003; http://www.line56.com/.

Blake, R.O., Jr., The United States and India: Building Strength in Diversity, remarks of chargé d'affaires, U.S. Embassy, New Delhi, at Lucknow Universit, Jan. 16, 2004; http://newdelhi.usembassy.gov/.

Bureau of Economic Analysis, Industry Accounts Data, Gross Domestic Product by Industry, U.S. Department of Commerce, Washington, DC, 2002; http://www.bea.gov/.

Bureau of the Census, E-Commerce Statistics Section, E-Stats Archives, Washington, DC; http://www.census.gov/.

Bureau of the Census, Report FT900 (92) (CB-93-97), Foreign Trade Division, Washington, DC; http://www.census.gov/.

Bureau of Transportation Statistics, Airline Information, Fuel Cost and Consumption 1977–2004, Department of Transportation, Washington, DC; http://www.bts.gov/.

Bureau of Transportation Statistics, General Aviation Profile 2002, Department of Transportation; http://www.bts.gov/.

Business Process Outsourcing Continues Growth, *Outsourcing Pipeline*, May 5, 2004; http://www.outsourcingpipeline.com/.

Business Programs Directorate, Food Beverage and Entertainment Assessments, U.S. Army Community and Family Support Center; http://www2.armymwr.com/.

California Integrated Waste Management Board, Used Oil and Filter Facts; http://www.ciwmb.ca.gov/.

Cargill Industrial Oils and Lubricants, Cargill, ERMCO, Waverly Form Alliance to Sell Biobased Transformer Oil, press release, Minneapolis, MN, July 16, 2002; http://www.techoils.cargill.com/.

Casanova, J., 747 Airport Planning Document, Boeing Airport Technology Group, Dec. 2002; http://www.boeing.com/.

Celento Henn, Ecology fact sheet; http://www.celentohenn.com/.

Center for History and New Media, A Defender of the Bastille Explains His Role; http://chnm.gmu.edu/.

Centers for Disease Control, Nursing Home Care, 1999 Data, National Center for Health Statistics; http://www.cdc.gov/.

Chang, A., Feeding Uncle Sam's Army, ABC News, Feb. 26, 2004; http://abcnews.go.com/.

Chinese Culture and Education Foundation, The Great Wall of China, 2002; http://www.ccefoundation.org/.

Clagett Farm, From the Farm to the Table, Transportation; http://www.clagettfarm.org/.

Department of Environmental Protection, New York City's Water Supply System, history, City of New York; http://www.nyc.gov/.

Department of Occupational and Environmental Health, Case 3IA20 Report, College of Public Health, University of Iowa, Iowa City, Oct. 10, 2003; http://www.public-health.uiowa.edu/.

Department of Veterans Affairs, Facilities Directory; http://www1.va.gov/.

Duke University, Health Sector Management Program, Fuqua School of Business, Durham, NC; http://faculty.fuqua.duke.edu/.

Economic Downturn Took Toll on Coatings Output in 2001, *Phaenomen-Farbe*, Feb. 11, 2002; http://www.phaenomen-farbe.de/.

Economic Research Service, Crop Production Practices Data, 1996–2000, U.S. Department of Agriculture; http://www.ers.usda.gov/.

Economic Research Service, Food Industry Costs, Profits, and Productivity 1950–1997, U.S. Department of Agriculture; http://www.ers.usda.gov/.

eFoodletter, Foodservice Research Institute, Apr. 2003, June 2003, Aug. 2003; http://www.fsrin.com/.

Environmental Research Foundation, Chemical Accidents, Sept. 22, 1994; http://www.ejnet.org/.

Eskimo Words for Snow, College of Engineering, Computer Science, and Technology, California State University, Chico; http://www.ecst.csuchico.edu/.

Federal Aviation Administration, Cockpit Control Knob Shape, Federal Aviation Regulation, Sec. 23.781, FAA, Washington, DC; http://www.airweb.faa.gov/.

Fifth Estate, Biographical Sketch of Lord Timothy Dexter; http://fifth-estate.home.comcast.net/.

Fizz in the Air: Coke Holds Cola Exclusivity on Most Airlines, American Juggles Two Colas, *Beverage Digest*, Dec. 8, 2000; http://www.beverage-digest.com/.

"Food Grade" Anti-icing Fluid Reduces Auto Rust too, *Aerosp. Technol. Innovation*, 5, 4, July/Aug. 1997; http://nctn.hq.nasa.gov/.

Francis, R.T., II, opening statement at Oversight of Aviation Maintenance Forum, National Transportation Safety Board, Washington, DC, Aug. 30, 1999; http://www.ntsb.gov/.

Frank, M., Moneyball Your Business, *Portals Magazine*, Mar. 2, 2004; http://www.portalsmag.com/.

Freedonia Group, Lubricants to 2006: Industrial and Automotive: Market Size, Market Share, Demand Forecast and Sales, Market Research, June 2002; http://www.freedoniagroup.com/.

Freedonia Group, Paints and Coatings, Market Research, Aug. 2002; http://www.the-infoshop.com/.

Glenn, T.F., What is the "Lubricants" Business?*Compoundings Mag.*, Jan. 2002; http://www.petrotrends.com/.

Globe Ranger, Strategies for Deriving Value Beyond RFID Compliance, Globe Ranger, Nov. 2003; http://www.globeranger.com/.

Green, W., The Man from CHAOS, *Fast Company Magazine*, Nov. 1995; http://www.barn.org/.

Growth vs. Package Cost, Food and Drug Packaging, June 2002; http://www.findarticles.com/.

HAZMATPAC®, Product Catalogue 2004, Houston, TX, 2004; http://www.hazmatpac.com/.

History Learning Site, Canals 1750 to 1900; http://www.historylearningsite.co.uk/.

Hodgson, J.H. and Cheshire, C., Coca-Cola Uses Emulation to Improve Throughput, *Control Engineering*, Oct. 1, 2002; http://www.manufacturing.net/.

Hohner, Color Analysis for Liquid Flow, product catalog; http://www.instant-analysis.com/.

How Much Fuel Does an International Plane Use for a Trip? HowStuffWorks.com; http://travel.howstuffworks.com/.

HowStuffWorks.com, The History of Plumbing; http://science.howstuffworks.com/.

Hughes, J., The Hazards of Household Cleaning Products, *Share Guide: Holistic Health Mag. Resource Directory*; http://www.shareguide.com/.

Hutchinson Response Project, Kansas Geological Survey at the University of Kansas; http://www.kgs.ukans.edu/.

International Water History Association, Sextus Julius Frontinus; http://www.waterhistory.org/.

Itronics, Itronics Announces New Gold'n Gro Product, press release, Apr. 8, 2003; http://www.mirrepel.com/.

Kevan, T., Calculating RFID's Benefits, *Frontline Solutions*, Jan. 2004; http://www.findarticles.com/.

Laboratory for Interactive Learning Technologies, TWA 800 Materials, University of Hawaii at Manoa; http://lilt.ics.hawaii.edu/.

Lawson, S.D., Disney Does It Again, *Daily Press Travel Guide*; http://www.vvdailypress.com/.

Lerner, I., Architectural Coatings Survive Bad Economic Times, *Chemical Market Reporter*, Aug. 20, 2001; http://articles.findarticles.com/.

Lovins, A.B., Battling Fuel Waste in the Military, *RMI Solutions Newsletter*, Fall 2001; http://www.rmi.org/.

Maginot Line, Wikipedia Encyclopedia; http://en.wikipedia.org/.

Mariner-Volpe, B., The Evolution of Gas Markets in the United States, Energy Information Administration, U.S. Department of Energy, Washington, DC, May 2000; http://tonto.eia.doe.gov/.

Methanol Institute, Methanol: North America's Clean Fuel and Chemical Building Block, fact sheet; http://www.methanol.org/.

Metropolitan Sports Facilities Commission, marketing material, Hubert H. Humphrey Metrodome; http://www.msfc.com/.

MIL-STD-1247C, Markings, Functions, and Designations of Hoses, Piping, and Tube Lines for Aircraft, Missiles, and Space Systems, Integrated Publishing, Draftsman; http://www.tpub.com/.

Mineart, S., *A Commonplace Book*, 2004; http://www.commonplacebook.com/.

Modernising the City's Networks, *World Report*, Feb. 24, 2001; http://www.worldreport-ind.com/.

Moss, J., The Bridgewater Canal, Papillon Graphics' Virtual Encyclopaedia of Greater Manchester, Manchester, U.K., 2003; http://www.manchester2002-uk.com/.

Muralidharan, R., The Soft Drink Industry in 1996: A Case Study for External Environment Analysis, Indiana University–South Ben; http://mars.wnec.edu/.

NASA, Propeller Propulsion, NASA Centennial of Flight 1903, National Aeronautics and Space Administration, 2003; http://wright.nasa.gov/.

National Association of Convenience Stores, Economic Impact of Convenience Stores, fact sheet, 2004; http://www.nacsonline.com/.

National Association of Manufacturers, Manufacturing: the Force behind the Economy; http://www.nam.org/.

National Inventors Hall of Fame, Jet Engines, induction information; http://www.invent.org/.

New York Public Library, Print Collection, Section X: Brooklyn Bridge, Humanities and Social Sciences Library, New York; http://www.nypl.org/.

OilPure Systems, Industry Overview; http://www.oilpure.com/.

On a New Order of Things by Machiavelli, The Gurteen Knowledge Web site; http://www.gurteen.com/.

Pafko, W., Case Study: Petroleum: Origins of the Industry; http://www.pafko.com/.

Partington, E.R., Beer Barrels: From Roman Times to the Present Day, Nickel Institute; http://www.nickelinstitute.org/.

Pepsi Bottling Group, prospectus, Pepsi Bottling Group; http://www.pbg.com/.

Pour It On! — Beverage Service in Restaurants, *Nation's Restaurant News*, Aug. 31, 1998; http://www.findarticles.com/.

Praying Each Day, July 4; http://www.prayingeachday.org/.

Price, C.C., The Foodservice Industry at a Glance, 1985–1995, Economic Research Service, U.S. Department of Agriculture, 1996; http://www.ers.usda.gov/.

QED Systems, Active and Passive RFID Systems White Paper, Cedar Rapids, IA, 2002; http://www.autoid.org/.

Roberti, M., RFID: the Cost of Being Smart, *CIO Insight Magazine*, Sept. 15, 2003; http://www.cioinsight.com/.

Rorres, C., Archimedes Web site, Department of Mathematics and Science, Drexel University, Philadelphia; http://www.mcs.drexel.edu/.

Rowterra Distributors Ltd., Bale Wrapping; http://www.rowterra.bc.ca/GUIDE1.html.

Schreiber, C., Declining Market Share Forced Frito Lay to Make Big Changes, *Livestock Weekly*; http://www.livestockweekly.com/.

Shays' Rebellion, Supreme Judicial Court History Society, Boston; http://www.sjchs-history.org/.

Short, N., "Creature from the Black Lagoon," review, *DVD Verdict*, Aug. 23, 2000; http://www.dvdverdict.com/.

Shriner, R., U.S. Military Consumption, International Environmental Problems and Policy Study, University of Wisconsin–Eau Claire, Spring 2003; http://www.uwec.edu/.

Siddhartha, The Literature Network; http://www.online-literature.com/.

Silk, C., Why Did Kitty Genovese Die? The Objectivist Center; http://www.objectivistcenter.org/.

Singer, P., *One World: The Ethics of Globalization*, Yale University Press, New Haven, CT, 2002; http://www.iaed.org/.

Spectrum Laboratories Inc., chemical fact sheet; http://www.speclab.com/.

State Board of Equalization, Staff Legislative Bill Analysis, Bill Number SB1520, State of California, 2003; http://www.boe.ca.gov/.

Sun Tzu, *Korean Web Weekly*; http://www.kimsoft.com/.

Syracuse University School of Management, Research Guide, Syracuse University, Syracuse, NY, Fall 2002; http://libwww.syr.edu/.

Tennessee Solid Waste Education Project, The Problem Is Too Much Trash! University of Tennessee; http://eerc.ra.utk.edu/.

Testaccio: A Mount of Used Amphorae, Centro Para El Estudio de la Interdependencia Provincial en la Antigüedad Clasica; http://www.ub.es/.

Texas Restaurant Association, NRA 2002 Industry at a Glance (National Statistics); http://www.restaurantville.com/.

The Roman Aqueducts and Water Systems, Bowdoin College, Brunswick, ME; http://academic.bowdoin.edu/.

The Scandal of Cork Taint, *Wine Anorak*; http://www.wineanorak.com/.

Transport Canada, Hazards of Incorrectly Identifying or Mixing Aircraft Fluids, Airworthiness Notices: B048, Edition 1, Dec. 11, 1998; http://www.tc.gc.ca/.

U.S. Census Bureau, First Flight Centennial, Special Edition, Washington, DC, Dec. 3, 2003; http://www.census.gov/.

U.S. Centennial of Flight Commission, Hans von Ohain Material; http://www.centennialofflight.gov/.

U.S. Department of Defense, Compliance Strategy for Executive Order 13149, Alternative Fuel/Hybrid Vehicle Requirements, Department of Defense, Jan. 2003; https://www.denix.osd.mil/.

U.S. Department of Energy, Decision and Order, Case No. RF272-89296, Washington, DC, June 17, 1997; http://www.oha.doe.gov/.

U.S. Geological Service, A Tapestry of Time and Terrain, USGS; http://tapestry.usgs.gov/.

United Soybean Board, Screen Printing Ink Cleaners for Substrate and Textile Screen Printers, Sept. 1997; http://www.ag.uiuc.edu/.

Vapor Pressure, Baltimore County Public Library; http://www.bcpl.net/.

Whitman, C.T., administrator U.S. Environmental Protection Agency, remarks to National Water Infrastructure Forum, Washington, DC, Jan. 31, 2003; http://yosemite.epa.gov/.

Winter, J.P. and Alonso, A.M., Waste at Work: Prevention Strategies for the Bottom Line, INFORM, Inc., and Council on the Environment of New York City (CENYC), New York, May 2000; http://www.cnpl.cl/.

Wisby, G., Chicago Ranked among Top U.S. Water Wasters, *Chicago Sun Times*, Aug. 29, 2002; http://www.greatlakesdirectory.org/.

Wood, D., Designer Water Becomes an Undesigned Logistics Problem for the Army, *Newshouse News Service*, 2003; http://www.newhousenews.com/.

Wood, J., Bridgewater Canal, World through the Lens, 1995; http://www.worldthroughthelens.com/.

World Book Encyclopedia, Various Entries.

Wukitsch, T. and Dean, M., Mount Testaccio; http://www.mmdtkw.org/.

Yale University School of Management, Beverage Industry Report, Yale University, New Haven CT, Nov. 3, 2003; http://www.som.yale.edu/.

Index

Total quality management, 41, 391
TQM, *See* Total quality management
Transitioning
    case study of, 287–294
    description of, 285
    employees' role in, 291–293
    equipment and mechanical aspect
        control equipment, 298–299
        customer sites, 294–295
        data transmission, 299–300
        description of, 294
        on-site tanks, 296–297
        piping, 297
        product analysis, 295–296
        sensors, 298
        supplier analysis, 296
        truck tanks, 300–301
        trucks, 300–301
        valving, 297–298
    organizational aspect of, 285–287
    waterline approach to, 291–293
Truck and trucking
    combination, 225–226
    configuration of, 300, 312
    control equipment for, 301
    costs of, 362–363
    delivery of products
        description of, 130–131
        process involved in, 311–314
        report, 313
    description of, 127–129
    design of, 300–301
    driver of, 314–315
    environmental effects, 383
    loading of trucks
        description of, 127–128
        report about, 312–313
    multiple-use, 226
    piping of liquids from tank to, 150
    programmable logic controllers on, 301, 314–315
    regulatory issues, 247
    remote telemetry unit on, 301
    route planning, 337–338
    staging of products for, 129
    in Supply Chain, 127–130
    in Supply Chain for Liquids, 151–152
    tank systems on, 194
    touchpoints for, 399
    tubing used by, for external port connection, 246–247
    two sets of, 225
    unloading of trucks, 128–130
    variable-capacity, 226
Truck tanks
    description of, 247, 300–301
    pressurization in, 300
    reverse flow, 273
Tubing, 246–247
Tunnels, 3–4
Turbine flowmeter, 256
Turbulence of liquids, 90–91

U

Ultrasonic sensors, 254
Unloading of trucks, 128–130
Users
    Adapted Supply Chain effects on, 138, 140
    cost reductions for, 133
    definition of, 232, 235
    information about, 337, 353–354
    multiple, 222–224
    Optimal Supply Chain for Liquids effects on, 232
    planning and control activities for
        in Supply Chain, 134–135
        in Supply Chain for Liquids, 156
    product information access by, 234
    Supply Chain effects on, 132–133, 230–231
    Supply Chain for Liquids effects on, 155, 182–183, 231–232, 235–236, 237, 318–319
    target, 344

V

Valving, 297–298
Variable-capacity combination truck, 226
Vendor-managed inventory, 152, 181, 326
Vetruvius, 142
Viscosity, 89–90
Visibility
    customer behavior, 169–170
    description of, 328
    product demand, 167–169

W

Warehouse and warehousing
    automated, 408